LEARNING TO LIVE OUT LOUD

A Memoir

PIPER LAURIE

Crown Archetype
New York

Published in the United States by Crown Archetype, an imprint of the Crown Publishing Group, a division of Random House, Inc., New York.
www.crownpublishing.com

CROWN ARCHETYPE with colophon is a trademark of Random House, Inc.

Library of Congress Cataloging-in-Publication Data is available upon request.

ISBN 978-0-8230-2668-5
eISBN 978-0-8230-2677-7

PRINTED IN THE UNITED STATES OF AMERICA

Photographs courtesy of the author's private collection
Jacket photography: John Springer Collection/Corbis

10 9 8 7 6 5 4 3 2 1

First Edition

For *Anna*

If you asked me what I came into the world to do,

I will tell you: I came to live out loud.

—Émile Zola

Contents

Preface

When I was fourteen, a mustachioed middle-aged agent took me to meet Howard Hughes. Mother didn't come along. She believed there would never be hanky-panky if I were alone with a truly successful man. She said, "He wouldn't be stupid enough to get into trouble." She also thought the encounter would be good practice for my speaking skills. I rarely spoke. And never with strangers.

A few days before, the agent had asked my mother for permission to take me to a coffee shop for lunch and then repeatedly asked me if I had a boyfriend. All I could muster in response was a sound that I hoped would be taken for a giggle.

Three days later the agent and I were driving slowly through dark studio streets. I tried hard to control my panic. Nothing is as mysterious as a deserted studio at night. We passed many soundstages until we reached the very back of the lot and parked in front of a small frame bungalow. The agent helped me out of the car and escorted me up two steps, directly into a tiny, dimly lit office.

Hughes was sprawled back in his chair, his feet in sneakers resting on the desk with ankles crossed. He was long and thin, to my "art student's eye" his head seemed a bit too small for his body.

They told me to sit in the chair close to the desk. I sat. The mustachioed man who had delivered me quickly disappeared, saying, "This is

Rosetta. She's not quite fifteen . . . and doesn't she have beautiful red hair?"

Hughes barely looked at me, but he would sneak a peek from time to time. Neither of us spoke; the room remained so very quiet. After a while Hughes mumbled something to me that I couldn't comprehend. I heard the words but couldn't make sense of them, and I waited for an explanation that never came. The two of us just sat there silently in the dim light, waiting. For what, I had no idea. But I was grateful he didn't ask any questions.

A long time passed, perhaps a half hour, when the agent finally reappeared looking surprised and suggesting it was time to go. As I rose from my chair, Hughes stood up and moved over to me, mumbling something. He looked me in the eye for a few warm and dazzling seconds. The look seemed to say, *It's all right, dear. Don't worry.* We shook hands, and I walked out the door feeling he was a kind man.

Years later I would understand that this was at the beginning of Hughes's period of extreme isolation and illness, and that many young girls were being brought to him for his enjoyment. Perhaps my silence that day, my own isolation, was a reflected image he preferred to avoid. In my naiveté, I fantasized all the way home about how wonderful it would have been to speak out whenever I pleased, as others did. Not for a moment did I sense the sordidness of the aborted meeting or recognize we were two socially crippled travelers going in opposite directions. I simply sat there in the car, wondering how disappointed my mother would be that my "speaking practice" had failed that day.

1.

Home

Mother loved to tell everyone about the night before I was born, when dear Uncle Schmule came to the foot of her bed and spoke: "Hello, Charlotte . . . or do you prefer Sadie?"

Uncle Schmule had died the week before, but Mother said she saw him quite clearly, with his magnetic blue eyes that pierced right through her body. He was a handsome, bearded, wise man whom everyone loved, and he told her that her child would be born in the morning and be a good and blessed person. I've always felt slightly burdened by the implicit challenge in the story, and wished I'd never heard it.

A male midwife delivered me in a one-bedroom walk-up on Tyler Street in Detroit on January 22, 1932. Father declared that night that childbirth was much too difficult to abide and they would have no more. In spite of all the drama, I appeared to be a healthy child, unlike my fragile older sister, Sherrye. They named me Rosetta and called me Sissy, but later most would know me by another name, Piper Laurie.

Like most Americans, our family had come to America in search of a better life. My father's parents had traveled across the Atlantic from Poland in a boat filled with Jewish immigrants. Our *zaddi* changed his name from Abraham Jacobovitch to Abraham Jacobs and settled in Detroit with my *bubbi*, Deborah. Together they had eleven children, nine of whom survived. My father, one of the oldest, quit school after eighth grade and went to work in his father's bakery so that his seven younger sisters and brothers could finish high school. It was not unusual at the time for young men to forgo their education so they could help support their families.

My mother's parents, Samuel and Anna Alperin, had emigrated from Russia. Their three children, including my mother, were born in America. After the birth of their son, Manny, my grandpa left his family and became an itinerant cowboy, roaming the West on his horse. Grandma carried on supporting the family with her sewing. My mother could never forgive her father for deserting them, and my grandma never forgave him for not giving her a Jewish divorce, called a "get." The essential meaning of the "get" is, *You are hereby permitted to all men*. They were legally divorced, but that was an entirely different thing.

My mother retained a code of ethics completely her own. When she was ten, a car ran over her leg, and she considered it an honorable act not to tell her mother and to suffer the damage quietly. When she began to work, she turned every paycheck over to her mother, who must have been something of a tyrant in those days.

One night my mother met my handsome and gentle dad, who danced divinely. Mother was smitten. She broke her engagement to a wealthy young attorney and married my father instead. They had little in common except for a love of ballroom dancing and a need to survive. My sister Sherrye, born a year later, was sickly with asthma and had to be taken to the hospital several times close to death. I was born two and a half years later.

Supporting two babies wasn't easy in the middle of the Depression. My parents lightened their life by turning on the radio and dancing in their tiny apartment.

I think my mother used magic to make her delicious soups for us. I was told "more soup" were my first words, but not too many followed. My parents took it for granted that I seldom spoke. I don't know when people first noticed my silence. It was bewildering to find the right words. I could hear them; they seemed to be flying all around me but not where I could grab on, especially when I knew someone was waiting. People's patient expectation caused me to panic inside. It would be almost a lifetime before I found out that my "difficulty" had a name: acute anxiety disorder. It's not an uncommon or traumatic burden nowadays, if attended to.

True, our family struggled through the dire financial times, but our lives overflowed with sensory stimulation. Mother sold pies from a baby buggy to help bring in money. She'd bury my sister and me under her freshly baked pies and cakes in the large carriage and push us down the street, selling her wares, calling out, "Fresh baked! Fresh baked!" Mother tried to keep a kosher home for us, but she finally had to give up, and for a while we lived on the traditional hard-time potato diet. But Mother liked to celebrate and laugh, and she would sneak us into Detroit's magnificent Fox or Michigan Theater to see the stage shows she was crazy about. We didn't have to pay because we weren't staying for the movie, and it was there we witnessed many of the vaudeville greats as that era was ending.

I was about two and a half when I heard a full orchestra play for the first time. The thunderous volume, the vibrations from the brass, and the sweep of the strings turned me inside out. I crawled to the cold theater floor in terror and then onto my mother's lap, where she held me as I wept. But I remember quite clearly that when Mother asked, "Shall we go?" I did not want to and said, "No, please, no."

A year later I saw the great Ted Lewis come out in his top hat and tails, pushing a shiny red-and-white peanut stand. He was singing and shouting "Is e-v-v-r-e-e-body happy!" as he tossed real peanuts in their shells to the audience. Children were encouraged to come on stage and take all the peanuts they could carry. Something inexplicable made me walk down the aisle and up onto the stage. Perhaps it was Mother who told me to go. Once there I don't recall seeing the audience at all, only the colorful people on stage. For years afterward my sister talked of how embarrassed she was seeing me there, her three-year-old little sister holding her skirt straight out, exposing her underpants as the people on stage filled her skirt with peanuts and the audience howled with laughter.

Another time I saw the talented child star Jane Withers on that stage, speaking with such vitality and intimacy to the audience. She was wearing a frilly blue dress, and lit up with pink footlights, as she accepted the enthusiastic applause from the audience. Out of what cloud had she come? Fantastic! How did this happen? It was unfathomable to me that a child could get that kind of attention and adulation.

One hardly ever saw my dad except at night. He was one of the fortunate ones, always away working. He expected dinner to be ready the moment he got home, and didn't want to wait a minute longer than it took to wash up and change clothes, and he grumbled if food wasn't on the table. It was a small thing to ask, he reasoned. When we sat at the table, dinners were quiet, with most of the conversation in Yiddish, so we children wouldn't understand. Unlike later generations, children and adults still lived in separate worlds. If we were fortunate enough to have fish for dinner, we weren't allowed to speak at all for fear we'd choke on the bones. Twice a year for a treat, we'd have hot dogs that had been boiled for two hours and skinned, followed by a dose of milk of magnesia. We so loved the hot dogs, we didn't mind the follow-up ritual.

At the time I just thought of my mother as someone who kept making lots of rules. Looking back, I realize the struggle to survive had taken a toll, and she had come to distrust everyone and everything.

The year I turned four, Mother suddenly packed a bag and took my sister and me on a broken-down bus almost three thousand miles to Tucson, Arizona. She hoped Sherrye's asthma would improve in the desert air. There may have been other reasons, perhaps difficulties in the marriage that she could never share with us. Or maybe she just wanted to get away. Whatever the reason, my dad stayed behind to keep his job.

In Arizona we lived in an isolated shack in what seemed to be the middle of the desert. There was nothing around us, not a building or a house. We had to walk a great distance to get to the store or to the bus. If we didn't get back to the shack before dark, our only light was from the flashlight Mother carried. Mother insisted on carrying the groceries, too, and repeated over and over, "Hold on to me. Hold on to me," for fear she'd lose us in the sand. I could tell she was terribly frightened, and I suppose I was, too. She'd pray when we couldn't find the shack. After about a month, Mother moved us to a one-room stucco house with a porch, right across the street from Sherrye's school. My sister took me with her one day and told the teacher that she had taught me to read and write as she was learning. I felt so proud.

Sometimes Mother would take us to a small concrete building, where we would sit on benches under bluish light and breathe ozone. It was supposed to be a cure for Sherrye's asthma. Her asthma did not improve, however, and God knows what the "ozone" did for the rest of us.

I celebrated my fifth birthday in Arizona. A few months later, without a cure for Sherrye's illness, we took the bus back to Detroit, where I started kindergarten.

I was desperately in love with my mother in those years. One day she appeared at the door of my kindergarten class to bring me a forgotten lunch. She was wearing an elegant suit topped with an astonishing gray hat, on which different colored gray feathers were sewn horizontally. The feathers looked alive, and for a moment when she moved, it seemed she was balancing a real bird. Her long dark hair was slicked up into a nest of braids under the hat, and she wore her small blue-glass earrings, her only earrings, which, everyone said, perfectly matched the color of her eyes.

That day she was the most interesting person I'd ever seen. Mother wore only wash dresses at home, and somehow I knew she had dressed herself up so beautifully just for me. Everyone stared as she walked to my desk, leaned over, and gave me her kiss, murmuring, "Sissy, dear." The aroma of Mother enveloped me, a department store scent that was very pleasing and that I could remember for years. She handed me my lunch and left. I was overwhelmed with pride and with love for her that day. I had no idea that by the end of the year, we would be separated by thousands of miles in a move that forever changed my life.

One day when I was still five, Grandma Anna, who somehow managed to have small homes in both California and Detroit, wrote to my parents about a sanitarium called Reslocks, an institutional home for children in the northeastern portion of the San Fernando Valley, about twenty miles from downtown Los Angeles. The sanitarium was in the mountains, in a place called Tujunga. The air in Tujunga was supposed to be beneficial to children with asthma, epilepsy, and allergies. The children lived in dormitories with nurses supervising. If the children were fit enough, they were driven daily to a nearby public school.

For reasons I can only surmise, for it was never talked about, my parents decided that both Sherrye and I should go to Reslocks. One day they came to me and said, "You can choose to stay home with Mommy and Daddy, or you can go to the sanitarium in California like a grown-up girl and keep your sister company." Though I was an inarticulate child, I knew what it meant to be asked to act like a "grown-up." With all my heart I didn't want to go, but it was clear what they wanted of me. I knew I wasn't really being offered a choice.

Grandma came to take Sherrye first, traveling cross-country on the train and spending time in her little stone house in the mountains to test the air, literally. After several weeks Mother and I followed. I was told to pack lightly and take only what could fit into my small cardboard suitcase. I treasured my colored-sand set more than anything I owned. There were eight glass test tubes, each with a different color of sand. With cardboard and clear glue, I could sprinkle the sand and make pictures. When I tried to pack it, I found that the flat box was too wide to fit into the suitcase by about two inches. A small but deeply felt sacrifice.

Mother and I traveled across the country by train, and the journey was thrilling. The ever-changing scenery and then the glorious mountains. The excitement of seeing Indians in full dress at the stops. Eating in the dining car. I was five years old but had never eaten in a proper restaurant before. Now my life was bananas and cream; I was just sitting there—eating—and watching the great beauty of the world go by.

When we got off the train in California, there was a brief respite at Grandma's house in Tujunga before we entered the sanitarium. I passed my time there blocking out the unthinkable, as children can do.

I found some scraps of wood in the backyard and built a little table with a hammer and some nails left behind by a worker. Somehow I managed to pound nails into five pieces of wood. When I finished, I had a small table about a foot square that tilted sharply, with loose, uneven legs. I sat out there in the yard eating my meals off my table as often as they'd let me, holding on to my plate, trying to keep it from sliding off the table. I loved that table. It was the first time I had the pleasure of creating something useful with my hands, imperfect as it was, and the feeling of self-reliance it gave me was delicious.

During that respite I was sent on an errand by myself across a field bordered by very tall eucalyptus trees, when suddenly a powerful wind came up. The trees' wild gyrations in unison, like giant dancers, the whistling of the leaves moving against one another, the pungent aroma filled me with ecstasy. The sight of a tree in movement, or of people moving in a beautiful or interesting way, still thrills and touches me deeply.

The reprieve ended, and the day I had shut out of my mind inevitably came. Sherrye and I were taken to the institution that was to be our new home.

Nothing about the Reslocks Sanitarium was welcoming. The functional one-story building was in the middle of two flat acres of hard, dry soil. The grounds were covered with a few desertlike plants, including goatheads—a kind of weed that spreads out with thorns that you had to watch out for when you were barefoot. It was bordered by a half-dozen live oaks, a few pines, and a walnut tree. There were lots of red ants and an occasional horned toad. Two dormitories were housed in the flat building, one for the boys and one for the girls, with about two dozen children living in them.

While we were waiting to be admitted, Sherrye asked Mother and Grandma how long our stay would be. "We don't know, we'll see," they said. Being open-ended made it seem to be forever, to a small child.

We must have said goodbye but I have no conscious memory of it, only blackness. Sherrye told me years later that I had fainted. I only remember, afterward, standing in the girls' dormitory, watching Mother and Grandma go arm in arm up the stone path leading to the road. I waited for them to turn around and look back. I thought perhaps they'd change their minds and realize a mistake had been made. But they continued on, talking to each other, turning at the road and then passing out of sight.

That curved stone path became indelibly carved into my being. I looked out of that window almost every day for the next three years, hoping for a sight of my parents. I would conjure up a vision of them returning on that path in their brown and gray coats to take us away. And sometimes, if I were alone and sure no one could see me, I would cry.

Sherrye and I were each assigned a bed in the girls' dormitory, which was a narrow room with a dozen beds, six on each side. Sherrye's bed was at the end away from me. We were taught to make our beds first thing before breakfast, with tight "hospital corners." Every night we were led in the Lord's Prayer. We recited it in unison out loud, but when I got to the "God bless" part, I always completed my list silently with "and let them take us home."

The boys and girls did everything together except sleep and bathe. All activities were in the dining hall, with its worn beige linoleum. Regular meals were mostly a lot of gray, tasteless food served at two picnic-style tables, the only furniture in the room. In the morning the oatmeal was sometimes heavily salted by mistake, instead of sugared. Food was not to be wasted, so we were told to eat all of these "mistakes." If we refused, as my sister often did, we were penalized by having to stand in the corner for long periods of time, sometimes on a high stool wearing a dunce cap.

Other times we lost the occasional privilege of listening to the children's programs on the radio on Saturday mornings. We sat on the floor and hovered over that tiny radio for the weekly fifteen minutes of entertainment, the only entertainment that we didn't provide for ourselves. We cherished those fifteen minutes.

Despite all the restrictions, we managed to find a few unauthorized snacks. There was a gigantic walnut tree on the grounds that bore perfect nuts, and we children would dig holes in the ground and hide them like squirrels. We felt great satisfaction and power hiding the walnuts from the nurses and administrators. We also had a small fig tree that bore magnificent figs. No one seemed to know or care when we ate them. We took great pleasure in having snacks whenever we pleased, a habit that persisted throughout my life. The children were weighed regularly. So many were sickly and thin from ill health that gaining weight was a major goal. Sherrye and I were considered the "chubbies." Sherrye was always sweetly round, and I was average to slim. I was never overweight, but the label of "chubby" was implanted on both our brains forever. We were also considered freaks because we both had red hair. Not just one of us, but both.

We children were never touched or hugged; it was against the rules. If I missed my parents' cuddling, I didn't allow myself to think about it.

The nurses were very strict about everything. No one was allowed to drink water during the night. In extreme cases, if you were very thirsty and dry, you could wet your lips, but they watched over you to make sure not a drop got into your mouth. The only exceptions were for the children who had seizures. The nurses would allow them a little water now and then because they hated the commotion; it could be very dramatic and scary to the younger children who had never seen an epileptic seizure. After a while we just took it in stride and could help a little by holding the children's heads or getting something to put in their mouths.

Mr. and Mrs. Reslock owned the place. Mr. Reslock, or "Poppy," as we were told to call him, drove us to Pinewood Elementary School every day during the week. (During our last year there, Poppy ran off with Miss Baker, one of the nurses.) Out of perhaps two dozen children, only eight or ten of us were fit enough to go to public school. We were squeezed into the smallest car I'd ever seen and Poppy would drive all over the empty country road, deliberately zigzagging and throwing us all around inside the car. This was long before seat belts, of course, so there was nothing to keep us from being thrown wildly. Most of the children loved the sensation, but it frightened me. I didn't like my body moved about without my permission, but I couldn't speak the words to ask Poppy not to do it.

The public schoolyard was large, and I liked playing tetherball. When the rope and ball were removed, we children used the thick pole for climbing. I was very good at it and could climb up quickly with my strong arms and legs. One day just as I was reaching the top of the pole, an extraordinary thing happened. A richly pleasurable sensation began to grow in me, then flood my groin and pour into my whole body. I clung to the top of the pole, ten feet off the ground as if my life depended on it. The children below were shouting "Come down, Rosetta, come down. It's our turn." But nothing would move me till the miraculous throbbing had stopped. And so I first experienced God's gift to a lonely child.

We'd get a phone call from our parents every few months and would take it in the tiny office at the front of the dining hall. The owners stayed with us during these conversations. Long-distance calls were very expensive, so they were never longer than two or three minutes.

The dismal days were broken up by the frequent turnover of nurses, though the head nurse, Mrs. Schwartz, was always there. She was the strictest of all, and extremely unpleasant, even cruel. Mrs. Schwartz was a large woman with brown hair rolled into a knot at the back of her head. She always wore her nurse's cap, even in the middle of the night. I had nightmares about her—that she was actually Hitler in disguise. I began to have a series of fantastical, grandiose dreams in which I killed Hitler, aka Mrs. Schwartz. It was a potent outlet for my feelings of powerlessness. I slew both of them at least three times. I knew who Hitler was. I don't know how I knew. And I knew that I was Jewish. This was 1938 through 1940, and the Second World War had yet to start for the Americans, but sometimes children would come back from visits with their families and talk about what they had heard when they were *out there*. Curious, how a small child living in the mountains of California knew what was happening to the Jews of Europe at that time, even though many Europeans claimed they didn't.

I overheard a conversation between some children at the home who were saying that many Jews were being killed in places called concentration camps. Alarmed, I found my tongue. "Why are they killing the Jews?"

The other girl said with great authority, "The Nazis are jealous because the Jews are so smart." I didn't feel particularly smart, but I felt a strong sense of pride in being Jewish. Being smart was something to strive for. I had no idea how many of the children in the home were Jewish other than my sister and me. I know many were not, because they all observed the Christian holidays. On our first Christmas morning there, the children had lots of presents on the foot of their beds. It seemed to Sherrye and me that their families must be very rich and loving. We'd never received presents at home, except on our birthdays. So, of course, we received nothing now, a hard thing for a young child to accept.

The following year we got one present between us. It was a very sophisticated professional puppet with dozens of strings. *Oh, for heaven's sake!* Far beyond our capabilities, it was unusable within fifteen minutes, the strings impossibly tangled. *What were they thinking? Had they forgotten who we were?* Later there was another impersonal present, a croquet set that was sent for all the children, not just for us. It felt like we had disappeared. But it was a very nice croquet set. Frank, the handyman, rolled out a court. It took many days, but the children had learned to be patient. We were excited to have something new to do.

I did make a friend, a little girl named Bonnie Ann Goodflower. Even her name was delightful, as if she came from a fairy tale. She had straight yellow hair, blue eyes, and big white crooked teeth that crossed over sharply in front. She was closer to my age than my sister, and she didn't seem to mind that I had little to say. We always found something to giggle about when we were together. Bonnie was always ready to play a game or climb a tree with me. I can still picture her dancing with joy in front of the fig tree because we'd squashed ripe figs on our faces. When I became an adult and recalled Bonnie in my mind's eye, I realized that she may have had Down syndrome. Perhaps that's why she was such a dear and uncomplicated friend.

There was a long period one summer when Sherrye and I were the only children at the home. The others had gone on vacations with their families, who lived locally. Of course, we were envious, but I tried not to think about it and kept as busy as I could, swimming and collecting pretty rocks. I glued bright red geranium petals to my fingernails with spit and pretended I was "a fancy girl all dressed up." I swam every day, my supersize orange-brown freckles gradually overlapped one another until they looked like one massive tattoo on each cheek, and I watered the pine seedling that I had planted on Arbor Day.

When the other children returned, Sherrye and I were genuinely happy to see them and hungry to hear about everything they had done. One of the boys had gone to Catalina and taught us songs he'd learned there, like "K-K-K-Katy" and "Sleepy Lagoon." The melodies still thrill me.

Unlike the other children, Sherrye and I had almost no contact with our family. I had no idea what was happening with my parents. They must have been suffering in ways they believed we couldn't understand. I did know that my mother's health was not good. She had fallen and had signs of early arthritis. For the most part, though, their lives were a mystery to me.

Apart from the rare phone calls, our only means of communication was by letter, and that communication was one-way. Each week all of the children had to write to their parents while the nurses stood over us in the dining hall to make sure we did. I could never think of anything to say, so the nurses coached me and tried to get me started. I dutifully wrote down what they told me: "Dear Mother and Daddy. How are you? I am fine." Then I just sat there frozen and helpless until the nurse would say, "Just sign off," and I would write, "Love, Sissy." The letters gave no hint of my real life. Sherrye, on the other hand, wrote bluntly of our unhappiness. Our parents never wrote back. Mother kept Sherrye's painful letters, and many years later I read them. I asked my mother why she had kept them all those years, and she replied that she thought we might want them someday. I also asked her if she hadn't understood how unhappy we were. Puzzlingly, she replied that no, she had not. How was that possible? Was it just a form of denial that enabled her to live with the separation?

Visits from my family were rare. Grandpa Alperin, our wandering cowboy, came to see us at the home three or four times over the years, but he wouldn't come in. Why, I don't know. I think my mother didn't want him to. She was ashamed of the way he looked, with his shabby clothes that were sometimes stained. Sherrye and I would meet him out at the road for about ten minutes, where he'd give us each a package of gum, tell us to make it last a long time, and leave.

Finally, about a year after she left us at the home, my mother came out and visited for a few unbelievable days. I melted into her and stayed as close as I could every moment she was there. Once she took us on the bus to downtown Los Angeles. We walked around Pershing Square and into the elegant Biltmore Hotel. The rambling lobby was filled with imposing portraits and landscapes. I'd never seen such paintings. My mother said we were in an art gallery, and I've always thought of the Biltmore Hotel as such. My father, who feared losing his job if he was gone too long, saw us only once. He was paid to drive someone's car cross-country.

It was shortly before my eighth birthday that my parents' fortunes must have begun to change. That year Mother arranged for Sherrye and me to take piano lessons. Every few weeks the music teacher would come to Reslocks and give lessons to the children. There was a piano in the dining room of the owner's house, on the far side of the property, where we had our lessons and went to practice.

My particular practice time was scheduled immediately after breakfast, and I was told to never be late, for if I were, some terrible punishment would be inflicted. I would go directly from the children's dining room to my practice session instead of the bathroom. I'd let myself into the unlocked house, and sit down at the piano, squirming in agony. I would never have dared to use a bathroom without asking permission, even if I had known where it was. There was never a soul in sight to ask, so I would suffer until my practice time was up and then race across the yard to the one in the girls' dorm.

After many months of lessons, a piano recital was arranged in someone's private home. The piano was on a small, raised platform in the music room. Each of us had to go up to the platform, announce the piece we had learned, and play it for the small audience. When it was my turn to announce the title of the simple piece I had learned, a fierce agony enveloped me, and I stood on the platform exposed and immobilized. I could not make the words come out of my mouth. I seemed to be in a kind of fugue state, enveloped in grayness until it was clear that I would not speak and was told to "sit and play, Rosetta." I was on fire with mortification, but I did play, and apparently not too badly. When it was over, I vowed with all my soul that I would find something to do in life, perhaps with music, that didn't require speaking in front of people.

Both my parents had promised to come for my eighth birthday. I don't know why that eighth birthday was so special to me. I'd had my sixth and seventh birthdays without them, but to me, becoming eight was a rite of passage into adulthood. I would be close to the same age Sherrye had been when we first entered the sanitarium. But more important, I was going to see my parents.

When the day came, I put on a clean dress and special clips in my hair to keep it neat. I was dizzy with excitement. Then a short time before they were to arrive, I was called to the little office, handed the phone, and heard my parents' voices on the other end. "Something has happened that was unavoidable, so we're not going to be able to make it," they told me. "We aren't sure when we'll be coming out, but we'll visit as soon as we can." They sounded cold and distant.

I hung the phone up feeling as though I would die. In all my adult years, I don't believe anything has ever disappointed me that much again. I somehow moved myself out of the tiny office into the dining hall. I stood in the middle of the almost-empty room on that ugly, stained linoleum, not knowing what to do with my body; it felt wounded. My despair was physically palpable. I went outside and hid in some bushes. I didn't die that day, but a part of me began to change.

Sometime after I turned eight, Mother finally did come to visit for a few days. She worked her way across the country, stopping in a half-dozen cities, selling wholesale perfumes to upscale department stores and then grabbing the next train.

I was outside walking with Mother when the owner, Mrs. Reslock, came to us and asked that I go somewhere else so the adults could speak. My guilty imagination told me I was in trouble.

Something had happened some weeks before when the nurses weren't around. All the girls in the dormitory, including me, had thrown off all our clothes and danced around in a circle, holding hands and singing, "We are a fairy circle, la la la la la," acting out the image of cherubs we'd seen in a fairy tale book and giggling. We were found out and punished in some way that I've forgotten. And sometime before that, about eight children had hidden behind a freestanding wall far from the main building, intended for a never-built handball court, playing doctor. I was too timid to participate because it required a bit of talking, but I found it titillating as an observer. Some days later I was summoned to the office and grilled as if I were a criminal. They demanded a confession from me that my sister was the "ringleader" of all the nasty things the children were doing. If I didn't admit this about my sister, they would tell our parents. That would be a catastrophe. They didn't physically beat me, but they did browbeat me for a very long time. They stood over me yelling, "Tell us the truth! Tell us the truth!"

I actually thought Sherrye was the ringleader; it certainly seemed to me that she was very bold, a quality that I envied. But somehow I felt a deep sense of loyalty to my sister. I sobbed and insisted, "It wasn't her, it wasn't." Defending my sister seemed more important than the truth. I never did tell. I already had great respect for truth, but I always felt I had done the right thing. As I got older, I asked myself what I would have done if my sister had been guilty of doing something truly evil and hurting someone.

So when Mrs. Reslock asked me to disappear so she could speak to my mother, I was sure she was going to tell Mother about the "nasty things." What else could it be about? I watched them from a stone bench at a distance. I could see Mother being told something, and her body language suddenly changed. They talked for quite a while, perhaps twenty minutes, and when Mother finally walked back to me, she seemed distracted and quiet, which I interpreted as coldness and anger toward me. Whatever Mrs. Reslock had said, I was tortured by the feeling that if we'd had a chance to be taken back, we had lost it.

But I was wrong. Almost a year later, after being at the sanitarium for three long years, Sherrye and I were told that we were going home. My father had been promised a job as a furniture salesman in Los Angeles, and my parents were moving to California to make a home. At last they were coming for us! I had dreamed of being with my parents for so long—it was the only thing in the world that I desired—to be cuddled and touched and held by them, to be tucked into bed at night.

Incredibly, though, instead there was an overwhelming feeling of disappointment and sadness that I was going home with them. This place, as hateful as it was, had been my home for a third of my life. It seemed that I had always lived here. I was shocked by my feelings and couldn't understand them. This feeling of dread was bewildering to me. I had expected joy. It was as if there were a beautiful present that I knew existed but couldn't unwrap. Was I simply preparing myself in the event they didn't show up? It would be many years into adulthood before I would understand why I responded that way.

The long-awaited day finally came, but when my parents arrived to take us away, it seemed we were leaving with strangers. The old parental ties had been mightily stretched during that period and grown gossamer thin by the time they took us out of the home. Children do adjust to their environment. The emotional separation from parents is not supposed to happen until adolescence. In my case it had come a bit early. I never overcame the feeling that my father was a stranger, and to a lesser degree my mother, though she eventually attached herself to me like glue. My parents and I seldom talked about those years apart, and afterward we lived together in a civilized way for many, perhaps too many, years. As for me, my exile had cultivated an imagination that grew like a giant sheltering flower. It was a lifetime gift.

2.

Mother

In the months that followed my departure from Reslocks, our lives gradually regained a sense of normalcy. The family moved around a lot in the beginning, but by the end of the first year, we had settled into a tiny one-bedroom apartment on South St. Andrews Place, near Western Avenue and Eighth Street in Los Angeles.

Ours was a front apartment with an iron-grilled balcony that later became my fantasy stage. We had a bedroom, a tiny bathroom, and a galley kitchen with a breakfast nook where we ate our meals. There was a half-size refrigerator placed over a cupboard and an old-fashioned built-in icebox at the floor with a little door that opened to the hall. The iceman no longer delivered ice, so its primary purpose was for storage, and for me to squeeze through when we were locked out. Our parents slept in the wall, as I used to think of it, in the good old Murphy bed that came out at night. Sherrye and I shared the tiny bedroom with just a few inches between our beds. Later, when we had bunk beds, there was three feet of moving-around space. I preferred sleeping on top where I could look out the peculiar little window high on the wall. Sherrye and I shared that room for six long years and fought over every inch of space, so much so that it wasn't until she married and moved out that I started to like her and we became friends. We lived in that apartment for almost ten years.

My mother devoted herself to Sherrye's and my improvement.

Clearly she was trying to make up for the years of separation. She thought Sherrye and I were too fat. I wasn't overweight; I just had no shape. Our food was carefully monitored, just as it had been at the sanitarium. Once I was supposed to memorize something and still had half a page to go. It was dinnertime, and everyone else was eating. I was hungry, too, but Mother would not let me sit down until I had memorized it all. It was extremely difficult to concentrate, especially since I had to stand next to the table, where my mother kept one eye on the text while she ate. But I finally succeeded and was allowed to have my meal. There are several ways to look at that. Was I building muscles of self-discipline? Or was it feeding rebellious behavior? At the time it just seemed arbitrary and cruel.

Mother even got a doctor to give me and Sherrye appetite suppressants. I remember walking to school one day feeling especially "good." This was long before people understood the dangers of "appetite suppressants," but it started me on a path of amphetamine use that would take years to escape.

I tried not to get in trouble and to do everything right. I was Miss Goody-Goody, but the honor system didn't work for Sherrye. To keep her away from food, a lock was put on the refrigerator door and some of the pantries. But nothing could keep Sherrye out. If she wanted it, she would get it. Sherrye didn't seem to care if she was punished or beaten. And she was, quite often, sometimes by Mother with a broom handle when my father wasn't at home. He wouldn't have permitted it. I was never physically beaten as my sister was when Mother was out of control, but I always expected to be next.

I could see early on how my parents' constant monitoring and criticizing of my sister, their inability to hold their tongues, only caused more anxiety and pushed Sherrye further into her sneaking and compulsive eating. I felt she'd do better if they'd just let her be. Every now and then I had an aberrant brave moment and confronted my parents with an uncontrollable outburst of anger and tears for what I perceived to be their stupidity and lack of sensitivity to Sherrye's needs. If I was also speaking for myself, I didn't know it yet. Where the words came from, I did not know. But my parents didn't punish me for my outbursts.

I think they were too shocked to hear such raw anger displayed by their usually silent, compliant child. Sometimes I would feel rage at my mother, to the point of wanting to strike her, hurt her physically, but I controlled the impulse and tried to work harder at whatever I was doing in an endless quest for my parents' approval. I was seldom complimented about anything. It was part of their Eastern European background. To speak of one's good fortune would bring punishment of some sort.

Mother could be quite cynical at times, but she believed her own family should always have principles of honesty and goodness. Her personal code of morality made for one of my most stunning experiences during those years. It happened right outside the A&P Grocery on Wilshire near Western. Mother, Sherrye, and I had just finished grocery shopping and were about to walk home when the manager came running out of the store, shouting at my mother.

"Your little girl has stolen a package of Red Hots!" he said, pointing at Sherrye and grabbing her arm. "I saw her put it in her pocket."

Mother's face got beet red, and she looked as if she could hardly breathe.

"Sherrye?" And then louder, "Did you take them?" She put her hand in Sherrye's pocket and pulled out the bag of tiny red cinnamon candies. But before handing them back to the manager, my mother did one of the most amazing things I'd ever seen.

In the middle of Wilshire Boulevard, with people walking by, my mother began beating her chest with both hands as animal-like cries rose from deep within her belly. Then, her arms outstretched, her hand still clutching the little bag of candies, she cried out in a deeply resonant voice that the great tragedians would have envied: "I WISH THE EARTH WOULD OPEN UP AND SWALLOW ME RIGHT NOW!!!" It was said with such intensity that for a moment I thought the sidewalk might actually open up to envelop her. She meant it. She was so mortified that her child had stolen something. It was hair-raising. The manager disappeared as quickly as he dared, but I stood rooted to the spot, terrified by what I was witnessing. Part of me was horrified, but another part of me admired my mother's ability to express her deep despair so passionately and in such a public way. My own despair was still trapped in silence.

From time to time I would be overwhelmed with a depression that I didn't understand. I had no clue as to why I felt that way, but it could become physically painful. More than a few times I stood at the fourth-floor window, alone in our bedroom or on the roof, wanting to fling myself out to the sidewalk below, wanting to stop what I was feeling. I don't know what stopped me. My relationship with God was a struggle. My faith was fragile, and sometimes I had no faith at all. Part of me loved life, especially nature, which always seemed to me to be connected to God. I was always curious about life and what was going to happen. Ending my life then would be as sacrilegious as looking at the last page of a book before reading it. I wanted to live my life to the surprise ending.

At times my mother would ask why I seemed sad. All I could say was, I didn't know why; I just felt like crying. In those moments Mother would hold me on her lap and say, "Cry, Sissy, it's all right. Go ahead. Cry. Let it out." And I did. But only for a short time; I was too ashamed to do it for long. I was deeply grateful to her for her words. I felt she was trying to be my mother again. She could be so warm and nurturing in those moments, filled with sensitivity and innate intelligence.

I longed to talk to my sister. I suppose it was because of the age difference, but she never seemed interested in what I thought or said. Instead of bringing us closer, the years in the sanitarium had driven a wedge between us. Sometimes I lay in bed in the dark, my sister in her bed just inches away, yearning to know what it was like to be Sherrye. *What was it like to see what she saw? How could it be that Sherrye, whom I knew so well, spent her whole life being someone else? Not me. Were we not the same? I wished I could float over . . . drop down . . . and look out through her eyes. If I did that, would I disappear? Or would I float out and back again and remember where I had been?* These were the thoughts of an embryonic actress, though I didn't know it yet.

A year or so after we moved into the apartment, a bad fall Mother had had in Detroit while we were in the sanitarium gradually developed into severe arthritis, limiting her movements and bringing increasing pain. Finally she couldn't walk at all and had to sit in a small, straight chair, day and night, for many months. She left the chair only when she shuffled to the bathroom, using the chair as a walker. Sherrye and I became responsible for keeping the household going. We cleaned the house, did the wash, dusted our father's pipes, shopped for food, and cooked simple things. All of this had to be done before and after school.

I am ashamed to say that I resented my mother's illness. Inside I was very angry. From time to time I had the evil thought that my mother was exaggerating her physical pain. I thought the way she moved was so grotesque and dramatic that it couldn't be genuine. It was deeply unkind of me. I hated myself for thinking such thoughts, yet they continued to recur. Perhaps it was the "actress" part of me that thought she was overdoing the performance a bit. She was hurting, and if she did play the drama of it, why shouldn't she? After a lifetime of hardship, it was natural for her to cry out for some attention and rest. Her whole life had been a struggle, working hard and pinching pennies from the time she was a child. I know now that her arthritis was undoubtedly stress related. She was ill for the better part of a year, but eventually she recovered and resumed her role as a full-time mother once again. More accurately, she became a full-time stage mother.

It was my mother who first suggested that I become an actress, though she didn't use the word. One day when I'd been back with my parents for about a year, Mother lifted her head from the newspaper and said, "Sissy, would you like to be in the movies?"

I don't know whether she had divined my deepest wish or simply projected one of her own. Whatever the case, I felt a sharp pleasurable sensation in my stomach. *Oh my, how did she know this?* I had never dared speak about it. I had deliberately misled my family when they asked what I wanted to be when I grew up. I would tell them I wanted to be a manicurist or anything that happened to pop into my head at the time, but the truth was, I wanted to be a movie star.

I had seen my first movie while we were living at the sanitarium.

Grandpa, our cowboy, got permission to take me and Sherrye out to a movie one afternoon. We went by bus and streetcar to a theater and saw *The Blue Bird*, with Shirley Temple. It was an extraordinary but disturbing experience. I entered deeply into the world of the movie and the happy "children in heaven" scenes. It seemed to me that children had to be dead and in heaven in order to be happy, and the idea had troubled me.

Now I began to slowly catch up and see as many movies as our parents would allow. We went to see the great Technicolor musicals with Betty Grable and Alice Faye, as well as black-and-white comedies starring Joe Penner, Charlie Chaplin, Hugh Herbert, and the Marx Brothers. When we finally had a little car, the whole family drove to Hollywood to see the scary films like *The Cat Woman* and *I Walked with a Zombie*. It still cost only ten cents to get into our neighborhood movie theaters, and we could stay as long as we liked. On Saturdays, Mother would pack a lunch she considered healthy for Sherrye and me to take to the movies. This was long before outside food was banned from the theaters. A lot of people brought sandwiches, but Mother always packed lots of crunchy things, carrots and celery that infuriated the other patrons each time we chewed, along with cottage cheese in waxed paper, and fruit. We were never allowed to buy candy, but somehow Sherrye always had some money and bought it anyway. After a while I occasionally joined in her criminal ways, though I felt too guilty to do it very often. We would stay for the two features, then watch them all over again and get home in time to help with dinner.

I had so many crushes. I was in love with Paul Henreid, Warner Baxter, Betty Grable, John Garfield, Joan Leslie, and John Hodiak. I had the thrill of a lifetime one day while walking to elementary school. I was turning the corner at a stop sign and glanced up at a man waiting in his car across the street. It was Warner Baxter! I must have done a double take when I recognized him because he looked amused and gave me a great warm smile. All those teeth and that mustache smiling at me! No one believed me when I told them about it later.

Sometimes Mother, Sherrye, and I went on the bus to Hollywood and walked down Vine Street or around the area near Grauman's Chinese Theater, hoping to catch a glimpse of movie stars. Occasionally we did see someone we recognized from the movies. Mother bought me a little pink autograph book, and over time I collected several signatures, the first being Sid Grauman himself.

I longed to be part of that magical world, but I kept my desire a secret. It never occurred to me that it was possible. It was a complete mystery to me how people in life got to be up on the screen. Most people in those days, even in Los Angeles, had never seen a movie camera and had no knowledge of the mechanics of it all. Most people did not yet have television; we certainly didn't. They didn't know agents or people who had been in the movies. All they knew was that you paid your dime and walked into a golden, darkened palace, and suddenly there on the screen were gigantic images of incredibly beautiful, perfect people, living extraordinary lives. I told no one of my desire. I couldn't bear the ridicule if I spoke the truth: that I wanted to transport myself into that gilded, mysterious unknown.

The day my mother voiced my deepest wish, I thought, *She knows my secret—it's out.* I was very excited.

Mother continued, "Here's a coupon in the paper that we can fill out. It's a contest, and if you win, you'll get a screen test for the movies." It was the Better Babies Beauty and Health or Talent Contest, sponsored by the *L.A. Herald-Express*, a local Hearst newspaper.

Oh, so that's how it's done, I thought. *How clever of my mother to have found out.* So my mother filled out the coupon entering me into the Beauty and Health division of the contest. We often entered contests, but we had never entered anything like this. Most of the contests were letter-writing contests, and Sherrye usually wrote the letters. There was one I was still yearning to win. The prize was a charming $25,000 two-bedroom house. It was made of beautiful red bricks and stucco. I kept a picture of it in our room on top of the chest of drawers.

This time we had to send in a snapshot that Sherrye took of me with my mouth closed, so the judges wouldn't see my crooked teeth. We would be notified in about six months about whether I should come downtown and be inspected for health and beauty. There were many prizes, but the grand prize would be given to six lucky children. It was a screen test at Warner Bros. Studios. In the meantime, I prayed to win the red brick house, which would mean, among other things, we could have a dog.

About this time my friend Corrine, who lived across the street in a real house, started taking harp lessons on Saturday mornings at a converted church, the Guy Bates Post Academy. I would walk with her to her class just a few blocks away, come home, and wait for her to return to play with me. Then my mother heard that the academy gave elocution lessons as well. I was still an uncommunicative, silent child, shy with anyone other than Corrine and my immediate family. The constant excuses in front of friends that Sissy was "shy" simply made it worse. My mother had done the best she could to change this. She made me practice by insisting I go up to strangers in the park, of course with her standing close by, and asking, "Would you please give me the correct time?" Each and every time I had to do this, it was increasingly humiliating. When the talking practice failed, elocution lessons seemed to her to be a logical next step.

Corrine and I would walk to the academy and back home together every Saturday morning. It was very nice. While Corrine was learning to play the harp, I was given a "diction" lesson: a list of words and how to pronounce them ("Teuuessday, not Toosday"), and I learned to recite two monologues, a comedy and a dramatic piece. When my parents had friends over to play cards, I would be asked to practice by reciting for them while standing in the little space behind the couch. The friends were tolerant, but most continued to play on.

One day in public school we were told to memorize a poem or speech about anything and be prepared to do it in front of the class. I thought, *How lucky—I already know something by heart!* I decided I would do the comedy monologue, called "The Old Maid." I would play an old maid on a shipboard cruise who talks about all of the men in her life and impersonates them with various accents as she talks. It never occurred to me that it was odd, a ten-year-old playing an old maid. I didn't think I was especially good at it; others in my elocution class were quite skillful and polished. But I knew the piece by heart, and I did find it fun to slip behind those people.

On the day of our recitations, when my name was called, I went to the front of the classroom, took a deep breath as I was taught, and started my piece. About three lines into my English accent, there was a sudden roar of surprised laughter and some stomping of feet. The teacher called, "Quiet!" But the laughter continued as I performed, becoming so loud that the teacher had to silence the children a number of times. When it was over, there was thunderous applause, whooping and hollering and stomping of feet. I couldn't believe what was happening. I began to tremble; my body got so weak, I wasn't sure I'd make it back to my desk. But I managed and sat down, still trembling, not yet comprehending that the whole world had just opened up for me.

After that day, whenever our class had finished our work and had free time, instead of asking the teacher to read us a story that we loved, the children almost in unison would shout, "Oh, let Rosetta do her piece again! Let Rosetta do her piece!" I did the piece dozens of times. And always they would roar with appreciation.

When the time came to cast the school play, *Hansel and Gretel,* I was asked to play Gretel. I said I would rather not, that I would rather direct. And they let me! I have no idea why I thought I could. A small but real confidence came over me. I had no trouble talking to the children about the work. I knew what I wanted, and the words flowed un-self-consciously. But when rehearsals were over, I reverted to my inhibited, silent self.

Hansel and Gretel was a success, and I decided to write my own original play. These were the war years, so naturally it had a patriotic theme. I called it *The Hoarder*. The main character was a selfish citizen who hoarded flour, sugar, coupons, butter, rubber tires, and stockings—anything and everything that was rationed. I brought children home to our apartment to rehearse. Again, I had no trouble talking to the children. My mind was focused on the work. I couldn't get a boy to play the lead, so I cast a very tall girl named Carrie who had short blond hair to play the hoarder. The children finally learned their parts, and we put the play on in our homeroom with great success. The performance was so well received that the teacher across the hall heard about it, and my teacher invited the other class to double up in the seats with us, to see the play again. The following week the principal invited us to put on the play in the auditorium for the whole school. I was sorry my sister had graduated to junior high and missed the performance. I would have liked showing off for her.

My mother must have been pleased with herself for having made the decision to send me to elocution lessons. Following my success as director of my original play, she suggested that since there was still time to make a change, we should move me from the Beauty and Health section into the Talent division of the Better Babies Contest, and I could recite one of my monologues. Not long afterward we received a postcard that invited us to go downtown to the Eastern Columbia Department Store Auditorium on a certain day to "show them my talent."

The large auditorium was filled that day with perhaps a dozen little boys and what seemed like hundreds of little girls in fancy dresses and costumes, many of them wearing rouge and lipstick. Tap dancers, singers, and acrobats. Since my entire wardrobe consisted of two nice cotton school dresses, I had little choice about what to wear. I told myself I was glad not to have to wear a fluffy costume, though I secretly loved them.

My mother said, "God's with you," before I went on stage. She said that so often during the course of any day that it had lost any spiritual connotation for me. It was just something she said when I tripped, before I hit the ground. It was said as one word, "Goswiyou," the instant something might be going wrong that she couldn't stop. The sound of it was the equivalent of stroking or hugging me. I never ceased to be both annoyed and comforted by it. Even as an adult, I was touched by it.

I followed an acrobat and did my dramatic monologue. It was about a little Italian girl, with accent, who pleads with a judge to release her though she stole five dollars to buy "d'medicina" for her dying mother. It was easy for me, as it is for many children, to bury myself completely in the role. I was very moved by the story of the girl's love for her perfect mother. I genuinely sobbed as I pleaded with the judge. When it was over, some of the adults seemed touched, and the children seemed bewildered. *Why is that little girl crying on stage?*

Many weeks later we were informed by mail that I was in the semi-finals. I would have to perform again. After that, if I made it, I would be one of six children getting the first prize of a screen test. My parents told me not to get excited, as I would not likely be a winner. It was the old Eastern European curse again: Don't brag, or something bad will happen. Several weeks later I again went to the auditorium and decided that this time I would do my comedy piece. I'd never had such a large audience before. Most of my competitors and their parents laughed in the right places, and my mother seemed proud of me. Not long afterward my parents received a letter informing us that I was one of the six winners. I had won a screen test.

The screen test was to be shot in the darkness of a soundstage at Warner Bros. Studios in Burbank. I had no idea how a screen test worked; I was so ignorant of the whole process that I had never even heard the term "soundstage." I knew nothing about the mechanical aspects of making movies. I had never even seen a movie camera. There were no studio tours or television shows to learn from, so when I walked onto the soundstage that day, I walked into a nightmare of the unknown. I don't remember how we got there. My father had the car, so we must have gone by bus or streetcar, but I have no memory of it. My anxiety pushed me into a kind of fugue state. I do remember being very cold in strange, very white, brightly lit rooms filled with what seemed to be dentist's chairs. I was told to sit in one, and they patted my face with something wet. Pancake makeup?

The only part of the experience that is totally clear is the moment I was finally perched on a high stool that someone slowly turned. A monolith that they called the camera (they were huge in those days) took movies of every angle of my face. Then I was turned to face the monster squarely, and the director started to ask questions, "to see," he said, "what kind of personality you have."

With the first question, "Tell me your name, darling," something agonizing and powerful crushed me from inside. As if pulled down by a powerful magnet, my chin dropped to my chest and I could not lift it. Nor could I speak. There was a place deep in my body that flooded with pain, and I had an overwhelming need to weep like a small child. If I dared speak a word, the pain would be unleashed, and I would sob uncontrollably. So I sat immobilized, my chin glued to my chest.

The movie star Dennis Morgan had strolled onto the set during the test and saw my distress. I saw him out of the corner of my eye and recognized him. He was very jolly and, with great warmth, tried to cajole me into lifting my head. His speech seemed a little slurred, and I could smell alcohol on his breath, but I felt his kindness. I could not, however, lift my head until they said I could go home. These attacks of anxiety would continue without warning for many years, far into adulthood, and I could neither stop nor control them. Needless to say, my first screen test was an abject failure.

Never one to give up, Mother thought more classes would help me grow out of my shyness. Sherrye, who was thirteen, had a beautiful natural singing voice, and Mother hoped to develop that as well. She drove us to classes almost every day after school. There was tap dancing with Johnny Boyle for a few months and a few ballet classes with Nico Charisse himself at his studio, a half block from the Charlie Chaplin Studios on La Brea. Nico's young bride and protégée worked in the office and answered the telephone. We never saw her dance until years later, when she appeared in MGM musicals as the beautiful Cyd Charisse. Sherrye and I also went to "charm" school, where we actually walked around with books on our heads like they do in the movies and worked on our posture and speech. When there was no money for private lessons, we took group singing and acting classes from third-rate teachers.

My mother did not want to be seen as a stage mother, and she often talked in front of us about not wanting her kids to be "Hollywood kids." If she saw that we were changing, she said, she would stop our lessons. Mother seemed to enjoy talking about me and for me, which was okay with me. I didn't want people to know what my thoughts were anyway. In those days, spoken words seemed to be used hypocritically and dishonestly by most of the adults I encountered. I would rather say nothing than speak ignorantly or untruthfully, and it was easier to remain silent than to fight through my fears. And so I let my mother speak. I think she liked things that way. She appeared to most people like a benign stage mother, not at all like the loud, pushy mothers we saw who put makeup on their kids and dragged them everywhere. My mother was always ladylike and soft-spoken in public, and most people believed the image she created. I instinctively knew better. She had a plan for her girls, and nothing was going to stop her. We would be successful in show business, financially independent, with careers. She had constant battles about the cost of tuition with our father, who felt his very hard-earned money was being wasted.

But it wasn't only my mother's ambition that drove me. I wanted very much to be noticed and praised. Ever since I had seen the young Jane Withers on stage in Detroit, bathed in that warm pink light, I had secretly and guiltily yearned to be that unfortunate creature, a "child star." (Jane Withers actually grew up to be a lovely and dear woman whom I have had the pleasure to know.) Child stars, it seemed to me, got so much more attention than adult stars. Think of all the power I would have! I never thought any of this out intellectually, only intuitively. I think I liked the path Mother had chosen for me. Though I would never marry for anything but love, I was more than willing to work toward a career in the movies.

Sherrye continued taking private singing lessons, but she never liked to practice. I never thought I'd be good enough, so I worked harder. Sherrye and I started doing singing and dancing comedy skits, entertaining wounded soldiers at the Sawtelle Veterans' Hospital and at many Red Cross and war bond rallies. We also performed for the people at the original Jewish Home for the Aging, when it was still east of downtown L.A. in Boyle Heights. In one of our most well-received numbers, we sang, "When it's sweet onion time in Bermuda, I'll breathe my love to you. We will frolic among the garlic. . . ." We'd sing several choruses, and during the second one I'd skip around and toss green onions to the audience that were hidden in a pretty basket I carried. We stole the idea from the Duncan Sisters, the vaudevillians who did "Topsy and Eva" at a theater on Hollywood Boulevard.

We were constantly entertaining somewhere on weekends. It wasn't just for the experience; Mother actually believed in public service. And I did, too. We wrote a letter to President Roosevelt volunteering my services for just about anything and enclosed a homemade recording of one of my tearful monologues. An assistant responded almost a year later, without an assignment, just a thank-you.

We also entered the regular Friday night talent contest at downtown Clifton's Cafeteria. Clifton's is a Los Angeles landmark that's still there after all these years, serving free sherbet in a little dish that comes sliding down a chute. One night Sherrye sang a patriotic song, and I did a monologue about a little girl whose father was not coming home from the war. I won the first prize of five silver dollars for my monologue. For years mother kept the silver dollars in a box labeled "Sissy's first earned money."

Sometimes before we performed, I was aware that my mother was quite anxious. She would then pull a small bottle out of her purse. It contained wine diluted with honey and water. The wine was normally used for my mother's Passover sponge cake. Sherrye and I were told to take a sip to clear our throats and to relax us. The wine always went right to my legs. Mother never drank any herself, though she was the one who appeared to need relaxing. No one actually drank at home, either, though we did keep a bottle of schnapps under the kitchen sink for Grandpa when he came to visit. It's a miracle Sherrye and I didn't grow up to be alcoholics. I suppose we chose other vices.

Always on the lookout for good teachers, my mother heard about a German actress named Hermine Sterler who had escaped from Europe just before the war and occasionally gave private lessons. She was living in Hollywood at the Tower Apartments on Highland Avenue, just north of where the famous Kodak Theatre is now. Miss Sterler was the first fine teacher I ever had. She helped me to lose the "tricks" that I had picked up as a child performer. It's easy for children to fake things. Miss Sterler had me work on a scene from a play that required a little girl to walk into a room with her doll and speak to someone. The text informed us that the girl had come from a place that was hot, and the girl was tired. Over and over Miss Sterler had me enter the room until I had recalled, with sense memory, what the girl was supposed to be feeling. If I truly recalled that sensory memory, something extremely subtle changed in the way my body moved, the way my face rested, the way I breathed, and the way I behaved in the next moments. Of course, part of the art of acting lies in knowing how far to go with the internal work and the choices one makes. In any case, she made me understand the importance of bringing something genuine with me into the room from offstage instead of just starting from zero when I appeared. She called my attention to the importance of simplicity. These were important lessons for an eleven-year-old. For reasons that I did not understand at the time, Mother stopped the lessons after about six months, saying that "the woman" was feeling too close to me. I couldn't understand why that was a bad thing. Miss Sterler made me feel I had a future if I worked hard. There was nothing strange about her affection for me. I was bewildered, but I had no alternative but to accept my mother's decision. Mother often seemed competitive with women around her own age. Whatever my mother's reasons for cutting me off from her, Hermine Sterler was the first person to ask me to use my own truth in my work.

In later years I saw Miss Sterler a few times in movies, playing small roles requiring an intelligent-looking woman with an accent. I assumed she had gone back to Germany after the war or had died. I thought of Miss Sterler many times through the years but never tried to contact her. Somehow to do so seemed disloyal to my mother.

During the long years in the sanitarium, I had felt like a motherless child. Three years after leaving it, my mother consumed my life. For better or worse, my life had become hers, and I didn't know any other way to live it.

3.

The Real Thing

When I was twelve, Mother heard that a small professional theater in town was looking for a young girl to be in a play. Perhaps one of my teachers mentioned it. An appointment was made for me to meet Harry Hayden. He was a well-known character actor who owned the theater together with his actress wife, Lela Bliss. The play was *Guest in the House*. It was to be given at the Bliss-Hayden Theatre on Robertson. The theater is still there, now called the Beverly Hills Playhouse.

Mother and I arrived for our appointment and were both invited into Harry Hayden's tiny office. I recognized him from movies I'd seen. He asked me to read a scene from the play. And then another. He asked me to come back, and the routine was pretty much the same. More reading and suggestions. Mother sat quietly, watching from a chair against the wall. I must give her credit—she never interfered with the actual work or tried to coach me. Not once, not even at home, when no one was watching, did she ever suggest a line reading for me. When we finished, Harry Hayden said, "I want you to play this little girl, but I know for sure that someday you'll be a famous leading lady." I wondered if he meant what he said. It was hard for me to tell if people were sincere. I almost never believed them completely. But I think on some level I was storing up some of the votes of confidence.

For now, I had a part in a real play, a professional play. I had many scenes throughout and was excited by the responsibility to be where I needed to be for entrances at exactly the right time. I was to play an innocent little girl in the psychodrama starring Marissa O'Brien, a pretty actress in her late twenties who happened to be Margaret O'Brien's aunt.

I got my first Actors' Equity card that year. Well, it was actually a "working permit" card. It was dated 1944, with a big FIRST YEAR stamped in red, diagonally across the front. It certified that "ROSETTA COBB" was a member in good standing. Sherrye and I had been performing together as the "Cobb Sisters," using the last syllable of our real name minus the *s*, Ja-*cob*, as our last name. I had changed my name for the first time, and not the last.

We played only on weekends for several months. It was an exciting time for me, and I was learning so much. Margaret O'Brien, who was a few years younger than me and a big star at Metro-Goldwyn-Mayer, came to one of the performances. We were not introduced, but I watched very carefully afterward as she walked out to the street, holding hands with her mother. She had on shiny black patent-leather Mary Janes. She didn't look as happy as I thought she should, wearing those shoes. Could it be that being a child star wasn't that much fun?

A lot of people saw me in the play, and by the time the run ended, I had a "part time" agent, someone in a little office at the end of the Sunset Strip. The agent arranged for me to have another screen test. This one was almost as much of a trauma for me as the first had been. I felt like I was walking through fog, terrified to be on a movie lot once more. After a series of meetings and auditions, I was screen-tested for the part of Jane Powell's little sister in an MGM musical called *Three Daring Daughters*. Jane was so polite and confident and seemed very grown up. She's still such a tiny little thing, but at the time she was a good head taller than me. I remember little about the screen test, except sitting on an ottoman saying my few lines to Jane. I didn't know the circumstances of the story or what the scene was about, and I was very uncomfortable. I wasn't even sure when the camera was rolling.

I didn't get the job, but an appointment was made for me to be interviewed by the highly regarded talent and acting coach for the studio, Lillian Burns. Lillian Burns was the star maker for all the young contract players at MGM. I sat in an antique armchair in the large office. It was beautifully furnished as if it were a living room, with lush carpeting and paintings. After she had asked me a few questions, and I mumbled some answers, she suddenly said, "You can't do pictures, my dear. One of your eyes is lower than the other." What a blow.

I slunk out of the office, feeling a little embarrassed that I had inflicted my face on her. Who knows why she saw what she did? Perhaps she'd been looking at too many Picassos, or I may have slept on my face the night before. I was very affected by the remark. My mother, who was waiting in the car, assured me it was not true, and I guess I trusted her enough to forget about it. Besides, I figured, so much else about my appearance was unlike a movie star, what difference did that make?

About a year later I signed a test-option contract at Fox studio and was filmed doing the Elizabeth Taylor part in *Life with Father*. I watched it and thought I was really quite awful. Clearly, I didn't know what I was doing. The performance was so erratic. One moment would be fine, and then I'd lose my concentration, and the character would be gone. Even I could see that I was just Rosetta. It was so painful to watch. Truthfully, watching myself has gotten only a little less painful through the years, and I do it as little as possible. When it was all over, I went to see Elizabeth Taylor in the movie. I had deliberately held off doing that because even I knew it wouldn't be good to do an imitation of her. She seemed so skilled and poised. I didn't think I'd ever be able to do that, seem to be a real person on the screen. And it was becoming too late for me to be a child star, which had been the whole point. But that was something I could never tell anyone.

I walked to Hebrew school every day that summer. It was a five-mile walk that was self-imposed. I enjoyed the opportunity to be at a geographical distance from my mother, who seemed to be all knowing, all seeing. There were lessons to prepare for my bas mitzvah (we called it confirmation at that time), and I wrote my own speech. Our tiny Orthodox shul (the Mogen David) was in a lower-middle-class neighborhood on Gramercy Place near Venice Boulevard. (Years later it moved to a nicer part of town.) Rabbi Marin officiated at all our family events.

I was growing up. The braces that I'd worn for two and a half years came off. More important, I was successful in convincing my mother to cut my hair! I had been wearing my thick red hair in little-girl braids far longer than was appropriate.

The cutting was done in a ritualistic way. My freshly washed hair was braided one last time. Holding large scissors tightly in hand, my mother, with clenched teeth, savagely cut through each braid at shoulder length. She saved the braids, wrapping them carefully in tissue paper and giving them to me years later. When my hair started getting darker, the studio used them for a color match.

Now that I was transformed, I deliberately made myself late to school so that I could make a grand entrance. I'd always hated being late, having to walk from the back of the room to the front to hand my excuse to the teacher. All eyes on me. Weird red hair. Not many people dyed their hair red in those days, so the red was clearly something we couldn't help, like a family disease. My gigantic freckles, an absolutely square body, and not yet a sign of breasts. And to top it off, I could not move up the aisle between the seats without hitting them all, bouncing from one hip to the other.

But now I wanted them to look. I arrived ten minutes late. It was like being on stage. I walked slowly and carefully up an aisle, not hitting a single desk, tossing my shoulder-length bob a little until I caught someone's eye. Someone whispered, "Oh, look at Rosetta! Look at her hair!" Someone else said, "Oh, yeah, she cut it. Ohooooooooo." I felt I had joined the land of human beings.

A few months later Chickie, a popular girl who had never spoken to me before, walked over to me in the schoolyard at lunchtime. She said in a confident voice, "Oh, Rosetta, you're getting to be really cute now." She studied me for a moment, looking a little troubled. "If you just had some personality."

I wanted so to be like the girls who talked to boys. They wore cashmere sweaters and rode bicycles to school and always seemed to be laughing and having fun. I had never laughed out loud in my life. I would just shake a lot and make little sputtering sounds. I was still known as "quiet little Rosetta" and continued to have a lot of difficulty forming personal relationships.

I was hitting puberty, becoming interested in boys, and starting to cool to the idea of having a career. I hadn't done any acting for a while, but my life seemed full. I was valedictorian of my junior high graduation class. There were no more lessons, and my attention was increasingly focused on my personal life.

My sister Sherrye had lost a lot of weight and now looked voluptuous and beautiful. Only seventeen, she became engaged to an ex-sailor whom none of us liked. My mother became obsessed about his family: "They aren't good enough for Sherrye or our family!" I myself believed my sister was marrying him just to get out of the house. I kept my mouth shut, but I didn't like him, either. I thought he was kind of stupid, with a weak character, and was ashamed of being Jewish. He had had his nose fixed and changed his name from Ginsberg to Wade. I had little tolerance in those days.

Despite their misgivings, my parents gave Sherrye a beautiful wedding at a big hotel in Santa Monica. It cost my dad $5,000, a small fortune for us or most anyone in those days. I was the maid of honor and sang "The Anniversary Waltz" at the dinner. I was very nervous, but my sister and parents insisted that I sing. I wore high heels and a silver metallic dress that was much too grown up for a fourteen-year-old, and I fixed my hair like Veronica Lake, over one eye. My parents were so preoccupied with the wedding that they paid little attention to me, which was probably a good thing. I needed a little breathing and growing space.

The marriage did not go well from the start. My sister, however, was heroic. She worked full time, got her husband through pre-med and medical school, and cooked and baked for his friends when they came over to do homework. She became the perfect doctor's wife and gave all the expected parties. She hid her unhappiness under her steadily increasing weight. They had the first of three children after ten years of marriage. He left her after twenty years because he couldn't deal with her obesity.

With Sherrye's wedding behind her, my mother turned her attention back to me and my career. It was impossible to figure her out. She was always worried about the boys at school getting "fresh." She would tell me, "Just make sure they keep their hands to themselves." I was bewildered about what she thought was going on. The boys my age were actually quite shy and timid. She and I never talked about sex. There was never any "the birds and the bees" conversation. None of my friends knew anything about it. A girl in the schoolyard once told us that you had to be careful about kissing boys too much, that the boy's "thing down there" would "blow up." I didn't know if that meant like a dynamite explosion or like a balloon reaching large proportions. It was disturbing, to say the least. Of course, I couldn't imagine my parents ever having sex, so there's a possibility they thought the same about me. And it was true for quite a long time. I was lucky because I was never once chased around a desk or faced with a casting couch dilemma.

My mother never suspected the true intentions behind the visit with Howard Hughes, and I was still a naïve fifteen when another agent took me to Charlie Chaplin's beautiful home in one of the canyons. Chaplin was looking for a girl to be in *Limelight*. He lived in a mansion, or so it seemed to me. I didn't go inside, but the grounds that I saw were magnificent, and I was taken to a sun porch overlooking the tennis court. A few of Mr. Chaplin's friends were enjoying themselves on a Sunday afternoon, watching him play tennis. After a while Mr. Chaplin and his friend came up to the porch to say hello and get something to drink. He was quite jovial, and his cheeks were flushed as he chatted with everyone. When we were introduced, he seemed genuinely pleased to meet me and treated me like a guest, not like an unknown to be judged. He made sure I had something cold to drink and took great pleasure in patting me on the cheek.

Nothing specific was said about work, and after about an hour we left.

I was too naïve to realize how demeaning the whole thing was—the agent dragging me around, putting me on display. If Chaplin knew why I was there, he didn't let on. But at least I didn't feel I was on display. I was grateful for that. I didn't yet have the maturity or discipline to play the part anyway. But Claire Bloom was indeed lovely in the role.

I was blowing with the wind as far as my career was concerned. These meetings with such accomplished strangers were scary and unpleasant, but I didn't feel I was permitted to say so. A couple of times my mother asked me straight out if I wanted to continue, and I was afraid to say that I didn't or even that I didn't know. I knew in my heart my mother would be profoundly disappointed if I gave it all up. I would probably never be forgiven. It would take many years for me to see I was getting this all wrong.

Not long after that at a place called Highland Springs, I met the man who became my manager. Highland Springs was an inexpensive resort in the desert that Mother and I went to where I could swim and ride horses all day long. The cowboy in charge of the horses, John McNamara, was in his eighties. He was also a poet. He and I would go out on a trail or up in the mountains, he'd hold my hand and recite poetry to me. I was so very comfortable out there in the mountains with John and felt released from all the guilt I carried. I would ride Bonnie, a pinto who had eaten locoweed and occasionally tossed me off for no reason. I found myself suddenly on the ground at least a dozen times, no broken bones, but feeling accomplished.

In the evenings we would square dance and sometimes I would participate in the comedy sketches put on by the entertainment director. It was fun being in "show business." The sketches were a little like the vaudeville I'd seen as a small child. A man named Ted Raden saw me in the sketches and introduced himself to my mother. He had a job as an executive assistant at Enterprise Studios and he told my mother he would like to be my manager. Ted told her that if I wanted to have a career in show business, she should buy "flashy" clothes for me to wear wherever I went, attention-grabbing clothes in loud colors. I listened to his suggestions with a lot of discomfort. Luckily for me, my parents weren't about to go out and buy me a new wardrobe. Mother did, however, buy me a long woolen coat of Day-Glo chartreuse. People stopped and stared, all right, which was the opposite of what I desired, except when I was acting.

Ted would come to the apartment frequently for dinner. It was an opportunity for my parents to grill him and see if he was honorable. He was very careful not to step over the line with me in a physical way. I was fifteen, although we told him I was eighteen, and he was in his thirties. My mother told me to lie about my age. She didn't want people to know how young I was because somehow she thought being older would make getting acting jobs easier. I lied about my age so much in those days that I was never able to celebrate my sweet sixteenth. I just skipped it. No regrets. At one point I told Ted my true age. He didn't seem surprised.

Ted arranged for me to sing a newly written song called "Under the Arch" at the wrap party for the film *Arch of Triumph*, which starred Ingrid Bergman and Charles Boyer. I dreaded the whole idea, but it was something he had gone to some pains to arrange, and he and my mother expected me to do this. There was a small band, and I wore the silver metallic dress from my sister's wedding, high heels, my hair upswept, and mascara and lipstick. The fifteen-year-old was trying to look twenty-five. No one paid any attention to me or the song as I sang nervously with the band. There were several hundred people at the party, but the stars were out of town, and I was not "discovered."

One day as I waited for Ted in a small outer office at the studio where he worked, the ground-floor window was suddenly opened from the outside, and a dashingly handsome John Garfield climbed through, appearing delighted with himself for his audacity. He looked so different from the way I had always seen him in the movies: tense, troubled, and in black and white. Now he was shiny and rosy-cheeked, as if he'd just stepped out of the shower. Most likely he had; he'd been shooting on the lot. After cracking wise to the secretary and laughing at his joke, he disappeared behind the producer's door.

Ted told me one evening that he had thought of a good professional name for me and handed me a scrap of yellow paper with "piper laurie" written on it. He'd not capitalized it, so it looked strange. I didn't care for it because it didn't seem to be a name. He couldn't explain how he'd thought of it; he said it just came to him! I had used a variety of professional names by then. In those days it was understood that Rosetta Jacobs was not a name that could be used professionally. Everyone advised us so. Not because of its ethnicity, I never thought of it as such, but because it didn't sound like Lana or Cary and was hard to remember. It never occurred to me that I didn't have to change my name. For the last twenty or thirty years, I've admired and envied all the performers who have proudly used their real names. The longer and harder to pronounce, the better.

One serendipitous evening a few months later, Ted took me to see a production of Euripides' *Medea*, starring Judith Anderson, at the Biltmore Theater downtown. My eyes were opened that night and have yet to close. I had never before seen a legitimate play, much less a Greek tragedy of such power. We sat so far up, we could hardly see Miss Anderson. If she exposed her breasts at one moment, as rumored, we certainly couldn't tell. What moved me was her inner nakedness. I could hear her and feel her power. The whole experience of the play was life-changing for me. It was so clear—the beauty, creativity, and especially the courage of the theater and the actors were what I wanted. My dreams were now being transformed into another vision, completely my own.

Ted continued to look for opportunities for me. One evening he told me that he'd heard about a class of professional actors headed by Benno and Betomi Schneider. They had come from Russia by way of the Habima Players, who were the Hebrew-speaking part of the Moscow Art Theatre. The Habima Players had moved to Israel and become what is now the State Theater of Israel. Benno and his wife, Betomi, later moved to New York and then out to Los Angeles, where they worked with the Actor's Lab and privately coached stars who worked for Samuel Goldwyn and Warner Bros. They were also conducting classes for working actors. On the West Coast the Schneiders' group was considered one of the very best. Ted made arrangements for the Schneiders to interview me.

That evening Ted drove me to their studio on Yucca Avenue in

Hollywood and waited in his car. We both had grave doubts about my being accepted into the class. They were all working professionals, and I was an inexperienced unknown. Betomi was the one to interview me in the small office. She was a striking-looking woman with stringy blond hair that was not quite shoulder length. She was not as old as my mother, but her face showed that she had seen and experienced everything in this world. With her thick but intelligible Russian accent, she asked me about myself, and I told her I wanted to become a good actress. She asked how old I was. Though I was still fifteen, without makeup and sophisticated clothes, people thought I was perhaps thirteen. I told Betomi I was eighteen. She scrutinized my face, trying to see beneath the makeup.

"I don't know what I'd do with you in the class," she said. "The others are quite a bit older. What kind of scenes could I find for you to work on? I'm sorry. I think this will be difficult if not impossible."

I held my breath as she looked at me for a long moment, and then she said, "Perhaps we will try—just for a few weeks. Are you agreeable for a trial?"

I was beside myself with excitement and fear when Ted picked me up and dropped me off for the first class. The studio was a good-size room with a small, elevated stage at one end. There were three rows of students sitting on folding wooden chairs, about twenty-five in all. Some had faces that I recognized from films. All were ten to twenty or more years older than me. I remember thinking that I was truly out of my element, that everyone looked so grown up and professional. I sat in the middle row on the very end, the better to hide.

Betomi brought the class to order and asked if anyone had a scene they wanted to do. There was total silence. Anyone who has attended an acting class taught by a highly respected teacher knows the kind of silence I'm talking about. It's filled with terror and insecurity. After a moment Betomi went on: "We have no scenes? No one is ready to do their scene?" Everybody seemed frozen. It was like people at an auction afraid to make a false move, afraid the smallest movement will commit them to something irrevocable and dangerous.

"All right, then," she said. "We will do improvisations. Who will go first?" Silence. "Yes? . . . Who will go?" More silence.

Betomi was seated in the middle of the front row. She turned around and looked at all the students. "There is no one—no one who is brave?"

That was my call. Her words went right through my gut. In a flash I knew I must jump off the fifty-foot diving board and die if necessary. My whole life's desire was compressed into this moment. Live or die. I forced myself to put up a hand, and I kept it there like steel.

Betomi saw my hand and said, "Oh . . . we have the new one . . . all right." If she looked surprised, I didn't notice. I was already walking to the edge of the cliff in my mind.

Betomi called me to join her in the corner of the room. She quietly told me some of the circumstances of the improvisation, but not all. My partner, a woman in her thirties named Irene Vernon, would be told the other part.

This was a kind of madness. I had never before done an improvisation. It meant relying on my ability to verbalize, which hadn't improved significantly. I don't remember the specifics of the scene. What I do recall is Irene coming in and accusing me of stealing her watch. That was all I needed. I had suffered for years from guilt about an apple I'd taken from the Reslocks' personal dining room table without permission. It was the only thing I'd ever stolen. Now my potent imagination just overcame me, and in my raw emotion I somehow found the necessary words. At some point, when we'd gone as far as we could go, the scene was stopped. I could see that Betomi was pleased that I had worked that fully. That night she assigned me a scene to work on with Irene. It was the scene from *The Children's Hour* where the child is falsely accused of stealing a watch.

Mother would take me to Irene's little house in Culver City, and we'd rehearse while she waited in the car. Irene had been under contract to MGM at one time and still lived near the studio. We worked on the scene for about two weeks and then presented it to the class. Betomi was wise; it was a good choice of scene. The class gave their critiques. One could learn a lot from those critiques, most especially about the people giving them. Betomi gave the final commentary, which was the one we waited for and took most seriously. She said I was an excellent "listener." As far as I was concerned, listening was the only thing I could do. I felt safer if I really engaged and focused on what was being said. My concentration and imagination, out of necessity and opportunity, had developed so fully during my childhood. It was one of the gifts from those years.

I got to stretch a bit with older parts like *Street Scene*, *Awake and Sing!*, lots of Tennessee Williams, and of course, *Our Town*, plus improvisations in every class. All the reading of plays was a social education for an unsophisticated young person.

I was in Betomi's class for almost three years, and she never actually told me that I had been accepted. It never came up. We just kept going on with the work. Only once did my lack of life experience trip me up. I did an improvisation with the thirtyish, handsome, and overtly confident actor Dale Robertson. I was playing a diseased, end-of-the-road streetwalker in the improvisation. My goal was to get him to hire me. Unknown to me, his "action" was to arrest streetwalkers because he was an undercover officer. I was seated on a "park bench" when he strolled by. I flirted, he sat down, and after a little conversation, he asked how much I charged.

Dale probably expected me to say a dollar, or even fifty cents, which at that time would have been about right. I tried to think of the lowest possible figure for such an act, to give away one's body at the cheapest price. So I said, "A hundred dollars"—in the money of that time, perhaps enough to buy a cheap secondhand car. Along with Dale's double take and guffaw came raucous laughter from the entire class. It went on for about five minutes, and finally the improvisation had to stop. I had no idea what they were laughing about until Irene told me.

In addition to the scenes, every two weeks we had body movement. Gerri, a dance and movement teacher, gave us stretches and strengthening exercises. Then we would improvise to music and tell a story with our bodies in any kind of dance form, using the whole room as freely as we could—alone or with a partner. Most of us were not dancers and were pretty clumsy. It took courage to do these exercises without inhibition.

Just as Hermine Sterler had tried a few years earlier, Betomi kept hammering out my "tricks," which I would go to when I hadn't really done my homework or didn't know what to do. She made me work to be "specific" about subtext and to be honest in every moment, intellectually and emotionally. Not in the self-indulgent, masturbatory style of some misunderstood so-called methods that encourage actors to *feel* everything, to forget to really *listen* to each other and forget that it is primarily the *audience* that's supposed to *feel*. Every good actor I know understands there are many methods, and every actor must find for himself pieces from all of them.

As anyone knows who has worked in an environment of mutual trust for a period of time, close relationships are formed, sometimes lasting a lifetime. It was true with my dear friend and classmate Bob Richards. Bob endeared himself to me right away when he told me I was a chatterbox. At first I was sure he was teasing me, but he stuck to his story through almost forty-five years of friendship. He knew it pleased me. The ease and confidence I felt with him might explain it.

Bob wanted to direct me for class in the Tennessee Williams one-act play *This Property Is Condemned.* It is a two-character play for a young boy and girl. The girl is at a railroad track, walking along an embankment carrying a banana and doll as she describes her older sister's "wonderful life," a life she dreams of having one day. Her sister is in fact a prostitute, but the child is oblivious to it. (The movie, which was made decades later, never showed the young girl but focused solely on the older sister, who is never seen in the play.) It was essentially a one-person play for me. My classmate Bob played the part of the young boy and had just a couple of words to say. It always reminded me of the inequality in length of the two parts in Beckett's *Happy Days*, which is a virtual monologue for the woman. *This Property Is Condemned* was one of those pieces of material that seemed so organic to my spirit and experience that it made any intellectual understanding irrelevant. I hadn't had enough life experience to understand the play, yet I instinctively understood the little girl and her choice of words from moment to moment. I didn't know that I was exactly the right person to speak those words, but my friend Bob helped me to trust myself. The play is so beautifully written, and I probably didn't get in the way.

We rehearsed for a long time. When we presented the play, which ran about twenty-five minutes, Betomi had only positive things to say about it. Not one criticism. *Was it real? It seemed so. How extraordinary.*

Not long afterward, for some family reason, we all had to go to New York City. While we were there, we had the rare and special experience of seeing Lee J. Cobb in the original *Death of a Salesman.* At the final curtain I saw my father cry for the first and only time in my life. If the theater could do that, I knew I was touching something wonderful.

I had just turned seventeen. My manager, Ted, had long before drifted out of my life. For a while he continued to take me to class twice a week and wait for me, taking me out for coffee afterward. Eventually, though, he grew tired of waiting three hours for me to finish class, so my mother, and sometimes my dad, took his place. One night my dad picked me up from class and when we got home he parked outside the apartment so he could get something off his chest. He begged me to stop all the classes and give up my ambition to be an actress. "There are thousands wanting to do this. The odds are so against you. What makes you think *you* have a chance? It's a waste of time and money. Forget it, Sissy. Just forget it."

I don't remember if I said anything. I couldn't look at him. I just stared at the glove compartment, not knowing how to respond. But I knew with my whole being that I would prove him wrong. My dad didn't realize he had succeeded in doing just the opposite of what he had hoped.

Some nights Benno, Betomi's husband, would take over the class. He was tougher than his wife. It was stimulating having a new teacher. He taught the more advanced class of movie actors, who were putting on a production of one-act plays and scenes at the Las Palmas Theater. I was not in that class, but I did get a phone call one evening around six o'clock from Benno. That was an event. My teacher was calling me!

Benno told me that one of the stars, Jayne Meadows, could not do the show for some reason. He asked, "Do you think you're ready to do the Williams play in public and replace Miss Meadows?"

I knew myself well enough to know I'd have a hard time forgiving myself for being a coward, so I said, "I think so."

And he said, "All right. Please come down immediately to the theater and rehearse on stage. You'll do the performance the night after tomorrow."

I said, "Yes, I'll be there."

That night, in fact, I had a special appointment with one of the two Hakim brothers, who were producers. I had never met Mr. Hakim, and I didn't know until later that he had a rather unsavory reputation. As far as my family knew, a nice man with an accent had called and said he was a friend of someone from the synagogue. He had spoken to my father and then to my mother, asking permission to take me to the opera. All we knew was that he had a famous name, produced movies, and sounded courteous and respectful on the phone. My mother seemed to think that this famous person with an accent would never risk doing anything bad, especially to an underage girl.

For my part, I was excited to be going to my first opera and Mother was excited for me. I had borrowed a tiny fur wrap from Irene for the occasion. Benno's call came a few minutes before Mr. Hakim was to arrive, I had no way of reaching him but there was no question in my mind that I must go to the rehearsal. I didn't like being rude, but naïvely I was sure my "date" would understand my decision. The show must go on. Surely he knew that.

I started getting into my rehearsal clothes and collected my props: the doll and banana. I was almost ready when we heard the doorbell. A chauffeur was standing in the narrow hall near the icebox door. "Mr. Hakim is waiting in the car," he informed us.

I said, "I'm so sorry, but I won't be able to go because, you see, I have an emergency rehearsal."

The chauffeur looked surprised and said, "Yes, ma'am, I'll tell him," and left. The tiny four-passenger elevator took about five minutes round trip, and suddenly we heard pounding on the front door.

My mother opened the door, and there stood Mr. Hakim in his tux, looking apoplectic. He pushed his way in and expressed his outrage.

"How dare you? Who do you think you are?"

He was beside himself with rage. And of course, he was quite justified, but I certainly didn't think so at the time. What about my art? Nothing was more important than that. I had never heard anyone speak as he did, had never heard some of the words. There were many terrible arguments in our house, but no one ever swore. His words were upsetting, but I stood my ground with the utter confidence in being right that only an adolescent can manage. We finally got Mr. Hakim to leave just minutes before someone from class came to take me to the rehearsal.

When I got to the theater, I was asked to go on stage and just block for lighting. I did little bits and pieces of the dialogue and waited as they lit for those spots. Benno seemed pleased with what I was doing and said he looked forward to seeing me the next day for a full rehearsal. I loved the feeling of being on the big stage. The warm stage lights went right through me to my heart.

When the morning came, however, Benno called and, with what I thought was genuine sorrow, said the problem that had existed for Jayne Meadows was no longer a problem. It appeared she would be able to go on after all. It was impossible to tell her that she couldn't. My legitimate debut on the big stage would have to wait. I was deeply disappointed, to say the least.

Tony Curtis, who was a new member of my acting class, drove me to the theater to pick up the props I'd left the night before. The air was heavy, and Tony tried to cheer me up. He had silently flirted with me outrageously since the first night he joined the class. Whenever I'd turn around that first night, he would make sexy eyes at me from the row behind. He looked as though he would die if he couldn't have me on the spot. It almost worked. We had gone to a few movies together. The first time he arrived at our front door, he announced to my mother, "Where's that crazy mixed-up kid?" a popular saying at the time. My mother was highly indignant at what she considered his crassness. Tony was under contract to Universal and had only done some bit parts, but girls were already coming up to him on the street and screaming with delight when we went to movies. He had a big, flashy convertible. It was the first time I had been out with someone who was in the movies. So exciting. I had kissed a few boys before, playing kissing games at parties, but Tony kissed better than any of them. I think actors practice. I thought he was very handsome, except for the shape of his mouth. It looked just like my awful brother-in-law's.

It was fun going out occasionally, but the work in acting class was still the most important thing in my life. I attended Los Angeles High School during the day, but after-school and weekends were devoted to rehearsals. I used to tell my acquaintances in high school that I couldn't go to football games or other school activities because of dental appointments and anything else I could think of. I didn't want them knowing about my theatrical ambitions. It was still a fragile thing to me. Plus, kids in those days who did "special" things after school were considered freaks. Only my friend Karlyn knew the truth. Though I had yearned for film stardom as a child, over the years I had grown to seek something else. My dream for the past three years, never expressed to anyone, had been to go to New York, study, and seek my fortune in the theater after high school.

Some of the casting people from the studios monitored Betomi's classes and admired the students' work. After a number of meetings and auditions, I was offered a test-option contract at Warner Bros. It was 1949, when they were ending the contracts of all their great stars. Solly Bianco, in particular, was very supportive and wanted to give me a test anyway, so there would be film of me that I could use. I didn't mention to him that somewhere in their archives might be a piece of film of a ten-year-old child in extreme distress.

I did a scene from *Mildred Pierce*, a film starring Joan Crawford in the title role as a woman who raises a spoiled daughter who grows up to steal her mother's lover. I played the daughter, the Ann Blyth part that got her an Academy Award nomination. It was a very meaty role. They had a skeleton crew shoot it, with the Joan Crawford part read off camera by one of the executives, a very young, blond, and handsome Bill Orr. Talk about using my imagination!

Shortly after I turned seventeen, my agent, Herb Brenner, showed the test to Universal-International, as it was called in those days. I was asked to come in for an interview. After an initial interview with the casting people, Millie Gussie and Bob Palmer, I was asked to prepare a three-minute audition scene for Sophie Rosenstein. Sophie Rosenstein had been the superb coach for all the great actors at Warner Bros. When she left Warner Bros., she was asked by Universal to work with their contract players. If she were working today she would have been a fine film director but for women in those days, it could not be. Ida Lupino was the sole woman director in this country during that period, the first we had had in decades.

I discussed the audition with Betomi, who suggested I do *This Property Is Condemned.* Knowing the routine at Universal, Betomi said I would be allowed to do three minutes only. The casting people or Sophie would stop me when the time was up, but I should start the audition at the beginning of the play anyway. My friend Bob Richards, who had directed it for class, would come with me and play the other part.

Bob picked me up in his little old car. When we got to the studio, we parked off the lot on the street. There was a pass waiting for us and we walked in and found Sophie's office up on the hill. In the office were the two casting heads, Bob Palmer and Millie Gussie, and of course, Sophie Rosenstein. Sophie was a tiny, large-breasted, birdlike woman with a slightly humped back, beaklike nose, full lips, piercing bright eyes, and more charm than a whole chorus line. Supremely intelligent, she had endless brilliant and handsome men at her feet. After brief introductions, Bob and I started the scene.

I had brought my little doll and a banana for props. I began walking along the imaginary railroad track singing, "You're the Only Star in My Blue Heaven." After going along for a little while, we reached the three-minute mark, and a small part of my brain was open to hearing *Thank you very much.* But it didn't come. We continued on, and still they did not stop us. So we kept going until suddenly the play was over. It was twenty-five minutes later, and everyone was applauding with shining eyes.

Sophie asked if we would come back and do the play again for the contract players' class. I felt as though I'd successfully climbed Mount Everest.

A few days later Bob and I came back. This time the room was crowded with young actors, many of whom we recognized. I held on to my banana and doll and tried to stay focused. Bob and I went through the play again, and when we finished, the room was silent for a few moments. Then the very good young actor Richard Long said in a profoundly serious way, "That's the best piece of work I've ever seen in this room."

I was beginning to feel very strong inside. I had gained some confidence verbalizing my thoughts in Betomi's class because I felt respect from my classmates. I had begun to trust my aesthetic judgment a little. But my confidence was fragile in the outside world.

While I was waiting to hear from Universal, Diana Douglas, who was in my acting class, must have mentioned me to her ex-husband, Kirk Douglas. He was preparing to produce a movie starring himself and was looking for a young girl to play opposite him. He asked if I would meet him for a cup of coffee. We met at a little coffee shop in Hollywood. My mother dropped me off and waited for me in the car. Kirk and I sat at a tiny table opposite each other. He was, of course, so very handsome and extremely intense. As best I understood it, I would be under contract to him for this movie and possibly others. The movie he described, and the part, sounded exactly right for me. I would have to choose between Universal and Kirk Douglas, whose plans (as I understood it) were not yet firm. I was seventeen and had no experience to draw upon, so I had to rely on agents to advise me. They advised me to wait for Universal. Knowing what I do today, it's entirely possible I missed a wonderful adventure with Mr. Douglas. But I regret little in my life, even the mistakes.

4.

Breaking Me In

Universal-International wanted to do their own screen test before deciding to put me under contract. I would take the test with another actor they were considering, Rock Hudson. Rock was six foot four, handsome, immensely likable, and (like me), a beginner. For our screen test, the casting people chose something from a screenplay the studio owned called *Thunder on the Hill*. Though undeveloped, I had the beginning of some judgment that I trusted. I knew that the role was much too sophisticated for me and that the script was melodramatic. Perhaps they were trying to see if I could play grown-up parts, but it all seemed so silly. One of my lines was "I love you like this, all stirred up with fire in your eyes." What seventeen-year-old of that period would say that? Neither Rock nor I could keep a straight face when I tried, but somehow we got through the test. Then, of course, we waited. . . . And waited.

Rock was always broke, and my mother loved feeding people, so he spent a lot of time at our apartment. He was a big eater and a big laugher, and we did a lot of both. Of course, I had to limit my food because I was trying to be slimmer for the camera, and I still couldn't laugh out loud. While Rock laughed, I'd just vigorously, silently shake. But we had a good time together.

How can I forget the day I got word? Universal decided to sign both Rock and me to seven-year contracts! Getting a studio contract in the 1950s meant a regular substantial paycheck and an opportunity for greater success. It was like having a small regular part on a television series today. We were joyous, moved to tears, and thrilled for our futures. We felt that this contract was a meaningful acknowledgment of our abilities. I would actually be paid to create interesting things with my art, to enlighten people with it and give them pleasure.

Three gorgeous guys—Rock Hudson, my friend Bob Richards, and another contract player, Jimmy Best—took me out with them to celebrate that afternoon. While I was waiting to be picked up at our apartment, I noticed I was sitting on our old royal blue upholstered rocking chair, wearing my royal blue suit. That struck me as silly and meaningful. Perhaps they'd come for me in a royal blue car! Everything in the spirit of the day! We all went to the circus. It was my first circus, another missing part of my education. What a day! Three handsome and warm friends, the circus, and the feeling that someone had tapped me gently on the shoulder and said, *You're a serious artist*.

How little I understood the mistake I had made, that I had naïvely committed myself to years of a sort of prison that shielded me from creativity. Eventually I would learn that Universal-International made mostly low-budget B westerns, program pictures like *Ma and Pa Kettle; Francis the Talking Mule;* and *Arabian Nights* films. They had the formula down pat: they were mostly entertaining, and they always made money. But there were no serious writers or directors who knew or cared anything about actors. The few potentially good ones were limited, like me, to inferior material and brief schedules. Occasionally a big star would bring in their own project with a decent director, but it was rare.

The standard beginning actor's contract at that time was $100 a week for women and $150 for men. A man always got more. At that time it was also a given that even if parts were equal in size and importance, the male name almost always came first, unless the female was someone like Garbo. No one questioned it, at least not out loud. A hundred dollars a week doesn't sound like a lot, but the biggest stars in those days, Clark Gable and Cary Grant, were only making $200,000 to $300,000 for an entire film. Since I was still underage, a big chunk of my salary would be put away in trust until I was twenty-one. After withholding, the Screen Actors Guild pension, health insurance, Social Security, etc., my weekly take-home pay would be around $40. A year from then, I would be getting $150 minus the deductions. There would be yearly options and raises, but only if they wanted to keep me. The option was only one way. At the time I was ecstatic getting anything. I couldn't believe this had happened. I was going to be in the movies! I was learning so much now, often able to speak more freely with friends without someone else's words to hide behind. I was doing good work in class, where I expected to continue.

When it was time to sign the contract, a family friend suggested we visit a semiretired judge, an elderly acquaintance of his, and have him take a look at the contract. I had read it myself very carefully at home, thrilled that all these pages concerned me. The judge would witness the signing since I was underage.

We met him in his small office at a courthouse in Glendale. After looking at the contract, the judge watched as I signed my name about fifteen times. I felt very important, having never signed a document before. In addition to the sections on salary and my responsibilities as an actress, the night before I had read an ominous-sounding morals clause in the small print. It concerned my personal behavior. This was serious stuff. I would not only have to be a good actress; I would also have to be a good person. It was a somber vow that I took when I signed. When I had finished, the judge said, "I'm going to give you some important advice. Something that you should remember the rest of your life. Don't ever let men know that you are smart. Always let men feel that they know more than you." What an evil and unfortunate thing for him to have told this seventeen-year-old girl.

I hadn't yet graduated from high school when Universal made their offer. I had another semester to go and six months before I'd turn eighteen. My agent, on my behalf, asked the studio if it would be possible to delay the beginning of the contract until after my graduation. I had final exams and didn't want to be distracted. The studio said they would agree to that if I transferred to the little studio schoolhouse on the lot and finish my studies there. That way I could finish high school on schedule and still have time in the day to take photos and meet some of the people at the studio. I would be the only student of Mrs. Gladys Heaney, the lovely teacher who had been there for decades. And so I left my high school without time to catch my breath or say goodbye, and transferred to the studio school.

Mrs. Heaney and I had class alone every day in the tiny schoolhouse that held five desks in addition to the one I occupied, plus a larger one for Mrs. Heaney. Every morning promptly at ten-thirty, and then again at one-thirty in the afternoon, she would call recess. Student and teacher would rise, walk to the small office in the back, and smoke cigarettes. I had managed to avoid smoking during most of high school, thinking my friends were silly and just showing off, but when I wanted to smoke correctly for *Street Scene*, which I was working on in Betomi's class, I chose Betomi's brand that came in a nice little box and didn't stop for fifteen years.

My life had taken a surprising turn. I had never expected to be offered a studio contract. After all, I had been turned down after screen testing quite a few times before. I was just going through the motions. But now I was being swept off my feet, and my vanity made me so helpless that I hardly noticed. It was incredibly flattering to be offered money to practice the only thing I felt I was good at. I had never had any money; nor did I really want it. But receiving money meant that I was truly valued. My parents seemed to be impressed with me, and that in itself was seductive.

Visiting the soundstages, the various technical departments, and the permanent structures on the back lot was like traveling the world. I was the youngest person under contract, and many people were being paid to mentor me. Millie Gussie, one of the casting directors, took me around to various offices and introduced me to people. She took me to meet producer Leonard Goldstein, a man somewhere in his late forties. We went into his office and I was seated by the side of his desk. Leonard looked particularly gruff and was holding a small baseball bat in one hand. He reached out with the other as if to shake my hand. I gave my hand to him and he pulled and pulled until I was out of my chair and almost on the floor. He must have sensed my shyness and was trying to loosen me up. He was behaving outrageously, but I could see "Marx Brothers" in his eyes, and I liked him immediately.

I also met producer Robert Arthur, a man in his forties who was casting an upcoming movie named *Louisa.* I had worn my hair down that day, wanting to look as old as possible out of habit, covering half my face like Veronica Lake as always. Millie asked me to go into Mr. Arthur's office bathroom and pin my hair back on the sides with bobby pins. That did the trick. He seemed satisfied that I was the teenager he was looking for to put in his new project. I was living the dream.

The studio put me through a boot camp of training to become a shining ingenue. I was sent to the "still gallery" almost every day after school, where people constantly changed my clothes and hairstyles. I despised those gallery photo shoots. I was stiff and self-conscious and had to be cajoled into a smile. I'm still that way. If you want me to smile, tell me not to.

The publicity department scheduled me to appear at public relations events, where I tried to get used to being the focus of attention in front of a crowd. It's a very different skill from acting a part on stage. Once they asked me to model sports clothes at a charity event with some other girls under contract. They urged me to "please smile" before I walked out and around the hotel pool, but I had such bad facial spasms and twitches as I walked that someone mercifully removed me from the show. Obviously the three weeks of modeling classes when I was twelve had not worked.

A few weeks later they took me to a "medical fair" being held at the Long Beach Convention Center. I was introduced on stage as "Universal's new young star" to lots of applause, though I hadn't yet made a movie. After I took my bow, my handler, a public relations man from the studio, told me I could walk around the large convention hall with a little basket they'd given me and fill it with samples of anything I wanted from the booths. The handler disappeared for a while, so I wandered around, happily dropping items into my basket to take home. Band-Aids and medications didn't appeal to me, but some pretty little packages with the name "Trojan" and another called "4XXXX" looked like they might contain bubble gum or something yummy, so I popped many of them into my basket. When the handler returned, he removed them quickly with a mixture of horror and hilarity before they were spotted by the public or the press. The only condom I had ever seen had been filled with air like a balloon and hung from the flagpole at Los Angeles High.

I also attended my first Hollywood social event during this time. Twenty-one-year-old Jerome Courtland, a popular young actor, was asked to escort me to a charity dinner given on a large studio soundstage. The wardrobe department dressed me in a formal dress that had a pretty flower on the shoulder. I would miss going to my high school prom, but I felt a little like Cinderella that night. All of the very young movie stars and personalities were seated at one long narrow table, away from the older ones. There must have been thirty of us. Sitting directly opposite me was Shirley Temple, so close we could have played kneesies! She looked absolutely perfect, with flawless skin. Oh, my goodness gracious! Beautiful and famous young people to the left and to the right! About twenty feet from me, at the other end of the table, stood a young man staring at me. It was twenty-one-year-old Roddy McDowall. He was asking someone, "Who is that?!" and pointing directly at me, the new girl in town. There was nothing Machiavellian about it; he was just incredibly curious. Roddy always had to know everyone.

The next day there was a half-page, extremely flattering colorized picture of me in the Sunday paper, with my name spelled correctly. Very heady. I had also been discovered by Roddy, who would be a lifelong friend. After that evening Roddy began asking me out. I remember sitting outside my parents' house after dates, necking with him in his car. It was a *long* time ago.

By then my dad's small furniture store was doing well, and he had finally saved enough for a down payment on a house in a nice neighborhood. The first house of our lives. Buying the house was a tremendous achievement for him. We moved into it just as I was getting enormous amounts of publicity in the press and beginning to earn a little money. It was a sensitive point with my dad that people assumed *I* had bought the house. My mother and I tried to make it clear to our friends and family that it was my father who had bought the house, not me. I paid only for my own expenses, and the studio furnished me with clothes.

Our new house was in an upper-middle-class neighborhood on the border between Los Angeles and Beverly Hills, on a street called Schumacher Drive. Karlyn and I had once taken the bus to look at Schumacher Drive—it was where Rick Eller, my "Prince Charming" from junior high and high school, had lived. Perfect Rick Eller had never acknowledged my existence. Perhaps he still lived there! But now I was too busy to find out.

I wanted to pay for help for my mother, who was now taking care of a large house as well as doing many things for me. I didn't yet have a driver's license, so she had to take me everywhere, and my studio contract made additional demands on her time. My parents agreed and allowed me to pay for a housekeeper. Her name was Edna. She was married to Lewis McCarver, a man who worked for my father in the furniture store. Edna was magnificent to behold; over six feet tall, black as onyx, and exquisitely beautiful. She was probably in her late thirties at the time. Edna had no children and decided, probably for that reason, that it was her destiny in life to care for me and make me happy. She looked for ways to spoil me. I loved all of her excessive warmth and loyalty and tried not to question it. I had become a sponge for the good things in life. I did, however, have my own personal line of right and wrong that I knew could never be crossed.

Meanwhile I had completed my high school courses at the studio school. The Los Angeles Board of Education instructed Mrs. Heaney to give me my final exams quite formally in the schoolhouse, with locked door and no interruptions. I did pretty well, mostly A's and one B. Because I wouldn't have a high school graduation ceremony, the publicity department said they would photograph me in cap and gown to commemorate the event. When the wardrobe department brought my "graduation clothes" over to the schoolhouse for the photo, to my horror I saw a graduation cap, shorts, a tight sweater, and high heels. I was mortified. I didn't know how to protest. Wearing abbreviated clothes in my private life had never been easy for me. My mother's preoccupation with physical perfection was challenging for me. I felt I could never achieve it. Appearing in brief clothes for the studio would be a humiliation. *Where were some words, some vocabulary?* My head was empty. If I refused and simply said no, would they fire me before I'd even made my first movie? I felt very infantile, very cowardly, and I was. But I did what my elders asked of me. I put the clothes on and tried to pretend no one was there. I still cringe when I see those pictures, not only because I didn't have Rita Hayworth's thighs, but because the photos are symbolic of how I'd allowed myself to be used.

It would be a very long time before life would teach me that it was okay to fight for what I wanted. At seventeen, I still thought that being a good person and working hard were enough. In many ways I was so taken care of. The spaces inside me, however, were being filled with nothing that could last. Nothing like a real education, or even the blessed real-life experience of a waitress job.

Officially, my contract went into effect right after my eighteenth birthday. A few days later I was scheduled to start shooting my first movie, *Louisa*, playing the teenage daughter of Ronald Reagan. The script was charming. The parts for the adult members of the cast were well written if not the most original. A pretty and single grandmother, played by Spring Byington, comes to live with her married son, played by Ronald Reagan, and his family. She is pursued by both Edmund Gwenn and Charles Coburn and ends up acting more like a teenager than her teenage granddaughter, me.

I had an important featured part in my first movie and was assigned a dressing room on the set. I had the same kind as everyone else, with big wheels that could be moved anywhere on the soundstage. It was a cozy little thing with a built-in sofa, a small closet, and a dressing table. I didn't yet drive, so Mother was still my chauffeur. She took me to work and came back for me, spending hours each day waiting for me in the car, sewing or reading. She never went in with me, never sat on the set or went into my dressing room. She took care to be the good, noninterfering movie mother.

Bud Westmore, of the famous makeup family, was assigned to me.

Bud was a friendly man with a good sense of humor, though he wasn't joking when he made me over. He used every trick he knew to "improve" me. There was some fancy shading on my nose, a thick dark base, and lots of shading on my jawline to make my face look slimmer. He drew funny round eyebrows unlike my own and penciled red marks at the inner corners of my eyes, which was supposed to make them look bigger in black and white photography. "Who is that?" I asked when I saw myself in the mirror. I didn't recognize myself; nor did my friends when they saw the movie.

Ron Rondell was the first assistant director. He showed me the ropes and gave me some primary rules of behavior. Number one: Every minute wasted on a set costs a small fortune. Although two hours were allowed for makeup and hair in the morning, reporting to makeup five minutes late almost always meant being five minutes late to the set. Nothing of their routine could ever change. Number two: Never leave the set without telling an assistant director where you are going. Not even for a bathroom trip. Those rules have been imprinted into my gut. I still ask permission to go to the bathroom, and I try to time it to be the least intrusive.

I met all the stars of the movie for the first time when we did the wardrobe tests: Spring Byington, Edmund Gwenn, Charlie Coburn, Ruth Hussey, and Ronald Reagan. They embraced me emotionally, though not physically. People in those days mostly just shook hands and were not so demonstrative with strangers. I had just turned eighteen and was playing sixteen, but they didn't treat me like a child, more like a beloved little sister. Spring Byington, who was quietly cheerful, bought me a little book that she thought I would enjoy. It was called *Miss Ulysses from Puka-Puka*, a sweet story that I read right away. Edmund Gwenn, or "Teddy" as we called him, would step up into my dressing room and sing songs because he knew I enjoyed them so much. A favorite was "I've Got a Lovely Bunch of Coconuts," and we would sing it together. He was such a joyful person, and his joy empowered his work.

Charlie Coburn didn't stay in his dressing room very much. He liked to be out on the set in his chair being social, even taking naps in the middle of all the action. Charlie would sit on the soundstage, puffing on his cigar, and stop me if I walked by. "Come sit down, Piper," he'd say. After teasing me for a few minutes to make me smile, he'd coach me, saying, "Now when you holler up 'Mother!' you shouldn't say it with the hard 'r.' You don't want to give away your Detroit background. This girl would say 'Mothaaa.' It'll sound better if you say it that way." I had already worked hard on my diction, but obviously not hard enough. I did my best to follow Charlie's advice.

Ronald Reagan was especially kind and friendly and held my hand for a long time when we were first introduced. He had broken his leg, or perhaps it was an ankle, a short while before, and his cast had come off just days before we started to shoot. By then he had only a slight limp. He was no longer married to Jane Wyman, and as far as I knew, had not yet started dating his beloved Nancy Davis. In a very charming way he told me that, even though he was playing my father, he would prefer I not call him Mr. Reagan and to please call him Ronnie. Later, by invitation, I called everyone in the movie by his or her first name.

There were times when the whole cast would sit around on the set and tell stories. Teddy, Ronnie, and Charlie were great storytellers, and they all loved to talk. They never actually told me that they'd often worked together, but their closeness was apparent. I realize now what rich bodies of work these people had, but at the time I had seen so little that I didn't yet understand what a rare experience I was having.

The only difficult thing in making the movie was my actual part. The script called for my character to constantly behave like a shocked Mother Superior. I couldn't find any reality in what my character did in the script, or in the words she used. Every line and moment for the girl seemed like a cartoon. It seemed to me that a real girl would be amused and appreciate her grandmother's behavior. Perhaps in a more clearly stylized screenplay, I could have found a way to make this caricature of a teenager live. I kept trying to think of ways to make her real for myself, but it was a constant struggle on the set.

I was genuinely surprised when I went to the veteran director, Alexander Hall, and asked his advice about the girl I was playing. I assumed that since he was the director, he would be like Betomi, interested in grounding my character in reality. To the contrary, he seemed quite surprised and impatient at my question, replying, "Oh Piper, just learn the words and forget about it." I was shocked and naïvely thought at first that he was joking. That was the first overt attack on my expectation of doing excellent work. It's one thing to have poor material, but one has to at least try to make something of it. It took a while before I understood that Hall's admonition was the norm for that studio during those years. I was completely on my own. Ironically, years later, I would be grateful for the director with a light or sometimes nonexistent touch. But at the time I was desperate for some guidance and had no time off to visit Betomi and ask for some.

The relentless publicity campaign that had taken over my life continued. Fred Banker was the publicity man on *Louisa*. I'll never forget him because his "bright idea" branded me for years; because he did his job so well; and because I genuinely liked him. There was a scene in the film when Edmund Gwenn is showing off for Spring Byington and prepares a salad for the family. In the course of the scene, Teddy tosses some marigold petals from a centerpiece on the table into the salad. When Fred saw the scene, he looked up at me with his eyes blazing and said, "I have an idea!"

He called all the wire services and told them, "Universal's new contract player—Piper Laurie—eats nothing but flowers," and offered them all "exclusive" interviews with the flower-eating girl. I thought I had no choice but to play Fred's game. So day after day at lunchtime, I sat in the commissary with a new reporter, eating a meal that was some sort of flower or plant life arranged prettily on a plate, prepared in the kitchen especially for me. Sometimes there were colorful sweet things in jars purchased from the rare health food store. I didn't know what some of it was, but I tasted everything and ate most of it. It was certainly more interesting than the role I had in the movie. I threw myself into it, playing my new part with gusto, nibbling on orchids, rose petals, and marigolds—"Oh yes, they're really delicious!" Each day there was a feature story in one of the newspapers (we had quite a few then) about my eating flowers. But when I got home at night and my parents asked me how my day had been, I couldn't speak about it. It was exhausting and ultimately sad getting up the energy to play the lie every day. The whole arrangement sounds pitifully tame compared to today's publicity stunts, but for many years to come I was marked as little more than "the girl who ate orchids." My expectations to make art were beginning to crumble.

As filming progressed, Ronnie Reagan took an increasing interest in me. He began calling me into his dressing room when I passed the door. I was quite flattered by his fatherly attention. He'd invite me to sit down and ask how I was feeling about everything. Was I comfortable? Could he help me with anything? He was the president of the Screen Actors Guild at the time, and sometimes he asked me to just sit there while he did guild work and I studied my script. Occasionally he would step into my dressing room, sit down, and chat. I was very shy at first with this immensely appealing and famous man. But gradually our relationship seemed more like one I'd have with someone in my acting class. He was becoming quite a friend and was sympathetic about my frustrations with the script.

One day while we were still shooting the film, Robert Arthur, the producer of the movie (and later a Reagan supporter), called me into his office. He said, "Piper, it doesn't look nice, going into Ronald Reagan's dressing room on the set. I don't want you to do that anymore."

Embarrassed, I managed to explain, "But he invites me to come in."

"I don't care. It doesn't look good," he went on. "You're still a teenager, and my God—he's your father's age! So stay away. And while I'm at it, the director says you're asking too many questions." That was a line I recalled hearing in a spy movie. I really didn't know what to make of any of it. After that I made excuses for not going into Ronnie's dressing room when he'd invite me in. I'd read or pretend I was studying my script.

I was even more confused when soon after my talk with Mr. Arthur, Ronnie said he'd like to take me to my first movie premiere. When the studio found out, they quickly decided they would chaperone us. A limo and a publicity woman picked me up at home and drove me to the Hollywood Brown Derby, where Ronnie was waiting for me. I had tried to dress as sophisticatedly as I could, in high heels, a navy silk suit, a little hat and veil, and white gloves. Ronnie and I sat by ourselves in one of the famous big leather booths and tried to eat while people stared and fan magazine photographers took pictures. After dinner we were driven to one of the big theaters in Hollywood. The publicity people followed in another car. I don't remember what Universal movie was being premiered; I was too excited to really see it. When it was over, Ronnie took my hand and led me to the limo, where he gave me a little kiss on the cheek, and the publicity woman took me home.

When we finished shooting *Louisa*, the writer of the screenplay, Stanley Roberts, who was an elegant man in his thirties, invited me to my first Hollywood dinner party at his home. I was surprised. I had the feeling that he didn't think much of me. I discussed Mr. Roberts's invitation with my parents, and my mother thought I should go. I decided to wear my all-purpose sleeveless black linen dress and a beautiful white shawl crocheted by my grandma.

My father drove me to Mr. Roberts's large home in the hills overlooking Los Angeles. When I walked in and saw the other guests, I thought I was dreaming. The small group of eight or ten included Ronald Colman, Greer Garson, Claudette Colbert and her doctor husband, and a few more equally accomplished people. Greer Garson was magnificently and expensively dressed, as they all were. These were people who were normally thirty feet high. I will never understand why I had been invited. I was the only civilian, so to speak, but I decided to just accept it and float through this dream. I was enthralled by the luminaries' ease with themselves, the comfortable conversations. I did try to think of things to say, but by the time I worked up the courage to speak, the topic would have passed. They graciously made no mention of my quietness, and I felt happy and comfortable.

After dinner three or four of the women, including Miss Garson and myself, sat outside on the porch on beautiful white wicker furniture. In the middle of another thought, Miss Garson suddenly interrupted herself and looked at me. "My dear, it's only because you're pretty and so young that you can get away with wearing that thing." She gestured toward my grandma's shawl. I was a little off balance for a few minutes but recovered. I believed that my grandmother's work was beautiful and chalked up Miss Garson's comment to plain meanness. I told my mother about it when I got home, and she was outraged. For the rest of her life, Mother feigned forgetfulness when speaking about "What's her name? Oh, yes, yes, Kit Carson!" However, when I myself had passed the age of Greer Garson that evening and found myself in the company of younger, attractive women, I realized that I had misjudged her. I understood that she had meant it as a compliment, and an expression of her awareness of time passing.

Several months after finishing *Louisa*, the entire cast was asked to do a radio show called the *Lux Radio Theater*. The program broadcast hourlong versions of current popular movies using the original casts. We rehearsed for a few hours; then the audience was brought into the large theater in Hollywood, and the show was broadcast live, coast to coast. It did not challenge our memorization abilities because it was radio, and we held the scripts in our hands. It was good to see everyone again and fun to do the show with an audience. When the broadcast was over and we'd taken our bows, Ronnie came over to me and said, "Would you like to go and have some dinner?"

I looked around, thinking he meant the group of us, but everyone seemed to be on their way. I didn't drive yet and my mother had brought me as usual, so I told him, "Oh, that would be nice. I'll ask my mother. She's waiting for me outside in the car." Did I detect a slight lift of his eyebrow? Perhaps it was my imagination.

We gathered up our things, and Ronnie came with me to the parking lot. My mother rolled down her window, looking apprehensive. Perhaps she was shy in his presence. It was the first time they had met. He asked her, "Would it be all right if I took Piper to dinner? I'll get her home safely."

My mom hesitated briefly, then said, "Oh, that's fine. Just see that you drive carefully." She said that to everyone.

As we walked over to where his car was parked, I was aware that my heart was racing a little. He was almost forty, more than twice my age, and I thought of him as a friendly father figure. He was certainly a man to admire, so appealing and highly respected, exuding a quality of decency that inspired trust. He was also quite fit and at an age that

I think is the most attractive for a man. I was thrilled that this lovely man wanted to take me to dinner.

As we reached the car, he smiled with such warmth and said, "I'm glad you're joining me." He took my elbow gallantly, helped me into the car, and came round to his side to sit beside me. It was a big car. I don't think it was brand new, but it was clean, and it smelled nice.

He hesitated before starting the car, then turned to look at me in a surprisingly grave way. Had I seen that look before? I thought I had, once or twice during the months that we'd worked together. I wished I'd known what it meant. It confused me. Surely he wouldn't have been thinking of me in *that* way. He was, as Robert Arthur had pointed out, my father's age. But sometimes I had wondered.

He drove away very slowly and after a few blocks said, "Piper, how would you feel if I made dinner for you?" Now it was clear. My heart was beating so very hard, I was sure he could hear it. This was a kind of invitation I had always refused. But there was real chemistry brewing now that I could not deny. I made a decision, when I said, "Yes, I'd like that very much," that this would be my first love affair.

He drove up the hill on one of the small streets off the Sunset Strip and parked in the carport behind the apartment he'd been living in since his divorce. We went up the back way very discreetly and into his apartment. It was rather small and seemed crowded with too much furniture. I sat in a comfortable chair, and Ronnie asked if I'd like something to drink. I was now old enough, and it was legal. With as much sophistication as I could muster, I said, "Yes, that would be nice." He brought me a glass of wine, turned on some music, and began to cook, talking to me all the while from the kitchen. He did like to talk.

He made a very nice hamburger steak and salad. When dinner was ready, we sat at a small table in the living room. He lit some candles, and we drank special wine. I was eighteen and felt very much my own woman. When I thought about it later, I knew the reality was, I had picked him. He had stepped forward, and I had picked him as women can do sometimes.

I didn't know if Ronnie knew I was a virgin. I supposed he knew, but I'd be damned if I'd say the words. It seemed unsophisticated, unwomanly for me to say it. It reminded me of some of those second-rate comedy plays I'd read in class. Most girls my age were expected to be virgins and were. I didn't believe the stories about casting couches and how young girls were misused. At this moment the fact of my virginity seemed irrelevant, and I didn't want to be coy. I knew I wanted to make love with him. I wanted to be completed by this wonderful man who clearly desired me. He would know what to do. I expected something like the fantasy left over from a story I'd heard about Charles Boyer and the way he treated his women with their first experience. It was probably apocryphal, but it seemed so nice that it had stayed in my head. There had been great passion and playfulness, grapes by the bedside and violins playing.

The evening up to that point had been quite romantic. But the actual intimacy with Ronnie was without grace. I can appreciate it now; Ronnie was more than competent sexually. He was also a bit of a show-off. He made sure I was aware of the length of time he had been "ardent." It was forty minutes. And he told me how much the condom cost. In all fairness, I suppose that was to reassure me.

The experience was a stunning revelation for me, to be so physically close to someone, actually interwoven with another human being. So amazing to look up and see the familiar face and that naked expanse of chest above me. But more than a few times during intercourse, he said, "There's something wrong with you. You should have had many orgasms by now—after all this time. You've got to see a doctor about your abnormality." He used the word. "And maybe a doctor can find out why it hurt you so at first. There's something wrong with you that you should fix."

I was expecting a little pain the first time. Didn't everyone know that? And I was no stranger to orgasms, having discovered this miracle of our bodies when I was a young girl. But it had been a secret activity, and I know now that the uninitiated need a trusting environment to blossom.

I suppose I should have spelled out the mortifying fact of my virginity, but even now I still expect people I admire to know more than they really do. He was a lot less knowledgeable than I could have imagined, missing the obvious clues of my inexperience, even to the small traditional stain on the sheet. It's possible that even if he had known, it might not have changed things very much.

I don't remember anything about the drive home. I was numb from embarrassment and fearful for my future. This man I so admired had told me there was something wrong with me. I couldn't tell my parents what had happened. How could I possibly have access to a doctor if I needed one, as Ronnie said I did, without my parents knowing? Still, a part of me suspected he was wrong. When I eventually did make love to a man who treated me caringly, I knew he was wrong.

Over the years, from time to time I've thought about that evening. Ronald Reagan, famous for his unfailing sense of humor and good judgment, is admired more than ever today. He is sometimes spoken about in tones reserved for a saint. But that night I learned that he was indeed fallible. His words to me were cold and just plain stupid. And in a moment in my life when I might have benefited from it the most, he offered not the slightest trace of humor or kindness.

A few months later Ronnie and I were thrown together once again. I was sent to Chicago to do publicity for *Louisa*. Ronnie and I were the only members of the cast there. My parents had insisted there be a chaperone to watch over me, though I certainly hadn't told them what had happened with Ronnie. A public relations woman was hired to come in from New York and stay with me in the two-bedroom suite.

On the surface, things were fairly relaxed between Ronnie and me. We were professionals, after all, and I was still excellent at covering what I was feeling. We did radio shows, television, and newspaper interviews. There were hundreds of fans wherever we'd go. Some of the teenagers knew who I was because they had already read about me in fan magazines, but everybody knew who Ronnie was. We did autograph parties in department stores. Sometimes he would jump up onto the store counter and talk at length with great passion and earnestness about the undeservedly bad reputation of Hollywood. He compared the number of divorces in Hollywood to the number across the country. He knew the statistics. He told the admiring fans that Hollywood could hold its head up. I remember Charley Simonelli, a Universal executive and later a close friend, who was with us on the tour, admiring Ronnie's easy oratory style. "Boy, look at that guy go! He is *good*! He looks like he's running for president!"

On the last day Ronnie and I had to appear on stage at the Paramount Theater between showings of the movie. We had a little patter that we did together at the microphone—we'd rehearsed it for a minute before in the wings. It was a somewhat embarrassing exchange of lines similar to the ones they sometimes do at award shows. The studio wardrobe department had found a beautiful purple chiffon gown for me to wear on stage for the two performances. It was strapless, and I knew I looked well in it.

After our last show a few of us went back to the Ambassador East Hotel, where the Universal people always stayed, to have a goodbye drink. Ronnie sat on a couch by himself in the middle of the room, holding his drink. He was unusually quiet, just staring at me as I sat on another couch against the wall. The others were in various places in the room, chatting. The head of the Universal publicity department, Al Horowitz, sat next to me sipping his drink. I recognized that special look that told me Ronnie was not listening to the conversation in the room. He seemed very relaxed and unable to keep his eyes off me—or perhaps it was the strapless purple dress.

It was getting late, so I excused myself. After I said goodbye to everyone Ronnie followed me, or should I say followed the purple dress, into the hallway. He asked if he could escort me to my room. Not wanting to presume anything other than a gentlemanly gesture, I naïvely said, "Well, all right, thank you."

As quickly as I spoke the words, I knew it was a mistake. When we got to my door, he wanted to come in. Gathering some newfound feminine power into myself, I said, "I don't think that's a very good idea. Shall we take a walk instead?"

Ronnie at once agreed, and we went down in the elevator and out into the night. He took my hand as we walked through the beautiful tree-lined side streets of Chicago around the Ambassador East Hotel.

Our conversation covered a lot of territory, including what I thought about our age difference. Apparently it troubled him that I was only about nine years older than his daughter Maureen. But he said not a word about the evening we had had together.

We stopped under a streetlamp. He looked at me with that nice face and those warm flirty eyes, and I let him kiss me. Then he steered the conversation to the possibility of our being together. I told him I couldn't possibly because I was dating someone else. It was partly true. I had been going to the Chez Paree almost nightly with my chaperone, where I was serenaded by the handsome, glorious-voiced Vic Damone, and going out with Vic afterward. But the truth was, I no longer found Ronnie to be someone I wanted to be close to. His insensitivity had been wounding and, in retrospect, even cruel.

It was an awkward moment, and I didn't have the courage to just leave it at that, or to tell him the truth about how upset I had been. He was after all, still very much an authority figure to me. He looked so disappointed and hurt. I was embarrassed to be turning him down and wanted to say something kind, so when we started walking again, I said truthfully, "I'm very honored that such a respected and admired person was my first lover."

He stopped quite suddenly when I said that, almost did a double take. There was a quizzical look on his face. Was it possible he still didn't know? Even with the colorful evidence I had left behind? Perhaps at that moment he got it—perhaps. He was very quiet as we walked back to the hotel. I wondered what he was he thinking. Whatever it was seemed impenetrable, and I didn't try to break through. He saw me to my door and looked at me so strangely as we said goodnight, as if he hardly knew me.

Many years later, at the end of Ronnie's last term as president, I was invited to the White House to attend a "goodbye gala" for all of Ronald Reagan's old friends. I declined. I told myself it was because I didn't agree with him at all politically, but that wasn't the complete truth. I hadn't seen him since before he'd become the governor of California. After all those years, it seemed odd to be invited. I assumed the guest list had been put together without his input, and that I would simply be one among a large group of actors with whom he'd worked. That would have made me uncomfortable. As disappointing as it was, the relationship had been more important to me than that, and I wished to save myself embarrassment. Who knows? I might already have been wiped from his memory.

5.

About the World

Three months after becoming eighteen, and about one minute after completing *Louisa*, I started my next movie. It was a "comedy with music" called *The Milkman*, starring Donald O'Connor and Jimmy Durante.

I had no time to reflect on anything. I just moved forward. My part was the cliché ingenue whom Donald falls for. My big scene would be dancing a romantic soft-shoe in the park with Donald. My agent had told the studio that I was a dancer. Yes, my sister and I could do a terrific Irish jig, but I was not a trained dancer. I'd taken a few lessons when I was younger, but that was about it. Now I was going to be dancing with Donald O'Connor in a feature film and I tried not to panic. Rehearsals were scheduled every day with Hal Belfer, the choreographer. He had a tough job getting me ready but I worked very hard. I thought I was slow and I had to repeat the steps many times to retain them, but I think I was just very nervous. Everyone kept telling me I moved well, that I was as good as Betty Grable. They'd say anything to keep me going. Donald was very patient and supportive. He would hold my hand in such a dear way to give me confidence. I had a deeply felt crush on Donald. We became good friends and remained so until the day he died, almost fifty years later.

Working with Jimmy Durante was an extraordinary experience. When he wasn't performing he was quiet, sweet, and thoughtful. One day the three of us, Jimmy, Donald, and I, were in the milk truck shooting a scene in front of the commissary, which was doubling as the milk company. There was a large crew and perhaps a hundred spectators, many of them visitors to the lot who had just come from lunch. People were used to seeing Donald working around the lot, but never Jimmy Durante. It was a treat. The scene required Jimmy to stick his head out of the truck and whistle really hard, a contrivance to make the truck go forward without a driver. When Jimmy did the whistle on the first take, his whole upper plate flew out of his mouth. It sailed across the street, at least twenty-five feet. When it landed, everything stopped. Not wanting to acknowledge that it had happened, people tried to pretend they hadn't seen it. Donald and I were frozen. There they were, the half circle of teeth, sitting out there smiling at everyone. Nobody knew what to do. Should somebody pick the damn thing up?

After what seemed like an eternity, Jimmy finally jumped out of the truck and scampered over to his teeth. He picked them up, brushed them off, threw them back into his mouth, and jumped back onto the truck as if nothing had happened. Then he said, in that gravelly voice, "Okay—let's do that again!" Jimmy gave us permission to laugh by leading the way. We'd all been immobilized because we loved him so much. When the movie wrapped, this kind and generous man gave a fifty-dollar bill to every crew member, a lot of money in those days.

I was still eighteen, and the studio was about to turn Tony Curtis and me into "real" movie stars. When I first arrived at Universal, I had been disappointed that Tony seemed more stunned than happy to see me there at the same studio. I thought it was nice, my friend from acting class and me getting our big break together, but Tony had seemed a little distant. It didn't help that I had gotten real parts and a major publicity buildup before he did. It had never occurred to me that a guy could feel competitive with a girl. In retrospect, I guess he felt it was his territory. Up to then Tony was being used only in bit parts, though he made more money than I did, and he had already attracted hundreds of fans. Reports of his mounting fan-mail count were sent to the front office. Now we would be together in our first starring movie, *The Prince Who Was a Thief*. It was Tony's first real part. I was hoping that his coldness toward me would pass now that he was getting a break and we were costarring in the same movie, and so it did. We were both happy for each other now.

Once again I was working with extraordinary actors whose bodies of work I wasn't aware of: Everett Sloane, from *Citizen Kane*; Betty Garde, from the theater; and Jeff Corey, a terrific actor and highly respected acting teacher. My role was again a cartoon, but at least it was a rather charming cartoon. The studio had hired a director from off the lot, which was a very unusual and smart thing to do. His name was Rudolph Maté. Rudy was an artist and had photographed many fine European and American films. This was his second time as director. Rudy encouraged me to do things in my own way and applauded and laughed like a child when he was pleased. For the first time, I felt free in front of the camera. I was allowed to wear more natural makeup, so I looked like a real person in my first Technicolor movie. I had one of those can't-miss parts—the gamine thief who's in love. The movie was supposedly based on a Theodore Dreiser story that the studio owned, but it was actually only the title that was Dreiser's. It was essentially a Pygmalion story. Some people thought my role stole the movie. I wove myself through the bars like a serpent into the "treasury house" in a scene that people of a certain age still ask me about.

The movie cost around $200,000, was eighty-eight minutes long, and was a huge financial success for Universal, making many millions of dollars. The exact amount they kept secret from Tony and me. Tony and I were treated by the studio like golden treasures. The very young and the not-too-discerning loved the film. At the time I thought it was pretty silly. It had lines such as "Son of a nose-less mother" and "Maggot-brained child of a jackass." Seeing it years later, I understood why so many kids loved it. The Technicolor was so pretty to look at, my part was foolproof, and Tony looked great with his athletic body and handsome face.

Only a few months had gone by since I'd started making movies, and I had just finished my third one. Things were happening so quickly.

A twenty-foot-tall picture of me in a bathing suit had been displayed in New York's Times Square, which impressed our New York relatives. I even got my first fan letter, which I opened with great excitement. The message read, "The wages of sin is death." It made me feel creepy and brought me down to earth.

Despite my success, I was frustrated and confused. I thought the studio had respected my ability to do serious work. I thought that was why they had responded to my audition, screen-tested, and signed me. But everything they asked me to do was superficial, and the parts were so poorly written. The publicity campaign was working. A lot of people in the public were beginning to know my name, especially the young people. But practically no one had seen my work. Of course, I was a prime target for critics when the movies finally came out. They had a lot of fun at my expense. How could they know that I thought the work was even worse than they did?

Around this time, nine months after starting with Universal, my old contract was torn up. I was now making $250 weekly, the equivalent of several thousand today and another year was tacked on to the end of my contract. I had no say in the matter.

Not long afterward my ex-"manager" Ted sued me. That was disappointing. He had lost interest and disappeared well before I auditioned and screen-tested for my Universal contract. I guess he felt I was probably getting very rich and owed him something. I did feel gratitude toward him for finding Betomi's acting class for me and for the inspirational experience of seeing *Medea*. He settled for $5,000, and I never heard from him again.

A short while later I had a brief moment of hope that I would still be able to do work that mattered. Incredibly, my agent told me that the great Vittorio De Sica, the Italian director who had made the extraordinary *The Bicycle Thief*, had requested to borrow me from Universal for his next film! De Sica was an artist whose work I knew and admired. I was ecstatic. I was going to be saved. I couldn't imagine how the great director had heard about me or what made him want me; perhaps it was someone in my acting class, perhaps Betomi herself. But before I could find out, Universal turned De Sica down. Why did they do that? How could they do that? I asked everyone I knew, including my agent, but I sensed they didn't really care. Why should they? I was working. I didn't yet understand that Universal was a picture factory then, specializing in disposal product for the double-feature market.

Instead of going to work in Italy, I spent a lot of my time being photographed in short costumes, celebrating every holiday that came along—Miss Firecracker for the Fourth of July, Miss Thanksgiving, Miss Easter, Miss Mud Bath, and then Miss Milk Bath (for which I donned a flesh-colored bathing suit and sat in a tub of milk that had been warmed for me, courtesy of a sympathetic prop man). Every week these photos appeared in the newspaper. Once a picture of newcomer Marilyn Monroe, who was a little older than me and getting the same sort of treatment at Fox studios, appeared in the paper with my name under it. And vice versa.

The Prince Who Was a Thief was screened for servicemen going overseas, and it was very well received. Abe Lastfogel, who was head of both the William Morris Agency and the USO, asked me if I would go to Korea to entertain the troops. The government was still calling the Korean conflict a "police action," though in reality it was a full-blown, bloody war. I wanted very much to go. At nineteen you feel you're immortal, and it would give me an opportunity to be useful at last.

My mother and father were dead set against it. Over the next few weeks the studio executives put pressure on my parents, who had never before said no to them. The studio said I would be cared for and protected, that I would always be safe and they shouldn't be worried for a moment. I think the studio people believed what they were saying. They were all actually quite naïve. When my parents finally relented, I was excited.

At my mother's insistence, the studio had hired a full-time chaperone for whenever I was on tour. She was a wonderful woman named Gail Gifford. In spite of the pin-up pictures in shorts, swimsuits, and tight sweaters, the studio had taken great pains to protect my image as a sexual innocent. A fan magazine had proclaimed me one of the "last six virgins in Hollywood." I jokingly threatened to sue, but I was personally unhappy with the hypocrisy of the label. I took pleasure in knowing that I had had some womanly experiences, though I had never confided the fact to anyone. I had no girlfriends, and even if I had, I don't think I would have talked about something that was so private. This time, however, my parents acknowledged that I could not take a chaperone into a war zone. I would travel with the other performers under the auspices of the USO.

There were great preparations to be made. I needed material. I wasn't going to be one of those girls who just showed up looking attractive, with nothing to do. I had seen a wildly comedic, two-character musical play called *Pals* that ran about twenty minutes, written by a man named Richard Morris. Richard was a young man in his late twenties under contract to Universal as a jack-of-all-trades, including acting and writing, who eventually went on to write successful musical comedies for Broadway and the movies. I asked him if he would do the skit with me in Korea. He was thrilled at the prospect of going overseas with me. We rehearsed for several weeks in the rehearsal hall with someone at the piano and on drums, though there would be at least six musicians going with our troupe.

Meanwhile, the wardrobe department went to work making our costumes. I was playing a cowgirl smitten with a cowboy, and the skit had a clever, satiric *Duel in the Sun* ending. They made a nice cowboy outfit for Richard and two (just in case) beautiful cowgirl outfits for me. My costume had a divided skirt to give me freedom of movement and look feminine, a hat, and matching boots made by the famous Nudie.

The day before we left, while I was packing, Rabbi Marin unexpectedly came to the house to give me a special blessing and to bring me a tiny gold mezuzah. (The Ten Commandments are on a scroll inside.) It had an inscription saying, "From the Congregation of Mogen David Synagogue for Piper Laurie," which meant they were proud of Rosetta Jacobs.

We had another completely unexpected visitor come to the house that day—the legendary Danny Kaye, whom I'd met briefly a few weeks before at a USO meeting. My father, who had obviously never met Danny, answered the door without missing a beat, as though he were expecting him. Dad casually said, "Oh, hi, Danny," as though Danny Kaye dropped by our house every day. It delighted me to see this very cool side of my father. As passive as my dad was, occasionally he surprised me. Danny had brought fabric for me to give to Jimmy Fukasaki, the man who would be coordinating things in Tokyo, our stopover before Korea. The fabric was to be made into shirts for our mutual friend Leonard Goldstein and picked up on my way home.

A group of perhaps fifty excited entertainers gathered at Burbank Airport early on a December morning. My parents had driven me, and I saw they couldn't conceal their fear. By then I could read their faces far more easily than I could have only ten years before, when they'd taken me out of the sanitarium.

I think a band was playing—someone made a speech—and then about twenty of us boarded the C-54 transport headed for the Far East. The rest of the group was going to Europe, Iceland, and Africa. The first hop of our flight to Hawaii would take sixteen hours nonstop. This was before jets, of course. Jets were only starting to be used in Korea as fighters, so ours was a four-engine propeller-flown plane. We were a distinguished group. Paul Douglas, Jan Sterling, Mala Powers (who was Roxane in *Cyrano de Bergerac*), Julia Adams, Beverly Tyler, the extraordinary Molly Picon from the Yiddish theater and movies, her husband, Yonkel, our six musicians, and Johnny Grant. This was Johnny Grant's first trip to entertain the troops. It was long before he became the Mayor of Hollywood. He had primarily been a radio personality interviewing celebrities out of his truck as they exited nightclubs. After that first trip with me, he did it sixty more times over the next fifty years, traveling the world entertaining the troops. He was heroic.

The sixteen hours did not seem long. None of us had ever been to Hawaii and from the air it was unreal; water of blues and greens I'd never, ever seen and after we landed, it was even more so. The air was perfume, truly intoxicating. I'd never, ever experienced anything like that. As beautiful as it remains, and some I suppose will argue this point, but thanks to environmental changes, I've never seen it like that again. We stayed about two hours, long enough to refuel and have a lemonade.

Now we had sixteen more hours to fly to Wake Island, site of a historic and horrible battle of World War II. Attacked on December 8, directly after Pearl Harbor, it was held by the Japanese until the war's end. Most of our group was aware of its recent history. Just one year before, in 1950, President Truman and General MacArthur had met on Wake Island to discuss the Korean situation, which had just escalated. We were not allowed to get out of the plane and observed this flat, sparsely inhabited place from our windows. After a couple of hours and fuel, we took off for another sixteen-hour hop to—Japan.

The night before I left Los Angeles, I had stood at the edge of the ocean and told myself that within days, I would be standing on "the other side of the world." And now I was here! Impossible! I stood at the Tokyo waterfront on that first evening trying to absorb this, make sense of it to myself. Was it my imagination, or did the sea indeed smell and sound different?

We were all so unsophisticated. The first landing on the moon was still eighteen years away, but perhaps for the first time I had the tiniest understanding of the physical world.

We had the rare experience of staying at the Imperial Hotel, the mysterious, imaginative hotel built by Frank Lloyd Wright. It was one of the few structures that had survived the 7.9-Richter-scale earthquake of 1923 and it had gone almost unscathed through World War II. Few people now alive have had the privilege of staying at the hotel. Sadly, it is gone now, demolished in the name of someone's idea of progress. Primitive in feeling, it was very spread out. The public areas were large and magnificent, with many dark, narrow, mazelike halls that twisted and turned to get from one place to the other. It was an adventure just to find the way to one's room. The rooms themselves were small, with low ceilings, and the smell of incense was everywhere. There was a tiny bathroom with a deeply sunken bathtub and torrents of hot water that gushed from a faucet as thick as an elephant's trunk. I treasured the comfort of that tub. We saw very little of Tokyo outside of the hotel.

Local food, as beautiful as it looked, was off limits to all army personnel, and to us. Human fertilizer was still being used at the time.

Not long after we landed in Japan, I found out I had a problem—a big problem. My carefully made cowgirl costumes and props had mistakenly been put aboard the plane headed to Europe! The bag would never catch up with us before we left for Korea. The only things that had arrived with me were my underwear, a skirt, a blouse, a sweater, and a sewing kit. As my mother would say, "Thank God for small favors." But these precious few personal items didn't solve the problem of what Richard and I would wear on stage.

I had only twenty-four hours to replace the missing items. I went with a Japanese man to a costume shop, and with rough sketches and sign language, I tried to describe the sort of outfit and props that we needed. English was rarely spoken at that time, but somehow I made myself understood. The costumers were absolutely brilliant and in a little over a day created a truly bizarre but practical version of what we needed. My new costume was a bit like a large male bird. The costumers had done "cowboy and Indian" research and concluded that fringe was appropriate—at least twenty-inch-long fringe. We clipped off much of the fringe and added a hat and pair of boots. The Universal prop department's machine shop had designed a finely made "arrow holder" that was hidden under my shirt. The "hidden" arrow holder was now a four-inch metal pipe that would be seen from the beginning of the skit as some inexplicable appendage. The arrow itself was attached midway through the play, offstage. It, too, was gigantic, but so what? The whole thing would work, and I was elated and relieved to have it!

We would all be dressed in army clothes except when on stage, and they gave us heavy parkas and boots in preparation for the subzero weather. We carried ID as "Captain" so we wouldn't be shot as spies if we were captured. The evening before we left Japan for Korea, I took the needle, thread, and scissors that my mother had packed and altered my army regulation pants. They were a size small, but were still huge on me. It pleased me that it was necessary, and also that I could do a good job of it. I always found relief from tension when I could use my hands.

I cut away chunks of fabric. The stitching was very strong and held up for the whole trip.

On the five-hour flight to southern Korea, we were divided into three groups that would travel in different directions. We drew straws for the musicians. Somehow my group ended up with the guitar player, which should have been wonderful. Unknown to anyone, however, the guitarist was blind or very close to it and was very dependent on his brother, the accordionist, who had been traveling with him. When we drew straws, the brother was assigned to another group. The brothers had not anticipated being separated and, wanting very much to go on the trip, hadn't told anyone there might be a problem. All the music cues for our act, about thirty of them, were visual. Our sheet music was now useless, and we had to find a way to change all the visual cues to sound cues. Richard and I ended up having to stomp heavily or hit things to make noise or create a vibration. We had no choice but to make it work, and work it did. I'm sure we looked a bit wild and frantic, inexplicably stomping around, but it seemed to add to the energy of the piece.

For everyone who has had the privilege of performing for servicepeople anywhere, the experience is the same. The troops are appreciative to an unbelievable level. And if you have the fortune to have good material as well, you feel you've gone to showbiz heaven. I froze my butt off outside, having to change offstage into my nice skirt, blouse, and heels in the middle of the show, protected only by a couple of sheets held up by the other girls to preserve my modesty. But it seemed a small price to pay for the amazing experience I had been given.

In between shows we moved a number of times a day in small two-seater planes, tiny helicopters, and ambulances. One time the ambulance we were traveling in broke down and we were stuck for many wasted hours on the ice, waiting to be rescued. We lived in tents and never saw a real structure after we left the south. And there were no women, not one, not even female nurses. They may have arrived later on, but we didn't see them at this time in the battle zones.

Our living conditions were very primitive. We were given a shallow pan to keep under our cots for washing up in the morning. Some nights I just couldn't brave the elements outside the tent to go to the latrine, so I quietly used my pan as a chamber pot and stashed it till the morning. Our nights were short, but it was amazing that we all slept so deeply, even though guns and bombs could be heard in the near distance.

The MASH hospitals were pathetically primitive, very different from the ones in the movies and on television. They were improvised and moved around frequently. We tried to visit them as often as we could in between shows. I had never seen such blood and pain and heroism. I was nineteen, but often I was looking at boys younger than me. Many of them had seen me in *The Prince Who Was a Thief*, and it meant a great deal to them that I was there. I was a brief distraction from their horror, and I felt purposeful at last.

There was one boy named Gus, who had been shot on his twenty-first birthday. He was a medic who had been rescuing somebody when he was attacked. His face was covered with shrapnel wounds, and his body appeared to be seriously wounded. He had heard I was in the area. He especially liked me in the movie and hoped he'd get to see me, so I made it my business to go to him as often as I could. There was something about him that drew me to him. His words were so optimistic, but I could see something else in his eyes. For as long as I was in the vicinity, about a day and a half, I would run to his tent between shows to sit with him and hold his hand. Sometimes we talked a little. He told me he lived in Richmond, California, across the bay from San Francisco. He asked if I could call his parents when I went back to the States, tell them I had seen him and that he was doing great. I promised I would and went off for about an hour or so to do another show. When I returned, he was dead. He had gone just a moment before. I gave him a kiss for his parents.

There were many others whom I grew close to in this intense and passionate time who did not survive. I didn't have the luxury to feel too much. There was so much to do, and feelings had to be postponed to do it. I knew how to do that. A valuable gift from my childhood. There were bombs and constant gunfire around us. Sometimes in the middle of a performance, a group of soldiers would suddenly rise, lift up their rifles, and leave. They were needed for a nearby skirmish. And we heard when they hadn't survived.

On Christmas Eve, after our last show that evening, a chaplain told Mala Powers and me that he was going into enemy territory to a little outpost of American soldiers that night. I don't think he actually asked if we wanted to go; no, he wouldn't have done that. But Mala and I did ask if we could go with him. He thought about it for a few minutes before saying we could and told us to keep it to ourselves. He also warned us that we would be riding in an open jeep so that we could jump out quickly in case of an attack, with no headlights and only a flashlight to guide us.

Mala and I sprayed ourselves with cologne, and we all left within the hour. The chaplain drove, and a soldier sat next to him in the front with his flashlight pointed straight down to the ground. We were told to be very quiet. There was very little moonlight, and we went slowly over the rough terrain. I honestly was frightened. I felt God's presence this night and asked him to protect us if he could, and if not, for my parents to forgive me. But there was no question that I must do this. During the journey Mala and I did not murmur one word to each other, and I don't recall our exchanging even a glance. I suppose if I had seen that she was frightened, it would have unnerved me. As far as I know, she was trying to be brave, just as I was.

We had been traveling for over an hour, maybe two. We were now within a few hundred yards of the enemy, perhaps surrounded by them. They seemed to be shooting in our general direction because we saw lights from the explosions. And then we saw a dark area that became even darker as we approached. We saw that it was a very small tent. We got out of the jeep and were led silently through the side of the tent, carefully and quickly.

The only light was from a small, wood-burning stove in the center of the tent. There were perhaps a dozen soldiers, boys, packed closely together, looking astounded at our arrival. Not high spirited and filled with exclamations of "Wow!" as the others had been. They were somber and thoughtful and very timidly would touch our arms or lean over and breathe our aroma, as if we were apparitions. They talked very quietly. Someone kissed me on the cheek. Someone else on the back of my head. Perhaps it was the cold, but they all had tears in their eyes.

We stayed maybe forty-five minutes or an hour, sipping coffee, whispering. Then we carefully sneaked out of the tent and made our trek to the open jeep, back through the woods and the hills on the dirt road with the flashlight and got back to our camp safely. I thanked God again, as I had many times during this trip.

I saw Mala from time to time through the years, but we never, ever talked about that night. Perhaps it was too intimate and sacred. I have seldom spoken about my experience in Korea until now. I understand why most returning soldiers, who are battle-weary way beyond anything I have known, are silent. No one wants to go back there.

When the trip was almost over, I was approached by a soldier, who said, "I'll bet you're missing getting showers, aren't you?"

"I certainly am."

"Well, the general is out of town, and he has a shower rigged up in his truck." I was given a flashlight, a bar of soap, a .38 revolver, and was escorted to the truck. It was a little improvised thing, something like a pail with holes in the bottom that was strung up. When you tilted it with a piece of heavy string, a little warmed water trickled out. It felt luxurious! There was a towel for me, and I dried off quickly, dressed, and stepped out of the truck. Two armed soldiers were waiting to escort me back to the girls' tent. I was happy to give them back my gun. I didn't have a real bath again until we got back to Tokyo.

We spent several days in Tokyo, culminating in a show at the Ernie Pyle Theater. It had the widest stage I'd ever worked on. All of us who had spread out over Korea were reunited and put on a wonderful show for the men, with all the musicians working together. I shall never forget it. It was the first indoor show we had presented. It was a huge theater, and the applause after the act with Richard and me must have gone on for ten minutes. You would have thought we'd just sung an opera. Everyone was terrific and some were fabulous, especially tiny Molly Picon, who was getting up there in years and stood on her head in the middle of her act. (Years later, inspired by Molly, I learned to do it myself on stage.)

One afternoon before we left, I made a date to meet Molly and her husband, Jacob (Yonkel) Kalich, at the Kabuki Theater. I was sure I could get there on my own; the directions seemed simple. I started out walking and soon realized I was very lost. Remember, the Second World War was just barely over. Japan had not yet exploded with architecture and subways, and many people still wore traditional clothes. Very few spoke English. And there was something else: people would not look at you—make eye contact—not even the people who worked in the hotel. We were the conquering Americans, and there was an element of fear and distrust toward us. I felt so bad about that, but I didn't try to force my feelings of goodwill on anyone. They didn't seem ready to accept them.

I kept walking, lost in a sea of people packed together, moving steadily through the streets. It was the most delicious experience I'd ever had, the first time in years, really, except when I was a child, that I'd been alone. No one in the whole world knew where I was, and I felt independent and free. The freedom was exhilarating, and I walked, and I walked, and I really didn't care that I was lost.

Then I spotted an American sailor, towering over everyone around him. I went up to him in his white uniform and said, "I'm lost, and I'm looking for the Kabuki Theater."

He said, "Oh, I know where that is," and he led me there. I found Molly and Yonkel in their seats and sat next to them. I had brought my camera and managed to take movies of some of the miraculous plays. The stage was literally twice as wide as the widest conventional stage I'd ever seen, far wider than the Ernie Pyle Theater we'd just played.

Where shall I begin? The colors. The artistry. The play I saw featured an old man who was unpacking plates from a box. That's all he did, for several hours. He unpacked the plates—with such concentration, such focus. He was so interested in each and every one that they became interesting to us and pulled us into his world hypnotically and then far deeper into our own. I heard a little rustle of paper from behind and turned to see that many of the audience members, who'd come there to spend the day, were eating their wooden box lunches. It reminded me of the long Saturday afternoons at the movies when our mother packed Sherrye and me food for the whole day.

We did one more show on a battleship anchored in the harbor, and then it was time for us to go home, all of us barely managing to fall into our seats on the plane. I hoped I'd be able to come back to Japan someday and really see it.

Going home, we flew to Midway Island first, a sixteen-hour flight. The Battle of Midway was regarded by many as the most important naval battle of World War II, as most of us were acutely aware. Attacked six months after Pearl Harbor, the Americans managed to hold on at great cost, which very likely changed the outcome of the war. I don't remember if anyone got off while we were refueling, but I didn't. I was so full of unprocessed emotions, I couldn't deal with any more. I was content to look at the native gooney birds through the window.

There were another sixteen hours of flying before we reached Hawaii and stayed overnight. The women in our group slept on cots in the army nurses' barracks, where I saw the biggest cockroach I'd ever seen. I gave thanks that my sister wasn't there. She had so despised the desert cockroaches in Tucson when we were children.

Off to Los Angeles in the morning, another sixteen hours. It's a blur to me. I know my parents were there to greet me. I was exhausted to the core, emotionally and physically. They took me home, and I went to sleep and slept, they told me, for three days.

When I was finally up and around and feeling I had my strength back, I started making phone calls and writing letters to the parents of the soldiers I had met. I wrote to the Estradas, the parents of Gus, the boy who lived in Richmond, California. I got a letter back saying that they would love it if I had time to come visit them and that they would cook the most wonderful Mexican dinner I had ever had.

Several months later I had a break and went to see them. It was a five-hundred-mile trip up the coast. My friend, producer Leonard Goldstein, who liked to spoil me, offered his car and driver, Wilbur, to take me and my chaperone, Gail, to San Francisco. Her presence seemed silly after the relative independence I had experienced, but she was a lovely and interesting woman, and it was fun to have her as company. She was actually my only woman friend, though I still kept my personal business to myself. It would be years before I had more close women friends. The only women I met were actresses under contract to the studio, and I did not know how to encourage their friendship. They certainly did not open their arms to me, and even if they had, I had little leisure time.

Gail and I stayed overnight in a San Francisco hotel and the next day drove to Richmond. The entire Estrada family greeted us: Mr. and Mrs. Estrada, the sisters, brothers, in-laws, and several babies. They lived in an attractive middle-class two-story home. We sat around for a while having hors d'oeuvres and wine, and I met everybody, including the neighbors.

Shortly before dinner was ready, Mr. Estrada came to me and said, "I want to show you something. Would you mind coming upstairs for a minute before we sit down to eat?"

We went upstairs into one of the bedrooms, and Mr. Estrada picked up a large framed portrait of their son Gus. It was a college graduation picture. Handing it to me, he said, "I need to know, is this the boy you saw? Is this the boy you saw that died? I must know this before we sit and eat."

I felt the weight of what this vulnerable man was asking. I had never felt so responsible for another person's feelings. But he was depending on me, and so I told him the truth. After a moment he said, "Thank you" and held me, the last tangible connection to his son, and wept.

About ten others were already seated at the large table when we joined them. They had waited for us before starting to eat the delicious feast. I noticed Mrs. Estrada looking to her husband. Their eyes connected, and he told her what she needed to know. There was great unspoken sadness at the table, but there was also great warmth, and it was true—it was the most delicious Mexican food I'd ever eaten.

We kept in touch for a long time. Mrs. Estrada sent me beautiful, hand-embroidered linens and towels every year for my birthday and for

Christmas. I entertained them when they came down to Los Angeles and gave them a tour of the studio. We lost touch after many years, when I moved to New York. But one of Gus's sisters wrote to me just a few years ago, and we've communicated by notes and phone calls. Her parents are gone now. Her young brother Gus would have become eighty years old in January 2010.

My empty persona was starting to be filled. The Korean trip had opened my heart and my eyes. But when I got home and returned to the business of show business, it seemed I was wasting my life. The efforts made by my agent to get me some freedom to work at other studios, or on television or on the stage, were rejected. Even my requests for time off to work in Betomi's class were denied. When I wasn't on tour "selling," I was shooting.

I made fifteen pictures for Universal over a six-year period. Leonard Goldstein produced four of them. His movies were "program pictures," costume dramas on a shoestring. They cost little and made big profits. *Weekly Variety* called Leonard "Hollywood's top moneymaking producer."

The gossip was that I was Leonard's "girl." I wasn't, though he was definitely my friend and mentor. I pretended I wasn't affected by the talk, but it did get to me. I could put up with it because I genuinely liked Leonard and felt protected by him. Like my mother, Leonard was the child of Russian Jewish immigrants. He told us stories about his father arriving from Russia and pushing his scissors-sharpening cart until he reached Bisbee, Arizona, where he married and raised five children. Leonard had two sisters who lived with him in his apartment, and two more brothers, one of whom was a twin (Bob) whom I met a few years later.

My parents liked him, too. He was a real friend to everyone in my family, including my awful brother-in-law. They were all comfortable with one another. Whenever Leonard came to call for me, my father would answer the door and Leonard would say, "Hello, son," because he was a year older than my dad. There was real affection between them.

Leonard and I would have dinner together at least two or three times a week, sometimes at my house (where he loved my mother's cooking) and often at the Chinese restaurant that one of his brothers owned. He was my dear and best friend. I'd never had one like him.

Sometimes when I was feeling lighthearted and silly, Leonard indulged me in my favorite childhood game of Hide and Seek after we returned from some elegant affair. My parents were already in bed and out of sight, but they could hear us running around the house. I can't imagine what they thought. Leonard seemed to understand I was still working out part of my childhood. I had never talked about those years in the sanitarium, but he instinctively seemed to understand my need to play. This man, with the tough demeanor of a Bogart or Edward G. Robinson, whom many people feared, found me to be a nonthreatening and relatively inexperienced female whom he could trust. Leonard believed in my talent and encouraged me not to give up my ambition to be in the theater. He'd say, "Watch out, Helen Hayes!" I clung to his words of encouragement because the small creative world that I knew thought I was an embarrassment. They did not hesitate to say as much in the press and in reviews.

Leonard had regular Sunday morning brunches in his Beverly Hills apartment. His sisters, Della and Phyllis, did the cooking. You never knew who would show up on these Sundays. A lot of sports figures. Joe DiMaggio, who was as quiet as me, sat directly across from me at the small table for a long time, eating his bagel. I wanted so to engage him in conversation, but inhibition and shyness are contagious. We didn't exchange two words.

One Sunday Leonard asked if I wanted to go along to a football game with the group. Leonard and his sisters had already expressed some concern about who would meet their uncle Moe when he arrived. He was expected that afternoon from out of state and someone would have to miss the game to greet him when he arrived. I was not interested in football, so I volunteered to stay and see that Uncle Moe was comfortable, maybe even go with him to get a bite to eat. I would certainly want someone to do that for my favorite uncle Morrie, who lived in New York. Everyone left for the game and perhaps an hour later Uncle Moe's taxi arrived. Uncle Moe was a nicely dressed gentleman in his fifties. He seemed like a family member to me, so I felt comfortable. I apologized for Leonard and his sisters and asked if he'd like to go to dinner. He said he'd like that very much, and I explained I'd have to stop home first to change my clothes.

Leonard's driver, Wilbur, drove us to my house. Uncle Moe said he would wait for me in the car, but I asked him to please come in and meet my parents because they liked to know whom I was with. He hesitated for quite a long moment and then said, "Well, all right."

I took him down the long hallway, back to the den where my dad was reading the paper, and said, "Daddy, this is Leonard's uncle Moe."

My dad jumped up, about to shake hands, but then he pointed with his finger at Uncle Moe. With a funny grin on his face, he said, "I saw you on television!" Dad knew he'd seen him, but he couldn't quite place him.

Uncle Moe suggested we go to the elegant restaurant La Rue's. During dinner many people stopped at our table to say hello. I thought, *My goodness, Uncle Moe knows a lot of people. Maybe he didn't need my company after all.*

It wasn't until after Uncle Moe and I had left for dinner that my father finally realized who he was. "Uncle Moe" was the notorious gangster's gangster Moe Dalitz, one of the major figures who helped shape Las Vegas in the twentieth century. If Dad had any problems with my going to dinner with Uncle Moe, it was too late.

Uncle Moe had just come from testifying at the Kefauver Committee hearings in Washington, D.C., where, it was said, he'd held his own. I didn't find out who he was until Leonard told me the complete story the next day. Everyone had a good laugh, especially when they heard Moe's reaction to the evening. He told them he'd felt like a schoolboy having to come into my house to meet my folks and was genuinely embarrassed at my father's greeting. I thought it was pretty funny, too. Many years later I read that Uncle Moe had left millions to charity.

Little by little I was becoming more independent. I learned to drive and had my first car. I was no longer dependent on my mother or the studio to take me everywhere. The car was a nifty little black Chevy hardtop convertible with red leather upholstery. It was the first place of privacy I'd ever had, and I treasured it. For a while, I kept a giant-size Hershey chocolate bar in the glove compartment. I never ate any, but I felt powerful knowing it was there.

6.

Becoming Movie Stars

Before *The Prince Who Was a Thief* was released, Tony and I started filming *The Son of Ali Baba,* a rip-off of the movie we had just completed. Instead of "Tina," this time I was "Kiki," and Tony was once again some sort of prince. We were both unhappy about the film. *The Son of Ali Baba* was seventy-five minutes long and became known primarily for Tony's line in his Bronx accent, something like "Yonda lies d'castle of m'foddah," which he swears he never said. All I know is, when we shot it, we were sitting on our horses on the back lot and had to do a great many takes while Tony struggled to get his Bronx tongue wrapped around an impossible line. The movie made a fortune for the studio and Tony and I each got another huge raise. My guilt turned into depression.

All the years of nothing but hard-boiled egg whites, carrots, and celery had taught my body to hold on to whatever it could get. Even five pounds made a difference on my small frame. The wardrobe department would scold me and at home I got the same treatment. I went back on "diet pills," the amphetamines prescribed for me by any doctor and delivered to the house.

Fear of following in my sister's footsteps kept my weight from getting completely out of control. Sherrye had given up fighting her morbid obesity. At five feet two, she already weighed close to four hundred pounds in her early twenties. It was a very sad thing to see. She pretended to be the jolly fat lady, but she hid herself from my professional acquaintances. I knew she'd have been thrilled to meet them, but she seldom came up to Los Angeles. If I wanted to see her, I'd drive down to Long Beach. Leonard Goldstein was the exception. In spite of the lowbrow pictures he produced, she sensed his humanity. She felt free to join us when I'd bring him to family dinners with my parents.

My own fight with the weight devil continued. In the commissary at lunchtime, I would sit against the wall at a single table like many of the contract players. As the studio heads passed my table, they'd stop and check on what I was eating and then make comments, as if they were my parents.

"Watch it there, Piper. Do you really need that?" Then they'd continue on to the large, round executive table in the corner. I was sure they were still watching me. Did they not know how rude and humiliating that was? I'm sure they didn't understand how sensitive I was about it. None of them had ever met my sister.

I was told that my next movie would be *Francis Goes to the Races*. It was one of a series of *Francis* movies, all of them revolving around the adventures of Francis the talking mule, with the humans playing second fiddle to the mule. Those films were farcical, occasionally funny, and very profitable for the studio. I was considered the female lead opposite Donald O'Connor, who was always adorable and terrific, but my part was inconsequential.

The only good thing about shooting the *Francis* film was hanging out at Santa Anita racetrack when there were no races going on. One day a jockey asked me if I wanted to "inspect the stalls." I said I'd love to, and when we got to the barn, he asked if I wanted to go for a ride. Of course, I said yes, and we both hopped onto the big Thoroughbred in front of us and whizzed around the track several times. Leonard Goldstein spotted us galloping by and frantically ran out onto the turf, waving us to a halt. The studio standard for my safety was so inconsistent. I could never figure it out. Apparently their insurance that day didn't cover me riding during my free time. It was perfectly all right for me to do my own stunts in the movies, even quite dangerous things, but only if the camera was rolling. It was also fine for me to be upgraded constantly to a bigger, feistier, "better" horse, sometimes within the same scene, as long as it was the same color. Those big black stallions looked wonderful on screen and required a very strong, confident rider. The wranglers felt I looked better on a horse than most of the stuntwomen, who were daredevils rather than refined equestrians, though they were trained to do a lot of things I couldn't. I did as many stunts myself as I could. I loved using my body, running fast and jumping down from high places, and I took pride in knowing how to fall without hurting myself. I was proud that the wranglers and stunt people trusted me with the beautiful animals. The crews are especially appreciative when an actor or stunt person does well with a physical challenge. They will applaud and show their admiration openly, though they rarely respond to acting scenes.

Once I wanted to rear my horse instead of having the stuntwoman perform it. It was a necessary thing for my character to do in order to escape from the villain who was holding me captive. The horse was specially trained to stand up on its hind legs in response to the slightest featherlight pull on the reins. This sensitivity was exquisite, but if you used too much of a pull, the horse would respond and possibly go completely over onto his back. I had beginner's luck, and it went well, but I found out afterward that my stunt double didn't get full pay because I had done her stunt. After that, with a few exceptions, I let the stunt people do their work before I made my attempt.

The permanent stable was on the back lot. Most of the contract players were required to take weekly riding lessons as a group. But because I was experienced, I got to ride whenever I wanted and as often as I had the time. The wranglers would give me a nice horse and I'd go all over the hills that have now become the Universal Studios Theme Park. Believe it or not, as you entered the main gate in those days, you could see sheep grazing on the hill in the distance. Universal had an arrangement with a sheep farmer and therefore didn't have to pay to have the grass cut. A little time out there in the hills on a horse helped me to stay relatively sane. Being close to nature has always sustained me, and thank God, even as a small child, I was never blind to it. After I'd ridden for a while, I'd stop at the man-made lake, which was surrounded by fake trees, and take a swim. Then I'd shower off at the studio gym run by Frankie Van, the well-known boxing referee, and end the pleasant morning with a Goetz salad in the commissary (named after Bill Goetz, a studio head).

My agent had had no luck changing anything concerning work for me. The studio stubbornly took the position that I was "damn lucky" to be earning all that money and to have "a name." Several times I tried talking to the studio heads myself about my frustration. I would request a meeting and make great preparations to meet with whomever was running the studio. I actually wrote out lines demanding more interesting work and memorized them. Incredibly, when the hour arrived, the woman of the world who knew what she wanted reverted to being the silent child. In the face of authority, my chin would involuntarily drop to my chest and remain there as it had at my first screen test. I would walk away in tears, unable to defend myself against the condescending pep talk I inevitably received.

Universal decided to have the world premiere of *The Prince Who Was a Thief* in my hometown, Detroit. It was held at the magnificent Fox Theatre that I'd gone to when I was a child. The publicity department arranged for my extended Detroit family—my mother and father, the aunts and uncles and cousins, even my *bubbi*—to meet us at the train station on arrival. Zaddi had passed away a few years before. I had such mixed feelings. I was excited, but I was not proud. I didn't believe I deserved any of this celebration. I hadn't done anything of worth, and I knew it.

Tony and I did a little skit on stage between showings of our movie. It was just like in the old days of the theater, when I'd watched the vaudeville acts with my mother and sister and seen Jane Withers. The skit was written and directed by the brilliant Jay Presson Allen, who later became famous and successful as a Broadway writer-director. The rehearsals back home had been exciting. I'd never worked with a director as strong and sure of herself as Jay. On stage, after our skit, Tony asked my family to stand and take a bow, which I must say he did with great good humor. The entire balcony of that huge theater stood up. There were several hundred of them! Incredibly, they were all truly my relatives: cousins, aunts, and uncles. Later we heard that a theater in the Bronx, Tony's hometown, had a marquee advertising Bernie Schwartz (Tony's real name) and Rosetta Jacobs in *The Goniff and the Maidle*, Yiddish for *The Thief and the Girl.*

After the premiere, my aunt Goldie gave a family party at their modest home. To my surprise, Tony came along. I always remembered that and thought it was dear of him. After he'd gone back to the hotel, all the young cousins took turns using the bathroom that Tony Curtis had used.

Now the touring began in earnest. From city to city we did an endless round of department store autograph parties; signed thousands of pictures supplied by the studio; did interviews on radio and television shows; had dinners with dignitaries; had press conferences; then hopped a late-night or early-morning train or plane to take us to the next city. Press and photographers greeted us at every arrival no matter the hour. And one always dressed up to travel in those days.

I was afraid to appear in public without my full makeup, terrified the fans would find out that it was only Rosetta Jacobs. Once I lied to a second cousin who asked if my eyelashes were real. I had learned to put on false eyelashes even as a train rattled me up and down. Of course, all of this took time, almost three hours of what could have been sleep time. As we trooped from town to town, from train to plane, I became increasingly exhausted.

At the end of one long day, when I had bathed and washed my hair, my chaperone, Gail, suggested that I think about arriving just the way I looked then—with no makeup and my hair curly. She implied that I was wasting time and energy on my beauty regimen. One brave morning I tried it: I appeared wearing just my lipstick. To my astonishment, no one seemed to notice! The photographers didn't seem surprised or horrified, taking their pictures as before, and people were just as friendly. Their acceptance somewhat eased the burden of my fake life. Nevertheless, I was envious of Tony when we had a precious spare half hour to freshen up and rest between appearances. He would take a quick shower and change his clothes and be completely refreshed. I could never manage to put myself together that fast in those days. After a shower I had to deal with hats, jewelry, straight seams in my stockings, a few minutes on my face, and a few more if my hair got wet. It wasn't worth the effort, so I stayed as I was—hot and exhausted.

Tony and I had been thrown together for a long time by then—making two movies, touring the country, doing fan magazine photo shoots of us on fake dates—and we'd gotten along pretty well through the whole grueling process. One day, not long after we had come home for a little while, Tony grabbed me and pulled me into a cubicle in the publicity department. Holding both my arms, he looked at me with tears in his eyes and said, "People who are envious of our good fortune might try to destroy our friendship." He made me promise that we would always check with each other if we heard anything upsetting about the other. We embraced and vowed that we would always be friends. I was deeply touched and considered him to be my only real friend besides Leonard.

Soon afterward Tony and Janet Leigh, whom he'd been dating for real (and whom I found delightful and warm) decided to announce their plans to marry. I was excited and happy for them. At the same time the studio was making plans to send Tony and me back on the road, this time for a twenty-six-city personal-appearance tour covering all the major openings of *The Prince Who Was a Thief*. When the studio found out about Tony and Janet's plans, they thought it would be better if Tony and Janet postponed their marriage until after our tour, as if in some way their marriage would invalidate the movie. I was outraged when I heard that the studio wanted to stop such a personal thing. I thought such thinking was ridiculously old-fashioned. Even then, movie fans were so much more sophisticated than the studio gave them credit for. Of course, the fans knew our movie relationship was not real. I spoke up strongly to Leonard on behalf of Tony and Janet. He listened carefully and seemed convinced. I was thrilled that my words had apparently carried some weight because I soon heard that Tony and Janet had gone ahead and married in the East.

Occasionally in the following weeks, Tony joined me on the tour. I did double duty when he wasn't there, participating in at least twenty interviews and appearances, plus the big premieres at night. It was a rough schedule to carry on my own, but I was happy to do it for a friend. I learned a great deal and at that age, I had the stamina to survive it.

However, as the tour progressed with me alone, I began to hear stories, too frequent to ignore, that Tony was telling people I had personally tried to stop his wedding because it would "spoil my tour." Tony was reportedly saying that he was the "real draw" in our movie and was "carrying me." I was upset and bewildered when I first heard these things. Tony was on his honeymoon and impossible to reach. Then I began to feel some anger and, I confess, a little pleasure in the fact that I drew as many people on my own as when Tony and I appeared together.

I didn't really believe the talk at first, it was so preposterous, but as the stories continued, they began to hurt me. I had no way to confirm any of the gossip and I thought about the pact Tony and I had made. When I got back to Los Angeles, I tried to talk to him and clear the air, but he would walk away or leave if we were in the same room. His open hostility and coldness were bewildering. I was frankly afraid to confront him. I had never ever confronted anyone before, so I chose what seemed the easier road and did nothing.

Tony Curtis and I made a total of four movies together at Universal. While making the very last one, the tension between us grew until we spoke not one word to each other, except when necessary in the scenes.

Since that final movie decades ago, I laid eyes on him only once: in the 1980s, when I went to see him on stage at the Mark Taper in L.A. I had planned to go backstage to see him if I liked his performance even a little. I figured thirty years was long enough for both of us. But when I reached the theater, I was apologetically told that they were changing my seat to a row farther back for fear he'd see me in the audience. Whether I'd just be a distraction or really disturbing to him wasn't clear. In any case, I did not go back to see him.

As someone who had great fondness for the very young Tony, I regret we weren't able to come together before he left us.

I was now nineteen and starting my sixth movie in less than two years. I was billed over everyone in *Has Anybody Seen My Gal?*, even over my friends Charles Coburn and Rock Hudson. Many people envied my good fortune, but it all embarrassed me, especially in front of Charles Coburn. I know now it probably didn't bother him; he'd been around so long and seen it all before. All the young ones come and go, but he'd still be around. I loved Charlie, and he loved pinching ladies' bottoms. It was like a tic; he couldn't help himself. If you were female and under a hundred and five, you had to move fast around him. No one ever seemed offended. Not for a moment did we consider reporting him for sexual harassment.

No one was particularly aware of the boy at the end of the counter when we shot the drugstore scene. A very young James Dean had been hired as an extra and sat there quietly. Years later my uncle Morrie spotted him while watching the movie on TV and called from New York to tell me.

Rock Hudson had good billing but was miscast in a small part as my boyfriend. Rock was not yet getting good opportunities, but at least he was being used. Most of the contract players got no work at all except in bit parts or background. Tony and I were the exceptions. Rock and I spent a lot of time together "hanging out." At the time I had no inkling that Rock had a sexual preference one way or another. I didn't think about it. There was no particular chemistry between us, and he never made a pass at me. I just figured I wasn't his type.

Rock was as vulnerable as he was big. One night all the contract players performed scenes on Stage 28, the old "Phantom Stage," where the original 1925 *Phantom of the Opera* had been shot. The Paris Opera House and some of the boxes had become a permanent set, redressed for a number of pictures. The urban legend was that three separate times over the years, the studio had made an attempt to dismantle the set, but each time a worker suffered a serious injury caused, they said, by the ghost of Lon Chaney. Rock was so frightened backstage that he was almost out of control. He wasn't afraid of the ghost, but of appearing on stage in front of the audience, mostly studio personnel and agents. I held on tightly to this huge man, who was shaking and sweating in front of me. I tried to make him believe with all the conviction I possessed that he was wonderful in his scene. I'd seen it, and he truly was. He managed to pull himself together and was really quite fine.

The only A movie I ever made at Universal was *The Mississippi Gambler,* with Tyrone Power. Rudy Maté, who had done *The Prince Who Was a Thief,* was going to be the director. I had seen Tyrone Power and his beautiful wife, Linda Christian, walk into the commissary the year before. We had all literally gasped at the sight of the two of them, dressed in white, tanned, and looking like gods. I never imagined I would be asked to work with this matinee idol. I was told that I was competing with Linda Christian for the lead opposite her husband. Power was also one of the producers. I didn't think I had a chance.

Linda and I would both be making screen tests. I was given a scene to study for a day or so, then sent to wardrobe and fitted with a nineteenth-century ballgown. On the day of the test, makeup was plastered on me, my hair was piled up and swirled, and I was sent to the soundstage to meet Mr. Power and shoot the scene. As I walked in, Mr. Power was standing in his costume in front of a backdrop suggesting the nineteenth century. I was so tightly laced into my costume I could hardly breathe; so when I found myself face to face with Tyrone Power, eighteen years my senior and still gorgeous, I thought I would faint. I struggled to catch my breath, said, "How do you do?" and put my hand out.

With a very small smile he took my hand and said, "Shall we?" Very businesslike.

Someone said, "Roll 'em," and not skipping a beat, Tyrone Power gathered me into his arms and gave me a great big movie-star kiss. That was how the scene began, and we played out the rest of it. It apparently went all right. I was in such a state that I really didn't know. I heard later that Linda Christian had done her test at another time, either later that afternoon or the next day, and it had gone well. I was told that no one would discuss the part with me for at least a week, and that I would do well not to ask.

I was ecstatic when I received word that I had gotten the part. Not because it was a good role, only because I had "won" something. The part was still a cliché, like all the others, but it was longer and had more potential than anything I had done before. I was informed that I probably wouldn't see Mr. Power again until we started to shoot. Well, that was okay with me. I would be making preparations myself.

I had almost twenty changes of costume. I had fantasized about wearing those period dresses when I was a young girl; I'd even drawn pictures of them. But the actual fittings were something else entirely. Standing absolutely still for five, six, seven hours at a time was surprisingly difficult. In fact, it was torture! I found out that all the real prima donnas were in the wardrobe department, especially the fitters and seamstresses. They were superb at their work, really the best; they'd been doing it for years and didn't give a damn about hurting the feelings of the stars. When everything was finally done and we were ready to shoot, I felt I had *earned* the right to wear those beautiful dresses. I wore a new gown almost every day, but of course I couldn't sit down in any of them. Instead of a chair, I had to use one of those slanted reclining boards that fit under the skirt in back to lean against. The most beautiful dress of all was the bridal gown for the big church wedding. Brilliant costume designer Bill Thomas had outdone himself. He was an elegant man who had designed my clothes on several other pictures. I liked him very much. I never felt disapproval from him about my curves, as I did from most of the other designers.

Tyrone Power had a good sense of humor and immediately warmed up to me and to everyone else. He asked me to call him "Ty." Ty preferred borrowing chewing gum from me to having his own supply, like people who enjoy eating off other people's plates. I tried weaning him away by having packages of various flavored gums delivered to his dressing room. But truthfully, I enjoyed giving the quintessential movie star something that I had and he wanted, even a stick of gum. I doubted he would have asked for more. There wasn't any overt chemistry between us, which was probably a good thing for the work. I may have been suppressing it because of our relationship in the movie. My character was very young and spoiled and didn't show feelings for Ty until the very end, when she realized she'd been in love all along.

The lavish church wedding was shot on Universal's largest soundstage. Ty, who is in love with my character, has to watch me being married to someone else. I'd made seven movies in three years, and this would be the fourth time I'd been married on screen, but never like this. I invited my grandma and mother to be on the set the day of the wedding. They had never been to a set before. There would be hundreds of extras there, and I knew that if Grandma said anything out loud, the crowd would cover the sound. She had often talked out loud to me on the screen in quiet movie theaters, just like in the Yiddish theater, where the audience constantly talks to the actors on stage. She had said endearing things to me, often in Yiddish, like "*Oi, mayn ketzalah*." ("Oh, my little kitten.") Grandma thought nothing of saying whatever she pleased to anyone at this time in her life, and I expected she would exclaim something when she saw me in the beautiful wedding dress. To my surprise, she was well behaved on the set, and when she was introduced to Ty she even got herself a kiss. I think my mother must have enjoyed that day too, although if she said so I was too preoccupied with the work to hear.

We shot the movie almost chronologically and did the second-to-last shot last. I loved doing that scene. It was on the big back lot lake that had been built just for the movie. A stuntwoman should have done it but I wanted the challenge of doing it myself, and they let me. The riverboat was actually pulling away from the dock as I came flying down a long path and leaped aboard. I was aware of a lot of water underneath me as I sailed over it with my long skirt and all the petticoats. As my toe touched the deck, someone grabbed me to stop my momentum. I got applause for that one.

One night we were shooting a scene involving hundreds of extras watching some native dancers in New Orleans. The purpose of the scene was to see the awakening of the hidden passion in my character as she watches the dancing. The lead dancer happened to be Gwen

Verdon, who would become a legend on Broadway within a few years in musicals like *Sweet Charity*, *Can-Can*, and *Damn Yankees*. Her dancing and the music were so terrific, it was easy for me to get into what my character was feeling. My cheeks became very flushed and later, when the rushes were seen, the front office and makeup department accused me of secretly adding to my rouge and ruining the footage. They were very angry and never let me forget it. Their low expectations and lack of respect for the actors' work continued, especially for the ones they owned.

When I finally saw *The Mississippi Gambler*, I was deeply disappointed in my performance. I felt I had failed an opportunity. I was not quite as harsh on myself watching it thirty years later. Wanting to seem sophisticated and being in over my head were exactly right for the part. Rudy Maté was smart to have cast me.

Shortly after we finished shooting *The Mississippi Gambler*, I was asked to go to South Africa for the opening of *Has Anybody Seen My Gal?* The foreign market was immense, and my films always did well abroad. I was thrilled at the prospect of going to Africa until I heard that the audience would be segregated. There was still apartheid. I told the studio I would not go. It was the first time I had said no to them. Doing something I believed in felt good. I had dipped my toe into the water.

Costarring with Tyrone Power made me an even more valuable commodity. I was given another new contract, the *third* since I'd started at Universal. I received a raise of thousands of dollars, to as much as many major movie stars at that time were earning. It was an obscene amount of money for a twenty-year-old. My head was spinning. I was expected to wear something different every time I was in public because I would always be photographed. The studio said they would no longer supply me with clothes since I could afford to buy myself almost anything I wanted.

My mother took care of my clothes and saw that they went to the cleaner after wearing. (She despised the fact that I smoked and often said "A lady should smell sweet.") She even saved me the trouble of shopping for new clothes, something I hated to do. She would bring home dozens of designer dresses for me to try on. She loved the fact that I could afford to buy beautiful things, and it was nice seeing her vicarious enjoyment. I was fulfilling her image of me as a movie star. She bought almost nothing for herself. There were aspects of the clothes that I confess appealed to me. I appreciated the sculptural quality of a few of them, as art objects, and I loved the fine fabrics. I would have enjoyed them even if someone else were wearing them. My father built an extension onto the house, a room that was an enormous walk-in closet just for my clothes. I was touched that he did most of it himself, with his own hands. I had never seen him build anything before. He'd always been away at work.

My parents and I never discussed what any of us were feeling about all this "success," never talked about what any of it meant. It seemed to be taken for granted.

Our only rich relative was Aunt Bergie, who lived elegantly at the Essex House in New York with Uncle Harry. She was a perfectly nice woman, I suppose, whom I'd met briefly once or twice, and who through the years had sent my mother beautiful and expensive hand-me-down clothes to wear. My mother despised being poor and the idea of taking anything from Aunt Bergie and her well-dressed and educated daughters was painful to her. It was so hurtful to her that she would give the clothes away rather than wear them. She proudly wore her own inexpensive dresses.

When I suddenly found myself comparatively wealthy, Aunt Bergie happily volunteered to help me spend my money long distance. She wrote to my mother that she would have her furrier in New York, the famous Ben Kahn, send me some "suitable" fur coats to choose from. She also had her jeweler send a selection of elegant watches "because Piper should have these things." She chose not to call me Sissy or Rosetta as the rest of the family did. To her I was Piper, her movie-star niece. I played her game because I could tell it pleased my mother. I picked out two beautiful watches and a full-length Aleutian blue mink coat that cost a small fortune. I still have one of the watches and I wore the coat for years, until wearing fur was no longer acceptable to me. I let the storage bill at the cleaner in New York lapse, and the coat disappeared, where it is traveling somewhere in space.

In the midst of all this "success," I was suffocating spiritually, but at the time I couldn't have told you that. With the aid of the amphetamines, I continued to function, but all my real feelings seemed to be on hold.

There was one creative outlet that relieved some of the pressure. With the help of the makeup and wardrobe departments, I would dress in elaborate disguises, a hobby that would become valuable decades later when I made *Twin Peaks*. I went home one day done up as an Asian girl and for about five minutes fooled Edna, our housekeeper. She wouldn't let me into the house. On another occasion I worked as a cowboy extra on the back lot for almost a full day. Another time, covered by a beard, I lined up with the unsuspecting men, including Rock Hudson, waiting to pull a sword out of a column. An assistant director fired me at the end of the day for causing too much trouble. My disguises gave people a good laugh. I secretly wanted to be Harpo Marx. I still do. Wearing someone else's skin all day gave me a chance to escape. For a few hours, no one knew who I was. I was free of the identity others had imposed on me.

I had lots of dates—some arranged, some not. I could go out with almost anyone I chose. I didn't even have to do the asking; someone else would do it for me. If anyone said no, I was never told about it. I never had to personally ask for anything.

One evening my friend Leonard, who had just produced a very nice movie called *Meet Danny Wilson* with Frank Sinatra, took me to the famous Cocoanut Grove at the Ambassador Hotel to see Sinatra perform. His voice and singing were never better, and in between shows he sat at our little table and talked to Leonard.

We left before Sinatra's second set. As we were walking out of the Grove, an extremely tall and handsome young man approached Leonard and said he hoped we'd enjoyed ourselves. Leonard introduced me, and as we walked away he said, "Now, there's a fellow for you."

I said, "Oh really, why?"

Leonard said, " 'Cuz he owns the joint. And a lot of other joints. And he's a nice Jewish boy."

A few days later Leonard called to tell me that the young man I'd met, Mr. Schine, had phoned asking if it was all right to call me. Leonard had told him that he would ask, and I said, "It would be nice to spend time with someone not in show business."

And so G. David Schine, who together with Roy Cohn would become a notorious figure in the Army-McCarthy hearings a few years later, called me, and we made a date to go to dinner.

David was prompt, but I was not. I kept him waiting, not deliberately, for about fifteen minutes while my mother entertained him—my usual panic at meeting someone new. When I came down the hall and into the living room, I felt some ice in the air. I had expected my mother to be impressed with this six-foot-four, extremely handsome young man. I felt somehow that she didn't like him, and I didn't know why.

When we went outside, I looked for his car. There was none. Perhaps he had a chauffeur who had gone around the block? Instead he said, "We'll go this way," indicating up the street. I thought perhaps it had been hard to park, and he'd left his car around the corner. We walked one block, two blocks, and finally he said, "Do you mind taking the bus?"

Not wanting to be a bad sport, I said, "Of course not." So we boarded the Wilshire bus and took the twenty-minute ride to the Ambassador Hotel. We had dinner at the Cocoanut Grove before the crowd came and danced a little. Afterward David drove me home in a fairly ordinary car that appeared from somewhere. He was extremely polite and seemed genuinely interested in my work, not feigning condescension as some people did. He asked if he could take me to dinner the following night before returning to New York.

Leonard called the next day to see if I'd had a nice time and informed me that, in case I didn't know, David's family owned not only the legendary Ambassador Hotel but also all of the luxurious Schine hotels in Florida, not to mention 150 movie theaters, one of the largest theater chains in the country at the time. David's wealth meant nothing to me. Perhaps it meant something to my mother, but by that time I had received offers of marriage from many wealthy men and a few princes as well. Almost all of the young actresses did.

It was the same routine with David the next night. It was appealing to me that he tried hard not to show off and seemed to want to be a regular guy. It was still daylight when we once again walked to Wilshire and took the bus. All the seats were taken that evening, and this time we had to stand. Some of the people on the bus recognized me and looked a little confused. This was not New York, where actors commonly ride the bus and subways. As we rode, David handed me a small gift-wrapped box. *Oh my,* I thought, *it's too soon for jewels.* Since he had presented it to me in public, I opened it while everybody stared at us. It was a tiny pink electric shaver. What could I say? Quaint. I am not a hairy person, but of course, I thanked him with all the passengers looking on with interest. When we got to the hotel, we sat in a booth again, and this time his charming and genuinely witty younger brother Richard joined us. David and I danced a little and had a little wine with dinner. At the end of the evening, he drove me home and kissed me sweetly at the door.

When I wasn't working and David was in town, we'd see each other at the Cocoanut Grove. Interesting people would join us, like the great actor Edward G. Robinson, Jack Lemmon and his wife, Mike Todd and his date. We'd have dinner and stay to see the entertainment. Sometimes David's friend Roy Cohn, who always had a pretty girl on his arm, would join us. We saw more and more of Mr. Cohn over the next few years. Thus began a three-year, rather slow-moving but ultimately dramatic relationship.

My pal Rock Hudson and I were cast as the leads in an Arabian Nights fantasy called *The Golden Blade*. Good for Rock. This time I would have to perform a dream dance sequence in the film, and I embraced the challenge. The famous choreographer Eugene Loring was hired to train me. I started working with Eugene several months before shooting, training for eight hours every day. Besides keeping my weight down, working hard at anything made me feel more comfortable with the privileges that I had. Eugene demanded that I eat a steak for breakfast every morning before I left the house. That seemed impossible because my breakfast was usually black coffee and a cigarette. Eventually, though, I began to enjoy the ritual. When I got to the studio, there were ballet stretches and strengthening exercises for hours. In the afternoon there were basic modern dance movements that I repeated and repeated until I collapsed to the floor. Gradually I became stronger. During the last few weeks of training, I was given the actual choreography. We shot the sequence in one day, and Eugene and I both thought it went well. It was exciting to move like that, and the crew was very impressed.

When I saw the finished film months later, to my shock, most of the dancing was done by a double! They must have gone to some pains to make sure I wasn't on the lot when they shot it. I suppose if I hadn't been so numb emotionally, I would have been angrier, but I never felt my efforts had been wasted. My body felt disciplined and strong. The experience of working with Eugene was a gift to me. I didn't like the deception, of course, but somehow it didn't surprise me.

I despaired that things would never change. Producers at other studios were making excellent dramas about real young people that were more suited to my abilities, but Universal still refused to loan me for those projects. I was constantly ridiculed by the critics and press, who said things like "Universal's perky starlet outdoes herself—even less talent than imagined." I was spared from reading many of these comments because my mentors and family kept them from me, but the essence of their truth got through anyway. I had signed my life away to Universal when I was seventeen years old, and as far as I could see, there was nothing I could do about it.

About this time I gave an interview to a fan magazine in which I talked about how much my life had changed. I talked about my teen years and mentioned my schooldays' idol, Rick Eller, who hadn't known I existed. I told the interviewer how five years before, my girlfriend and I had taken the bus across town just for the thrill of passing Schumacher Drive, where the perfect boy lived. Now I, too, lived on Schumacher Drive.

Lo and behold, not long afterward I got a letter from Rick Eller! He said he had read the magazine article, still lived down the street, and asked if he could come visit. This was truly a fairy tale. Of course I said yes, and we actually had a few dates. Rick was just as nice and bright as I had imagined. He was still quite handsome, with perfect features and thick dark hair. But there was an unreality about all of it. At twenty years old, he was still a boy, and I had become accustomed to being with men, or at least people I thought were men. Rick was the same age I was, but it felt like several lifetimes lay between us. His mother invited me to a going-away party she gave for him before he left for Korea, and after that I lost touch. I know he returned safely, got married, and became a successful attorney. I had lunch with him years later with another friend from school and saw him again briefly at our fortieth high school reunion. He was still perfect.

It was 1952, and the "police action" was in its third year in Korea. A year and a half had passed since I'd been there. When the USO asked me to go again, there was no question about it. I said yes right away. The extreme cold during the first trip had been grueling, but it was springtime now in Korea and I assumed it would be a little easier. I couldn't have been more wrong.

The first time the endless flying had been exciting, but the second time—I wondered how we'd done it. It seemed sooooo long. Everyone was tense and irritable. One of the actors, Keith Andes, who was sitting behind me, exploded when I bummed too many cigarettes. He was quite right. It had never occurred to me that one didn't always share, and I was just too lazy to dig out my own. Most of us were smokers then, so the cabin was cozy with smoke.

The haze of cigarette smoke was nothing compared to the dust-filled air that hit us the moment we got off the plane in Korea. The whole army had respiratory problems, and of course, we did too. No one knew why the air we breathed caused infection. Even our hands were splitting open with cuts that didn't go away. Major wounds would simply not heal. The MASH hospitals were having a time of it.

I had asked Johnny Grant to come with us again. Johnny worked nonstop, giving the fellows a laugh wherever we went. He was "on" twenty-four hours a day. In addition to his own stand-up routine, I had asked him to do a little skit and soft-shoe dance with me. He resisted the soft-shoe, but in the end he rehearsed and did it with me. Later on in the show, I'd bring a soldier up, tie a flowery Easter bonnet on him, and sing "In your Easter bonnet." When it was over, of course, I'd give the soldier a big kiss. It was not a particularly original thing to do, unlike the musical play I'd done last time, but the soldiers seemed almost as enthusiastic. Between shows I went to see as many wounded soldiers as I could.

Not long after we got to Korea, I received word that my friend Dick Contino was in the vicinity. I had dated Dick a few years before, and our families had spent some time together enjoying the Continos' homemade Italian food. I had even slept over at their house one night, sharing a bed with his sister, and gone to mass with the family in the morning. If I had been born a Catholic, I think I would have been a great one. The color and theatricality of the rituals is very appealing to me. But we all get to heaven in our own way.

Dick had achieved fame and adoration. He had been a great star for a few years, playing his accordion with unusual sensuality and brilliance at all the top clubs with tremendous success. Then the draft board summoned him to appear for a physical at Fort Ord. When he failed to report, he was arrested, tried, and put in prison for six months. During that time all of his showbiz friends completely deserted him. It was not politically correct then to be a draft dodger. After his trial, my mother and I went up to San Francisco to see him briefly before he went into prison. Surprisingly, my mother was not afraid of the "stigma" that my supporting Dick might bring. When I think of it now, it was quite remarkable.

When Dick was released from prison, he went through basic training and then was quickly shipped to Korea. He was allowed to share his gift of music when some brilliant person said, "Put him in Special Services and let him lift the spirits and morale of the others." Dick traveled constantly in Korea, giving shows everywhere. He was hard-working and so passionate; it was obvious he was trying to make up for his mistake. The soldiers were grateful and forgave him, but the public never did. It would have been different today. These days you can be forgiven for almost anything if you're straightforward about it (though it always helps to have a good lawyer and a press agent).

Dick was there with Special Services when we had our reunion, and he asked me to sing with his band for a couple of shows. What a thrill that was. We had never been physically intimate except for a few kisses, but the music brought us together in a different kind of intimacy. Amazing how it can do that.

After a couple of weeks in Korea, the "crud in the air," as we called it, got to me, and I became sick. I started to lose my voice, but when I could no longer speak or sing, I was gifted with the miracle of "performance" adrenaline. Bolstered by amphetamines and aspirin, I was able to croak a few words into the microphone and sing for every show. Singing is much easier on vocal cords than speaking. I remember sitting on a cot in a tent, trying to put makeup on before going out onto the improvised stage to perform in front of a few thousand soldiers. I was perspiring and wishing I could stop hurting and breathe. I didn't yet know I had pneumonia and I just wanted to go home. But then, who didn't?

Many days later we left for home from Tokyo, flying sixteen hours to Midway Island again. We stayed only a few hours and then underwent the long flight to Hawaii. Sixteen-hour hops between each landing: after what seemed like days (and really was) we finally reached San Francisco before the short hop to Los Angeles.

By the time we got there, home was a blur to me. The doctor said I had pneumonia and should go straight to the hospital, but my parents thought I'd get better care at home. Poor Johnny Grant had pneumonia too, but he went to the hospital.

I had a high fever and couldn't really move or breathe for days. I have no recollection of that time except one: beautiful Edna, on her knees beside my bed, praying and sometimes weeping. That touched me so much. When I was able to sit up a little, she started bringing me little booklets from her church that were nondenominational and positive in their message. With that, and my mom's chicken soup, in a few weeks I became strong enough to move around.

Leonard Goldstein wanted me to recuperate in a nice dry place and rented a big house in Palm Springs for my family and me. When I was well enough to get around, I thanked him and insisted on paying for it myself. Leonard also had his driver, Wilbur, pick up my sister and brother-in-law in Long Beach and drive them to Palm Springs for a week's visit. My mother stayed with me the whole time, cooked, and took care of me. A very healing time. My father came on weekends. I don't remember Leonard coming but once, to check that everything was all right. He had six movies going in L.A. The weather was lovely then, not yet summer, so it was pleasant and quiet. I did lots of drawings of the desert, and of my dogs in the pool. I collected rocks and minerals, as I always had.

When I was stronger, I started writing and making phone calls on behalf of the boys I'd met in Korea. It was difficult having communication with anyone if you were in the service back then. This was before laptops or cell phones. Phone calls were impossible, and the mail was very slow. I was able to serve as a connection between the boys I'd met and their families back home. I, who was still waiting to find my own voice, found ease and privilege in speaking for them.

7.

Gaining Independence

When I had recovered from my bout of pneumonia, I often saw David Schine when he was in town. I found his quirkiness refreshing, and I admired and envied his good education. He was bright, I supposed, having graduated from Harvard at such a young age. He was rather quiet and thoughtful when he was with me and had a way of looking at me with what appeared to be pleasure and affection. And he wasn't afraid to tell me what he liked about me. I confess I enjoyed that. A lot of men withheld praise, thinking it diminished them in some way. He struck me as a very simple person with simple needs. I thought perhaps he had no money of his own. We eventually stopped taking the bus, but his gifts to me were few and far between and always just a little bit odd. The flowers he sent were always birds-of-paradise because they reminded him of me. Frankly, I preferred seeing them outside in the ground. I don't care for exotic flowers in the house except for perhaps calla lilies. I did enjoy dancing with David, one of my favorite things to do, and the Cocoanut Grove seemed to be our private club.

Some months after we started dating, David told me he wanted me to meet his mother, Hildegarde, the next time I was in New York. When I did, I found her to be a beautiful, accessible, and charming woman who seemed bewildered by her entire family, especially the men. She never seemed sure of what they were going to do or say, and I felt in some ways she didn't approve of them. It was strange. I knew she was fond of me. She put a color photograph of me and my puppy Sukoshi in a silver frame on the piano, alongside the family, and she hand-wrote many kind letters. She often had me up to their apartment in the Waldorf Towers for teas and musical afternoons when I was in town. It was very elegant and precious, a life I'd only seen in movies. David enjoyed the fact that I dressed at least as well as his beautifully dressed mother, a fact that she did not overlook. He told me she coveted my fur coat.

On the other hand, David's father, Myer Schine, was a tough, seemingly humorless man who made an effort to tolerate me. I supposed he thought everybody had designs on their family fortune. He needn't worry. I was dating four or five other people at this time. I was intrigued by but not particularly serious about David.

David's friend Roy Cohn started joining us regularly for dinner at the Cocoanut Grove, with or without a girl. It was often just the three of us. As long as I wasn't put under pressure, I had learned to get by socially with a little conversation. I even thought for a brief time that Roy Cohn had a yen for me. He tended to show off a bit and laughed too hard at anything vaguely witty I might say. I knew nothing about Roy Cohn except that he was a lawyer. He was not so unattractive then; the evil hadn't yet flowed out over him. May God forgive my ignorance; it would be quite a while before I would learn about his sins with the Rosenbergs and his vile acts with Joe McCarthy.

Soon after I met David, he had showed me a little four-by-six-inch pamphlet that he had created, with an American flag on the cover. It was called *The Communist Threat in America*. He told me he was putting one in every room of the Schine Hotels, "in the drawer next to the Bible."

I saw the flag and thought, *Something patriotic, isn't that nice?* and never bothered to look inside. I had never actually bothered to look inside a newspaper, either.

It is very hard to write about my ignorance and isolation, which are so mortifying to me now; my lack of awareness of those profoundly affected by the blacklists—the suicides, the ruined lives—was total. I was as blind as the blind in Europe before World War II. Completely ignorant politically, I rarely understood issues relating to anything but my so-called career. All I knew about politics was that my parents had been Roosevelt Democrats, and Roosevelt had been my beloved president until he died.

My awareness that David and Roy Cohn were collaborating on something together began slowly. We had had many pleasant meals together, but now before dinner we sometimes met in a large bungalow at the Ambassador Hotel, where Roy Cohn stayed when he was in town. There would be a lot of joviality between David and Cohn that I didn't understand. They were often talking about someone named Joe—"I talked to Joe, and he said . . . such and such." Then there would be lots of laughter.

One evening before going to the Grove for dinner, Roy, who was on the phone, said, "Piper, you want to talk to Joe?"

I said, "Who's Joe?" There was more laughter.

"He's on the line, and he wants to talk to you," Roy replied.

Always the good sport, I said, "Well, all right . . . Hello, who's this?"

"This is Joe McCarthy. Senator McCarthy. Nice to meet you, Piper. Having a good time with my friends there?"

I mumbled something. It was awkward making small talk on the phone with someone I didn't know. I gave the phone back to Roy, and after hanging up, he asked, "You know who that was? That was Senator McCarthy!" More laughter.

At that moment he and David struck me as adolescent schoolboys. Perhaps they thought I would be impressed to speak to a senator. I was not impressed. I had met Adlai Stevenson, many senators, and Vice President Alben Barkley when I was in Washington on tour. When Roy and David stopped laughing, we went to dinner. Little did I know I was dining with the devil's disciple.

Why didn't I ask "What's going on? What are you two working on?" Unless it was about my own work, or about love, I rarely asked questions of people. My mother's motto was "People's business is their own" or "Familiarity breeds contempt." So I didn't ask questions, and that, of course, doomed me to ignorance.

Except for flashing his pamphlet, which I was too lazy to read,

David never once talked to me about communism or anything vaguely political, for that matter. He talked about the theater and movies and about how great Sammy Davis, Jr., was, and he asked me if my work was important to me. When would I have it "out of my system and give it up"? When would I come to Florida to see their other beautiful hotels and visit with his family? He also talked about making a permanent life with me.

The idea of marrying David—or anyone else—felt like a death. I was just beginning to explore my life, my sexuality, and I found that I could choose my partners just as a man did. The fact that society did not yet support that kind of freedom for women was not a concern that I had. And although I had never done any work as an actress in public that I could be proud of, I still had hope. I still believed my creative life was ahead of me.

The studio sent me out on tour for several weeks to promote *The Mississippi Gambler*, most notably to New York and New Orleans. My life was filled with such extremes. I'd traveled for weeks in Korea in jeeps with just a duffel bag, but now my mother and Edna packed all ten of my red alligator bags, plus one for shoes and another for hats. I didn't lift a finger. In New York I stayed in fine hotels on the park, with great room service, and had my clothes cleaned and pressed by truly skilled people. I overtipped everyone, as I'd been taught. A car and driver were always there to take me wherever I wanted to go. I never had to scramble for a taxi after the theater. I knew these privileges were the result of the machine that had created me. My helplessness, or perhaps lack of courage, grew, as did my self-loathing. I spent most of the trip doing the interviews that I despised. The questions were addressed to a fictitious creature that I had nothing to do with: Pretty Perky Piper Laurie, the girl who ate flowers. I felt pressure to take on the persona of that girl just to get through the interview. I despised the persona, but it helped me control my anxiety.

"Oh yes, they're quite nutritious," I would explain when the interviewer asked me about my "flower diet." It was a complete performance, not a very good one to be sure, but it at least allowed me to hide behind someone and get words out. As Piper, I knew what to say; as Rosetta Jacobs, I was still struggling. Most writers and critics of my movies seemed unable to distinguish the material from my performance and assumed I was the one at fault. I tried not to read the comments, but sometimes it was unavoidable. The press continued to say things like "Be kind to us, and send this girl back to Detroit." When I dared think about my teacher Betomi and her expectations, I felt shame.

I was going to turn twenty-one while I was in New York, and the Universal publicity department threw a big press party in honor of the occasion. They never missed a tie-in. I was going to celebrate my birthday in a way most young women never do, at the chic 21 Club in Manhattan. It was an elegant place, and I'd never been there.

I used the occasion to at least wear a dress I liked. It was my favorite: ankle length, made of yards of pale gray-green organza, with a large, soft pink silk flower at the waist and a wide, dark green velvet ribbon hanging from the flower. It made me feel as if I were in a garden. There must have been 150 people there for my "birthday celebration," all press or publicists. It was astonishing that so many well-known journalists showed up to have a glass of champagne and congratulate "the young starlet." Even Mike Wallace was there. I still have a photo of a very young Mike in the foreground. I put on my "charming perky act" and had two glasses of champagne, but on this birthday, I was yearning for the company of just one personal friend.

The next day I was off to New Orleans for the first time. My weight was down, so I filled myself with great meals, in particular, a twenty-course meal served at my induction into the Ancient Order of Creole Gourmets. They were now getting my name right at these events. When I had first started out, I would get wildly enthusiastic introductions at the "creamed chicken luncheons" or at the local chambers of commerce that ended with ". . . great pleasure to introduce Miss . . . Piper Cub!" And in the next town it would be "Miss Piper . . . Heidsieck!" But the one I loved best was "Miss . . . Peter Lorre!"

When the tour ended and I got back to Los Angeles, I was stunned to learn that Universal had actually agreed to loan me to another company, RKO. At last! How much they got for me, they wouldn't say, but I knew it was a lot more than they paid me. The movie was *Dangerous Mission*, starring Victor Mature, the wonderful Vincent Price, whom I got to know better years later, and me. The producer was *the* Irwin Allen. This would be the first of his so-called disaster movies; the next one, *The Poseidon Adventure*, was to come a bit later. Every disaster he could possibly create for the movie on the relatively small budget happened in this one.

Irwin Allen wanted to approve everything himself, which made the wardrobe fittings an adventure in themselves. He sat right outside the fitting room while I tried on my costumes. I tried on one dress, and when I came out to show it to him, he whispered to the wardrobe woman, "Can you put in some falsies?"

Now, I was always considered by the costumers at Universal to be quite nicely endowed naturally, but I thought it would be interesting to try the pads and see how it looked. The last time I'd padded my bra was in junior high, and I'd used socks. So I went back into the fitting room, stuck in a pair of spongy things, and came out for Irwin Allen's approval. He scrutinized my figure for a moment and then said, "More . . . *more* falsies!" He was drunk with some kind of screwy sexual power.

So we ladies looked at one another, unsure of how to handle it, and went back into the fitting room, where I stuck in another pair. They looked really grotesque, and I removed them all before returning to Irwin Allen. I was about to protest the entire thing when he said, "Well, that's looking better! How about one more pair?"

We were wild! Stifling our laughter, we flew back into the fitting room and did absolutely nothing. I just waited a few moments and returned. Allen looked at me with a big grin and said, "Now that's what I wanted! That's great!"

We shot part of the film on location in Glacier National Park, the most spectacular natural setting I had ever been in. We stayed at an enormous rustic lodge. Groucho Marx, who was an acquaintance of Irwin Allen's, came to the location for a few weeks and joined us for some meals at a big round table in the dining room. He was quiet and pleasant and occasionally witty, but for the most part he behaved like an ordinary and slightly shy man.

I liked my leading man, Victor Mature, immediately. He seemed more manly and "grown up" than most of the actors I had played opposite. Like Tyrone Power, he was at least fifteen years older than me. Victor was an honest man with a reliable sense of humor who definitely didn't take himself too seriously. He never felt comfortable unless he had food stashed away nearby. When we got back to L.A., Vic always had to have fresh sandwiches and fried chicken hidden in the chest of drawers in his dressing room. He didn't always eat it, but he liked knowing it was there. A childhood hunger. I understood that.

We shared something else—a sexual connection that was very intense without our acting on it. It lived powerfully without us literally touching each other. Years later, in the play *Bent*, there was a prime example of that kind of gift. Vic was a hell of a guy, and I liked him so much. I knew he had a crush on me. I was just his type. (He told me he had been in love with June Haver.) He was big and brawny, with workman's hands, really sexy and sensual. He could be very naughty and bold.

While we were working on the film my girlfriend from school, Karlyn, was getting married in San Francisco at the Fairmont Hotel. I wanted very much to be there, and RKO arranged for me to have a three-day weekend so that I could comfortably go to the wedding and get back. Universal would never have allowed me to cross the street while shooting a movie.

It was so nice having a few days off on my own. My family and Leonard drove me to the station in downtown L.A. and saw me off in the late afternoon. It was an overnight trip, and at Leonard's suggestion, I had taken a bedroom on the train. The train would make very few stops, the first one in Pasadena, just ten minutes outside of Los Angeles.

When we made our stop in Pasadena, only one passenger got on. The passenger found his way to my compartment and knocked. To my utter astonishment and delight, it was Vic, looking for an opportunity to be really alone with me for the first time.

I said, "Come in."

I found him irresistible. I'd always loved trains but never so much as this. We stayed together all night on the way to San Francisco, and when we got there, he checked into the hotel diagonally across the street. He waited for me while I was at the wedding, and we spent the next two days together before taking separate flights home.

Back in Los Angeles, we were finishing the filming of *Dangerous Mission*. The lobby of the Montana lodge we'd stayed in had been recreated at the studio, using the largest soundstage on the RKO lot. The set was enormous and expensive to build. We had scenes to shoot with the cast principals that tied in with many interior and exterior scenes already shot in Montana. Several hundred extras had been hired for just one morning's filming.

I had been in quite a few scenes that morning when I realized I had on the wrong clothes. In fact, all the principal actors were wearing the wrong clothes. Since the scene tied in with many we had shot in Montana, the costumes had to match. If the costumes were wrong, nothing we'd shot during that expensive morning would make sense. When I brought the mistake up to the wardrobe woman, however, she dismissed it as nonsense. Several times I tried to explain the complicated story and time-line for the actors involved. It was absolutely clear to me that all of us—Vincent Price, Victor Mature, William Bendix, Betta St. John, and myself—were working in the wrong clothes. The wardrobe woman wouldn't accept it. As far as she was concerned, I was just a twenty-one-year-old troublemaker.

So I went to Irwin Allen, the producer, who was sitting nearby in a high director's chair, and explained the problem to him. It was obvious he wasn't really listening. I repeated my logic to Allen very carefully. This time, though, I didn't revert to my usual "child speaking to authority" role. I knew I was correct, and it never crossed my mind to give up. How did I become so brave? Was it because I was out from under Universal's parental influence?

After repeating the scenario three or four times, during which he never once looked at me, Allen's face suddenly turned pale. Grabbing his script, he looked at some pages and then jumped out of his chair and bellowed, "Stop!—stop! Oh shit! Shit! Shit! God! We have to reshoot everything!"

The first assistant director came running over, looking at Allen as if he'd gone mad. Allen continued, "We have to do it all over. Damn it! Keep the extras! Don't let the extras go home! Tell the extras they have to come back after lunch! Tell the demolition crew to hold it. We can't tear down the set!!" They had been scheduled to start pulling the lodge down after lunch. Even if it were possible to rebuild the set and bring back all the actors and extras, it would have cost a fortune. If we'd moved on and the mistake not been caught, eventually they would have found they couldn't put the movie together. I thought I deserved at least a bunch of posies.

I guess nobody likes to say thank you to a smartass. Irwin Allen could never bring himself to say it, and he avoided my gaze whenever possible after that. That was okay. In spite of myself, I was beginning to spread my wings a little.

Eternally hopeful, when the movie wrapped and I returned to Universal, I thought perhaps they'd offer me a decent part. Instead they offered me a little home on the studio lot built especially for me to live in and reflect on my new star status. It had a bedroom, dining room, kitchen, and living room. It was my extravagantly large "movie star" dressing room when I wasn't using the one on the set. It was sleek and modern, and I felt quite grown up. They built it next door to the studio hospital, which also meant someone was there day and night. I wondered if they did that to keep an eye on me, even though I was now twenty-one.

My work calls in the morning were always early. I began spending nights in my little home at the studio to save myself almost two hours of travel. I'm not sure what my parents thought about my staying away overnight. Most girls who were twenty-one were already married and those who were unmarried still lived at home. My parents seemed to tolerate my living part time at the studio as long as it was not widely known. I supposed they thought I was still innocent, as I was expected to be. I didn't have a lot of communication with them about it. Mother never talked with me about these things, and certainly not my father. They were probably afraid to know the truth.

Through all the changes, Leonard Goldstein continued to be my closest friend. He had moved his production company over to Fox and was doing terrifically well. Leonard was part of my family, and my parents loved him. We had an affectionate but basically platonic relationship.

One evening Leonard came to the house and told me very slowly and with great difficulty that he had gone to see his friend the jeweler. "I told him I wanted the best rock in the joint." He patted his pocket. "It's right here." He looked at me very seriously. "You know what I'm saying to you, don't you? Tell me if you want it. Should I take it out of my pocket?"

I was touched, but I was also frightened because while I hadn't yet thought it through, accepting the ring didn't feel right. I had real love for Leonard, and I didn't want to embarrass or hurt him. I didn't know what to say. For lack of anything better, I asked him how he felt about having children. I told him I had always supposed I'd have at least ten, and asked him how he felt about that. He told me children had never occurred to him. We both got our answer. Always curious, I confess I would have loved to have seen the ring, but it had to stay in his pocket.

Leonard and I saw each other less often after that evening. Instead of almost every day, he came by only once or twice a week. He no longer phoned every day. I had hurt him, and I felt wounded myself. I was surprised to discover how much, and how I truly missed him.

Mother was also going through some difficult times. Perhaps she was disappointed when I told her that I had turned Leonard down; I don't know. She wasn't sleeping, just roaming the house all night; talking loudly nonstop; letting out her anger about my sister's weight; her unhappiness with my dad's partner; my dad's passivity; and the world in general. She never mentioned me. Why I was off limits, I don't know. I wasn't treated as part of the family. I was her star. "Sissy doesn't have time to do that," she'd say, or "Sissy needs her rest."

My poor father had to endure the constant roaming, weeping, and angry speech-making. Selfishly, I could at least close my bedroom door at night and try to get some sleep while my mother ranted. I always feared she'd open my door and inflict it on me as well, as she had when I was a child, but she never did. When I did open the door in the morning, she was still going strong. The sound of her voice had become hideous to me. I remembered years before, when I had loved my mother so intensely that I'd prayed to have her birthmark (which was displayed like jewelry in the middle of her upper arm). It was about the size of a dime. When I was four, I got one in the same spot. It stayed there for a number of years and began to fade when I no longer needed it, just as mysteriously as it had come.

Today we might have insisted on some psychological or medical help for my mother. It's altogether possible that whatever the problem, it was exacerbated by menopause, but women just "got through it" in those days. My father remained completely passive. Mother was not a person who trusted doctors. She trusted almost no one now, and she unconsciously did her best to teach me to do the same. I never thought of my mother as someone who was mentally unbalanced. How could I? She was just damn angry.

I was grateful when I had to leave town again to go on location. I was going to Utah to shoot scenes for my next film, *Smoke Signal,* with Dana Andrews. A few days before leaving, Leonard called and told me to turn on the news. He said my friend G. David Schine was in a lot of trouble. I had been out of touch with David for a few weeks because I'd been out on the road selling a movie. The events that Leonard told me about were shocking to me.

Leonard said that David had been working with Roy Cohn as an unpaid consultant for Senator Joe McCarthy—the "Joe" I had talked to on the phone months before. They were investigating the "communist infiltration" of the United States. Now David had been drafted into the army, and Cohn had tried to stop it by getting David put on

McCarthy's committee officially. Cohn wasn't able to pull the necessary strings to do that, so he started trying to intimidate the secretary of the army, Robert Stevens. He threatened to investigate the army for possible communist infiltration unless David got released from army duty or, at the very least, was given a light job so that he'd be available to work on McCarthy's committee. Secretary Stevens didn't go for the intimidation or blackmail. He said no, he wouldn't do that. Roy Cohn then maintained that the army was holding David "hostage" to keep McCarthy from looking for Communists, and Joe McCarthy started an investigation of the army.

Leonard warned me that the press might be trying to find me and talk to me about David. I said my dates with David had been very quiet and that only the hotel photographer had ever taken our picture, so I thought it unlikely people knew about us. Leonard was relieved to hear that I was scheduled to leave for location. Nowadays almost any kind of publicity is thought to be a boost to a career, but in 1954 it would have been scandalous and hurtful to be associated with such a controversial and despised person.

Not long afterward I got a quick call from David, telling me to read a certain newspaper that would explain his innocence. He said he thought his calls were being monitored. I got the paper and read it, then I went out and got *all* the newspapers. At that time Los Angeles had quite a few but I'd never, ever bought one. I read them all. It was a brand-new and exhilarating experience for me. Each one had a different version of what had happened, what McCarthy was really doing, and what David's relationship with Roy Cohn really was. There was no way to know the truth. Perhaps Cohn had a "crush" on David, as some of the papers implied, and just wanted him around. I thought it was entirely possible Roy had romantic or sexual yearnings for David, who was a handsome six-foot-four Adonis, but the speculation that they were a homosexual couple was silly to me. Everything I knew about David from our relationship of over three years told me any sexual feelings Cohn might have had were not reciprocated. David was an ardent lover of women's bodies and loved making love. Perhaps I was naïve, but that's what I felt. I was astonished by what I read, but I kept reading, reading, and asking questions. I was in turmoil, conflicted because David was my friend and sometimes lover. I had no idea what David had contributed to McCarthy and Cohn's evil work. I chose at that time to believe it was nothing, that he was naïve and had been manipulated by Cohn.

The hearings in Washington began the day I left Los Angeles to go on location in Utah. Millions of television viewers tuned in to watch the dramatic encounters between McCarthy/Cohn and the brilliant counsels for the army, Joseph N. Welch and John G. Adams. Leonard knew there was no television or radio in Moab, Utah, so he gave me a shortwave radio to keep in touch with the hearings and the world. As it turned out, we were in such an isolated spot that the shortwave didn't work either.

It was frustrating to be leaving Los Angeles, but I had no choice. On the morning of my departure, a car and driver picked me up at my parents' home at about six a.m. Our next stop was Toluca Lake in the San Fernando Valley, home of Dana Andrews. From there we'd drive to the airport.

I hadn't yet met my costar, and I was extremely excited at the prospect. Dana Andrews was one of my idols from adolescence. When I was thirteen, my girlfriend Karlyn and I had gone to see his film *Fallen Angel* at least six times. We really only wanted to see the scene where Dana Andrews kisses Linda Darnell. We had been dumbstruck seeing it the first time, checking with each other that they had really done what we thought they had done. They had opened their mouths ever so slightly as they kissed, and we thought that was wonderfully scandalous. We couldn't tell for sure if he had put his tongue in her mouth, but we chose to believe that he had. At thirteen years of age, we found it exciting and provocative. Karlyn and I went back over and over to see that scene; I had been in love with Dana Andrews ever since. Now I was to be playing opposite him.

We drove up to a glamorous-looking home with a circular driveway and parked in the middle at the front door. We were just on time. I had made a point of looking as well as I could at six in the morning, and I quickly sneaked a peek at myself in my pocketbook mirror. My lipstick was still on straight. I sat back while the driver went in and came back, saying that Mr. Andrews would be out shortly. We waited for a good half hour before Mr. Andrews finally appeared. He was draped over someone who appeared to be dragging him out to the car. The person opened the door, and Mr. Andrews fell into the backseat beside me. Someone said, "Have a nice trip," and we were off. Mr. Andrews seemed to be out cold.

I was stunned and disappointed. My sexy, sensitive hero was slumped beside me, reeking of alcohol. We were very late by then, but we still made the plane. In those days the airlines waited for celebrities. Someone helped Mr. Andrews to board, and by the time we landed in Utah, he was sober enough to acknowledge my presence.

In those days Moab, Utah, was a desert town of just a few buildings. We were housed in a half-dozen motels spread out for about a half-mile. Our living conditions bordered on primitive compared to today's standards. There was no air-conditioning, but we did have screen doors, so we kept ours open most of the time, hoping for a breeze. We ate breakfasts and dinners in a large building filled only with long tables, benches, and cooking equipment. Our second day there, we started shooting. The working days were very hard. To get to our location, we drove in rugged vehicles to a mountainous area where the temperature was 120 in the shade. We were given salt tablets, and there never seemed to be quite enough water. Despite the discomfort, the actual work went well.

Back at my motel after a long, hot day of shooting, I had eaten and showered and was getting ready to settle in and study my script when there was a knock at my screen door. My idol Dana was standing there—or should I say, leaning there—asking if I had anything to drink. I said that I was sorry, but I didn't.

"Will you come with me and help me find a drink?" he asked. There were no bars open in the town. I was afraid he might hurt himself out there alone, so of course I went. He threw his arm across my shoulders and I pretty much supported him as we stumbled from door to door, asking crew members if they had anything to drink. I'm sure some of them thought I was as drunk as he was. We were quite a couple. It appeared that no one but me was willing to be an enabler and that there would be no more drinks for Dana that evening. We stumbled back to my room, where he collapsed onto my bed.

Then an amazing thing happened. He began to recite the most beautiful poetry—biblical poetry, long Shakespearean soliloquies. For at least two hours, I was spellbound. Finally he had recited himself sober enough to get himself back to his room.

When I saw him on the set the next morning, he obviously had no recollection of the night before. He was very professional on the set, always on time, but extremely hung over. He needed to be fed by the oxygen tank brought in every morning by the prop man. After the oxygen fix, he was suddenly transformed into the terrific actor he really was. Occasionally at night he'd drop into my room quite smashed, wanting nothing more than an audience to listen to his beautiful recital. I was very touched, and slowly he began to know me as a friend. None of this was the relationship I had fantasized, but in a way it was better. When Dana finally got sober, he remained that way for the rest of his long, productive life. He became the president of the Screen Actors Guild and spent many years promoting the National Council on Alcoholism.

After weeks of filming, I returned to Los Angeles. The Army-McCarthy hearings were just finishing up. Leonard told me that my name had not been mentioned but that two other girls whom David had dated in the East had been. I watched reruns of the hearings and tried to catch up with all the news. I still knew little of the truth of the situation and wanted to know more.

David had been inducted into the army while I was gone and reported to Augusta, Georgia, for basic training. I had heard that the army was being as hard on David as it could possibly be. Not surprising—the press was watching him very carefully. There were so many reporters flying down there to observe and sneak photos of David's basic training and anything else they could.

After basic training, David was being shipped to Alaska. He begged me to come see him in Augusta before they shipped him out. I decided to chance it. My mother came with me. I wore a dark wig, cotton in my nostrils to widen them (which somehow transformed my face) and a kerchief on my head. There were several members of the press on board our plane; I recognized a few of them. I felt if we were found out, then what the hell, there was nothing wrong in being a loyal friend. I honestly didn't care if the studio heads were upset, *#^& them! When we landed in Georgia, Mother and I checked into a motel close to the base that David had suggested. After dark, David pulled up in the alley at the rear of our motel. I got in wearing my kerchief; we drove around for a while, then parked and talked.

I tried to get David to open up about his involvement with Cohn and the McCarthy committee. He was very emotional when I broached the subject. As soon as he'd start to talk, he'd shut down. It seemed very painful for him to face whatever was going on, and I didn't push it. I'd never seen him like that. I chose to believe that he was feeling remorse and anger at his own stupidity for having been caught up in something he didn't really understand. Mother and I flew home undiscovered. I think my mother enjoyed the drama of it all.

The studio was happy to have me back in L.A. in time for the second Miss Universe Contest. During the first Miss Universe Contest, I was named the "Spirit of Miss Universe." Romanticized pictures of me appeared on the posters all over the world. I traveled to promote the contest, as far as Mexico City, where I crowned Miss Mexico. I also went to Long Beach, California, to crown the very first Miss Universe: beautiful Armi Kuusela from Finland.

Now, a year later, I was to be one of the judges and again would be in Long Beach for several days. Susie Kirkpatrick (one of my favorite hairstylists, mother of many kids, and a very sweet lady) came with me to keep me company and have a mini-vacation. After checking in to the hotel, we spent a few quiet hours on the beach in the early afternoon. Late that afternoon we went back to the hotel and leisurely got ready for the big night. Susie called and asked if she could help with my hair. I almost always did it myself for real life. Being on the road so much, I had to be good with it. But it was a treat having her with me, and she came down and gave me a hand.

We were driven to the Civic Auditorium and greeted at the main entrance. Susie was taken to a seat in the audience and I was applauded as I went down the aisle. That was nice. I was seated with the other judges in a closed-off area on the side, down near the orchestra pit. It was lovely not to have any responsibilities during the pageant. Last time I'd had to make a speech and worry about getting the bobby pin on the winner just right, so that the crown would stay on. Once I was seated, introduced, and took my bow I wouldn't have to pretend to be a movie star. All I'd have to do was sit. There were about ten of us seated in three rows in the judges' section. I was on the aisle in the front row. Bob Palmer, who was also a judge, was seated right behind me. He was one of the heads of casting at Universal. I'd known him since I'd done my first audition for Universal when I was seventeen.

Most of the audience was in their seats and it was time to start when Earl Wilson, the famous columnist from New York, suddenly came running down the aisle. Earl was also a judge but was running late, literally. He jumped into his seat behind me and shouted to our group, "Did you hear? Leonard Goldstein just dropped dead!"

I thought I heard the words, but I pushed them aside and sent them out into space somewhere. A moment later I let them echo through my ears again . . . but I still wasn't sure I had heard them. I turned around to look at the source and saw Bob looking at me helplessly, his face telling me it was so. Almost everyone had known about Leonard's death that afternoon and had kept it from me because they wanted me to get through the pageant. At the worst possible moment, the secret they had been protecting me from all day had suddenly exploded in front of me. I turned back in my seat. All the insides had left my body and my heart had taken over, throbbing hard. The house lights were still on, and spotlights were on us. I was, in effect, on stage. My mind raced on without me. *Can I run up the aisle? Maybe I can climb the stairs to the stage and get out through the wings? . . . I can't. I can't even stand . . . my body has been extinguished. Don't move; no one will see you. Leonard, stay with me.*

I sat there immobilized, very still in the spotlight, not daring to break the fourth wall. Hours went by as the pageant dragged on. I didn't see it or hear it. I was with Leonard. I knew it had ended when I felt people's arms around me, and I burst open.

I have no recollection of where I spent the night or the next few days. I have only one clear memory. While riding down in the elevator at the hotel with my sister and brother-in-law, who'd come to my rescue, a smiling gentleman stared at me and actually said, "You look like you just lost your best friend." In a fog, I thought, *How curious that he knew Leonard was my best friend, and how insensitive for him to speak of my loss.*

Leonard had had a massive cerebral hemorrhage outside Darryl Zanuck's office while talking on the phone to publicist Frank McFadden. He died immediately. Leonard would have called it "a classy way to die."

Many people, including the Mexican president's young son Miguelito Alemán, came up from Mexico to attend the funeral. Miguelito's embrace comforted me. When the service was over, I went up to see Leonard, who was in an open coffin. I looked carefully at this complex man with the friendly gruff face who had loved me. I laid a rose in the coffin as gently as I could and then tried to take his hand. I was shocked by its cold hardness. I had only experienced fresh death in Korea, and I was not prepared for this. I knew now that he was really gone.

Leonard's spirit was very strong to me in the days and weeks that followed. When I slept, I had a classic recurrent dream that when I put the rose in the coffin, Leonard grabbed my hand and tried to pull me in with him. I could not walk into my bedroom until the portrait of him on my dressing table was moved to another room. His presence was so powerful and threatening. It had been just a few months since he had proposed. I felt unspeakable guilt that I had turned him down. He had taken it hard. Was I partly responsible for his body's attack on itself?

The first death one experiences of someone very close, someone who's a genuine part of your daily life, is perhaps the hardest. Leonard's love was as close to unconditional love as I'd ever had. I learned during this time that there is nothing useful one can say to someone who is deeply grieving. Better not to try. A physical touch is the best.

I sobbed through much of my life for almost a year. I worked, but if anyone said anything to me about Leonard, I would become undone.

One day I was sitting outside in the backyard, my mother having insisted I get some fresh air. As I sat there, a beautiful bluebird flew around me for a while and then dropped an exquisite feather onto my lap. It seemed so deliberate that I looked up. I saw the bird hover over me for a moment and then fly away. I felt Leonard's presence so strongly in that moment. I chose to take it as a sign that he still loved me and that he forgave me for all my imagined sins. I knew that the possibility that rough and powerful Leonard would be reincarnated as a little bluebird was sublimely ridiculous. But if it could be true, I hoped he was having a good time flying about and seeing the beauties of the earth, the things he'd taken little time for while he was here.

David was sympathetic about Leonard. He was writing to me regularly from Augusta, and then from Alaska, where the army had shipped him. But after a while he grew impatient because I rarely wrote back. When I did, much of it was about my sorrow and about missing Leonard. David was convinced that getting married to him and giving up work would make me feel better. That didn't make any sense. I needed to work.

The studio had a script that had originally been bought for Betty Hutton years before and they wanted me to do it. The film was *Ain't Misbehavin'*. The lead female role should have been played by a thirty-year-old with plenty of confidence and life experience. She was a tough and vivacious chorus girl, far from my own personality. Casting me was one of the rare brave things the studio ever did, though it wasn't really sensible or thought out. But I wanted to be challenged and to work hard. The problem was—the script called for me to laugh. It said in the script, "She laughs." I couldn't do it. I could still only shake up and down. I wanted to be able to laugh out loud, make mirthful sounds. There must be a way to learn.

If anyone could help me, it was my acting teacher, Betomi. I hadn't seen Betomi in more than four years by then, and it was difficult to face her. I was sure she couldn't be happy with the work I'd been doing. But we had a history of trust, and I hoped she'd open her arms to me. I drove to the sprawling ranch house in the Valley where she and her family lived. We were straightforward with each other.

I told her, "I have to be able to laugh out loud." It was hard talking to her about such a superficial thing. It felt almost sacrilegious to talk in terms of actor's "result." But I went ahead, and she met me with an answer without blinking an eye.

"We will do an exercise, a breathing exercise first. A large intake of air, and as if you are doing a vocal exercise, start up very high and say 'ha!' about five or six times, each time on a lower and lower note. Use your diaphragm each time to get a good strong 'ha!' Then we do the same thing again, starting at the bottom note. 'Ha-ha-ha-ha-ha-ha' all the way up to the top. Now do the whole trip together. Down and then up. Down and up. Remember to use your diaphragm! Now do it faster and faster, and now you are laughing!" And I was! I was laughing out loud! It was a little weird-sounding at first, but it was outside-of-my-body laughing. I was doing it! The sillier it sounded to me, the more the laugh became genuine. "Ha-ha-ha-Ha-Ha-Ha-HA-HA!"

I had to concentrate and work at it at first. But over the months, it became second nature to me, and finally it was completely mine. My ability to express my joy out loud became one of the higher pleasures of my life, a greater release than crying. Betomi had never failed me.

Rory Calhoun was cast opposite me in the film. We had done *Dawn at Socorro* together the year before. I'd also be working with Reginald Gardiner, one of the great sophisticated comic actors of all time. But the biggest news was that I would sing and dance five numbers myself. A choreographer was hired and I buried myself in daily rehearsals weeks before we were to shoot, dancing and singing all day. It was good medicine. They were all original songs except for the title song, "Ain't Misbehavin'," which Universal had owned for years. There were songs by Paul Francis Webster, Sammy Fain, Charles Henderson, and Sonny Burke. One song was written by my singing coach, Johnnie Scott, with Sammy Cahn. I pushed myself and worked hard to do the singing myself. I was determined. There was no way they would double me this time.

I continued to grow stronger with my dancing and heard through the grapevine that the fellow who gave us massages at the studio gym said I was in the best shape of all the females on the lot. Maybe it was all the laughing I was doing. But my feet were not laughing. They were not dancers' feet that had toughened with years of use. I remembered seeing the great ballerina Dame Margot Fonteyn walk into the commissary one day in moderately high-heeled sandals. She had walked right by my table, and I glanced down and saw her "weapons." They were not pretty, but they sure accomplished miracles.

The skin on my feet, however, was very thin. During rehearsals they became covered with blisters that popped and turned into open bloody sores. I covered them with the dancer's first aid, chunks of Chapstick topped with Band-Aids. During actual shooting my feet became so swollen that I had to use three sets of shoes in different sizes. Sometimes I would go to my dressing room between takes and cry from the pain. Mamie Van Doren, the perennial attention grabber who was behind me in the chorus line, was up to her usual tricks. I could have strangled her a couple of times when we had to reshoot because of her ill-timed desire to display herself. It took me a while to figure out the truth of the "technical problem" behind me. The crew, however, was having a good time. *But for heaven's sake, why now, Mamie, when my feet are bloody?* And all the while the director, Eddie Buzzell, kept shouting, "Smile, Piper, smile!" No matter how I tried, I could not smile on cue, though I was developing a hell of a laugh. When shooting was finally over, I was black, blue, sore, and wonderfully tired—but proud that I had stuck it out.

I heard there was a sneak preview of the film happening in Santa Barbara. We actors were forbidden to attend sneak previews and I, the "good girl," had never gone to one. This time, though, the rules weren't going to stop me. I had become a master of disguise by then and I transformed myself for the trip to Santa Barbara. As I'd discovered when I went to Augusta, cotton in the nostrils was a simple but really effective tool. After that a wig, a kerchief, some old clothes, and I was ready to go. My father agreed to drive me.

We drove up the coast to Santa Barbara and got to the theater early, before the studio executives arrived. After buying our tickets, we went straight to the dimly lit balcony, waited awhile, and finally the movie started. My heart was pounding so hard. I was about to show my dad where all his hard-earned money had gone. I was going to really surprise him with my singing and dancing. I knew most of my dialogue was stupid and unbelievable, but I had done the best I could and hoped nobody would notice the dialogue.

About ten minutes into the movie, my character made her entrance and had some witty banter with Jack Carson and Rory Calhoun. As I spoke my first witticism, there came a loud groan from the man sitting on the other side of my father.

"Oh my God, I can't believe how awful this girl is!" Five more minutes into the film, the woman with him said, "Oh dear, where do they find these people? She is *so bad*."

They continued being quite vocal. "This is a waste of time. I have an exam tomorrow, let's go."

"No, I don't want to miss the other film."

More scenes went by, and more groans. "She is . . . really . . . terrible!" I was beyond embarrassed. I was praying they would leave, but they stuck it out to the end. I dropped my head when the lights went on. Of all the horrible reviews I had gotten up to that point, none had stung so deeply as this because my father was a witness and somehow also a victim of their abuse. He was helpless to defend me. *Where are you, Harry Truman?*

When the movie was over, we waited as long as we could and then escaped to our car. My father said not one word to me during the two-hour drive home. My mind flashed back to the night we'd sat in his car and he'd told me to give up my dreams because I had little chance to succeed. This night I felt very fragile and small.

I saw the movie again recently. I marveled to see myself moving as well as I did, and I admired myself for being brave. I get credit for chutzpah and hard work. My voice sounded okay, too. Thank you, Johnnie Scott.

Once the intense work of the movie was over and I had time to think, the reality of Leonard's death loomed over me once again. I missed him so very much and couldn't fill the immense hole he had left. Meanwhile David Schine was still pressuring me to marry him. He called almost every day. "Come up here. It's beautiful in Alaska. We'll get married up here. I'll get us a place to live, arrange for a rabbi, and take care of everything," he kept reassuring me. "I'll take out the license, and all you have to do is get your blood test down there and bring the paperwork."

I began to think that maybe this was what Leonard really wanted for me. After all, it was Leonard who had picked David. Maybe marrying David would be the best thing for me. In a moment of weakness and loneliness, I told him, "All right, I'll come. Soon. Just a little while longer."

David found a little house for us near the base. He sent me many long, romantic, and loving letters. He had unusual gold wedding bands made—gold nugget, wide, roughly hammered, and beautiful—and he sent me mine. For the ceremony I found a lovely crème-colored Don Loper suit made of silk and a matching hat of very fine linen with a wide brim, trimmed with two exquisite pale-yellow silk flowers. I made an appointment for a blood test. We kept our plans secret from everyone but our families. I asked my grandmother to come with me to Alaska to be a witness and to represent the family at my wedding.

While I focused on my wedding plans, the studio told me I was to do a television show in New York in a few weeks. In the past they had forbidden me to do any television. I wasn't concerned about it because I knew I wouldn't be there. I'd be a married lady in Alaska and wouldn't be available.

David's family came to town from New York, and it was agreed that our families would meet at our house for dinner. David's father, Myer Schine, arrived for dinner accompanied by one of David's sisters and her doctor husband. David's mother, Hildegarde, of whom I was very fond, had stayed behind in New York. Mr. Schine looked particularly dour that evening. It seemed that was the way he always looked, and I supposed he was stuck with it. I felt the Schines had approved of me long ago. They had also driven by our house at least once that I knew of because I had been with them when they'd done it, but this was the first time they had been inside.

My mother was proud of her modest home and would normally make a feast of at least ten or twelve courses and several desserts for people she wanted to please or impress. But for the Schines, it was to be only six courses. Was it possible she was demonstrating her disapproval in some way? It surprised me. I thought this would be my mother's dream come true. Edna, who was going to help serve, arrived late, which was also highly unusual. She was behind schedule with everything, including a couple of dishes she was going to make herself. Nothing went well that night. In retrospect, it was a little like the hilarious dinner scene in *Alice Adams* with the brilliant Hattie McDaniel, but it was not funny living through it. My mother and Edna were so tense, I thought they'd explode.

Finally, with my family leading the way, it became clear that neither family wanted an elopement. They wanted a proper wedding ceremony when David returned from Alaska. Someone said, "How would it look? People would think you *had* to get married."

Then someone else said, "Just wait, and there will be a beautiful wedding." I was in no rush. I thought everyone made great sense.

David called while we were still eating, and I took the call in my bedroom. I told him how our parents were feeling and said that I agreed with them. We should wait and have a proper wedding.

David was calm but adamant. "We ought to stick to our plan and marry in Alaska." He talked about how wonderful it would be and told me I shouldn't feel frightened. I was frankly surprised and admired him for being willing to go against his parents. It gave me some real confidence in him.

So I said, "Yes. Yes, I'll come, don't worry."

I hung up and returned to the table and told everyone that I had spoken to David and that he and I were going ahead with our plans after all. Everyone took a deep breath and then proceeded to talk about the folly of our ways all over again.

"It would be so much nicer to wait. You could have a beautiful wedding and a beautiful home."

And then my mother said, "Just think, Grandma wouldn't have to make that long trip." They had me. Once again I was completely convinced not to go.

After the Schines left, I dragged the phone and its long extension cord from the den, across the hall, and into the far side of my bedroom and closed the door. I called David and told him I had changed my mind again. Why he didn't say "To hell with you" at this point, I'll never know. But he was angry, and we agreed to speak again the next day. Later that night I received the gift of an epiphany.

WAIT—wait a minute. What is this? It doesn't matter where or when you do it. Something's wrong! Why do you just go along, swaying in the breeze about something so important?? Obviously you don't know your own mind. WHAT THE HELL IS GOING ON HERE?! You're twenty-three years old. Grow up, Rosetta!! Get out of the house! TIME TO LEAVE!

In the morning I called David. I told him I wasn't going to marry him. I felt strong and clear-headed; I knew he couldn't dissuade me. He was very angry and asked me to send back his letters, which I did immediately. He said he would get his ring from me when he returned from Alaska in six months.

The truth was, the relationship with David had never felt right. I had been acting out some kind of scenario written by others again. David had fulfilled all of the superficial requirements for a husband, but I felt a darkness around him. He had never really opened himself up to me about McCarthy and Roy Cohn, and I couldn't understand or accept that. I was just going on instinct at the moment.

This was not the guy for me.

8.

Burning the Contract

I had allowed myself to be crippled. I didn't even know how to write a check. I didn't know how to get my clothes cleaned. I'd never kept a budget. I'd never waited tables or been kicked around and forced to take care of myself on the street. I'd never had to talk myself out of a jam. I'd never, ever stayed completely alone through the night. My emotional scars and education had been strictly internal ones and had not much use in this tough and complex world.

I spoke to my father confidentially and told him that I was planning to move out. I had come to him a few months earlier, when my mother had been on the warpath day and night. I told him that if he wanted to leave, even for a short time, he had my blessing. I could hold the fort alone. He had thanked me for understanding but ultimately chose to stay. Now I wanted to leave, and he gave me his blessing.

I went apartment hunting and got lucky. I found a place on Landale Street in a residential neighborhood five minutes from Universal. Everyone else handled my money, and I didn't know how to make a deposit on the apartment, so I borrowed some from my friend and chaperone, Gail, and her husband, Fritz Baumgarten.

Now that I wasn't marrying David, I had to go through with the NBC television show in New York. My elopement to Alaska would have made that impossible. I planned to tell my mother about moving out as soon as I returned. My dad agreed that it would be better to wait on telling her until I was absolutely physically ready to go. We didn't want to endure the weeks of haranguing and verbal abuse that would surely follow. We were also afraid my mother might become dangerous to herself or to us.

Mother seemed relieved that I wasn't going to marry David. I think she was in a celebratory mood. So now my parents decided they would go to New York, too. They would follow me a week later and see some relatives while I worked on the show. The studio reserved a large two-bedroom suite for us at the Sherry-Netherland.

I flew to New York and started rehearsals for *Broadway*, a play originally done in 1926, to be broadcast as the first of a new series for NBC called *The Best of Broadway*. Universal got a handsome sum of money for loaning me to NBC. The cast was exceptional: Joseph Cotten, Keenan Wynn, Gene Nelson, Akim Tamiroff, and myself. The director was Franklin Schaffner, who intimidated me enormously. He was so different from most of the directors at Universal. He was elegant and educated and seemed to know what he was doing. He would go on to do the original *Planet of the Apes* and win an Oscar for *Patton*. The show would be done from beginning to end without stopping, almost like a live show. It would be prerecorded, act by act, so that we didn't feel the terror of live television.

My part was an extension of what I had been doing at Universal all along: a cute, dumb girl who does a little musical number with Gene Nelson. Rehearsals were intense. I worked on my dance number with Gene, who also choreographed. He was delightful, so sunny and cheerful and motivating when it came to the dancing. We had met a few years before at an industry luncheon, and I remembered being blinded for a moment when he smiled at me. We had to do a hat-and-cane trick during the dance that I was determined to master. If I could master it, I knew it would look really fine. I finally got it! What pleasure I got out of that silly accomplishment.

Gene Nelson and I spent a lot of time together during those few rehearsal weeks. We ate in the little deli down the street at tiny tables that were squeezed together so that we were touching the legs of strangers. This was a first for me, being in New York and not eating in fancy restaurants. I couldn't stop giggling at the intimacy of the whole thing. The people that were so close to us as we ate seemed to be pretending we weren't there. The whole thing was hilarious to me.

We had so much fun. I hadn't felt this light in a long time, and of course, we became lovers. Even after my parents arrived, though their bedroom was separated from mine by only the living room in the suite, I had decided no more pretense. If they came into the bedroom while we were making love, I would just deal with it.

They never did come in, and Gene always left before morning.

When I returned to L.A. from New York, I asked my sister to come to the house and be there when I told Mother about my plans to leave home. I thought some support would help keep my mother from exploding in a destructive way. My mother had such firm beliefs that a girl who was unmarried must remain living at home. And for the last fourteen years, from the time my parents had brought us home from the sanitarium, she had dedicated herself to my career. I knew that if she were out of the picture, my picture, she would feel useless and irrelevant. Not a good thing for this lady who must have been riddled with guilt for having sent her children away. I was only partially aware of her side of things at the time. I only knew that I needed to be on my own and that just the sound of her once-beautiful voice had become hateful to me.

We arranged a time that was good for all of us. My dad and sister promised to help keep my mother calm and lend verbal support for my leaving. We all huddled in the tiny den. Mother knew I had something to say to the entire family. She sat on one couch with my dad. Sherrye sat opposite them on the other couch with her husband. I took a chair near the door. Smart.

I began and made a little speech about inner growth and my lack of maturity and worldly savvy. I allowed for several pauses in order for anyone to speak up and support what I was saying. Not a peep out of anyone. I continued and got to the part where I said, "I'm going to be moving out."

Up to this point my mother had been ashen in color and sitting absolutely still. She looked out of place, like a stranger in the house.

My sister sat silently weeping, as if she were watching a sad movie, but gave not one word of support. I continued on, and everyone remained as they were: my mother an alabaster statue; my sister "weeping buckets of tears"; not one word of support from anyone, including my father.

Where was everybody? They were supposed to say something! They were supposed to help steady my mother! It seemed clear I was on my own. All right, might as well start now. I told my parents that it would take me a few days to pack my things and move to my new place, and I hoped it would be all right to sleep at home for a few nights longer.

Since no one as yet had uttered a word, I started to get up to go to my room. Finally the silence was broken, and Mother said quite calmly, "You'll leave this house over my dead body."

It was scary to hear, but there were no histrionics, and I was grateful for that. The threat was a horrible one, but I had heard it before. I felt these were empty words spoken because she knew she had lost.

Her sadness must have been immense, but at the time I didn't dare let my guard down. I continued packing, and everyone let me be alone to do it. My sister and her husband went home to Long Beach, and my dad went to work the next day. I heard very little from Mother during those few days. Soft crying in the other rooms, but that was about all. As I write this, I feel so deeply sorry for my mother's sadness, which I understand much more now. I wish I could have comforted her somehow. But I had to go.

Two days later, when I was all packed and said my goodbye, Mother threw herself down in the hallway in front of the door, so that I had to step over her body in order to leave the house.

It was a beautiful thing, the first night I slept all night with someone. Gene came over the first night I had my bed. He had a golden body, whether he'd been in the sun or not, and beautiful smooth muscles for such an athletic dancer. It has been said that only men are turned on sexually by visual stimuli. Not so. After lovemaking, we realized we had all the privacy in the world and that there was no place he had to be but with me, so he stayed, and we slept all snuggled up and wrapped around each other. When I opened my eyes in the morning, this sunny golden boy was there smiling at me. It was like what a honeymoon should be.

I threw myself into decorating my apartment and loved using my own hands and taste to do it. I bought frilly white organza shades for my bedside lamps and saw Liberace shopping for lampshades, too. I had never cared about the decor in my room at my parents' home. I was not interested and turned all that over to them. But now I was interested in life in general.

Gene kept me dancing in the classes he taught. He also began to teach me archery, and I was not bad. We rode horseback several times a week in the evenings, and I started to learn to jump. And finally Gene bought me my own horse, a gorgeous palomino I named Sunny.

Gene and I had little in common artistically or intellectually. He had little appreciation for my serious approach to work as an actor. Of course, I had little to show for it. I thought his approach to his acting was superficial. But I didn't care. He was a superb dancer and lover, and I was having a wonderful time.

Gene had a birthday coming up and I wanted to surprise him with a party—the first one I'd ever given. I wrote a little six-character play that was a satire of a recent *Climax* television show he had done. I sent copies to all of his close friends and asked them to participate in the surprise party and *act* in the play. No lines to learn, just a reading.

Everyone said yes, including Blake Edwards, and we proceeded to have secret rehearsals at various locations. I had to make excuses to Gene for the times I couldn't be with him, and he began to be suspicious. He had someone follow me and report back to him. Then he confronted me with the information and demanded to know what I was doing and with whom. The scene he made was pretty sad and ugly, and I had to reveal I was planning to surprise him, but I didn't give specifics so there would be some element of surprise left. It was a nice party, but I was troubled by his jealous streak. Even so, we continued on with our athletic endeavors and had some lovely times.

Sometime after I moved into my own place, David Schine called. We spoke briefly about my returning his ring. He said he was coming to Los Angeles and would appreciate it if I'd send the ring to the Ambassador Hotel. I did that immediately.

When David got to town, he called and said he'd received the ring but wanted very much to see me and talk. I had been so confused for so long, and I thought all of that was behind me, that we had broken it off quite cleanly. I said I didn't think there was anything to talk about. I'd returned his letters and the ring. We were finished. He said, "All right, I guess you're right."

But after a day or so, he called me again. He called my parents' home, he called the studio, and he called my apartment repeatedly. I stopped answering the phone—not a difficult thing for me to do. After a week of this, the calls stopped, and I assumed he'd left town.

A few days after the calls finally stopped, I was upstairs in bed with Gene, asleep. It was about two in the morning when I was awakened by sounds downstairs. The window blinds were rattling a little, and it sounded like someone was trying to break in. I guessed immediately what that meant. Gene was now awake and started to get out of bed. I told him to stay put as I threw on my peignoir. I heard heavy footsteps walking into the living room and flew down the stairs, sure that it was David. It was. He reached the bottom step just as I did. I was actually still two steps above him, so we were eye to eye, so to speak.

He demanded, "Who's up there with you?"

"None of your business!"

"I'm going up," he said.

"Oh no, you're not!" I was furious. I grabbed at him as he moved past me, clutching at his jacket and holding on for dear life as he climbed three steps at a time with me still holding on. After a few steps I lost my grip, but I picked myself up and arrived at the bedroom entrance a few seconds after David did.

Poor Gene was sitting naked on the foot of the bed, looking surprised and vulnerable. David stood there with a torn jacket, staring at Gene. I moved into the room, stood next to Gene, and told David to leave.

He began to back away from the naked Gene and asked if I would please come downstairs so he could talk to me for a minute. I was grateful things were not escalating, so we went downstairs.

"How dare you break into my home!" I demanded. I was still angry as hell.

David begged me to meet him the next day. Wanting to be civil, I said I would meet him at the Smoke House, a nearby restaurant. He left by the front door. As I picked up several of David's buttons on my way back up the stairs, my heart was still racing. I went into the bedroom and told Gene I was going to meet David the next day.

The Smoke House is an old restaurant in the Valley, midway between Warner Bros. and Universal, that's always filled with people from the studios. David was waiting for me in the foyer when I arrived. We sat at a table in the middle of the restaurant, near a large potted palm. We were talking calmly and candidly when I noticed that the potted palm was moving strangely. I focused in the dim light and saw a familiar face between two large leaves. It was Gene, who'd come to spy on me. I pretended I hadn't seen him and hoped David hadn't, either. I wasn't up for more drama at the moment.

After David and I talked for a while, he felt satisfied that we had nowhere to go with our relationship. We said a final goodbye and wished each other well. It would be ten years before I'd see him again.

I no longer found Gene's jealous behavior amusing. It made me uncomfortable. I loved being with him and I loved spending time with his little boy, Cris, who was then about eight. He was a great little boy, and I was still able to enjoy rolling and tumbling on the floor with him. I had fun with all of Gene's family, including his mother, who was a perfect and sweet lady who made Swedish pancakes for us. I liked her so much that I went apartment hunting for her in the intense way that I did things that I was determined about and found a good one that I believe she was happy in for a long time. When Gene went away to Europe to make the movie *Oklahoma!* for several months, I was lonely, but I kept busy furnishing my rather underfurnished apartment.

One evening I received a new script from Universal. My last movie had been *Ain't Misbehavin'*, in which I'd been horribly miscast. I was told the reviews were punishing. Many times through the years, my agents and I had tried to change the structure of my contract, giving me some freedom to do other things. But they would not budge. Still, I was ever hopeful.

I read the new script. This one wasn't even a B western. It was a C western. The male star would be Audie Murphy, the most decorated soldier of World War II. He was a genuine hero, had a likable natural presence on the screen, and had become a Universal movie star, playing the lead in many movies. The woman's part was a prop and just barely that, possibly the worst part they had ever handed me.

I suddenly felt so deeply insulted, so unappreciated, so mortally wounded. This time they had gone too far. I calmly got up, walked over to the fireplace, and dropped their script into the flames. With it went a little of the humiliation I had endured in the last five years. Something was coming alive in me. Life seemed very simple at that moment. I picked up the phone and called my agent, Mike Zimring, at home.

I told Mike I would not do the movie. They could suspend me if they liked. They could suspend me forever if they wished. They could sue me. They could imprison me. I would not do this kind of work ever again. Even if it meant never working again.

Mike reminded me that my option had just been picked up, increasing my salary greatly.

"I don't care about that, and I don't care what you have to do. But you *must* break my contract." I told Mike not to call me until I was either free or they were coming to take me to jail.

Abe Lastfogel, the head of the William Morris Agency, called first thing in the morning to make sure I understood what I was doing. He told me that if I would reconsider and stay at Universal, I'd be making as much money weekly as Joan Crawford ever did at MGM. I wasn't the least bit moved. I wanted out. My parents, especially my mother, told me I was throwing my life away, and Gene thought I was being irrational.

A week went by, and the call finally came. Universal was releasing me! I was free! The penalty—I would have to do one movie a year for three years, for the token fee of $25,000 per movie. Sounded wonderful to me. I would have done them for nothing.

It was one thing to finally break free from the studio that had owned me since I was seventeen. It was another thing entirely to put the image Universal had created behind me. There were many months—almost a year—of being turned down for the jobs I wanted. Not one person would hire me for *live* television. It was too risky, they said. I was strictly a B movie actress who lacked depth, who might panic or not be able to learn or remember her lines. The only offers I got were a few movies similar to the ones I was escaping from.

It seemed a reasonable thing to cut back on my expenses, to survive as long as possible until something came along; so I had a strict budget. I bought nothing new and wore my jeans and shirts most of the time. No longer living with my parents and having a housekeeper meant I had to learn to run the washing machine in the back of the building and eliminate cleaning bills.

Fortunately, not having things came back easily to me, and I actually enjoyed it now. The last five years of being a fake movie star had been too rich for my taste. I certainly wasn't starving, but life now was simpler, and I never doubted I would find something of value to do. Gene took me out to dinner from time to time after dance classes, but often we'd have frozen dinners and watch TV.

I began to hear things from my agents about a Broadway play that was in the process of auditioning actresses for the lead. It was called *The Lovers*, and the author was Leslie Stevens. It was a heroic, romantic play that had a perfect part for me. I had heard Charlton Heston was considering playing the male lead. I wanted the part, but Abe Lastfogel absolutely forbade me to fly to New York to audition. "You're a movie star. You don't do that."

I went anyway. I prepared a few scenes and was asked to meet at the producer's office first, instead of going straight to the theater. When I arrived, there were a few people in the waiting room. I was told to take a seat. A short while later a man came out of the office, introduced himself as the playwright, and escorted me back into the hallway to talk privately. He whispered in a rather embarrassed way that they would not let me read.

"We can't afford to have a 'Piper Laurie,' and what she stands for, in the play."

I stood there trying to absorb what I had just heard. There was nothing for me to say. I couldn't argue with the truth of it. Feeling humiliated, I flew back to L.A. knowing that somehow I would have to change what "Piper Laurie" stood for. It would be easier to start from scratch than try to erase this negative perception. I wondered if perhaps I should start over, using my real name, Rosetta Jacobs.

Many weeks went by with the continuing frustration of not even getting to meet the directors and producers who were doing quality work. They were very set in their opinion of who I was and my lack of ability. Many of these people had never actually seen me in a movie. Their perceptions came from the enormous publicity buildup I'd been given. As far as they were concerned, I ate flowers, wore brief costumes, and was on the covers of fan magazines. That was that.

Offers of bad scripts continued to come in and I continued to turn them down. I would never do those movies again. The thought crossed my mind occasionally that eventually I might run out of money, but I didn't dwell on it. Someone out there would give me something decent to do. I still believed in myself blindly, in the way young people can.

Finally, one of my agents slipped me a script he had had to steal because the producers didn't think I was right for the part. Like everyone else, they said I was a glamorous bimbo. The girl in this story was a young, perhaps fourteen-year-old hillbilly girl. It was a half-hour gem of a script that would be done on *G.E. Theater*. I wanted so to play in this touching and simple story called "The Road That Led Afar" written by Hagar Wilde and adapted from an original story by Lula Vollmer.

The producers refused to consider me, but I kept pressing my agent to let me at least meet them. They finally agreed to see me. When I arrived for the meeting, instead of the expected dress, high heels, stockings, and little white gloves that one always wore to an interview at that time, I pretended I had just come from riding my horse. I came in wearing no makeup, old jeans, and a messy sweaty shirt, with my long hair all over the place. I apologized for not having had time to go home to change. I talked a lot about the role; I understood this girl, and I was the only one I knew who could play her. No false bravado there; I was convinced of it.

When I got home that day, I heard from my agent that the producers had called and said they were quite mistaken about me and that they wanted me to play the part. I had the part! A real part at last! A new beginning!

I had several weeks to prepare. One of the first things I did was to stop wearing shoes and get used to walking as this girl walked. I'd go to the market barefoot; I drove without shoes, visited my parents without shoes! I read the script over and over. I tried to stay with her mountain speech all day when interacting with people, which was especially hard while I was talking to people I knew. It embarrassed them. I understood this child-woman very well. I didn't have to invent anything to support the emotions. It was all there. I was full. I trusted that the character was there, and that all I had to do was watch and listen.

There were very few lines in this half-hour film. Most of the drama was in between the sparse lines. I could see that it wasn't just a tragedy; it also had very subtle humorous undertones. The fine actor Dan Duryea would play the older man who takes me without warning to live with his motherless children. He stops on the way to have the preacher, played by Edgar Buchanan, marry us. We rehearsed for several days on the set before shooting. I hadn't been this respectful of material I was working on since Betomi's class, and I felt blessed to have the role. This would mean a complete break from my past, enhanced by the absence of the superficiality of makeup and fancy costumes.

When the second assistant director came over to give us our calls for the first day of shooting, there was a crisis for me. He gave me the usual two hours for makeup and hair. I told the director and producer, who were both standing there, that it wasn't necessary because I wasn't going to be wearing makeup and that I had found something to use in my hair to make it look straight and unwashed. It would take only five minutes.

They all insisted that I must wear a little bit of makeup base because I was so fair and it would be impossible to light Dan and me in the same shot because he was considerably darker skinned than me. In my new life there was no place for compromise. I was determined to do things 100 percent my way, no one else's. My sensibilities, my integrity were on the line. It was my reputation and life that I was rebuilding. I insisted. They sent the cameraman over to the set to explain further. When I finally understood and accepted the technical reality, I was brokenhearted. I hid behind a wall on the set and sobbed quietly until some of the anger and disappointment were out of my system and reminded myself I still had this beautiful role. It was the last compromise I would make for years.

I overslept the first day of shooting, out of anxiety—a pattern that would continue for a long time. The producers' calls finally awakened me, and I rushed to the location, which was just minutes away. The makeup took about five minutes, and I'd already made my hair stringy. I threw on the torn and faded cotton dress that looked like it belonged to my character's mother and stepped into the studio car without shoes. I was driven to the back lot, where they were to shoot a long scene with me on the front porch, thinking the thoughts my already-recorded interior monologue (voiceover) was saying. The director and crew had been waiting for me for about five minutes, and I despised being late. I tried to stay focused and mentally ready to take my place on the porch as soon as I got out of the car. No wasted energy on apologies.

As I stepped out of the car, I spied my old friend Ronnie Reagan standing there in a gray business suit with his mouth dropped open slightly, staring at me! I knew that Ronald Reagan was now the official spokesperson for General Electric. What I didn't realize was that he did a short introduction every week in the first scene that led into the actual drama. The last time I had seen Ronnie was five years before, when I was eighteen and wearing the studio-supplied purple strapless dress. We had had our long walk and said goodbye at the hotel in Chicago. I felt I had lived five lifetimes since then. He looked bewildered at the sight of me, now looking about fourteen—shocked, actually. He couldn't seem to get his words together in a clear sentence. I thought for a moment he didn't recognize or remember me, but I knew that couldn't be, so when he finally took my hand I told him it was good to see him and went to my spot on the porch. From that moment I was totally involved in the work and didn't notice when he left.

The shoot went well. The director, Herschel Daugherty, and I worked well together. I heard they were very happy with the footage, but it would be months before it would be ready for broadcast. I was impatient. I wanted people to see it and perhaps think differently of me. Perhaps someone would even let me do a *live* television show. That was where all the exciting things were happening, with new actors, writers, and directors, some of whom would go on to have fifty-year careers. But I was still being turned down because I was Piper Laurie.

I held on to hope, and finally I got my miracle. A script for the very successful *Robert Montgomery Presents*, an hour-long *live television* drama broadcast from New York, was sent to my agent. I read it immediately and found it was a good story. It was called "Quality Town." My part would be substantial and highly dramatic, a challenging one like nothing I'd worked on since acting class. I couldn't believe it. Had someone gone crazy and decided to trust me? I was shaking with excitement and disbelief when I called to tell my agent, "Yes, yes, by all means, yes! How did this happen?"

He didn't know, so he suggested I just accept with thanks, which I did. Millions of people would see this show. I thought this might be the perfect opportunity to change my name and start using Rosetta Jacobs professionally, but the producers said, "Absolutely not! If she insists, then we have no choice but to use someone else with a name. Piper Laurie it will have to be. Take it or leave it." So of course, I took it. I would just have to be very good, good enough to change what "Piper Laurie" stood for.

I would be in New York for several weeks rehearsing before we did the live show. I didn't want to spend a fortune at a fancy hotel, so I called a woman who had briefly been my chaperone in Chicago years before. I knew she lived in Greenwich Village with her sister and she had mentioned that she had an extra room. She was very gracious and said I was welcome. I flew to New York, moved in, and for three weeks became a New York actress. It was all so unbelievable—what I'd been hoping for since I was seventeen!

I'd been too excited and busy until then to realize the terror of the situation, but once I settled into my room in New York, it all caught up to me. *LIVE TELEVISION! OH MY GOD! What have I gotten myself into? This is more terror than a thousand opening nights in the theater. I'd have only one chance to get it right. No chance to improve or fix anything.* In those days almost everyone who had a TV set in America would be watching! There were a few days before the rehearsals would start, and I was at my wit's end. In a panic I called Gene, who said he would fly to New York and stay with me in my little room for a few days and try to keep me calm. There was not much space, but I was glad he was there. Bodies can be a potent source of comfort.

When it was time to go to my first rehearsal at Central Plaza, I took a cab downtown. I thought I was on time, but everyone else had already arrived, including Lee Bowman, who would play my father. I was introduced to the director, Jim Yarbrough, and then to the cast. The actor who would be playing the role of my boyfriend in the show was looking at me from across the table with a silly grin on his face. I did a double take. It was Bob Richards! I was stunned. I had been out of touch for years with my acting class friend, who had directed me in the Tennessee Williams one-act play and come with me to my audition at Universal. I had no idea Bob had moved to New York and was working as an actor. And now there he was! Bob was the person who had told his friend the director that Piper Laurie was talented, that he knew my work and knew I could play this very demanding part. How my old friend had changed my life, more than he ever understood! Bob was a deeply feeling intellectual who hated revealing anything that might be interpreted as sentimental. He brushed off my expressions of gratitude, that day and in the years after.

The rehearsals for the live television broadcast were very much like rehearsing a play. I felt comfortable working at a slower pace than I had in the movies, being able to develop and explore scenes. During the dress rehearsals I had a tendency to play quite fully, especially the emotional scenes. My friend Bob whispered a suggestion that I hold back a little bit if I could, until "air." Otherwise I would be exhausted and have nothing left. I tried, but I had never learned to do that; it was all or nothing.

There was only one thing that I was not allowed to rehearse. In the climactic scene my character, who has been brought home from boarding school, rebels against her father. She unleashes her ferocious anger in a long scene that ends with her climbing up on a table, taking down an extremely large portrait of her mother, and throwing it across the room. The prop budget was small and they had only one painting. Therefore I could only actually throw it one time—when we were on the air. I wasn't concerned; I was physically strong.

I was told I looked okay on camera without any makeup and needn't bother using it, just a little powder. That was good; I was free to focus on the performance. My costume changes, which required perfect timing, still worried me. I rehearsed them over and over.

As the days passed, though, my fear of the actual performance continued to build. We all went to lunch together every day, and I marveled at everyone's composure facing, what was to me, death in a few days. I asked each member of the cast individually, "How many live shows have you done?"

Some would answer, "Oh, two or three," and others would say "Five." I'd watch them carefully to see if the battle scars were showing, for signs that they were telling the truth and had actually survived. I wondered what their secret was. When I wasn't acting, I had trouble catching my breath, my heart was racing so. I didn't know how I'd be able to cover it when we actually went on air. It felt like cold knives were going through me all the time. I remember wishing I'd get run over by a car, or that something would happen to save me from having to go through with this thing that was worse than any death. But as rehearsals continued, I was still alive, and I knew I had to face it.

Like a sentence of death, the night of the performance finally arrived. It was five minutes to nine, time for the countdown to "*AIR*" on the loudspeaker. Perhaps later it would be surpassed in degrees of tension and excitement by the first space launches taking off for the moon, but not by much. Four . . . three . . . two . . . one . . . *DEATH!*

I suddenly felt very calm, and all the work I had done fell into place. I was emotionally full when I needed to be. The costume changes were a little frantic, but the show went well until the last scene. There were three cameras on the floor being directed from the booth. When I actually threw the portrait for the first time, it was heavier than I had expected. It hit the camera that was shooting me! The camera shook as if there were an earthquake, and it gave the scene a very special effect.

At last the show was over, and I was still very much alive! Robert Montgomery himself rushed over to me, shook his finger, and said I'd have to pay for the camera I broke. I was in such a vulnerable state that for a moment I took him seriously and quickly figured that my salary wouldn't even come close to covering the cost. It wasn't broken, of course, and he was kidding. My friend Bob told me I had done well, and we all went out for something to eat.

The next day I went to meet my agents in the New York office of William Morris. I had never been up there before; there had never been a reason to. Their hands had been tied until now. While I was going up in the elevator a man introduced himself to me and said he was Marty Jurrow, the head of the New York office. He told me he had just come from having lunch with Joe Mankiewicz, the legendary Hollywood figure who had received numerous Academy Awards for writing, directing, and producing (*All About Eve, A Letter to Three Wives*, etc.). He was among the most honored and creative people making films.

When Marty and I got off the elevator, he continued, "The first thing Joe Mankiewicz said as we sat down to eat was, 'I saw the most marvelous performance last night on television, a young girl on *Robert Montgomery Presents*. She was sensational, some of the best work I've ever seen on television. Who was it, do you know?' And I said, 'She's our client! That's Piper Laurie!' "

As he told the story, my knees began to buckle, and I felt a sob beginning to escape. I didn't want to make a scene, but I was overwhelmed with disbelief and hope. "I don't believe you," I said.

He took my arm, pulled me into his office, and said, "I'll get him on the phone." He dialed quickly and said, "I have Piper Laurie in my office. She doesn't believe me. Tell her what you said at lunch."

Marty sat me in his office chair and handed me the phone. I said, "Hello." Mankiewicz pretty much repeated what Marty had said, and I mumbled, "Thank you so much."

I hung up the phone and let go with tears of gratitude. I never cried in public, but I didn't care now. These were tears of celebration. Someone who was respected by the entire creative world had just said he thought I was something.

Something very unusual was happening. Soon after I got back to Los Angeles, I received an offer to do another live show. It was an hour-long version of F. Scott Fitzgerald's "Winter Dreams." Ralph Nelson would direct it, and Anthony Perkins would play the young man. We would do it in the brand-new CBS studios in Los Angeles, next door to the famous original farmer's market. At first I questioned my incredible good fortune, but then I just opened my arms to it. I worked hard, as I always had, but this time with joy.

Tony Perkins was charming and highly enthusiastic about just about everything. He was scheduled to make his first movie, *Fear Strikes Out*, right after we finished our show. I had never worked with such a high-strung actor before. He would peel his cuticles till they bled before going into a scene. He was very dedicated to being good and didn't waste his time showing off.

Joe Mankiewicz's words had given me such a boost of confidence that the live aspect of the show seemed slightly less dangerous this time. It was the first time I'd had the opportunity to play someone *genuinely* glamorous. My character was a real person, not someone contrived. Once again, because of the type of camera used then for live broadcast, it was not necessary for me to wear makeup and I did my hair myself. I thought a lot of energy was put into the costume changes and not enough into the performance. But then, what did I know?

I was told the reviews were good. I didn't read them; I had stopped reading my reviews years before to protect myself. The reviewers thought the show was entertaining, but they didn't think it reflected the real Fitzgerald. Fair enough. They liked what Tony and I had done, though. I was even praised for letting my freckles show! After a childhood of wishing they would go away and five years of the studio covering them heavily, I really didn't care anymore.

Then another amazing thing happened. *The Road That Led Afar*, the half-hour filmed show I had done for General Electric, had been completed. I was told that the executives loved it so much, they had decided to run the show without a commercial break because they didn't want to "break the spell" of the beautiful performances. A commercial-free broadcast was unheard of in those days and is very rare now.

I was sent to New York by GE to publicize the broadcast, to do interviews and attend screenings. GE's spokesperson, Ronald Reagan, "interviewed" me at length for the radio. But peculiarly, instead of me meeting with Ronnie, Ronnie's recorded questions came to me on a big vinyl disk. I recorded my answers separately. He would speak his question, followed by a little pause, then speak his response to my answer, which he couldn't possibly have known. Obviously, someone thought they knew what I was going to say. Craziness!! My rhythms and tone and the substance of what I said were completely different from his, but they stuck the parts together anyway. My communication with the great communicator couldn't have sounded stranger. Perhaps Ronnie was embarrassed to sit face to face with me. No need. I had processed all that long ago. It was more likely that his early handlers were making those kinds of decisions for him.

For the first time, on the GE publicity trip to New York for the show, I didn't feel mortified watching myself on the screen. The cast of characters in my professional life seemed to have changed as dramatically as the characters I was playing. It seemed to me that even the level of intelligence of the reporters and the types of questions they asked me were totally different. It appeared they were either unaware of or had forgotten my past work. It was as if I were born anew. It seemed so strange; I was the same "bimbo" with the same handicaps as a few months before. The only thing that had changed was the material I had been given and the opportunity to be seen doing it. That "opportunity" is what thousands of actors hope for every day.

I received my first Emmy nomination as Best Actress for *The Road That Led Afar*, but I had trouble owning the pleasure. I still didn't trust it completely. Herschel Daugherty won the Emmy as Best Director.

Back in Los Angeles, Gene Nelson and I continued riding our horses, dancing, and having pleasant dinners at home with friends. One night John Frankenheimer joined us for dinner with his wife, Carolyn. John was a new director just out from New York who had been working in live TV. John and Gene seemed a bit competitive that evening. They quarreled about how a certain dance number should have been shot. Gene had just started to direct and wasn't going to let someone he considered an upstart from New York, whom he'd never heard of, tell him how things should be done.

A few weeks later I was at the CBS studios visiting Millie Gussie, who was now working in television. Millie told me I should come observe John Frankenheimer in action. She said he was phenomenal. The two of us sneaked very quietly into the booth where John was rehearsing a live drama to be broadcast later that evening. John's direction was an incredible display of an artist's intelligence, combined with the speed and power of a tornado. Watching him was like seeing a thunder and lightning storm conducted by a musician. It was brilliant the way he barked out seemingly infinite sensitive directions to the camera crew on the floor, moving them around with such fluidity. I had never seen anything like it. I left quietly, without saying a word, and then I began to breathe again.

Not long afterward I heard about a house that was available for lease in Rustic Canyon, an old and historic part of Santa Monica Canyon. The house was only $250 monthly. I could manage that. It was a Spanish house with a circular driveway in the middle of two acres of an experimental eucalyptus grove. There were at least fifteen different varieties of eucalyptus trees that had been there for decades. I could remove the French doors on two sides of the living room and feel as though I were in a giant tree house. The ocean was visible in the distance. After living in my little apartment in the Valley, I yearned to see the water. I told the owner I would take it. My landlords, who lived in the guesthouse, seemed to like me. At their suggestion, they put a panic button in my bedroom that rang in their little house. I never had to use it, but it was nice to know it was there. From my immense new living room, I could look out over the tops of the trees beyond to the mountains and to the ocean on the left. I was so happy, I never wanted to go anywhere.

Two years earlier I had risked everything, leaving my film career and my family to go out on my own. The gamble had paid off beyond my wildest dreams.

9.

A Difficult Actress

I continued being extremely selective about my work, turning down most things and working only a very few times during the year. I made good money when I did work, but I still had to watch expenses. I loved having breathing time between projects; to live in the real world, to be a person. I would have nothing but my childhood and my last job to inform my work if I didn't. The time I spent at Universal had been unnatural and useless. It did give me a "name," a value that I unfortunately had to fight to live down. But it was a value; I couldn't deny it. In the next few years I overdid living life a bit—a common fault among young actors. The emotional challenges in life will come anyway.

About six months after I spoke with Joe Mankiewicz on the phone in New York, he came to Los Angeles. Robby Lantz, Mankiewicz's partner in his production company at the time and later a powerful and respected agent, arranged for us to meet at the Beverly Wilshire Hotel and go to dinner. I was excited and apprehensive as I approached the door of the suite. Just as I got there, the door opened and I saw Don Murray and Hope Lange saying goodbye and leaving. That relieved my anxiety a bit; it took the onus off meeting someone I didn't know in a hotel room and made it seem more like a place of business. I managed to hide my nerves fairly well and to get through the introductions just fine. Shortly afterward we went to Chasen's for dinner.

I sat between Robby and Joe in a big booth. I immediately felt comfortable with Joe. He did have that gift, and it elicited superior performances from actors. I ordered Harvey's Bristol Cream sherry before dinner, served in an elegant little glass as I'd done many times since turning twenty-one. The name rolled comfortably off my tongue. I sensed that Joe and Robby seemed amused by my old-fashioned choice, but I felt very sophisticated and powerful ordering it at the time.

While we ate, Joe talked about our mutual work without the least bit of condescension. I liked him very much. He encouraged me to come live in New York where I could work in the theater. After we had been there for a while, he asked if I might be free to drive him to the airport after dinner. Something about the request didn't feel quite right. Surely he could get a driver. It seemed inappropriate for him to ask me. The stories I'd heard about Joe's womanizing ran through my head. My friend Bob, who never approved of any of my choices in lovers, had even told me that if I were going to have an affair with someone, it should be with an artist and intellectual like Mankiewicz. As much as I admired Joe's work, an affair was not a possibility I entertained. So I told Joe I had a previous engagement and couldn't drive him. Before I left them at the restaurant, Joe again warmly encouraged me to come live and work in New York.

A few months after my dinner with Joe, my agents said I'd been asked to come to New York to audition for a wonderful new play, to be directed by Joe Anthony. Best of all, I had been recommended by Joe Mankiewicz, who had told them I would be terrific in the part.

There was one long scene the producers suggested I do for my audition. Back then I was using a slow process to develop the characters I got to play. The memorization of the words came later, during rehearsals after blocking, quite naturally, almost as an afterthought. When all of these things came together and I was off the script, I was free to enter another world. My method of working changed over the years, but at the time that was my process.

There wasn't enough time to do that work or even memorize the long speeches, so I worked as well and honestly as I could in a never-never land; holding the script, reading, and trying to act. It was supposed to be a reading, after all. Many actors can do this very well, and through the years classes have been created to develop just that skill. Unfortunately, it is well known and mostly ignored, that a good auditioner is often a poor performer. For now I would do the best I could. I asked my dear friend Bob Richards to work with me and sometimes while I was working with Bob, the scene came to life. Perhaps if I were lucky, I hoped, inspiration would strike. But I really knew better. Inspiration only comes on the foundation of solid work.

I flew to New York, and because there wasn't time to find an apartment to borrow, I splurged because I could afford it at the moment. I took a room at the first hotel I thought of, the Sherry Netherland, one of the fancier and most expensive hotels in the city. That mindset was left over from my studio days. Perhaps that environment would give me confidence. The weather was cold, and since furs were quite acceptable at that time, I wore my full-length Aleutian blue mink and took a cab to the theater.

When I got to the theater, I deposited my coat somewhere and came out from the wings holding the script, shaking, and so pumped up that I overacted and lost my place several times. I knew it was bad. I asked for permission to start over, and someone out there in the darkness said, in a perfect and neutral tone of voice, "Of course."

I started over, but it was even worse. I seemed to have lost my ability to concentrate or focus or even simply read. Someone said, "Miss Laurie, would you like to come back some other time? Perhaps tomorrow."

Oh God—the condescending tone. I nodded and slunk into the wings, into the street, and into a cab, feeling at the moment very much like a Hollywood amateur. My agent called the hotel later in the day and said they were looking forward to seeing me at the theater the next morning at ten-thirty. I knew they were giving me special treatment; seldom is one given another chance. I knew this was most likely because of who had recommended me.

Having hardly slept, I went back to the theater the next morning. I was once again filled with enormous anxiety that I couldn't seem to cover this time, wanting so to be good and worthy of the recommendation by Mankiewicz. I started the reading again, but this time, if possible, I was even worse—over the top and completely empty. I was using the facility I'd learned as a child actor to cover the fact that there was nothing inside and that I didn't know what the hell I was doing! If you're skillful, you can fool a lot of people with that kind of performance, but it never allows for originality, nuances, or genuine spontaneity. I don't recall if I even finished the scene, I was so upset with myself. I remember throwing my pages to the floor in despair and running down the steps into the house, up the center aisle, out into the street, and trying to hail a cab.

My agent came running after me into the middle of the street, telling me to calm down, that it wasn't that bad, and urging me to please take my coat, which he'd picked up. "It's cold," he said. I grabbed the coat, jumped into a cab, and went back to my fancy hotel room.

Still wearing my high heels, I proceeded to crush and stomp on my full-length Aleutian blue mink, a symbol of a part of me that I despised. I then called the Mankiewicz office, breaking down, sobbing on the telephone. Robby, Joe's partner, got on the phone with Joe. I sobbed, "I'm sorry . . . I'm so . . . sorry—"

I think it was Joe who managed to interrupt me. "What happened?"

I was sobbing so hard I could hardly get the words out. "I was awful, I was terrible."

Joe said, "Where are you? I'll be right there!" In a fury I continued attacking my fur coat, kicking it, sobbing, and throwing things around the room. I wanted to destroy something in me, the inauthentic part of me.

Suddenly Joe Mankiewicz was at the door. I was truly hysterical by then, a state I don't think I'd ever allowed myself to be in before. It was all coming out. I was crying out the pain of not living up to my own expectations as well as his. "I was so superficial! It wasn't even bad *dreadful!* It was so *mediocre!!!*" Sobbing and moving about the room with anger and self-hate, I was out of control, and Joe did the only thing he could think to do.

He took hold of me and began to ravish me; that's the only thing to call it, taking off my clothes and reaching me in as primitive a way as one can imagine. A part of me knew he was taking advantage of the situation, but it was a distraction to say the very least, a really wonderful one that I found myself enjoying thoroughly.

Afterward I was spent, and so was he. And surprised. I could never have anticipated that this would happen. He held me for a very long time, and I noticed he smelled of Sen-Sen. Some time later we ordered something to eat from room service. I realized I hadn't eaten in days! I'd been so fixated on this reading I'd forgotten everything else.

After dinner, I looked over and there sat Joe Mankiewicz in his white shirt; he was leaning back from the room-service table in a small armchair, one leg crossed over the other, holding his pipe, asking me about my life, and telling me how a career can never really fulfill a woman. He said love and family were more important to a woman. It was a theme I suspect he had told many women before me. I heard it again later on when I saw his movie *The Barefoot Contessa*. But at the moment, I was sublimely happy. Only he could have made me feel—though the reading had been a disaster—that life was okay.

Kissing me goodbye, Joe asked me to please not go home to L.A. right away. "Please stay awhile longer," he urged me. I promised to stay one more day, and he came back the next day. We had a rather beautiful afternoon, no tears, filled only with love, laughter, and good conversation.

I spent the next week absorbing what had happened and writing passionate, grateful letters to Joe—telling him how much our being together had meant to me. But a little voice told me not to send them. They were not very good letters; they would have only burdened him, so I tore them up.

For many years, even after Joe Mankiewicz passed away, whenever I would see Robby Lantz, he would always ask, "Whatever happened between you and Joe?" It always surprised me that he didn't know. Or perhaps, always the gentleman, he did.

I read lots of scripts but didn't want to do any of them. I was clear-cut in my decisions. I was learning to trust my judgment. It was easy for me to simply hold out until the good material arrived. I just pinched my pennies and didn't buy things. If I had had children and a family to support, it would have been much more difficult, if not impossible. But I had only myself to worry about.

My patience paid off when the young and brilliant Sidney Lumet asked me to be in two live television shows, to be done almost back to back. Sidney had yet to make his first motion picture at the time. I had never met Sidney but had heard about his theater and television work. I don't know how or why I was picked to be in these shows, but I was thrilled. I was going to be working on intelligently written material that had the potential to surprise and enlighten the audience.

I'd be staying in New York for quite a while, and I needed to find a sublet with two bedrooms. I would need an assistant in New York, with the demanding roles and long rehearsal hours. There was simply no time to do everything for myself. I hired Edna's young niece Rose as my assistant. We called it "secretary" in those days. Rose had gone to college in Texas, where she had family, and now was out to see the world. Rose said she'd be happy to come with me. I found a place on West 55th Street, at the corner of Sixth Avenue.

The day before we were to leave, Rose decided she couldn't go. She missed her boyfriend in Texas. I suspect she'd actually lost courage because of all the unknowns for a young black southern woman in New York. So Edna stepped forward to uphold her family's honor, though she'd never set foot on an airplane before. She'd always said, "If I ever have to fly, it will be with one foot on the ground."

So Edna came with me, but on takeoff she locked herself in the lavatory and refused to come out. The stewardess kept pounding on the door. Knowing Edna, she was probably praying. She came out after we'd been in the air for about fifteen minutes, convinced, I suppose, that we'd stay up there awhile longer. She stayed in her seat with her eyes closed the rest of the way. I didn't disturb her.

Edna took good care of me. She was not intimidated by the city and found everything she needed. She quickly found where to shop and cooked healthy meals for me. Sometimes in the evenings, after a long rehearsal, I'd sit at her feet, and she'd massage my neck and shoulders as we watched TV. I felt very loved. I never, ever thought about the time in my childhood when that was not so. I was getting more than my share now.

The first show we were doing for *Studio One* was called *The Deaf Heart*, a beautiful, original hour-long play written by Mayo Simon. The broadcast was to be done live. The story was about a girl-woman who is the main caregiver in a family of nonhearing people. When she finds there is no longer any hope for her brother to hear, she gives up her own hearing, in effect, to be together with her family in their world. The story was constructed as a mystery about a psychosomatic illness, working backward, trying to find out why the girl had totally lost her hearing. I had to discover how to play her many moments of self-isolation, when people are talking around her, in a way that wouldn't tip off the ending, since physiologically she really can hear.

My dear friend Bob suggested I read Conrad Aiken's short story "Silent Snow, Secret Snow" as preparation. The story is about a young boy who more and more inhabits a dream world filled with snow, which he prefers to his own life. It's a psychological tale of escape from reality and incipient madness. When I understood where this boy went to escape, it helped me to find an active place for my character's mind to go in the seemingly passive moments of her deafness. The moments of self-isolation in my own childhood, though somewhat different, also helped me relate to the character.

The cast was superb, including the great Vivian Nathan, whom Lee Strasberg once called our best American actress; and the equally great Ruth White, who was in the original New York production of Beckett's *Happy Days* at the Cherry Lane Theater (a performance I had the good fortune to see). Richard Shepard played my brother. The now-iconic William Shatner, looking handsome and slightly adolescent (though he was really in his twenties) was one of the doctors giving me tests; and the brilliant Tony-winning actor Fritz Weaver, with the rich voice, was the head psychiatrist.

Real life always seemed more important than anything to Sidney.

When Fritz Weaver's wife, who was expecting their first child, went into labor on one of our precious rehearsal days, Sidney Lumet didn't think twice about it.

He said, "Take the day off." Fritz was ecstatically happy when he returned two days later as a papa!

I was surprised at the many breaks Sidney gave us to relieve tension during rehearsals. We'd work very intensely and emotionally for a half hour and then take out ten minutes to play and have a good laugh. Then back to work. The final "air" show was exciting. I felt we were all really good. I didn't read the reviews. I didn't dare, but I heard they were very good.

Without taking a breath, we started rehearsing the next show, again with Sidney directing. This time I would be playing three different characters. What a challenge! The show was called *The Changing Ways of Love*, with three love scenes from different plays and periods. The first was from *Awake and Sing!* by Clifford Odets. For that one I'd be playing opposite Jason Robards, Jr.

Like most really great actors, Jason was beautiful to work with. Relaxed, he really listened, played with me, always surprising me a little bit, and was spontaneous without violating the text. Our scene was quite emotionally charged and ended with a passionate kiss.

The moment the kiss ended, I would rush to a spot shielded by a backdrop a few feet away where I would silently change my clothes, put on a short glamorous wig, lipstick, and powder, then check myself in the little six-inch mirror taped to a stud and calmly walk out into a scene with a young and sexy Rip Torn, who was playing with me in a scene from Fitzgerald's "Winter Dreams." When that scene was over, I had about a minute and a half for the next change. Quietly, off came the dress, wig, and lipstick; a redo of my long hair with a couple of pins; on with a suit and hat; and then Richard York would pick me up to carry me over the threshold into a scene about a newly married couple in *Three Empty Rooms* by Reginald Rose! It was exhilarating to say the least!

The choreography of the quick changes was very important, rehearsed over and over. Nothing could be haphazard or out of sequence.

It must be the right earring first, so that a hidden helper could be fastening the left side of the dress, etc. Not one second or movement was wasted. The most difficult part of the changes was to fuse the physical choreography with an internal mental and emotional thread to sustain the character, to invent ways to integrate each offstage movement with the material so I could be in an emotional place to continue on.

When we were finally on the air and *Awake and Sing!* came to its passionate ending (the shot was just on our two heads), and I was tapped on my knee by an off-camera person. That meant it was safe to move and immediately change for the next scene. There was not a second to lose. But in the actual live performance I was overwhelmed with affection (and I don't know what else) for my fellow actor, Jason. When I was tapped on the knee and I pulled away, an impulse overcame me and instead of rushing off, I came back and gave Jason another kiss! I even managed to do the quick change in time. Years later Jason reminded me that that had happened. He said he'd never forgotten.

I was working on such stimulating projects by then, one right after the other. My agent said he wanted to introduce me to Maurice Evans, the British Shakespearean actor of wildly differing reputations. He'd become a U.S. citizen in 1941 and had done more Shakespeare in this country than anyone else, some admired, some not. My agent and I took a cab to Greenwich Village, where Evans lived in a converted firehouse with high ceilings, extraordinarily shaped rooms, and large comfortable furniture. It was very beautiful.

Evans was charming and asked me if I'd ever done Shakespeare.

I said no. He asked if I had ever seen *Twelfth Night* and I said, "I'm afraid I haven't." I was embarrassed.

He said, "How about coming into the library and reading a little bit from the book?"

I was so stunned at the notion of reading Shakespeare cold, without any preparation. It seemed preposterous, but for some reason I heard myself say, "All right." Sometimes my anxiety was eased when I was bold. I found my greatest strength and power when things were tough.

I felt giggly inside as Maurice sat down next to me on the couch, opened an enormous book, and pointed to a spot. "We'll start here," he said.

This is ridiculous. . . . Here goes.

I read out loud in a very undramatic way, trying to speak clearly, enjoying the poetry as I came to it. After a few minutes, we stopped. Maurice looked pleased; he said I had done very well for someone who had never done Shakespeare before.

He told me that he was producing *Twelfth Night* for Hallmark, to be done live, and that he would like me to play Viola. Beautiful Rosemary Harris would play Olivia, he would play Malvolio, and the rest of the cast would be star-studded with great comedians. The usual director for the Hallmark shows was George Schaefer, who was an excellent director. In this case, though, Schaefer was going on vacation and would be replaced by someone who, it seemed, was under the producer's thumb. The producer being Maurice Evans.

Bob Richards came to New York to help me prepare for the role. Edna insisted he take her room while she used the large living room sofa. She was always up at the crack of dawn and said she preferred having the freedom of the living room and kitchen. Bob and I worked every day, just reading aloud at first, getting used to the language. Then he had me analyze the play and what my character wanted in every scene. We broke down each of the speeches, making sure I understood every word that came out of Viola's mouth and the speeches of others as well. There would be no faking anything. The language was a difficult puzzle at first, but as I understood more and more, the speeches took on a real life for me. I found it a thrilling game.

The rehearsals were tremendous fun. They were just a half a block away from me, at City Center. Rosemary Harris was delightful to play with. She had recently come from England, where she'd just worked opposite Sir Laurence Olivier. I remember a couple of times, she and I walked to Central Park on our lunch break. One time I had brought an apple and cheese from home and she thought it so clever of me to chill my apple in the snow. When she said she wasn't sure she understood one of her lines, I was so excited to have a possible explanation. It was

In a Detroit photo booth with my parents and sister, Sherrye. I'm in the bottom right corner, about four years old.

At Reslocks, expecting my parents on my eighth birthday

Sherrye and me entertaining at a bond rally during World War II

I'm on the left, age nineteen, at one of my first Hollywood galas with Ann Sheridan, Leonard Goldstein, and Clark Gable

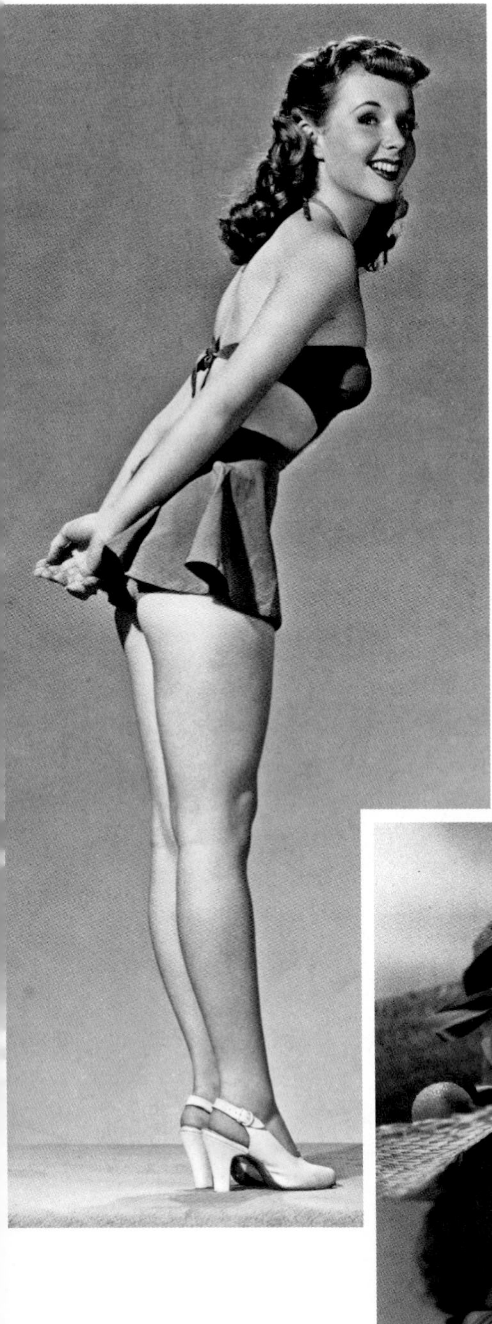

My first cheesecake pinup, 1949, age seventeen. The photographer made funny faces to get me to smile.

A Universal glamour photo, age eighteen

ABOVE: Ronald Reagan taking me to my first premiere, 1950
ABOVE RIGHT: With Tony Curtis on tour in 1950, appalled by the day's schedule

RIGHT: Celebrating my eighteenth birthday with Rock Hudson (above right) and Tony Curtis (below right) in the Universal commissary

BELOW: On a fake date with John Barrymore Jr., Debbie Reynolds, Roddy McDowall, Polly Bergen, and Jerome Courtland, 1951

Performing in Korea for the troops during the holidays, 1951 BELOW:
With G. David Schine on our first date at the Cocoanut Grove, 1952

Looking terrifed, before the ice was broken between us, with Tyrone Power in *Mississippi Gambler*, 1953

BELOW: At a costume ball with Rock Hudson, 1952. You can't see it in this photo, but I am holding a live baby pig on my lap, which I took to the ball.

As Princess Khairuzan in *The Golden Blade*, 1953

BELOW: The chorus line in *Ain't Misbehavin'*, my last movie before I broke my contract with Universal, 1955; (left to right) Lisa Gaye, me, Dannie Crane, Mamie Van Doren.

My lifetime friend Bob Richards

My great love John Frankenheimer, 1960s

An early-morning picture of my husband, Joe Morgenstern, early 1960s

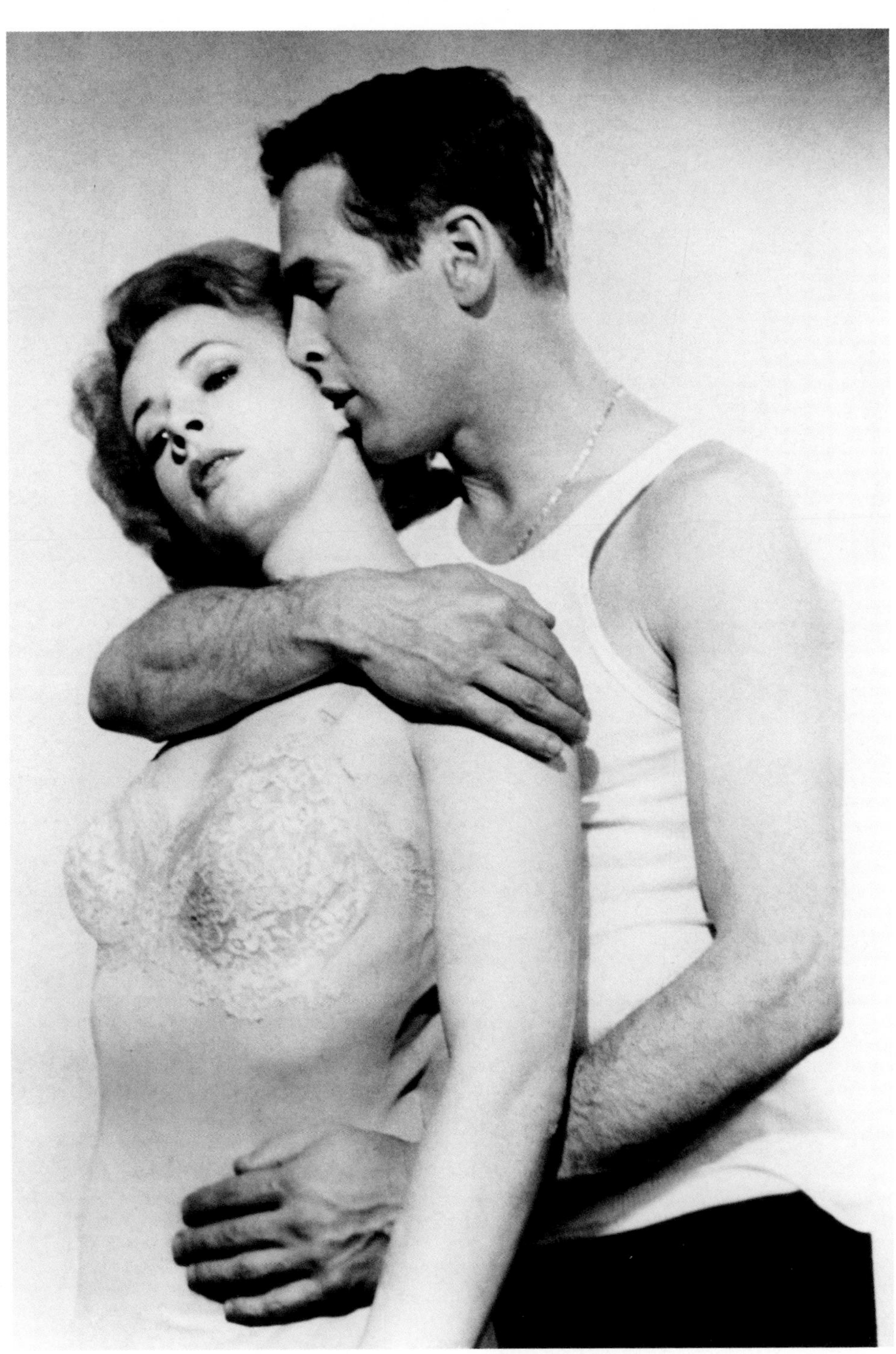

With Paul Newman in *The Hustler*, 1961

With Robert Rossen and George C. Scott in Washington, D.C., at a special screening of *The Hustler*

As Laura in *The Glass Menagerie* on Broadway, 1965

With Mel Gibson, as lovers in *Tim*, 1979

As Margaret White in *Carrie*

With Anna and Joe in Woodstock, 1971

With Anna, who visited the *Carrie* set the day we wrapped, 1976

During a moment of clarity in Paris, shortly before I separated from Joe, 1979

Anna assisting me with repolishing the Tennessee pink marble sculpture, 1982

Lane Slate, the great romance of my later years, holding his Emmy Award for writing *Tail Gunner Joe*, 1977

As Tojamura in *Twin Peaks*, with Derick Shimatsu, who played my assistant and was my assistant

As Dolly in *The Grass Harp*, 1995

With Jim Brochu at *Zero Hour* opening-night party at Sardi's, 2010

With Anna and my grandson

At a charity auction in 2007

one I had discussed at length with Bob, who was a scholar. The line was, " 'Tis not that time of moon with me to make one with so skipping a dialogue." I believed it meant she had little patience because she was having her period. Rosemary seemed shocked and delighted with the possible explanation.

Rehearsals went well until we were given cuts in the play. My part was left intact, and so was Malvolio's (Maurice's). We had timed the play and, even though it was still in rough form, it easily fit into the time allotted, so there was no justification for the cuts. It appeared Evans was behind the changes, which minimized the other comic parts and weighted the play toward Malvolio. I was indignant, outraged as only a passionate greenhorn can be. I felt this was an opportunity to bring a coherent and entertaining Shakespearean play to the mass American audience.

I had finally shed my life as a harem cutie and didn't think twice when I expressed my outrage for the love of art. I stood in front of the entire cast, most especially the director and the producer-star Evans, and told them: "The cuts are coming close to ruining the play. If you make any more at all, I'm leaving!"

When we returned from lunch the next day, we were all summoned to the table at the front of the room and told there were new pages with more cuts. Without a word, for I'd said my piece the day before, I picked up my big black bag, walked out the door, and walked down the street to my apartment.

The next three days were a test of my fortitude and belief in myself and in the artistic life I wanted to have. My tiny apartment was packed with lawyers from the network, from Hallmark, and from my agents—all telling me what trouble I was in. I sat curled up in a chair in the corner, very calm within myself, while they talked. There weren't enough chairs, so some people stood. Bob wanted to stay out of it and hid in the bedroom. Edna tried to keep up with the making of coffee and served homemade cookies to people. You would have thought we were having a party except for the worried looks on the faces around me.

In the middle of all this, on the third day, Rosemary Harris came over and with great passion pleaded with me to come back to work.

She told me how wonderful I was in the play, that it would be a pity for everyone to miss seeing me as Viola, and that I had a responsibility to my fellow actors to continue on.

But I said, as I said to all of them, "No, I don't want to be a part of the tragedy of what's being done to the play. If the play were Shakespeare's version and whole, I would come back in an instant."

I felt I could not accept compromise ever again when it came to art and principle. I suppose I was a terror.

My bluff was called. I was hoping they would back down and reinstate some of the material for the other actors and the play, but they didn't. Fortunately, they didn't sue me as threatened. Rosemary Harris played my part of Viola, which she had played before, and Frances Hyland came down from Stratford in Canada, where she had just played Olivia. My recollection is they still had about a week or ten days of rehearsal to go—difficult, but possible.

In the following weeks Maurice Evans blasted me in many interviews in the press, and it was widely covered with big pictures on the front pages of some newspapers. Maurice was very angry at me as "one of these Hollywood-type people who have to have their own way about everything. Spoiled brats! Unprofessional! To have walked out on a show—just like that!"

I refused to speak to the press about it. I was aware that there was something a little ludicrous about *me*, the ex-bimbo, defending Shakespeare's honor. But it was a genuine tragedy to me that I didn't want to talk about, and I didn't want to stoop to name calling as Maurice Evans had done.

When *Twelfth Night* was broadcast, the only positive thing in any of the reviews was "how courageous and intelligent Piper Laurie was . . . to have walked away from this travesty." I was disappointed, however, at not getting to play Viola and deeply sorry to have let the other actors down.

Bob went back to Los Angeles, I think secretly proud of me that I had remained strong. He knew where I had come from.

• • •

I'd been fortunate with work during the two years since I'd left Universal, but I wanted to learn more. I asked my agent to take me to meet the revered Sandy Meisner at the Neighborhood Playhouse. I was as nervous and serious as I had been when I was fifteen and met my teacher Betomi for the first time. Sandy did not show me any charm or warmth at our first meeting; I think he intentionally made it as difficult for me as he could. There was a long waiting list for his class, which would start in about two months, and he wanted to be sure that I would not leave the class prematurely. A few days after our meeting, he told my agent that I was accepted. Edna found relatives in the Bronx to visit and told me she was happy to stay on.

A few weeks later Gail, my friend and chaperone from my days at Universal, called from Los Angeles to ask a favor. She said an old friend and business partner of her husband was in New York and needed a date for a dinner party. Would I be willing to go out with him? Gail knew better than to ask me to go on a blind date. This person must have been very important to her husband for her to ask this of me. She said he was very respectable and that I might have a nice time. Out of my friendship for them, I said I'd do it.

The gentleman picked me up that evening and we went to an elegant apartment on the East Side, where about twenty well-dressed people were having cocktails and chatting. I was comfortable in my dress, a plain black-velvet with a V neckline, long sleeves, and pearls. It had been a long time since I'd been dressed up. There was something festive in the air and I was surrounded by charming men. One in particular was Conrad Hilton, whose son I'd had a date with just a few years before. The son had drunk heavily all evening and was a total jerk. But Daddy Hilton seemed dignified and friendly, as many of the gentlemen were. I had never felt so at ease in a social situation with strangers before. I felt I could do no wrong.

We'd been there about an hour when the hostess said very excitedly that "Aly" would be arriving soon. Someone else repeated it, then another. I could only assume they were talking about Prince Aly Khan, the adventurer and bon vivant who had once been married to Rita Hayworth. He was one of the richest men in the world and possible heir to his father, the "Aga." Only he could have stirred such excitement.

It was disgusting to me. I was so turned off by everyone's sycophantic response because it revealed my own. As an adolescent I had read all the movie magazines with my teenage girlfriends, and we had seen all those pictures of Princess Rita marrying Prince Aly. She was our idol and he was the man who had captured her. We had crushes on them and loved both of them in all their glamour.

Now I was thunderstruck by the idea that he would be at the party. I simply could not deal with the adolescent feelings that had surfaced so suddenly; so I chose, like an adolescent, to attempt to ignore his presence when I saw him coming out of the corner of my eye. I barely looked at him when we were introduced and immediately went back to an ongoing conversation with the person sitting next to me. Better that than my chin being glued to my chest. Perhaps.

A short while later about half the party of beautiful people piled into cars and went to El Morocco for dinner and dancing. I'd only seen photos of the place until then. I was seated at a gigantic zebra-striped oval booth, between Jack Warner and some other celebrated person. Aly Khan was seated at the opposite end of the table, a good twelve feet away. He was clearly staring at me whenever I looked up. I tried not to let my eyes rest on him, but he continued staring. I ordered my dinner as everyone did and had a conversation with Jack Warner. How about that!

Suddenly Aly Khan was at my left shoulder, asking me to dance. I was too stunned to say no and got up and walked ahead of him, as I was taught to do, till we reached the dance floor. I turned, and we were warm body to body in the impersonal way our generation was accustomed to. He stunned me further by not flirting with me in what I expected would be a cliché way. He seemed a little reserved and quite nice. He was an excellent dancer, a good height for me, and I did love to dance. We exchanged only a few words but danced for a very long time. Many people left the party and went home. We kept on dancing. It was not particularly romantic, just dancing. That's not true; it was quite romantic, as hard as I had tried not to feel that way. When the band took a break we went back to the table and found almost everyone gone, including my escort, who hadn't spoken one word to me since arriving at the party. Jack Warner was still there. He said my escort had been called away and asked if Prince Aly would see me home. Of course.

The cab dropped us off at the wrong place, so we walked the rest of the way, getting to know each other a little bit. When we passed City Center, he saw that there was a ballet company playing and said his mother had been a ballet dancer. Moments later he leaped up to touch the edge of the building's canopy as we passed. It was such a playful, lighthearted gesture, as if to celebrate his mother. When we got to my building, I told him I couldn't invite him up because I didn't live alone; we would wake Edna. He asked if we could meet for lunch the next day and go shopping at FAO Schwarz to pick out toys for his nieces and nephews. I said I would love to.

We met the next day and for many days and evenings after. It was glamorous and romantic, and I was having a wonderful time being with this handsome, intelligent, and very nice man. Not once did I think of Rita Hayworth, and I supposed he didn't, either. I met his son Karim, who was still in school at Harvard. A polite and shy young man, he later became the Aga Khan.

We often went to the theater. We saw *My Fair Lady*, which had just opened, though we got there late and had to sit in the back. Sometimes we had dinner with friends. One memorable night we had dinner with Danny Kaye and his wife, Sylvia Fine. The last time I'd seen Danny Kaye was when I was eighteen and about to go to Korea. I don't think he remembered that, but they had seen me in one of the live TV shows I'd done, and Sylvia Kaye was particularly complimentary. Aly seemed delighted that the Kayes considered me a good actress. He had never seen my work.

One evening we were sitting in a cab in the middle of a traffic jam on Central Park South when we both spotted Victor Mature, and another man I did not recognize, coming out of an office building on the other side of the street. I hadn't seen Victor in years, and I said, "Oh, there's Victor Mature!"

Aly said, "Yes. I like him. He's a good fellow, and he's with one of the most boring men in the world, Prince Rainier." (This was before Rainier's marriage to Grace Kelly.)

It was getting close to the time Aly would have to leave to do his princely duties around the world, visiting all the Muslim countries. He asked me to come travel with him. The first stop would be somewhere in Africa, on a photographic safari. We would stay in a beautiful pink palace, where he said his friends would love me. I wanted so to do it. But I had a commitment to start my classes with Sandy Meisner in a few days. I couldn't break my word.

Before leaving, Aly gave me some earrings shaped like flowers. They had petals of deep purple amethyst and a diamond in the center, and he said they suited me. It was a difficult goodbye, and we agreed to meet soon again. He was a very tender and romantic man and would call me from shipboard after he left. That was a thrill—speaking to someone in the middle of the ocean who told me he missed me. I received many affectionate letters over the next months. After a while I stopped answering them. Answering felt like a commitment of a sort, and the idea still frightened me.

A few days after Aly left, I started the classes with Sandy Meisner. He was a powerful and intelligent teacher and had not yet become ill, so while I was there, he had his full natural voice to use. Many of the people in class had worked with him before and understood his shorthand and vocabulary. It wasn't until long after I left the class that I fully understood some of the exercises, though I always found him inspiring. But I was running out of money and had to leave my classes and go to work. When I met Sandy again two years later, I was surprised to find he never blamed me for making that choice. He was warm and sympathetic.

I had been offered an A movie to be directed by Robert Wise at MGM. It was *Until They Sail,* a story from James Michener's *Tales from the South Pacific* about a family living in New Zealand during World War II. I would be playing the sister of Jean Simmons, Joan Fontaine, and Sandra Dee. It was Sandra Dee's first movie. I had an excellent part, that of the bad sister. Paul Newman was the leading man. I had no scenes with Paul, except for one in which I just sat six feet away and listened as he spoke to other people. I watched from a distance as he and Jean Simmons sat at a private table in the MGM commissary and had conversations about the work.

We had real rehearsals before the shooting began, with just people I had scenes with, at the Wises' home at the beach. That was a first for me on a movie. What they often call "rehearsals" end up being wardrobe fittings and possibly one read-through if you're lucky. Robert Wise was a sensitive and thoughtful man.

I visited the MGM makeup department, where my hair was dyed a very dark brown, almost black, and my brows to match. It was interesting how it helped me to get in touch with the part, more so than a wig. The famous Sydney Guileroff, who created all the MGM hairstyles, did my hair on most days and told me my hair should always be parted on the right. And I have done so since that day.

I tried to learn to ride a bike, a necessary element for the story. It was a missing part of my childhood education, and it was difficult now in my twenties to trust that I could balance on the flimsy thing. Some things simply need to be learned when one is very young. I practiced all day long around the MGM streets, sometimes riding way out onto the back lot and crashing to the ground frequently. People constantly stopped to ask, "Are you okay?" I rode every day, and by the time we started shooting, I was doing pretty well for a novice.

Shooting went smoothly. I loved acting with Jean Simmons, who was not only a fine actress but also the most beautiful of all. We had a scene in which she, my older sister, unexpectedly visits me, the promiscuous one, in my hotel room. The bathroom on the set was never seen in the movie, so I took advantage of its isolation from the crew to hang a douche bag behind the door. Though no one ever saw it, my knowing that concrete evidence of an active sexual life was just two feet away was a potent source of guilt and tension for my character and me. Sexuality was still quite hidden at that time. When the scene was over, I told Jean what I had done, and I think she was a little shocked and perhaps disapproving.

While we were shooting the film, a man approached me on the set with a handwritten scrap of paper with a message from Elvis Presley, who was shooting *Jailhouse Rock* on the stage next door. Elvis said he wanted to meet me and asked if I would please come next door and visit.

I told the message bearer, "Sorry, I can't break away." I could hear my mother's voice: *If he wants to meet you, he should come over to* your *soundstage*. Very old-fashioned etiquette. Sadly, we never met. (Many years later, long after I had become a real fan, and well after he died, I was tickled when I heard that a man who bought an Elvis address book at auction claimed in a television interview that it had my phone number in it.)

I had never been allowed to see rushes at Universal, but Robert Wise didn't follow that practice, so I went to see one of my most important scenes. Surprise—I didn't think my work was very good.

I approached Wise, expecting to be turned down, but I asked anyway: "Is there any way we can do it over?"

I must have been passionate in my request because he didn't turn me down right away and said he'd look into it. The following week he told me he had arranged to have a simple set put up, and the scene with my telephone call to my sister could be redone. I was stunned and overjoyed. Never before had anyone done that for me on a movie, respected me enough to really hear me. Having someone's trust is a gift and a responsibility. Thank goodness everyone agreed the work was better the second time around.

Until They Sail was underappreciated when it was first released; I don't know why. But through the years, because of television viewing, it's finally getting its due.

Shortly after the movie wrapped, I was given a script for *Playhouse 90*. It was the first year of the ninety-minute live drama on TV. The story was called *Mr. and Mrs. McAdams*, later changed to *The Ninth Day*, and written by Dorothy and Howard Baker. It was one of my favorite live shows. The script was beautiful, with lots of humor and humanity.

The cast was filled with incredible people: Mary Astor, James Dunn, Victor Jory, John Kerr, Elizabeth Patterson, and Nehemiah Persoff. John Kerr and I played teenagers growing up on the top of a mountain with a dozen adults, the only survivors from a nuclear holocaust. The teenagers have come of age and are the only potential for continuing the human race.

The show was live and complicated to do. Rehearsals were intense. One day at rehearsal I met some of the cast of the previous week's show, but I was so focused on my own work that I didn't realize till days later that I had met HARPO MARX *sans wig!* It was just as well. I would have embarrassed both of us.

John Frankenheimer was directing. This was the first time John and I had worked together, and we had a fine working relationship. He was the perfect director for me—sensitive, brutally honest, and imaginative. He was only twenty-six or -seven but appeared so sure of himself. He knew what he wanted but was always delighted when the actor found something even better. And just as Sidney Lumet knew when to find moments to release tension, to have a good laugh, so did John. John and Sidney had worked together in New York, with Sidney mentoring John. It was an absolute joy to go to work for them both.

When the rehearsals were almost over and the show was close to being ready, John invited me to have lunch with him and a writer friend at a nearby restaurant. Later he invited me to have dinner with him and his wife, Carolyn, at their house in Brentwood. It was quite a large house, underfurnished, and the three of us sat at a card table set up in the living room. I don't know who cooked the meal, but Carolyn served it on very large dinner plates filled with a lot of peas and very little food. When she asked if I wanted seconds, I said yes, I would, and my plate was brought back with a few more peas. I must have been an unexpected guest, and the food was being stretched. No explanation or apology was offered. It was all very strange.

After dinner we moved to the other side of the large, nearly empty room and had coffee. I was enjoying myself and felt very comfortable and free in the conversation. Just when it became especially interesting, Carolyn suddenly got up and left the room. It was still quite early, barely nine o'clock. Uncharacteristically, I really wanted to continue talking, so I said, "You must forgive me; sometimes I don't know when to leave. Please tell me when it's time."

I expected John to say, "Oh, stay a little while longer." But he didn't.

"I think this is the time," he replied. He seemed a little ill at ease. Something was going on that I hadn't picked up on. I felt somewhat embarrassed and left quickly.

The direct live broadcast to the East went extremely well, including an unbroken, beautifully written scene with John Kerr and me that ran more than twenty minutes. I felt I had really stretched myself and hoped Betomi had been watching. When the show was over, the whole cast and crew were invited to the Frankenheimers' house to watch the rebroadcast to the West Coast. My dad picked me up at CBS and came with me. We watched the show together with dozens of people, sitting on the floor in a large bedroom upstairs. Unlike my last, inexplicable visit, the refreshments were hearty this time. My dad seemed to love the show. He seemed impressed with John, shook his hand, and told him so but as usual said nothing to me.

After the broadcast of *Playhouse 90*, I went back to New York and met with Milton Perlman, who had produced the film version of Gian Carlo Menotti's opera, *The Medium*. Milton had seen most of my live TV shows and liked my work. He was about to produce a movie written by Paddy Chayefsky called *The Goddess*. Milton arranged for me to meet and have lunch with Chayefsky at the old Russian Tea Room. It was an uncomfortable meeting. Paddy had never seen anything I'd done and had great misgivings about me. He was very condescending to me, the "Hollywood starlet," and kept wanting me to prove to him while sitting there that I was a real actress. He was a difficult man.

It was finally decided that both I and the iconic Kim Stanley would make screen tests for the film. I had seen and admired almost everything this most exquisite and great actress had done on stage, and I was thrilled to be considered, even for a moment, in her company. I was also scared by the challenge.

I was twenty-five years old, and I had successfully reinvented myself. I had left my parents' house and a paternalistic studio far behind and created a life on my own terms. Along the way I'd been challenged personally and artistically, and I'd not only survived; in many respects, I'd triumphed. But then life stepped in. My period was late.

10.

The Twenty-fifth Day

I was always careful to use protection, but this time the condom had broken. The possibility that I might be pregnant was terrifying. This was 1957, and a strict, though hypocritical Victorian morality still prevailed. The man was a friend, but he was not someone I could depend on or with whom I could have a sustained relationship. No one that I knew personally had ever had a child out of wedlock.

I was in desperate need of solace and advice, but there was no one I could talk to. Gail was my only woman friend, and to confide in Gail was out of the question. She would be frightened and disappointed in me. She liked to think of me as an innocent, as everyone did. I certainly couldn't tell my parents or my sister. They would be shocked and judgmental. It is possible that I shortchanged the people close to me, with my low expectations of compassion and sophistication. But those were my genuine feelings, and they were intense. The person I could think to call was the woman who had chaperoned me briefly in Chicago and let me stay at her place in the Village. She seemed worldly and perhaps nonjudgmental. With some difficulty I told her the problem. She made the practical suggestion that I first find out for certain if I really was pregnant.

To do this discreetly was an involved process. I had to take a jar of my urine in a brown paper bag to be tested at a hospital up in the Bronx. I would have to take a cab, so I wore a kerchief on my head and no makeup for fear someone would recognize me. It was a scorching-hot summer day and the cab was an oven, even with the windows open. I worried the heat might affect the urine and spoil the test. When I finally got to the hospital and found the correct department, I gave them my real name, Rosetta Jacobs, and added a "Mrs." It never occurred to me to use a fake name for such an important thing. Why tempt the fates with dishonesty? I might get a fake result. I was told to come back in ten days. "Don't phone," they told me. I should come in person.

I returned home and spent the following days hibernating in the bedroom in my apartment. Edna was there, but she had no idea of what was going on. Ten days later, when I returned to the hospital, they handed me an envelope. I didn't open it until I was safely back in the cab. *Perhaps my life could start again.* But when I opened the envelope, the word on the paper was "POSITIVE."

My choices were all desperate ones. If I had the baby and wanted to give it up for adoption, there was no place I could go to have it quietly. I didn't have the kind of support system or money to allow me to disappear somewhere for nine months (as a few powerful and wealthy women did and later revealed). It would be impossible for me to stay in town and hide. People would know, and the personal consequences would be devastating. In 1957 women were shunned for having an illegitimate baby. Ingrid Bergman, the beloved star, had been banned from Hollywood for having a child out of wedlock. Her name had even been read into the *Congressional Record* as "a powerful influence for evil." In love with the father of her child, Roberto Rossellini, she had left the United States and continued to work with him in Europe. But I was certainly not in Bergman's league; nor was I in love with my friend. I would be unable to make a living. The stigma for both of us would be insurmountable. No doubt my family would disown me. They would never hold up under the public contempt and disapproval that would follow. I knew how important other people's opinions were to them.

Even if I could somehow overcome those obstacles, I knew I wasn't anywhere near ready to raise a child. I had observed from my own experience that being a good parent was the most difficult challenge in life and when it was time, I wanted to do it well. I knew almost nothing and understood less about the mistakes my own parents had made. I didn't want to give up the only thing I'd been trained for, the only thing I felt I was any good at in life. Clearly having a baby would be the end of both my career and my life. Today's young women may think I'm exaggerating and find all of this difficult to believe, but it was a different world then.

My options were limited. There was no morning-after pill and abortions were against the law. I knew that some women secretly had abortions, but I had no idea how or where they did it. I couldn't think of a single soul who might know. I didn't know of anyone who had ever had one. Trying not to panic, I called my lady friend in the Village and told her I had gotten the test results. I asked her if she would please try to think of someone who might know a doctor who would help me. Perhaps she could ask around. I had no choice but to trust her not to use my professional name. She didn't know anyone herself, but she agreed to try. I called her every day, and each time it was the same. People were too afraid to say they knew of such doctors. Four or five weeks went by, and no one came forward with information.

My terror grew with every day that passed and I shut myself off in my apartment. New York was in the middle of an unbearable heat wave. Those who could, had fled to the countryside. I had no air-conditioning and was having morning sickness. When I went out to get air and, hopefully, a breeze, there were so few people in the city that my world seemed hallucinatory. Then my breasts began to swell, which I confess I found very pleasant and unspeakably sad.

I still had the screen test for *The Goddess* hanging over my head. I called the producer, Milton Perlman, and told him to count me out. I was sorry, but I would not be available to make the test. The movie was made with Kim Stanley, who was, of course, remarkable. It took me a few years to view the film somewhat objectively, without the personal story of my pregnancy clicking in my gut. Though it was a truly great part, to tell the truth, I didn't really care about the movie anymore. I no longer returned my agent's calls. What was the point? I had no idea of what was going to happen to me. I felt like my life, certainly my career, was over.

Finally there were two possible leads through my friend in the Village. I quickly made the appointments. Both doctors turned me down with no apology. "Oh, no, no, I can't do that. Maybe you can find someone else. No, I can't tell you who."

Someone told my friend that an abortion might be available in Puerto Rico. I only knew how to get from L.A. to New York and back. I'd figure that out, but how would I find someone safe once I got there? The risk of a botched job, of infection and death, was a real one. I was frightened about going, but I felt I had no choice and started to pack a bag.

Then came another phone call. I was told to go see a certain Park Avenue doctor on the Upper East Side. I made the appointment. The moment I began to tell him why I was there, he stopped me and said, "Come back this evening at eight, and wait in the reception room."

I wandered the streets for a few hours and came back promptly at eight. The street door was unlocked, and I took a seat in the outer office. It was lit only by the streetlamp shining through the large window. I sat there alone and waited over an hour, thinking he had forgotten. Finally I heard sound coming from the doctor's private office. He must have gone to dinner and come in from another entrance. After a minute he opened the door and told me to come in. I sat on the other side of his desk. He asked all the pertinent questions and said if I could pay cash, $500, he would do this surgery in a small private midtown hospital. I was astounded that he and the hospital were willing to take such a chance, but that was a fair amount of money at the time. Today that would be many thousands. He said he could make the arrangements in about a week. It would be on a weekend, when the hospital would be low on regular staff. Easier to falsify records, I guessed.

If I had had no access to that kind of money, like most women, what would I have done? At that moment I felt only relief that my own life was going to be allowed to continue.

I hated lying to my business manager in Los Angeles when I called and told him to send me the money, and I always wondered if he guessed what it was for. I had never asked for a large sum of money before.

The week took a long time to pass, and when it did, I arrived promptly at the hospital (whose name, as well as the doctor's, I have completely erased from my conscious memory). I was taken into the operating room and told to bring along the envelope with the money. Just as I was losing consciousness on the table, the doctor stopped everything and said, "Wait! Did you bring the money?"

Pulling myself back ferociously from the edge of unconsciousness, I summoned all my effort to say, "Yes, it's there on the counter behind me." And I was out. I awakened in a small, clean room and felt fine. I was just a few days away from a back room in Puerto Rico and, without overstating, a good chance of losing my life.

Years later, when I had become a serious art student again and was studying sculpture with José de Creeft at the Art Students League in New York, my first piece of stone carving was an impressionist fetus made of Vermont marble, with a suggestion of the buds that would become arms and legs. It's about twenty-four inches high and weighs over a hundred pounds. I call it *The Twenty-fifth Day*, the day the heart begins to beat. My regret is in stone.

I believe in "life" and all its beauty. I am against destroying life, even in war. I am enthralled by the beauty of all living things; everything that is alive and growing, each with its own special gifts. As a woman and a blessed creature of God, though I have no wings or blossoms, I believe I was given the gift of intelligence and self-wisdom to choose when to be a mother to my child.

Some consider me selfish. But I could see no place to have this child, raise it, and be accepted by a community. Over the years I thought a lot about what I had done and thanked God for the chance to continue on.

After some months, I gave up the New York apartment and returned to California. Bob Richards, my friend since I was fifteen, and the director Jim Yarbrough, who had taken a chance and given me my first live TV role, had been living at my big house in Rustic Canyon while I was in New York. *If* they were actually in the closet, as so many were at that time, they hid it very well from everyone (including me) and they frequently went out with women. When I got back to California they stayed on at my house for many months at my invitation. There was plenty of room, and our dogs got along. I was very depressed and grateful for their company.

The three of us were pals, nurturing each other and enriching one another's lives. It was a most extraordinary, warm, and intimate relationship. We did everything together—read together, cooked together, argued together, loafed on the beach together—and eventually began sleeping together. We stayed close in my house for almost a year, confusing our friends when I'd always show up with both Bob and Jim at dinner parties. In those days the truth, that I had two lovers in my bed, would have been unimaginable to most people, so we never spoke of it to anyone. When I saw the movie *Jules and Jim*, which came out about five years later, I felt a little nostalgia.

Jim Yarbrough died in the early 1960s. The relationship with Bob changed over time, but we remained dear and close friends for another thirty-five years, until his death in the 1990s.

My life had become unproductive in recent months, too focused on myself. I did not feel very useful, so when a research doctor friend asked me for some help I jumped at the chance. He had a collection of sympathetic young actresses to take to dinner and also to help him with his research on cancer of the cervix. He needed low- or nonpaid woman power to help with some of the important, time-consuming surveys he was conducting. Some of us were more than willing to put on a white coat, sit in an office, and privately interview hundreds of low- and medium-income women. The questions were wide-ranging, but hidden in the long list of questions was the real question: "Is your husband circumcised?" and "How do you know?" Most of the women either didn't know or weren't sure. I thought it revealed a great deal about American women at that time. Curiously, not one woman asked me if she had met me before or told me I looked familiar. Their minds and focus were inward, in the self-protective, slightly fearful mode that doctors, white coats, and hospitals create.

I couldn't hibernate in my house indefinitely. I'd heard that Frank

McFadden had gone into the public relations business for himself after my dear Leonard died. I didn't want publicity, but I did want to give Frank my support in his new venture. He took me to lunch and told me that the Hollywood Chamber of Commerce wanted to give me a star on Hollywood Boulevard.

"Well, that's awfully nice," I said. Then he told me that I would have to pay for this honor. In those days a star cost $3,000. Today it's $25,000.

"Are you kidding?" I responded. I told Frank I thought it was outlandish to purchase an honor for myself. Besides, I had better things to do with my money than buy a star, including keeping my independence. (Today movie companies or networks promoting the star of a film or show usually foot the bill.) I told Frank no, and I think he was disappointed.

Frank had known me since I was a seventeen-year-old at Universal. Even though I was now almost twenty-six, he continued to think of me as a teenager and after a time I grew unhappy and wanted to end our business relationship. I was ashamed to tell him myself. It was hard to face him. So quite stupidly, I sent him a telegram. When I heard that Frank's feelings had been hurt, not by the firing but by my indifferent and cold method, I immediately realized how cowardly I'd been. Painful as it might be, I arranged to meet him face to face. We sat in a quiet restaurant where I offered, with great embarrassment, my deepest apology. Good friend that he was, he warmly accepted. From that day, I have rarely run from a necessary confrontation, and it is never easy. I have unhappily been called upon to fire a good many people through the years. But I do it myself. It makes me uneasy to hide behind someone or something.

Once I was ready to work again, I received an offer to do a three-hour version of Jean Anouilh's *Legend of Lovers* for *Play of the Week*. This show broadcast live productions of full-length plays to a television audience. And every night for that week, a tape of the show was repeated. The broadcasts made legitimate theater available to people who would otherwise never see it. Robert Loggia, Sam Jaffe, and I would be the leads. I had given up my sublet, so when I returned to New York I moved into Irene's little white apartment on West 55th Street.

We rehearsed for two weeks. Throughout the rehearsal period, I fought with Ralph Nelson, the director, and with pretty much everyone else. I strongly disagreed about some things that in retrospect were not very important, but at the time I fought hard for everything. I regret that I gave Ralph Nelson, with whom I'd worked before, such a hard time. We did not part friends. I had swung completely in the other direction since my timid, compliant days at Universal. I was empowered, all right. But I had not yet learned which battles to fight. I fought them all! I was earning a reputation in the industry as a "difficult" actress. My agents were often being questioned about my unreasonable demands and quick temper.

While I was in New York working on *The Play of the Week*, I was sent a movie script for *Miss Lonelyhearts*, a Nathanael West novel written in the early 1930s. I had read the book sometime before and been mesmerized by the story and the characters, but I didn't think the screenplay was very good. If the novel had been mediocre, a mediocre script might have been easier for me to accept. I told my agent I didn't want to do the movie, even though Montgomery Clift was the star. Of all the actors in the world, he was probably the one I wanted most to work with.

Monty was a friend of Roddy McDowall's, and we had met several times through Roddy. Monty found out where I was staying and made a surprise visit to Irene's apartment one very-early evening. He draped his charming self on the white couch and tried to convince me to do the movie, playing the romantic lead (eventually played by Dolores Hart). I sat in the big white chair opposite him for many hours as he approached the subject from any and every angle, appealing to me to change my mind. This went on until early the next morning. I was flattered beyond belief to have him go to so much trouble, but I believed very strongly in my opinion about the script. Monty finally confessed that he agreed with me but thought perhaps we could lift it a bit with our performances. At one time I might have agreed with him, but these were the years when I didn't want to compromise anymore. Monty finally left shortly before dawn, having cleaned out Irene's supply of refreshments. Though the movie was considered a failure, I sometimes think that missing the opportunity to work with such a gifted actor was a loss and a mistake. I might have learned a few things.

Despite my growing reputation for being difficult, I was still getting lots of offers for challenging roles. The legendary Mitch Leisen, director of many classic films, was set to direct the prologue to George Bernard Shaw's *Caesar and Cleopatra* for broadcast on *G.E. Theater*. Maurice Evans, who just a year before had claimed I was his mortal enemy, would play Caesar. I was asked if I would consider playing the role of Cleopatra opposite Maurice. In the wake of the *Twelfth Night* fiasco, Mitch was hesitant to ask.

I said, "It's fine with me, but you must ask him. Last year he said I was a pariah."

Apparently Mr. Evans's memory was short, for he gallantly responded, "It is absolutely fine with me *if* it's all right with her." So that's what it was going to be—a duel of grand manners with everyone on their best behavior.

Shaw's prologue in full, with just the two characters, ran thirty minutes, perfect for the time slot. The plan was to shoot the entire thing in 35 millimeter on a soundstage in Los Angeles. The script was distributed to everyone concerned for the initial meeting and read-through around the table. I took pains to be particularly gracious and grand when shaking Maurice's hand, and he was like a charming kitten wanting to please. I was aware of a lot of tension in the small room, with everyone watching Maurice and me to see if there was any sign of friction or animosity. They were obviously aware of the last disaster and seemed beside themselves with anxiety. I didn't expect any problems. It would be preposterous if someone wanted to cut or change anything; the script and length were perfect.

During a pause in the reading, I got up and quickly left the table to go to the ladies' room. I didn't bother excusing myself, not wanting to disturb the conversation. As I left, I was vaguely aware of a discussion about some minor alteration of one word of Maurice's for clarity's sake.

When I returned a few minutes later, I was astonished to find everyone standing, shouting, or talking frantically on the phone. They had all assumed I had "walked out" over the word change. Two people rushed toward me as if I were a returning war hero, anxiously reassuring me that nothing in the script had been changed, telling me "not to worry." Then everyone sat back down again. What a lesson that was for me in both power and insecurity! My whole world had been turned on its head since leaving Universal.

In addition to directing the production, Mitch also designed my costume. It was quite beautiful. I wore a long black wig for the role and held a white kitten as a prop. At the time Mitch was considered elderly for a director, but I found him direct and sensitive. Our only disagreement was over a stunt I wanted to do myself. I insisted on jumping down from the sphinx for all the takes. It must have been a good ten feet, but it was such fun for me to jump from that height into the sand. The stunt caused Mitch a little anxiety, fearing I could be hurt. He wanted the stunt double to do it, but I insisted, and all went well. Maurice and I got along fine during the production and even worked together again the following year. I thoroughly enjoyed speaking Shaw's lines, but I found the finished show a disappointment. It seemed slow and in need of more energetic editing. I have no idea whose sensibility determined the end product.

While I was working on *Caesar and Cleopatra*, Milton Perlman, the producer who had rooted for me to do the Paddy Chayefsky movie (which was done with Kim Stanley), called me. Even though I had turned down the screen test, Milton had continued being a supporter. He told me he was producing a new N. Richard Nash play for Broadway called *Handful of Fire*. Danny Mann, who liked my work, would direct it. They wanted me to play the female lead, a young bordertown prostitute who is loved by a pure young man. It was an amazing part. I didn't have to audition, and I would have a year to prepare. Heaven. A year's labor of love. I eagerly accepted.

I made several trips to Tijuana to do research. Tijuana is just over the Mexican border, a few miles past San Diego. On the first trip I drove down alone and checked into a sleazy hotel in the middle of town. From my second-story window, I watched the life of the town all day and night long. I saw the prostitutes being picked up by cabbies in the early mornings, always riding in the front seat as if they were longtime friends. On another trip, Edna packed a fried chicken lunch for me and my very good friend and agent, Lenny Hirshan. He drove us down to Mexico. Together with a local businessman, we arranged to be taken to a few of the brothels in the area known as the "shacks." We had agreed on a routine to expedite my research. A cabbie would take us to a brothel. We'd walk in and say we wanted to see "dirty movies." And just as they invited us into the next room to view the films, I would say I had changed my mind and didn't want to see them. The plan was for me to hang out while Lenny and the businessman went in to watch the movies.

Everything went just as we hoped. When I informed the man in charge that I didn't want to see the movies, he said, "Okay, the men go watch, and the lady can sit in the room with the girls." I noticed that the lights always dimmed slightly when the movies started in the next room. Meanwhile I sat with the girls, which was the whole point.

The girls were the "two-dollar whores," the lowest paid of the "working girls." They sat waiting for customers on small chairs lining three sides of the room. The first time I had the good fortune to sit with them, I was amazed at how young and sweet-looking they were. They seemed to be my age or younger; dressed in long-sleeved black or navy dresses with white lace or ruffled collars, high heels and stockings. Even little white gloves. They looked clean and refined, nothing at all as I'd imagined. Of course, when I sat down, they gave me the once-over. I was dressed in slacks and a blouse with a scarf on my head and no makeup. A few of the girls smiled shyly at me, and I tried to return a smile. One of them nodded at me and said in Spanish that I looked like a Madonna. A few of them agreed and gestured to my scarf. I said, "Thank you very much."

We were suddenly interrupted by a half-dozen youngish men, some of them sailors from San Diego, walking by a large opening where there had once been a door. They stuck their heads in, looking, making their choice of girl. I turned my head slightly away for fear I might be picked. Not likely, considering the way I was dressed, with my Madonna babushka. One of them gave me the *I've seen you before, haven't I?* look, before I turned away. He may indeed have seen me, not that long ago in Korea. There was nothing to be done about that.

I was sorry to leave the really dear young women; they were so warm to me, a stranger. When the businessman and Lenny returned from the "dirty movies," they seemed amused or embarrassed, I couldn't tell for sure which. Either way, I gave them my heartfelt words of appreciation and hoped it hadn't been too hard on them.

I had been preparing for *Handful of Fire* for several months when suddenly plans for the production changed radically. Danny Mann and Milton Perlman were out! Instead there was a new producer and a new director, the legendary Bobby Lewis. I was told my part was not secure and that I must fly to New York and audition along with several others. At first I was outraged, but I quickly realized I had no grounds to object. My friend Roddy McDowall was also going to audition, for the part of the boy opposite me. He was already a finalist, and one more reading would seal the deal. I ended up having to read on two separate occasions at Bobby Lewis's home in New York, both times with Roddy. Roddy and I were finally told we'd both be in the play. We were thrilled. No matter how much success you have, having to prove yourself never ends.

When I got back from the auditions in New York, my part once again assured, I plunged right back into preparations for the play. I drove down to Tijuana again, this time with Roddy. We drove in separate cars. I was pretty much conducting the tour and deciding where we would stay, and I recommended the fleabag hotel I'd stayed in before. When we got there, Roddy and I checked into our respective rooms. If possible, the place was even dirtier than before, though the view was greatly educational. I was tired and a little depressed because I was going to have to sleep on top of the sheets again, away from the bedbugs. I sat down on my bed in a robe and gazed out the window. I was still there when Roddy came in, carrying his camera as he often did.

He took a most remarkable candid photograph of me at the window. A very large print of that photo later appeared in Roddy's coffee table book titled *Take Two,* published in 1965, a collection of celebrity photos with accompanying text written by other celebrities. On the page facing my photo are Kim Stanley's surprising and touching words about me. I treasure them beyond any possible award. I only dare look at them every few years, to keep them fresh and shocking to my soul.

After almost a year of preparing for the Nash play, it was finally time to start rehearsals. I would be in the East for quite a long time, and again my old friend Irene Vernon loaned me her studio apartment on West 55th Street. I always seemed to find a home on 55th Street. The apartment was tiny, immaculate, and white, with white tile floors and a couch that opened up to a good-size bed. I'd stayed in it several times before, but now I would be there during the monthlong rehearsal period, the out-of-town trials in several cities, and then the run of the play in New York. My old classmate from Betomi's class was generous.

There was no doubt in my mind that the play would be successful. The love story was very basic and beautifully written, almost a fairy tale told against a backdrop of decadence. The girl I was to play was so simple and open, vulnerable and full of love, with nothing held back. I looked forward to going someplace new with this girl, experiencing it along with her, because up to this time I had never experienced that kind of love personally. I had never in my life said to anyone, "I love you." Not even to my parents. I had said and done many affectionate things, but I had never uttered the sacred words that to me expressed feelings that had to be profound if they were to be said. When they were directed toward me, they sometimes felt like a slogan coming from people's lips. Their words seem to come from their own neediness and their desire to manipulate me into responding in kind. I could never pull the words out of myself and say them lightly, so I never said them. For now, I would love this play and look forward to falling fully in love within the safety of its fairy tale.

Before rehearsals started, I was invited to dine informally with our director, Bobby Lewis, at his home. The only other guest would be Harold Clurman! Clurman and Lewis were both legends, among the most inspirational director-teachers alive. Clurman was one of the founders of the Group Theater. I had read all of Bobby Lewis's books on acting, as well as Clurman's books of criticism and acting and the theater, and found them exciting and provocative. I was ready to put all of it to practical use when rehearsals began.

What a life I was living! Two or three years earlier I could never have dreamed of what was happening, nor could anyone else. What an evening that was! The three of us sat in a cozy nook off the kitchen, with me squeezed into the middle. Clurman on my left, Bobby on my right. Clurman told me that my performance in *Awake and Sing!* with Jason Robards was far better than the one by the actress in the original Group Theater production he had directed. Later I realized the actress he was speaking of was his wife! I was so stroked verbally, I could have flown home.

Preparations for the play began. Before rehearsals started, my hair was dyed black, really black. I had never had hair that dark; it had been only dark brown when I played Jean Simmons's sister. I liked the black; it was another opening into the role for me. There was a preliminary wardrobe fitting, followed by a sitting in a photographer's studio, where head shots were taken of my new look.

Mark Rydell, the great actor who later became a superb movie director, was Roddy's understudy. My understudy was Patricia Bosworth, who became an outstanding journalist and biographer. Two other major parts were played by Kay Medford, the funny and unique actress (Barbra's mother in *Funny Girl*), and the gifted and handsome James Broderick, who would not live long enough to see his son Matthew achieve adult stardom.

On the first day of rehearsal, the entire cast of about twenty people sat on chairs in a semicircle spread across the stage of the Martin Beck Theater. There was an inspiring message from Bobby, who spoke for almost an hour before we started to read. If emotion was there naturally, he told us, we should let it flow. It could be dangerous to stuff it back down at this stage of the work when we were still exploring, finding out what was there. We wanted to be able to access it later on. When Bobby finished, we all held our scripts and read aloud in a simple way, not pushing anything, but not stifling it, either. Hearing the other actors speak their lines for the first time out loud was a stimulating feast for me. I had never actually spoken my own words out loud, waiting for this moment. I often found my tears falling onto my script when we read. I found it difficult to squash my emotion down, and so I let it flow without embarrassment. I'd find a way to put a lid on it a bit later.

Each day Bobby Lewis gave us a little lecture before we began, repeating in general his suggestion of working freely and simply at this stage. For the first three days, we all sat as before, sprawled across the stage. Everything seemed to be going very well.

One evening at about ten, I was walking alone back to my apartment after having dinner with Mark Rydell when I saw a man standing in front of my apartment half a block ahead. He was waving his arms at me. As I got closer, I recognized him as one of my agents.

"What happened?" he asked me. He looked stricken.

Totally at a loss, I said, "What do you mean?"

He said, "You've been fired! They wouldn't tell me why, only that you should not go to work tomorrow. They've fired you. I've been trying to reach you for hours. What happened?"

I was having trouble getting my thoughts clear. *What happened?* The words didn't make sense. I couldn't speak or answer the man. I felt like my body was losing its substance, turning into liquid.

He grabbed hold of me and said, "I'll take you upstairs." Once in the apartment, he said, "I think you need a Miltown. I have one. Here." I took it like a zombie, swallowing it with water as he said, "Get some sleep, and we'll talk in the morning."

He closed the door, and after what seemed just a moment, I heard soft shouting from the street. Someone was calling, "Rosieeee! Rosieeee! Rosieeeeee!" I went to the window, and three flights down on the street was dear Roddy on his motor scooter, looking up to see if he could spot me. He had known what building I was in but not which apartment. When he saw me at the window, he shouted softly, "Get your toothbrush and come downstairs. I'm taking you home with me."

I followed his directions like a sleepwalker. I came downstairs, mounted the scooter in the back, and held on tightly to Roddy as we whizzed through the streets to the apartment he was using while his friends were out of the country. The place belonged to Mike Todd and Mrs. Todd, Roddy's childhood friend Elizabeth Taylor. Roddy gave me their beautiful bed to sleep in, with wrap-around bookcases that made me feel secure. I slept a long time and awakened feeling heavy with pain in every part of me. The pain of humiliation, of knowing you're not wanted. Of failing in the adult world by being fired. My best wasn't good enough. When I spoke with my agent, he again said they gave him no reason, only that I was fired.

After a few hours, something ferocious kicked alive in me. I had given too much of myself to just walk away with nothing, no explanation, not even the decency of words face to face. I told my agent that if Bobby Lewis didn't speak to me directly, just talk to me, tell me where I had failed, I would stand outside in the street at the Martin Beck and shout and shout until he came out and faced me. I was so crazed at the moment that I was completely prepared to do just that and was getting ready to leave when I got a message that Bobby had agreed to meet me at a restaurant down the street on his lunch break.

We sat in a red booth. I did not want to make a scene; I wanted information. I asked him over and over why he had fired me, but each time he evaded the question. Every time I said "But why?" he'd answer with some kind of platitude, including "Someday you'll actually thank me for this experience. The first time you're fired is always the hardest." The fact that he didn't really care about the pain I was in wasn't important. What bothered me was that he had not one enlightening thing to tell me about my work.

When I left Bobby Lewis that day, I felt crippled inside. I don't recall what happened after that. Roddy told me later that I lay on the bed for three or four days and sobbed.

One afternoon a few days later, Roddy came into the bedroom and asked me if I would mind if he invited just two people over for dinner. He said they would be friends that I knew, people with whom I'd probably feel comfortable—John Frankenheimer and another man. If I felt well enough, I could join them at the table.

I liked John, and he greeted me that evening with just the right amount of empathy and straightforward information. He told me that he wanted me for a part in another *Playhouse 90* called *Days of Wine and Roses*. Anne Francis had been cast. He told me I was his first choice for the part, and that the minute he heard I was no longer in the play and available, he wanted to get a script to me. Out on the terrace that evening, he handed me a script that was all curled up in his hand. I put it away for later and promised to read it.

The next day, before Roddy came back from rehearsal, I pulled myself together enough to read the script John had given me. It took at least three hours. The script dealt with a young married couple's harrowing descent into rock-bottom alcoholism. It was a well-written story by J. P. Miller, with some speeches of my character, Kirsten, that sounded just like my mother (though she was not a drinker).

I always read very slowly and carefully if it was work-related, making notes of my first impressions and feelings, mostly in code so only I would be able to decipher such intimate thoughts. This time I made no notes. The last thing I wanted to do was work on another part. My heart was still with the young prostitute I'd left at the Martin Beck Theater. I had never played a drunk, not even in a scene in acting class. I supposed it would be a good exercise, but who needed another drunk? It had been done brilliantly a number of times in the last few years—Susan Hayward in *I'll Cry Tomorrow* and Ray Milland in *Lost Weekend.* Why do it again? Why be in it? When Roddy asked me if I would do the *Playhouse 90* with John, I told him I wasn't sure about anything.

That evening after dinner, while I contemplated the pros and cons of doing the new show, I did a sketch of Roddy on the back of the last page of *Days of Wine and Roses*. He was leaning on the piano, writing intensely into his script with his back to me. He was still rehearsing *Handful of Fire*. Roddy asked to keep the sketch; he later framed it and put it on the wall of the guest bathroom in his house, where it remained for many years, disappearing when he died.

I had been replaced in *Handful of Fire* by Arthur Miller's sister, Joan Copeland. Life was going on.

I had fallen into a deeply painful place, and I had to find a way to get out. Challenging, hard work had kept me afloat before. Roddy reminded me of what a treat it would be to work with John Frankenheimer again. Yes, that was a plus, but in the end when I told John yes, I'd do the show, it was really self-prescribed medication.

11.

Days of Wine and Roses

When I began to feel better, I moved back into Irene's little studio apartment on 55th Street. I had lost so much weight from stress that my skirt was falling off my hips. Before I left Roddy's place, I borrowed a belt from Miss Taylor's closet, which I regret to say I never returned.

I wasn't due back in Los Angeles for *Days of Wine and Roses* rehearsals for more than a month, but John Frankenheimer asked me if we could start working right away. He and J. P. Miller, the writer of the screenplay, were going to visit some AA meetings, some bars in the Bowery, and the alcoholic and psychiatric wards at Bellevue if we could have access to them. He hoped I would join them. Of course, I welcomed it. This was the best part of the work.

One day we were allowed to slip into Bellevue through a side door that led directly into the wards treating insanity and alcoholism. We moved fast and didn't stay long. Nevertheless, we were bombarded with information and tried to absorb everything we could. I found it very hard to take and wept when I got home. Another night John, J.P., and I went down to the Bowery and visited a number of bars. We saw such filth and sickness in roach-and-flea-infested places that I threw away the clothes I was wearing when I got home. But I also saw miraculously beautiful things, original things, especially in the body movement of some drunken people. It was almost balletic. I hoped I'd have the opportunity to bring some of that to the work. The three of us also found an AA meeting in midtown Manhattan. We walked in, trying to be inconspicuous though it was difficult; both John and J.P. were handsome giants. We took our seats toward the back. I felt guilty listening to the speaker, who was sharing with the group of about thirty people. I told myself that our presence was justified by our desire to do something enlightening and positive. We'd been listening for a while when I noticed John perspiring a lot. It was very hot in the room, and I took out a handkerchief from my purse and slipped it into John's hand. He wiped his brow and held on to the handkerchief. By the time we left the meeting, all three of us were overwhelmed with ideas.

J.P. said goodnight, and John said he'd take me home. We walked upstairs to my apartment. It was the first time he'd seen where I lived. I had hardly closed the door when John came over to me, gripped my shoulders tightly and said with the greatest of passion, "Rosie, I want to marry you! I've been in love with you for such a long time. I want us to be together, to be married to you." I realized later that after all the years we'd known each other, this was the very first moment we had ever been completely alone. I was stunned. I liked John so very much and really loved working with him, but I had never allowed myself to think of this handsome married man as a lover. Then he kissed me very hard, with more fervor than a woman likes to be kissed when the feelings are one-sided.

He went on, "My marriage with Carolyn is over. It's been over for both of us for a long time. It's done. Please marry me; I want to be with you!"

Oh my God, my recently wounded soul said, reaching out to the love and affection being offered.

Slowly at first, and then completely, John became the love of my life. It's hard to write about such a powerful obsession. Hard to avoid clichés and important to do him justice. We had already known each other well as friends and as director/actress when the gods willed we spend those weeks together in that little apartment, where we both became so vulnerable. We held back nothing from each other, revealed all our secrets, and there were many. No past behavior or present fantasy was censored. John helped me to get rid of a lot of the pain and humiliation I carried for being fired. He opened me up like a brilliant psychologist (and director), coaxed and pushed me to spew out my anger and hurt until it was gone. I was grateful to him for that. Any and all of me, anything I was, or might say, was all right. We were both so brave and trusting with each other. We became addicted to each other and couldn't bear to be apart for more than a half hour. Scientists have partially explained that kind of chemistry. I'm not sure I want to know. I was twenty-six years old and deeply in love for the first time.

John and I spent four intense weeks together. Then it was time for us to return to L.A. to begin rehearsals on *Days of Wine and Roses.* John's plan was to reveal to Carolyn his intention to marry me and to expedite their divorce. On the plane from New York to L.A., John and I sat next to each other barely speaking, trying not to think of the pain of being apart when we arrived. When the plane landed, we kissed once, and John let me leave first. We were to be met at the airport by Carolyn and our mutual agent, Lenny, who was also our close friend. He represented John occasionally because we were both with the Morris office. John and I separated in the crowd, and I didn't see Carolyn and John together at the airport. I was glad of that. I couldn't bear to see him with another woman.

A few nights later, at about three in the morning, the phone rang. It was John, who said, "I've just told Carolyn. Can you come over here?"

I struggled to get awake. I rarely took sleeping pills, but I had that night.

"Yes, yes," I said, "I'll come." I certainly hadn't expected this, but I was willing to be straightforward about it all. I quickly got into my clothes and gulped down an amphetamine with a lot of water, hoping it would work quickly on the way over. Ten minutes later I pulled up in front of John and Carolyn's house in Brentwood.

Carolyn opened the door and invited me in, asking if I wanted something to drink. My brain was still foggy, so I said, "Yes, a Coke, please."

We walked into the living room, where John sat in an oversize chair with his head in his hands. I sat down on the couch, and Carolyn returned quickly with my Coke and sat opposite John. There was a long silence, during which I gulped my Coke. Then I looked to both of them for a clue to what I had missed. Finally Carolyn spoke.

"I promised my psychiatrist, *our* psychiatrist, that I would not allow John to make a major change in his life until we were finished with therapy. John has told me what he wants, and I won't allow it. I cannot allow it. I promised our doctor."

There was not a word from John. He was a huge man, but now he was crouched over in his chair and looked so small and helpless. *Why had he asked me here? Why didn't he say something?* I felt somehow that he was waiting for me to fight for him. *How could I do that? Was I supposed to fight the psychiatrist?*

It was clear to me that the situation was far different than I had been led to believe. The marriage was not over, certainly not for Carolyn. I stood up and told them both that I didn't think I belonged there. I said there was much to resolve between the two of them, and I walked out. I'd only been there about fifteen minutes. The amphetamine and the Coke kicked in on the drive home. I was beside myself for the rest of the night, wondering if I had done the right thing.

The next morning Carolyn phoned me and asked me to promise to keep my distance from John. I thought it was an understandable request, but we had more than three weeks of preparations, rehearsals, and a show to do. I told her keeping my distance from my director was not realistic, but I would respect the intention of her request.

Rehearsals began for what would be one of the most celebrated live shows in television history. Despite our personal complications, John and I worked freely together, and I struggled with my feelings a lot. It was clear he did, too. I sublimated some of my feelings for John by making sure he ate something at lunchtime. Peeling his hard-boiled eggs became an act of sexual indulgence. We both poured our energy into the rehearsals. Once or twice we took a walk outside the CBS television city at lunchtime to get some fresh air and talk about the work.

In addition to the acting, *Wine and Roses* was a complicated show to do technically. John let me lie on the floor for one of the drunken scenes, so in order for the camera to be low enough, the entire scene had to be shot on a specially built four-foot platform. We had to climb up quickly to the platform that became the floor in our bedroom. How we climbed, whizzed around, and sustained our performances, I'll never know. John never held back from doing the difficult thing and from challenging all of us.

We also had to solve the problem of Charles Bickford putting me into a shower to be soaked in one scene, and a few moments later for me to appear in the motel scene, drunk as a skunk, with hair and clothes completely dry. John insisted on using a *real* shower where my hair, which was long and very thick, would actually get soaking wet. I remembered a special hair dryer, which was actually a gigantic blow dryer for pets, that I had used at Universal. I knew it could do the trick within seconds. So John and the producers rented this monstrous machine. (I heard Universal charged $1,000.) But because it made a thunderous sound and quiet acting scenes would be going on while my hair was being dried, the blower was set up in the wide hall outside the large soundstage. That meant I'd have to run in my wet slip across the set and through the massive door to the hall, which slid open just wide enough for me to pass through, then quickly closed behind me. Thirty seconds with the blower and my hair would be perfect, dry and wild looking. As I would fly back to the set, internally preparing for the drunken motel scene to come, someone would throw me the rest of my costume, a light robe.

Another problem was getting rid of my dyed black hair from *Handful of Fire*, which now had roots of light red showing. John sent me back to the beauty salon at least three times, each time saying, "Lighter, lighter!" before he was satisfied. I also had to find a way to "age" for the last scene of the show. I wanted to look worn and beaten by life in the scene, and I had about one minute offstage to accomplish it. So I started experimenting on my own. One night John dropped by my house unexpectedly to bring me new pages and caught me experimenting with one of my "quick aging" ideas. That night I was trying raw egg, hoping it would dry quickly and I could powder over it. When John arrived, I literally had egg on my face. He did not like the idea at all. I looked terrible, beyond what the character had suffered unless she had leprosy. John said we could accomplish the effect better with a hand-held light in just the right place for that scene.

I also asked John if we could have the prop man put a few drops of the real thing into the colored water I drank, just enough to give an aroma of alcohol but not enough to have any effect. I had heard that when Susan Hayward was playing an alcoholic, she had done that. But John was adamant. "Absolutely not," he told me. "What you're doing is fine! You don't need it."

I became worried about the lack of chemistry between me and my leading man, Cliff Robertson. As rehearsals progressed, I was having difficulty making real contact with him. I still don't know why this terrific actor was having problems. John and I had tried to be discreet, but perhaps Cliff sensed the special connection between us and felt left out. Years later I found out that John and the producers even considered letting him go. Thank goodness they didn't.

To relieve the tension during those weeks, I took every opportunity to drive to the ocean by myself and as far up the coast as there was time for. My life had piled crisis upon crisis, and I needed to exhale. I had fallen in love with a phantom. That didn't make John any less attractive. He was only superb.

On broadcast day we had a late call so I drove several hours away, through the rolling hills of the Valley, almost to the ocean. I was trying to deal with the terror that threatened to overwhelm me. I drove so far that I could not go farther without being late for the dress rehearsal. I was tempted to keep driving and miss the whole thing, this thing we'd been rehearsing and dreaming about for so many weeks. I looked around at the hills, breathless at the beauty of the world, and prayed for strength and guidance that my work could be a part of it.

The broadcast was that night. The countdown to air for a live show never gets easier. This was the time actors clung to whatever spiritual belief they had. I looked at Cliff across the room, in position for the first scene, and, with all the intensity I possessed, sent my energy across to him and asked him silently to play *with* me. And I was answered.

The miracles of this show: Cliff opened himself so beautifully to me and on air we played *together* for the very first time. I don't know if he had planned it that way all along, but he was really wonderful, and of course, this helped my performance. We also had good luck with a real baby who was sweet and well behaved while I held her in one scene. When it came time to take her offstage to a nonexistent crib, the real mother, who was hiding behind a backdrop, silently took her cooperative little angel from me and whisked her off the set. The only thing that went wrong was the handheld light that John asked for, to make me look haggard and worn in the last scene, was off just about one inch and actually was most becoming. I would not beat my breast about that.

It was bittersweet, the show ending. It felt like we'd done ourselves proud, but I was wiped out emotionally. Apparently there was no party planned. The show had been the only thing keeping me centered. It was just over, and I couldn't see any life beyond. I wanted so to hold John, to have him hold me and share our victory together. Instead, I found myself walking down the wide hall leading to the CBS exit, carrying my black drawstring bag of stuff, having no place to go. I turned a corner, and walking ahead of me were John and Carolyn. She was all dressed up in high heels, wearing a sexy low-backed dress and clinging to John's arm. She had probably watched the show from the producer's booth. The sight of them was too much for me. I got to my car, bursting with hurt and desire, and willed myself not to fall apart and feel sorry for myself. Instead I drove up into the Hollywood Hills to see my friends Bob and Jim and watch the West Coast Kinescope broadcast from their new home. They were happy to see me and gave me a *real* drink. By the time the show went on, I was really smashed. It was the only way I could bear to watch it. The only thing I remember is Bob using a word he had never used in connection with my work before. He was always so tough on me. As the drunk scene in the motel was happening, he actually said, "That's brilliant." That made me feel better.

When the broadcast was finally over, the guys reminded me that *Handful of Fire* was closing the following night. The play had gone out of town, opened in New York on October 1, and was now closing three days later. A total of five performances. I decided I would stay alive and fly to New York. I made the plane reservation that night. In the morning I grabbed my indestructible and still beautiful fur coat, flew to New York, and saw the final Broadway performance. I thought everyone was awful, stiff and bloodless. Even dear Roddy seemed lost. When I went backstage after the performance, to my great surprise, everybody in the cast began congratulating *me* on my performance the night before. They had watched it on a TV set backstage. (At that time, these live shows were an event.) My friends were so generous and happy for me. They had put up all my glorious reviews and pictures on the wall next to their own closing notice—very dramatic. They insisted that I at least read the *New York Times* review by Jack Gould that had been taped to the wall. I stood in front of the wall and read it:

> It was a brilliant and compelling work. . . . Mr. Miller's dialogue was especially fine, natural, vivid, and understated. Miss Laurie's performance was enough to make the flesh crawl, yet it always elicited deep sympathy. Her interpretation of the young wife just a shade this side of delirium tremens—the flighty dancing around the room, her weakness of character and moments of anxiety and her moments of charm when she was sober—was a superlative accomplishment. Miss Laurie is moving into the forefront of our most gifted young actresses. Mr. Robertson achieved first-rate contrast between the sober man fighting to hold on and the hopeless drunk whose only courage came from the bottle. His scene in the greenhouse where he tried to find the bottle that he had hidden in the flowerpot was particularly good. . . . John Frankenheimer's direction was magnificent. His every touch implemented the emotional suspense, but he never let the proceedings get out of hand or merely become sensational.

Afterward I found my way to Roddy's dressing room. He was surprised and thrilled to see me. Then in came director Bobby Lewis, chattering away as he entered. He looked horrified when he spotted me, whirled around in midsyllable, spoke to the wall for a moment, and then exited, continuing to talk on the way out. About forty years later

I had an emotional reunion with Bobby at a friend's home. There were embraces and inexplicable tears. I think we were congratulating each other on our survival.

The next few months were terrible. John continued declaring his love for me. He said his psychologist (the psychiatrist I was supposed to fight?) had told him our indulgent, uninhibited lovemaking was unhealthy because we were too much like children. Later I realized the doctor was most likely stupid or envious.

I never asked anything of John; I knew better than that. He told me he had formally separated and was working the details out with Carolyn. He convinced me things were different. So we began to see each other again, often at my house, or sometimes in the field and woods on the hill above it, where it was lovely and we had complete privacy. But then John said he was going away for many months to work on something in Europe. Everything was in the air, nothing resolved. My instinct told me Carolyn might still be involved. The situation was making me crazy.

I remember the day he left, thinking I'd never see him again, feeling angry and abandoned. I immediately did what I could never do as a child: I ran to a past lover for comfort. But a week later John unexpectedly came back with changed plans. He stood in my Rustic Canyon house and told me he was not going away after all. I was so overwhelmed with relief and love at the news. Of course I felt I had to confess that I'd gone to someone else, as some young and ignorant people do who worship truth at any cost. John took my confession hard and considered it a complete betrayal. I, of course, begged for forgiveness. He was, I suspect, still sleeping with his wife. My foolishness was complete.

John and I stopped seeing each other and I went into therapy for the first time in my life. For exactly nine months I saw a psychiatrist five days a week, trying to cure myself of a deep heartache and depression. In spite of the success of *Days of Wine and Roses*, I was still mourning being fired from the play in New York and, of course, mourning John.

Every day I told my Freudian psychiatrist of my inadequacies, of the terrible things I felt I'd done in my life. The doctor never said anything to me to suggest I might not be all that bad. Actually, he said nothing at all, and I sank deeper and deeper into depression. He did ask me to stop taking the sleeping aids that my stupid brother-in-law had given me, and I did. I was not able to stop the amphetamines, however, which I'd been taking for much of my life. Eventually I reached a point when I could not function at all, and I stopped talking again, even to my friends. I did nothing except go to my doctor appointments. Speeding dangerously through the streets, I was always at least twenty or thirty minutes late. That didn't leave much of a fifty-minute hour.

Looking back, I think it was a shame I didn't have a smart, caring friend to talk to about this along the way. A woman friend or two would have been nice, but that would be a few years coming. It took me many years to understand that I had thrown myself into the all-encompassing relationship with John to mend my broken love affair with *Handful of Fire*. But even when I understood all of that, the power of what I felt for John was not much diminished. He was an enormously talented and fascinating man.

I was finally saved from myself and given a new birth of freedom when the psychiatrist went on a European vacation at exactly the same time I was offered Maxwell Anderson's *Winterset* as a Hallmark TV show in New York. It was 1959, and I was twenty-seven years old when I arrived back in the city and moved into a small residential apartment-hotel (again on West 55th Street). The place had been recommended by my wealthy aunt Bergie and uncle Harry and was owned by a friend of theirs. My uncle sat in the hotel lobby sometimes, I think trying to keep an eye on me and perhaps report back to my parents, who couldn't understand why I was still not married.

It was a turning point for me. I was so happy to be in New York. It seemed like spring, even though it was October. I even had an occasional glass of wine, which I hadn't been able to do for a long time without becoming more depressed. Being there was such a breath of sweet, fresh air, and I went from feeling extremely fragile to slowly joining and enjoying the world again. My leading man in *Winterset*,

Don Murray, took me to the new Guggenheim on one of the opening days. The "teacup," designed by Frank Lloyd Wright, had just opened on Fifth Avenue.

We rehearsed *Winterset* in one of those huge open rehearsal halls with lots of windows, with tape put on the floor to indicate rooms and spaces. The director, George Schaefer, who had been on vacation when I left *Twelfth Night*, was back at work on this one. The problems with *Twelfth Night* and Hallmark seemed to have been forgotten. I was glad of that. George knew his stuff. I was playing Miriamne to Don Murray's Mio. Don was an extraordinary and warm man. My brother Garth was played by Marty Balsam. Charles Bickford, who'd been my father in *Days of Wine and Roses*, played the judge. George C. Scott played the gangster, Trock.

I was deathly afraid of George C. Scott in those days. Sometimes he'd show up at rehearsal a little late, wearing bloody bandages and bruises. He'd been in a fight or trouble of some sort with a woman the night before. He always stayed on the far side of the rehearsal hall when he wasn't in a scene. I stayed clear of that side. We never spoke, and I tried not to make eye contact. I'm not sure we were ever actually introduced. If we were, then it must have been from far away. It wasn't until many years later, after the second time we worked together, that we broke our silence, and I found out he was a pussycat.

Despite the joy of returning to work, the despair and fear at having been fired from *Handful of Fire* remained with me throughout rehearsals and I was fearful every day that it would happen again. The experience had cut so deeply, and I had been totally unprepared. It wasn't until we had passed a point of no return during rehearsal for *Winterset*, with probably not enough time to replace me with a new person, that I was able to feel confident I wouldn't be fired. That fear went on for years. I couldn't get rid of it. Sometimes I wasn't sure until the work was completely over.

We did *Winterset* live on tape, and it's all a bit of a blur to me. I think my increased use of amphetamines was distorting my perceptions, but I didn't believe I could get through the work without them.

Some of us got together after the broadcast and watched a tape of the show. I didn't care for it.

By holiday time a lot of my depression was lifting, but I was still having difficulty getting myself out of my little apartment to face the world. Roddy gave some dinners and parties at his new apartment and invited me to most of them. I rarely went. He had a big apartment on Central Park West that he'd pointed out to me a few years before while we were walking in the park. "That's where I want to live," he'd told me. He had invited me to his Christmas party, and after hours of indecision, I pushed myself into going. I called to let Roddy know I was on my way.

"Rosie, the party's tomorrow night!"

Not defeated, I went through the same struggle the following night: found a cab going uptown and arrived at the party at four in the morning, cold sober, wearing a pretty, brand-new dress.

I walked into a roiling sea of very drunk Broadway stars. In their midst, Maureen Stapleton seemed to be sailing slowly across the room. Jason Robards, whom I knew, and Christopher Plummer, whom I did not yet know, greeted me warmly at the door. I'd seen Christopher on stage a number of times. He was an actor gifted with power and originality beyond most I'd known personally. Both Jason and Christopher seemed more in command than most of the other guests. Seemingly enchanted by the sight of the newcomer, they each took one of my arms and escorted me into the noisy room. As chance would have it, Jason let go of my right arm while Christopher held on and found a cozy spot to the left on the floor, under Roddy's large desk. He invited me in for a chat. Sitting in our little cave under the desk, he talked about *Days of Wine and Roses* and said the show was much better than he had expected. He told me he had read the script at one point and turned it down. But he was generous with his praise for me and John. Even though Christopher was high, he was articulate and elegant. We talked for a few hours, and he came home with me.

Over the next month or so I spent time with Christopher. One evening as he and I entered my hotel, I spotted Uncle Harry through the glass door, sitting in the lobby as usual. We would have to walk by him to get to the elevator. When Uncle Harry turned away for a moment, we managed to scoot up the stairway. I found Christopher to be great fun, with a quick mind, though he could be terribly rude if he didn't like you. I cringed sometimes when he dealt with sycophants while we were out in public. But most of our time together was stimulating and loving. He was always dear and charming with me, if not a completely dependable beau. It could be tiresome waiting for him to return after a toot. Midafternoon on New Year's Eve, he dropped off a bottle of champagne and a recording of Sibelius's Second Symphony at my apartment, saying he'd be back in an hour. He returned three days later. Fortunately, I had my portable phonograph and the glorious and romantic Sibelius for company.

Christopher took me to some small parties where Sir Laurence Olivier was also a guest. He and Christopher were friends. I was afraid I might embarrass myself and have one of my extreme attacks of shyness if I were to actually meet Sir Larry. That had happened when I'd met Harry Belafonte only two years before. Abe Lastfogel had taken me backstage. When I was introduced to Mr. Belafonte, my chin involuntarily dropped to my chest and stayed glued there for at least ten seconds. Not a cool thing to do. In spite of all my years and experience, I could not control this response sometimes. So at these parties with Christopher, I deliberately moved myself from room to room to avoid being introduced to Sir Larry. We did meet many years later and spent a memorable evening together.

I'd heard that Jason Robards was about to do the new Lillian Hellman play. How I wanted to work with him again! The legendary playwright (*Children's Hour*, *Watch on the Rhine*, and *The Little Foxes*, among many others) had just written *Toys in the Attic*. My agents made an appointment for us to meet at her apartment on a Sunday morning. Kermit Bloomgarden, the great producer, was going to be there as well. Of course I was very nervous about the meeting. Twisting myself into a nearly hysterical knot, I arrived more than two hours late with a bloody cut on my cheek inflicted by a sharply bristled hairbrush that had slipped from my grip. My agent had left by then, but Hellman and Bloomgarden had waited patiently. Miss Hellman answered the door in a stunning red dressing gown, actually looking quite pleased to see me. She was gracious and kind and said, "These things happen sometimes." And then, "Would you like a cup of coffee?"

The apartment was big and warm, with beautiful furniture and lots of books. Coffee was served on an ornate silver tray on a large, low coffee table, and I stayed for more than an hour, feeling comfortable and grateful. Through the years I've heard so many stories about Miss Hellman's wickedness. I choose not to believe them.

I didn't get the part. But the same day I found out I was not going to be in the Hellman play, I got a call asking me to have lunch with Molly Kazan, Elia Kazan's wife, who was a budding playwright. I was only a half-hour late for that one. Molly and I liked each other right away. She was a warm, gentle lady with a marvelous sense of humor. She gave me a copy of two one-act plays she'd written called *Rosemary* and *The Alligators*. She was a member of the writers-directors unit at the Actors Studio and wanted to put the plays on there. It was purely experimental, and the actors would volunteer their time. Gerald Freedman, a talented member of the studio, would direct; Anne Bancroft and I would play the women; and Bill Daniels, Cliff de Young, and later Paul E. Richards, the men. I was not a member of the studio and was flattered to be asked.

I was so happy doing the work. We all got along well and rehearsed as often as we could, sometimes in the Danielses' apartment uptown, and sometimes at Anne's place in the Village. Her apartment was the narrowest one I had ever seen, but she decorated it with great style and bold colors. She'd just had a big success on Broadway in *Two for the Seesaw*.

In *Rosemary*, Bill Daniels and I played vaudeville performers who have come to rehearse at the beach. Our characters meet another couple there, played by Anne and Cliff. We arrive wearing our beautiful period clothes—Bill in a spiffy turn-of-the-century suit and me in a full-length pink organza dress, large pink hat, and parasol to match, designed by the talented and soon-to-be-famous Theoni Aldredge. Bill and I go into the changing tent on stage midway in the play and come out in our costumes dressed as children, me in old-fashioned pantaloons. Though it is essentially a dramatic play, we sing and dance and also (thank you, Molly Picon) stand on our heads.

Neither Bill nor I had ever stood on our heads before. We spent hours crashing to the floor in Bill's apartment while Gerry, the director, was trying to teach us. While we practiced, Bill's wife, the fine actress Bonnie Bartlett, would walk through the living room carrying bags of groceries to the kitchen, or the children to their room, trying to dodge us as she went. Afterward I'd go home and practice in the corner of my bedroom on top of pillows spread everywhere. At last I got it! We both got it! I could do it anywhere and did. It was a wonderful pick-me-up when I was tired. And we never failed to do it brilliantly on stage while singing our song, which incidentally was "You're the Only Star in My Blue Heaven"—the same song I'd sung in Tennessee Williams's *This Property Is Condemned* when I auditioned at Universal as a teenager. A good omen.

The second play, *The Alligators*, involved a woman, played by Anne Bancroft, who's in a hotel room in danger from the Mafia. After her long monologue, an innocent bystander in the room, a young bimbo dressed in body-hugging clothes (me), gets acid thrown in her face. A top newspaper reporter, Victor Riesel, had been a notorious acid victim a few years back and Molly invited us over to her and Gadge's (Elia Kazan's) home to meet Riesel and talk to him. The whole cast, including Molly and Gerry (the director), were plying him with intense questions.

Right in the middle of this, Gadge Kazan came over to me and told me I had a phone call. Who in the world beside my agents knew where I was? And why would someone call me here, while I was working? It did not please me having this sacred time interrupted. I went into the next room and picked up the phone.

It was John. I hadn't seen or talked to him for well over a year.

He said, "I have to see you tonight."

"How did you find me here?"

"The agent knew, and I just figured it out."

"I can't leave here now."

"I'll meet you when you're finished. There's a little café a block away. I'll wait for you there."

Did a heart ever beat so fast?

We finished our discussion in a little over two hours, and I trembled as I walked down the street to the café, wondering if John would still be there. He was.

I sat down opposite him. He seemed unsure of himself. After I ordered a beer, he asked me to take off the head scarf I was wearing. I told him I didn't want to. I had cut my hair, and I knew it looked awful. It had been a neurotic mistake.

He said, "Let me see it." I was always brave with John, so I took it off. Then he said, "I'm divorced now. I love you, Rosie."

And so it began—again. I saw John at my place, sometimes at the Plaza Hotel, then later at Judy Garland's grand apartment at the Dakota that John sublet for a time. I loved being with him. I liked the raw honesty between us, liked that he really listened to me and valued what I had to say. I liked his excitement at discovering the restaurant that was serving the first asparagus of the season (one had to wait for nature then). I liked going to the first Godard and Truffaut movies. I liked sewing an occasional button on his shirt and taking care of him a little. I didn't want any declarations or promises. I didn't want marriage. I didn't want any more than what we had. Things were fine as they were, and I was engrossed in my work. A couple of times John sneaked into our rehearsals. He told me he didn't care that the plays were not yet ready; he just liked watching me on stage. I believed that he did, and I felt very desired.

After a few months I decided to stay in New York and leave L.A. behind for good. I gave up my house in California and leased an apartment with many large rooms on the tenth floor of the Ardsley, on Central Park West between 91st and 92nd, overlooking the park and reservoir. I lived there for almost ten years. John stayed there with me when he was in New York.

We performed Molly's two one-act plays at the Actors Studio with great success. Many people I hadn't seen for a while, Mark Rydell for one, came to see what we were doing. I found out much later that the extraordinary writer-director Robert Rossen (Oscar-nominated for *Body and Soul* and *All the King's Men*) had also come to one of the performances. When plans were made to do the plays at the York Theater, a good-size off-Broadway theater that has sometimes been a movie house, I was sorry that Anne Bancroft couldn't go with us. She was a joy to be with and to play with; her warm smile would go right through you.

Anne was replaced by Jo Van Fleet, who had seemed so assured in her Oscar-winning role as James Dean's mother in *East of Eden* but was more insecure than me in some ways. In *The Alligators*, which was really a star vehicle for her, her character delivers a long monologue to the audience almost completely downstage. I was upstage during most of her speech, leaning on the sofa and listening, making it my business to be as still as possible. I knew my smallest movement could be distracting, and I was diligent about it. One night Jo changed her own staging to come upstage to me for a moment, nose to nose, and muttered, "You bitch!" I was shocked and bewildered until the stage manager later explained that when the audience had occasionally become restless during her monologue, Jo assumed I had been calling attention to myself.

After we played at the York for quite a few months, I indulged in some self-pity in the middle of a phone conversation with my parents. I inexplicably started to cry when I expressed my disappointment at their not coming to see me in my first New York stage appearance. I suppose that was coming from some place more deeply hidden than I wanted to acknowledge. To my surprise, and I was so touched by this, my mother flew out to be with me the next day.

I had almost no furniture in my apartment. There was a bed in the bedroom for me and a daybed in the large living room, where my mother slept. She stayed several weeks, until the closing, and a bit after. She spent time with me and came to see the show often, which I loved. I always knew she was out there because the unmistakable sound of her clearing her throat would catch my ear throughout the evening.

One night Christopher Plummer came backstage, enchanted with the plays and wanting to take me out. We were friends but no longer dating. John was the only man in my life. I explained that I had to go straight back to my apartment because my mom was visiting. Christopher wanted to meet her and say hello and said he'd meet me at the apartment. After a brief detour, he showed up an hour later. Mother had already gone to bed, and the living room was dark except for lights from across the park (I did not yet have drapes).

I think Mother was half-asleep when Christopher tiptoed just a little unsteadily across the hardwood floor, leaned over, gave her a kiss on the cheek, and said, "Hello, my love." She looked up at him and went right back to sleep. She told me later that she thought she was dreaming.

It was during this visit that my mother and I began growing into a new relationship. She almost never "suggested" or criticized, which was probably very hard for her. One morning we took the train to Stratford, Connecticut, to see *Othello* with Earle Hyman and made a day of it. We had lunch and then saw the play. She was so happy when we met Mr. Hyman afterward on the lawn, just bubbling with excitement and praise for him. I was so proud of her for not covering her strong feelings for this handsome and gifted man. She seemed to be a different person, and I was very grateful that she had made this journey to be with me. I guess I had been waiting for her.

One evening while my mother was still visiting, Robert Rossen came to another performance of our play, and this time he came backstage and was introduced to me by my agent. He was dressed very casually and seemed a little nervous holding the script that he presented to me. "I saw you in the plays at the Actors Studio," he told me. "I've written something I'd like you to read."

Most scripts I'd read recently had not been very interesting. I read them all very respectfully, giving them a careful, at least three-hour reading. One never knew; there might be a miraculous scene on the last page that could make the whole thing worthwhile. Finding a spare three hours when you're doing a play was not something that came easily for me, especially when the result was most likely disappointing. My friend Bob Richards thought this approach was a waste of time, but I persisted. I thought of all the hours the writer had spent, and I felt I owed them more than a hasty read.

I postponed reading anything until my mother left. When she did, I sat down and started to read Rossen's script. It was called *The Hustler*. My character, Sarah, didn't enter till about page forty, but around page five I already knew I wanted to be in this movie. I didn't care what the part was. The script was so clean and strong. It was all there, and I was excited. I had never before read a script where I could so vividly hear and see and even smell the characters and rooms. This was for me. I could pour myself into it and disappear. I hoped Robert Rossen hadn't gotten tired of waiting to hear from me. I told my agent right away that I wanted to do it. Thank God, Rossen had been patient. We agreed to meet.

He came up to my empty apartment, where the living room now had a chair in addition to the daybed, and we talked a little about this mysterious girl. Who she really was. I thought I understood her, even if I didn't know the particulars, the truth about her background. We talked about her being crippled and about how much that should show. Rossen didn't want it to be distracting and become a centerpiece of any scene. We decided to pick only the moments when it would add texture. Rossen told me that day that Paul Newman would also be in the film, which pleased me very much.

Meanwhile, my agents were trying to finalize the deal with the studio. The film was being produced by 20th Century-Fox. The studio had wanted Anne Francis again, a former contract player, to play the part. They finally relented and agreed to sign me but wouldn't move above a certain figure for me. I think it was $25,000, the token amount I'd agreed to per picture to get me out of my Universal contract (these supposedly confidential figures have a way of flying around from studio to studio). My agents and I stood firm on $40,000—not a princely sum, but a fair one for the time. Rossen took a stand on my behalf and insisted on my playing the role *and* their paying me the $40,000. I probably would have weakened if he hadn't insisted. The studio finally agreed.

Rossen asked me to go with him to meet George C. Scott, who was doing a play on Broadway. Rossen was interested in casting him. He had never met George and had heard unpleasant things about him, that he was difficult. He knew I'd worked with George and thought that would make the meeting more relaxed. Little did he know how frightened I was of George, or that we'd never, ever spoken, but I decided it would be counterproductive to tell Rossen and said I'd be happy to go with him.

Rossen picked me up at my apartment, and we went to see George's play, *The Wall*. His performance was quite powerful, and when we went backstage to see him, George quietly said he'd meet us at a café around the corner. Rossen and I sat together on one side of the booth, and when George arrived, he sat facing us. We all ordered beers. Rossen told him a little about the movie and handed over the script, just as he had with me—uncovered, without an envelope, rolled up a little, with marks from his fingers pressed onto the back pages, touched by the humanity of his hand. We'd been together perhaps an hour, and I hadn't uttered a word. I knew that if George played the part, these fearful feelings I already had toward him would be useful. George accepted the part.

When I began preparing for my role in earnest, I asked my friend Bob Richards to visit me in New York for a week or two and work with me on my character. Since my departure from Universal and our reunion, I had never worked without consulting him. Our relationship was now strictly platonic, but I sometimes worried that I was too dependent on him for finding ways to think outside the box. That changed, and he set me free in a very subtle way, allowing me to feel the student had surpassed the master.

After Bob went home, I started to experiment with superficial things like the way to get the right kind of limp. I tried many things, from a pebble in my shoe to having a lift put in. I walked around the park hurting so much that I knew my brain would never be able to concentrate on the acting. In the end I used nothing except an awareness of shifting my weight a bit when I wanted the limp to be visible.

Several times I hung around the Greyhound bus station at night, as Sarah often did. I thought it would help me to know what was going on inside her, why she behaved as she did. I would go downtown at three in the morning, walk around, and sometimes sit inside the station. I suppose I was fortunate that nothing out of the ordinary happened. Only once a man caught me by surprise after I had crossed the street and stepped up onto the curb. He leaned close to my ear and suggested what he would do for me, if I liked that. I think I said, "No, thank you."

I did things I wouldn't do today, and I suppose were not especially wise to do then. Perhaps because I've had so much more life experience now, I feel some of the research I did was a bit unnecessary, sometimes foolhardy, and occasionally downright dangerous. Certainly it wouldn't work today in this drug culture. Depending, of course, on what you're looking for, a little bit of research and a lot of imagination can go a long way.

Three or four weeks before shooting started, John asked me to come and stay with him in California for a little while. Though I was already beginning to wrap myself in the aura of Sarah and her insecurities, plus my own, I couldn't refuse John. He was quite anxious himself and wanted me there for support. He was getting ready to direct a new film, *All Fall Down*. He was also about to start meetings with Frank Sinatra for *Manchurian Candidate* and had real concerns about whether Sinatra would take his direction.

I understood and flew to California to spend time with him. He had rented a two-story house in West Los Angeles that was relatively modest, considering his growing taste for space and elegance. It had a gorgeous fruiting Meyer lemon tree in front. Every day I'd pick a gigantic sweet lemon for my tea with honey. There was a houseman to take care of almost everything. If I wanted to go anywhere, John insisted on hiring a driver to take me. When I first knew him, John's tastes had been much more down to earth. He used to drive an old, banged-up, cream-colored convertible with the top down. I guess he was not a terrific driver and would often bump into my trees in Rustic Canyon when he parked at my house.

While I was in California, I visited my parents at their new home in Orange County and went to see their furniture store, which was thriving. My parents' store was the first of its kind, selling only Naugahyde furniture. It appeared that everyone in Orange County at that time was yearning to have fake leather furniture and my folks became tremendously successful. When they showed me the store, I noticed they had one of the old Universal glamour shots of me hanging on the wall. Mother had finally found a place for all that energy and drive. She turned out to be a fine businesswoman and my parents became business partners, making a small fortune with their store. For the first time in their lives they didn't have to pinch pennies, yet ironically, that's exactly what they still did. My dad would bargain over trifles in a restaurant or store in the most brazen way. If he hadn't asked for rolls or bread to be served with the meal and didn't eat them, he'd ask for a reduction of the bill. I supposed he had a point, but he was so adamant about it, making up for all the years of not being assertive, that sometimes he'd leave the waitress in tears. My mother continued with her habit of rubbing money between her thumb and two fingers to make sure bills weren't stuck together. No matter where she was or how long it took, in a grocery checkout or a fancy restaurant, she took the time. It used to embarrass me, but now it just seemed sad.

John rehearsed almost every day during my visit, but we had the evenings and mornings together. The houseman left after dinner and we had the rest of the night for each other, to talk and make love. Everything seemed almost perfect—almost—until one day John asked if I would mind planning the shopping list and menu for the houseman to cook. Simple enough—but I was immobilized. I'd had almost no experience at planning entire meals for anyone, deciding what someone else would eat night after night. I realized I didn't really know that much about his taste in food; other things almost always seemed more important. I did know he adored Oreo cookies and I always had them available wherever we were, but that was it. Now I panicked.

It's heartbreaking and funny in a way when I think of how experienced I later became in the kitchen and home and, if I do say so myself, what a superb baker I became. But back then I didn't want the responsibility of choosing meals that might not please John. I was there to bring him pleasure. I finally just gave up and deferred to the houseman. I let him do the whole thing, buy and cook whatever he wanted.

I was sorry that I had disappointed John. I think he was looking to see if I could stay home for long periods of time and be content while he was working. He asked me if I was happy alone at home. Did I get bored? Was it all right for me? I wondered what he was getting at. Was he thinking of asking me to stop working? One night when we were to meet six or eight business associates of John's at a restaurant, I made us more than an hour late. If John was angry with me, he didn't show it much. He always seemed to be on my side, understanding, but we both knew something was up. Things were getting hard. A big part of me was saying, *Think about Sarah, about getting back for* The Hustler *rehearsals*. I was trying to feel competent during my weeks with John, yet inside I was becoming more fragile. I was cutting my hair shorter and shorter, the bangs in front unbecomingly so, much as it appears in the movie. The morning I left, John insisted on driving me to the airport, but we were both deeply involved in our own work and very quiet throughout the drive. I was feeling we were separating in an important way and would never come together again.

The official rehearsals for *The Hustler* were to start soon after I got back, and I needed to use my hands to dispel some of the anxiety. When I was six, I had built a small table to cope with the prospect of being taken to the sanitarium. Now I decided to build another table, this one with makeup lights, in the alcove of the dressing room in my apartment. I went to the local lumberyard and got sufficient wood to build a narrow table supported with sturdy brackets. I made a heavy frame of about three by five feet for the mirror and covered the surface with unusual tiles. I cut out the holes necessary for lights, and went to Rosetta Electric (a good omen) in midtown Manhattan for materials and instructions from the salesmen on how to wire and install the lights.

I've always been mystified and frightened by electricity, so I went back to the electric store several times to make sure I was doing the wiring correctly. I worked so very carefully, with my heart racing, and when it was finished, I held my breath, said a prayer, and pressed the switch. It worked! What a thrill! The lights were perfect, and I was still alive!

In the days before we started shooting, Bob Rossen and I had many walking conversations about the movie and my part. One early evening we walked over to the Ames Pool Hall in midtown Manhattan. Bob wanted me to meet Jackie Gleason (who was playing Minnesota Fats). Jackie practiced there every day, but that day he was gone by the time we arrived. As sometimes happens when making a movie, scenes were shot on different sets, so Jackie and I never met. Bob Rossen and I were getting to feel more comfortable with each other. At first I thought the talks were for my benefit only, but Bob told me later he had little confidence in his ability to communicate with actors. He felt he couldn't speak to an actor about what he wanted for a particular moment or scene in terms "useful to the actor," though he knew it when he saw it. If it rang true to him, he'd print. He also had a strong opinion about what I should wear in the film. In one scene he insisted I wear a sleeveless navy jumper with a long-sleeved white blouse underneath. A potent distant memory?

On the first day of rehearsal all the principal actors, with the exception of Gleason, met in a brightly lit hall in midtown. We sat around a large rectangular table. Rossen was in the middle. George C. Scott sat by himself at the far end. I was at the other end, toward the door, opposite Paul Newman. There was lots of controlled energy in the room, a not-very-successful attempt to keep things light.

I had to struggle to keep my focus. I'd done *Until They Sail* with Paul Newman two years before at MGM, but on that film there had never been an occasion for me to be physically close to him. Lifting my head from the script to speak my first line to Paul, I was met with the blinding force of his unearthly blue eyes. There was a nakedness about him in those eyes; surely I was seeing more than anyone was supposed to. After I'd gotten past my first line, I found myself luxuriating in the vision before me. It was more than the eyes; it was also of course the mouth, and the unbelievable grace of his cheekbones. Almost two weeks passed before I could do my work and just see a man.

I still found George C. Scott menacing and continued keeping my distance. I used my natural reaction to him, and much more, during our scenes together. I would see him as a large dangerous snake about to strike, instead of the large and handsome man that he was. Poor George. I don't know if he knew what I was doing, but he did nothing to discourage it. I thought of him that way for a good thirty years, until a mutual actor friend took me to dinner at his house, where George picked me up into the air and called me "Rosie." He was sober, sweet, and articulate. When I got to know him, I knew for sure how respectful he was of the actor's process. I finally asked him what he had whispered into my ear in the big party scene in *The Hustler* that elicits a violent response from me. We shot it perhaps three or four times, and I could never figure out what he was saying; it sounded something like "isha-pa-pishpo." He told me he chose to use just gibberish, knowing he could never invent words or phrases as powerful as what my imagination could summon up. Probably true. We worked together closely several more times over the years.

Working with Paul was a joy from the beginning. I'm sure he was unaware of the effect his beauty had on people. He was very serious about the work, often thinking he wasn't any good. But outside the work, he was generally easygoing and quite down to earth. When I arrived every morning, I would see Paul reading a newspaper in the makeup room. Up to that time, he was the only actor I had ever seen doing that. Not many actors read anything but the trade papers or their script that early in the morning. Just the sight of him reminded the rest of us there was a real world out there. Not a bad thing. It surprised me because generally Paul made an effort to come off as slightly lowbrow, cool, and casual. Clearly, he had a lot of interests. Was I seeing the budding philanthropist?

In an innocent way, I played house with Paul. Our cell-like dressing rooms were right next to each other, somewhere upstairs in the huge warehouse that was now our studio. We each had only a cot and a small table. I set up a hot plate in my room and brought soups for myself for lunch. One day Paul told me of a favorite imported dehydrated soup that he loved. (Obviously, tasty food was always important to him.) After that I made a point of getting that soup or something close to it, heating it up, and bringing him a mugful at lunchtime. I sat on his cot with him while we both ate. It was a silent bonding time.

One day Paul invited me to join him and his wife, Oscar-winning actress Joanne Woodward, at a fund-raiser ball for the Actors Studio. I had met Joanne only once. She visited the set for a brief time, wearing a beautiful red coat. I believe it was the only time she came to the set to see Paul. I thought it was very sensitive of her. John was shooting in California, so Paul and Joanne suggested their friend Gore Vidal be my escort to the ball.

The night of the ball we all met at the Newmans' apartment (I had heard about their dining room, and yes indeed, it was completely empty save for a large pool table). Joanne wasn't quite ready and invited me to come back to the bedroom to keep her company while she was finishing up. A couple of flourishes to her hair, a powder puff, and some jewelry. I doubted I would have been that open with a woman I didn't really know, but John, who knew her, was right; he had described her as someone I would like, "a really straight dame." Gore Vidal was charming and witty, and the evening seemed festive. It was a release for everyone, certainly for Paul and me.

Every morning while we were shooting, the hairstylist would come to my apartment and blow-dry my hair straight in front of the makeup mirror I'd created. Then she'd wrap my head carefully with fine tulle to protect it for the drive to the location or the studio. One day Paul asked if I'd like him to pick me up for work in the morning on his motor scooter. Oh, brother!—of course, I said yes. The next morning we flew through Central Park. It was beautiful, no traffic, round and around through the trees. Somewhere in Central Park my head covering floated away, but I didn't care. Bob Rossen greeted us when we arrived at the studio and gave us both holy hell before he sent us to makeup. Rossen forbade me to ride on the motor scooter ever again.

Bob Rossen was very caring of me, beyond my being the actress in his movie. When he found out I was not sleeping well, he hired a masseuse to come to my apartment a couple of times a week at the end of the day. It didn't help my sleep much, but it sure felt good. When I'd first told John I was going to do the movie, he'd asked about Rossen's interest in me. Was it personal or strictly professional? I told him I thought it was both. John said, "That's the best; I'm glad for you. In a creative endeavor, that's wonderful for both of you."

He didn't mean that it had to be overt and acted upon, only that the fact of its existence in a director-actor relationship somehow adds an extra element of energy and can enrich the work.

Occasionally during shooting I would have a long break between scenes and would get away for a swim at the Ansonia Hotel. I had loved swimming ever since Frank, the handyman at Reslocks, taught me how one summer. Once I had a two-hour break before I had to do the scene when Eddie returns to me with broken fingers. I wanted to look as if I'd been drinking heavily for days when I came to the door, so I went over to the Ansonia, which was just a few blocks away. I spent time swimming underwater so my eyes would be bloodshot and my face puffy. I'm sure the makeup man had something in his kit that would have accomplished the same thing, except for the joy of the swim. Rossen sent a car to pick me up when he saw I was missing, and I got back just in time to play the scene.

Paul and I had no trouble playing the written scenes. We believed in them, and there was plenty of chemistry while we worked. But one time Rossen asked us to improvise something lighthearted and fun in Sarah's apartment. Paul and I were so awkward on our own without the support of the strong written material in that apartment whose very walls seemed to have absorbed the tense atmosphere. The scene seemed inauthentic and proved unusable. Perhaps if we'd been in a different location or outside, we might have brought some life to it, but that set had begun to evoke powerful feelings that we couldn't escape.

There had been some unspoken but palpable anger between Rossen and Paul on the set. I think Paul may have been aware that he was not Rossen's first choice, and that couldn't have made things easier. Rossen once told me that his dream casting would have been John Garfield, if he'd been alive, or Peter Falk, whom the studio vetoed because he wasn't a big enough star. Peter was terrifically attractive in the days before he dressed himself down for *Columbo*.

One day I went to Rossen and told him that I didn't think I should be wearing clothes in the scene where Fast Eddie and I first wake up in bed. I should at least appear as if I weren't. The bedsheets would hide most of my body. The production code was still very strict at the time; even married people could not be seen sleeping in the same bed. But Paul and I would be in the same bed, and Paul, of course, wouldn't be wearing much, so why should I? I asked Rossen to tell Paul what I was planning to do beforehand so it wouldn't be a total surprise. Rossen said, "I don't think Paul is going to like that; he may be uncomfortable." But nothing more was said about it, and that's what we did. Rossen shot two versions: one for the foreign market, with Paul and me undressed under the sheets, and one for the United States, with me wearing a robe and lying on top of the sheets and Paul wearing a T-shirt. Interestingly, the acting in the clothed scene was far better, so that's the one that was used. If Paul was uncomfortable about the scene, I never knew it, nor did anyone else.

I think Bob Rossen won a lot of his battles. He did with me. We disagreed about the scene outside the restaurant after Fast Eddie tells me he's leaving town without me. I thought I should keep walking once I left the restaurant, but Bob wanted me to stop long enough for Paul to catch up with me. That seemed like a false, stagey wait, but Bob was adamant, and I guess I must have found something, perhaps the awareness of the rain, to justify my stalling for a moment. But I was pissed off at being forced to do something inherently dishonest to save two extra camera moves, and I stayed that way for several days. I think the other actors were having a hard time with him, too. Eventually the tension passed, and to his credit, I'm sure Bob hid a lot of money and production problems from us for our sakes.

Despite the insecurity I felt when we parted, John visited me several times during shooting when he had a break, and he was there when the film ended. There was a wrap party in a large room at the Plaza Hotel, and I was again surprised when he told me he wanted to come to the party. I never go to anyone else's wrap party; one feels out of place, even if half the people are spouses. But since a few people wanted to meet John, and John was extremely eager to meet Rossen, whom he admired so much, I agreed to let John bring me to the party. Afterward we'd have a private dinner with Bob and Sue Rossen in the dining room at the hotel.

When we got to the party, the cast and crew were relaxing—dancing, drinking, and chatting at small tables. Paul moved around the room, sipping on his tube of Coors as he socialized with everyone. It was obvious that John was uncomfortable and couldn't stand the party. I don't think he liked to dance. Perhaps he didn't know how. It's funny, after all the time I'd known him, I'd never realized that until that night. John left after a while, saying he'd be back. I was relieved that he returned. Our private dinner afterward was long, and I think the two directors were excited by each other's company. Their genuine admiration for each other was a lovely thing to see. They both seemed very happy and laughed a lot. John was only thirty years old at this time and just beginning his career. It meant a lot to him to sit down with the brilliant Robert Rossen. A few days later John went back to California to finish *All Fall Down*.

Paul had seen John coming to pick me up at the rehearsal hall after work when John visited. He used to say to me, "Why don't you marry the guy?" I didn't know if Paul was serious or not, but that idea, even with John, was frightening to me.

12.

Joe

I was twenty-nine years old and still unmarried, something almost unthinkable at the time. I had achieved my childhood dream of becoming a movie star and then left it all behind for a second career as a serious actor. Yet despite my success, I could feel myself unraveling. The years I'd spent in Reslocks as a child had made me resourceful and fiercely determined. But like all children who learn independence too young, I'd never had a chance to build the emotional reserves needed for adult life, and I was beginning to pay the price.

It was hard to end *The Hustler*. I again needed to do something useful with my hands to save me. I decided to build a massive kitchen counter across one wall of my apartment, above the radiator. It was mounted on heavy plywood and covered with dozens of two-inch tiles that I had collected in both brilliant and muted colors, some in interesting sculpture-like relief. They were the experiments of a unique tile company that I'd found downtown. When I finished the mosaic, I moved on to the already-existing counter on the other wall. The finished counters were quite beautiful. I had built them as independent units so that they could be removed, but when I moved ten years later, I chose to leave them behind. Actors are used to that. We often leave behind fabulous unrecorded stage performances. Perhaps it enriches the heavens.

I finally received word that *The Hustler* had been edited and was ready to screen. I was invited to attend a large screening the studio had arranged at Fox in midtown Manhattan, with hundreds of people invited. It should have been one of the high points of my career. Instead, I was so profoundly disappointed that it took years for me to recover.

It was the first time I had seen the completed film, and it simply wasn't what I expected. I had seen it all so vividly in my mind's eye when I'd read the script that I suppose I'd unconsciously made directing and editing choices as the story popped off the page and into my vision. While we were working, I believed I put all of that out of my head, and concentrated on my character, never really focusing on where the camera was, unaware of what the camera was "seeing." Some actors always know where the camera is; I don't like to. I'd be a better film actor if I did. My first subjective expectations of the film were so totally different from what was actually shot. That night as I watched it, the hard work was all I could see, not Fast Eddie and Sarah. Through my distorted eyes, it appeared that Paul and I were just Paul and I, struggling. I was much too close to it. It took fifteen years to pass for me to see the genius of what was done, of editor Dede Allen's brilliant work. How perfect the movie is. I saw how wrenchingly sensitive Paul's Fast Eddie was, and how brave. He made me weep over my own (Sarah's) death. It's a pity it took me so long to see it.

There were lots of subsequent screenings of *The Hustler*, and though I did not attend them, I heard about them. Everyone seemed to love the movie, even the critics. I couldn't understand people's reactions. It seemed to me that everyone had lost their ability to be discerning, or else it was a conspiracy of bullshit. Despite my feelings, I did some public relations for the film out of loyalty to Bob Rossen, including a press interview or two. One of the interviews was with Mike Wallace. He interviewed Rossen, Paul, and me separately, on camera in a little room. I remember I froze when facing his authoritative manner and powerful voice. I became quite tongue-tied, overcome by the old sense of panic, and ultimately it was a noninterview. A year or so later, at a charity event at Madison Square Garden, I saw Mike Wallace again. He put a microphone in front of me and inexplicably, as if we were old friends, gently said, "It's so good to see you, Piper, dear." His "dear" melted me. Had one of us changed? I wondered.

Without a new project to work on, I felt empty once again. Everything seemed to have ended, and I was missing John. He was still shooting in California, and I felt that if he wanted me there, he'd let me know. I was hardly in touch with him at all anymore. In my gut I knew our moment had passed. When Fox flew me to California for a gallery photo session for *The Hustler,* I decided to speak to him. John was just finishing *All Fall Down* at the same studio, so I called when I arrived at the lot and told him I was there and wanted to see him. We arranged to meet when we finished for the day on his soundstage, a re-creation of the exterior of a house. When I got there, the stage was deserted except for Warren Beatty, who told me John would probably be along shortly. We stood there for a few minutes talking, and the not-yet-married Warren said something nice about my mouth. I thanked him, and then John appeared, and Warren said goodnight to us both.

After a moment I asked John, "What's going on? Things are strange between us."

There was a short silence, and then he said, "I've met someone who is very good for me."

Sitting down on a fake tree stump, I predicted hopefully, "I think I have, too."

John said, "Her name is Evans Evans."

"Are you joking?"

"No, that's really her name."

I told John I had met someone as well, and we parted a few moments later. I don't remember if we kissed or hugged; I was just feeling a lot of pain and sadness. I didn't see John for another eighteen years.

John wasn't the man I chose to marry. I met Joe Morgenstern soon after I had seen the first screening of *The Hustler,* and I was still in shock. My apartment remained unfurnished, with not a thing on any of the walls. I was taking amphetamines throughout the day just to keep from disappearing, and I drank heavily to bring sleep. I don't know where or how I spent the days. In the midst of my anger and despair, Joe Morgenstern came to my apartment to interview me for the late, great *New York Herald Tribune*. On the morning of the interview, I'd just come from the dentist, and having refused Novocain, I was in pain. I excused myself while the publicist kept Mr. Morgenstern company, and I had a slug of vodka in the kitchen to get me through the interview. I did not normally drink during the day, but this interview was the last thing I wanted to do, and I was hurting.

Joe Morgenstern was the second-string drama critic to the highly respected Walter Kerr. He had come to interview me for a cover piece in the Sunday section of the paper. Joe was very young, so modest and shy, wearing slightly baggy trousers and a nicely worn jacket. I didn't know then that Judith Crist, his boss, had given him an assignment to see the Molly Kazan plays off Broadway months before, and Joe had gone back on his own to see me in my pink organza costume a second time. When we finished the interview and he left, I waited with him at the door until the elevator came. Standing there with his head down, he looked up at me for a moment, and I saw a flash of his deep vulnerability, which I'm sure he wished he had kept hidden. But I saw it, and it moved me very much.

A few days after the interview, Joe sent me a clever note and some glue-on picture hangers, a not-too-subtle suggestion that I put something on my blank walls. He called two weeks later and asked if I wanted to take a drive to the country and have dinner. I thought he had some courage to ask. In all the hundreds of interviews I'd done, no one had ever asked me out. Joe showed up for our date in a very small car that needed washing, and I found that refreshing. He was *very* smart, witty, and extremely articulate, the golden gift that I envied. I, of course, was on my best behavior because he was still writing his piece about me.

After that first dinner, he invited me to a gorgeous afternoon concert in the country that seemed to cleanse me. He continued to find ways to involve himself in my life, though I resisted. *The Hustler* was about to be released, and at the moment, during this time of immaturity, I despised everything wonderful that it had been for me. Waves of depression and anger would wash over me, and I only wanted to stay home, just working on my tile counters. Joe repeatedly called and tried to get me to leave the apartment, but I didn't want to see anybody and asked him to stay away. But he persisted, and sometimes I would weaken, and we would make love. He began to think he could save me from myself. At the time he didn't know who that self was, and I told him as much. He had no idea of the extent of sexual freedom I had enjoyed in that repressed time. Compared to me, he was relatively inexperienced. He also had no idea I relied on pills just to get through the days and that I just wanted to disappear. But Joe wouldn't have it. He wanted to fix everything, to take care of me. At that moment I actually wanted very much to be taken care of. I knew he was throwing me a lifeline, but it seemed dishonest to grab on, so I flailed about, sometimes thinking all I needed was new, stimulating work.

I was still being asked to do public relations for *The Hustler*. On a plane traveling to Washington, D.C., with Bob Rossen to screen the film, he asked me about doing another movie with him in Europe. It sounded like *Lilith*, from the way he described the story. He wanted to know how I felt about working with him again, and I said I'd love to. But then, because I considered him a friend, I told him I had decided to marry Joe. Bob's face suddenly fell and turned angry. The movie was never mentioned after that, and Bob made the movie with Jean Seberg. No comfort to me that it was neither a critical nor commercial success.

Depression and illness produce mysterious behavior. In the end, I agreed to marry Joe Morgenstern because I saw a glimmer of hope. He was completely unlike any of the men I had ever been close to. For one thing, he was a hell of a lot smarter.

I didn't want a big wedding. I had been married so many times in films, I thought a small ceremony would make it seem more real. We decided to get married in California, where my family was. The wedding took place the day before my thirtieth birthday in my sister's living room in Long Beach, with only the immediate family present. My mother and father; my grandma; my mother's sister, Ethel, and her husband, Uncle Phil; Mother's brother Manny; my sister, Sherrye, and her husband, Mel. Two of Sherrye's children, Michael and his sweet sister,

Robin, watched from the hallway while people took turns holding Sherrye's newborn infant, Steven. Joe's mother Molly, a genuinely gracious woman, flew in from New York to be there. Joe wore a suit, and I dressed in a simple, knee-length white silk skirt that my friend Theoni Aldredge designed for me and a pretty lace blouse I'd had for years.

Rabbi Marin officiated. He had been our rabbi since I was ten, confirmed me in the synagogue when I was thirteen, and married my sister Sherrye and her husband in an elaborate ceremony when Sherrye was seventeen. He had kept in touch with me after I left home, taking me to lunch occasionally when I was in L.A. to impress on me the importance of marrying young. I had resisted marriage for so many years; he must have been almost as relieved as my parents that it was finally happening. It was a traditional Jewish ceremony in both Hebrew and English, with a chuppah (canopy) covering us. Joe put the ring on my forefinger first, according to tradition, which says there is a vein in that finger that goes most directly to the heart. I moved the ring to the traditional ring finger of my left hand when the ceremony was over. Joe stomped hard on the glass (carefully wrapped in a napkin), breaking it with a loud crunch as everyone shouted, "Mazel tov!"

We left the house immediately after the ceremony, and Frank McFadden guided us through the press outside my sister's small home as they snapped pictures of me in my wedding outfit. Joe and I went directly to a nearby hospital to see dear Edna, who was too ill to attend. She was very weak but happy to meet Joe and gave us her blessing. Afterward we returned to the house for the reception. Still wanting to keep things as low key as possible, I had requested Chinese takeout food from a local restaurant. I wanted everything to be no-fuss, but Joe's mother was outraged by the lack of elegant food. She felt that the food should befit an important occasion and blamed my parents for the decision. She wouldn't believe it was my decision and never got over the "Chinese takeout reception."

We flew to Morocco for the honeymoon. I really didn't care where we went and I let Joe choose. I could afford a nice trip, and Joe picked beautiful Morocco. To me, it looked very much like the back lot at Universal where I'd filmed all those Arabian Nights movies ten years before. The highlights of the trip for me were picking samples from an abandoned amethyst mine to take home, and the day I looked up and saw one of my heroes, Winston Churchill, on his balcony overlooking the Hotel La Mamounia's garden. It was his regular vacation spot. I couldn't believe my eyes, but yes, he was truly there, probably for one of the last times.

When we got home from the honeymoon, I found I had been chosen to be "Woman of the Year" by Harvard's Hasty Pudding Club. I was dumbfounded and pleased. Joe and I flew to Boston and were entertained in a daylong celebration. There was a parade, a luncheon, and a stage production of *The Hustler*—in drag. What a marvelous day!

Despite my personal disappointment with the film, *The Hustler* was getting a lot of attention and critical acclaim. Unbelievably, I was nominated in 1961 for an Academy Award as Best Actress for my portrayal of Sarah. Paul was nominated as Best Actor; George C. Scott and Jackie Gleason for Best Supporting Actor; and Bob Rossen for writing, directing, and producing.

Sadly, the nomination meant so very little to me then. I'm sorry now that I wasn't at a place in my life where I could have enjoyed that sort of thing. I thought it was silly to measure performances in the first place. (I still do, but I have learned to accept an honor and, to some extent, enjoy it.) I hated the whole idea of performances in competition. There were more important things going on in the world. It was the early 1960s, a time of turmoil. The civil rights movement had begun. U.S. military advisers were beginning to participate in Vietnam. The fuss over a movie seemed all wrong.

I chose not to fly to California to attend the awards ceremony. The Academy told me I must ask someone to accept the award for me just in case, so I called Joanne Woodward, who would be at the presentation with Paul. I found her in the wardrobe department at Fox and asked her to accept for me in case I won. She said, "Of course, darling, I'd love to." "Darling" was said with such warmth and ease that I remember thinking I'd love to be able to use such words with people I cared about, and in such a natural way. From time to time I was still verbally challenged.

Joe and I remained in New York and spent Oscar night at my mother-in-law's apartment. We sat at a small card table in front of the TV and ate dinner while we watched the broadcast. When they announced my name as a nominee, I felt my face get hot and turn red, just as it used to in school. And there were only three of us in the room! I was so grateful not to be at the actual ceremony. Sophia Loren won that year for her extraordinary work in *Two Women*.

In spite of my Oscar nomination, good scripts just seemed to disappear around the time I got married. Suddenly there were no interesting offers. The ones I got were all similar to the character of Sarah in *The Hustler*, primarily sad or crippled girls, though the quality of the scripts was not as good and the characters far less rich. Apparently I had been stereotyped once again. Why was I surprised? Did I think the nature of the people producing and casting these things had changed? Later on I was told the reason was that *The Hustler* was in black and white, and I had made myself look drab and a little mousy in the role. I was told I should have worn a fitted slip and a push-up bra in the bathroom scene when I wrote on the mirror. I seemed to be just not quite sexy and attractive enough for standard American movies. This after my struggle to live down my glamour years at Universal. I had come full circle.

I decided not to wait any longer for other people to bring me good projects so we could pay our bills. Instead I asked my friend Bob Richards to direct me in a summer stock tour of a comedy in which I would star. Our relationship had long ago become strictly platonic. He flew out from California for the tour. I picked a comedy, *Wedding Breakfast*, and chose to do a supporting part because it was the comic role. Karen Sharpe, who later married Stanley Kramer, played the romantic lead. The standout performance that summer was when a bat came down to the stage one night and tried to make friends with Karen when she was out there alone. I could hear the audience screaming on the speaker in my dressing room as Karen dashed about on stage in her slip, the bat in hot pursuit.

When the tour of *Wedding Breakfast* ended, Bob returned to California, where he found our dear mutual friend, director Jim Yarbrough, in a depressed state. Jim had not had any directing offers for a long while. Though they'd had a bisexual period earlier in their lives, Jim and Bob had settled into a committed partnership, and they still shared a Hollywood Hills home. Though Jim never verbalized it, I think he felt particularly vulnerable with Bob away for weeks doing what Jim considered his work. I'm sure he understood that I was giving an opportunity to Bob, who also needed work and wasn't getting any as an actor. Jim had gone through weeks of torturous and expensive dental work while Bob was gone. No wonder he was depressed.

A few weeks after returning to California, Bob came home one day to find Jim unconscious. He had swallowed a bottle of sleeping pills. There was not yet a 911 to call, and it was a slow process getting help. Bob tried desperately to resuscitate Jim, forcing coffee down him, slapping him vigorously, and trying to get him on his feet and moving while he waited for help to come. By the time the police finally arrived at the house, Jim's face was swollen from the pills and beginning to show bruises from Bob's attempts to revive him. The police immediately jumped to the conclusion that it had been a "lovers' quarrel" and arrested Bob for Jim Yarbrough's murder.

Catherine McLeod, our mutual friend in L.A., called me in New York immediately to tell me that Jim had died and that Bob had been arrested for his murder. There was no time to mourn or dwell on the horror. I immediately called one of the smartest people I knew, Joe Strick, the husband of my friend Anne, and asked him to recommend a criminal lawyer. He said, "If my brother's life were at stake, I would hire Ned Nelson. He's the best."

I immediately called Nelson and hired him. In the long, drawn-out weeks before the trial, Bob remained in jail. When the case finally came to trial a few months later, it was thrown out in the first five minutes. We had been confident it would be; clearly Bob was innocent, and we had hoped it would happen earlier. But because of that one day in court, the full fee was owed to the attorney. It was a lot of money, and it would take a while for me to make that kind of money again, but it was a blessing for me to do this for a friend and to know that I could.

Bob never really recovered from the ordeal. He was devastated losing his partner and dear friend of so many years. He suffered for a long time. He finally gave up on being an actor; there had been a lot of bad publicity. He just wanted employment, any employment. But if he told the truth to potential employers, that yes, he had been arrested, and why, they wouldn't hire him. If he didn't tell and it was discovered later on, he would be fired. It was all deeply painful. Eventually he joined forces with his mother, and they moved into a small house in South Central Los Angeles. They were the only white family in a black neighborhood, but as the years passed, they became a respected and loved part of the community. They planted beautiful fruit trees in front of their house and grew their own vegetables. His mother was a dedicated baker who wouldn't think of buying a loaf of bread, and over the years I had many delicious, nutritious meals at their house. It was a humble home, but I think Bob found peace there. I visited him whenever I was in town. Bob and I remained friends for life, and I employed him as a coach and flew him east whenever I had a job.

Losing Jim took a toll on me. We had grown very close. It was difficult losing him in such a frightening and sudden way. He had been a generous man. He was the one who had dared to give me my first job on live TV, which changed the course of my career. He took a big chance for me and for Bob.

The stress of Jim's death put further strain on my new marriage, which was already rocky. Our first years together were filled with horrific arguments. In so many basic ways, Joe and I seemed to be ill suited for each other. I was sleeping with the enemy, for God's sake! I was an actress and Joe was a journalist, a critic, my natural enemy, and we disagreed on almost everything, including my career. Joe thought I turned down too many offers, that I wanted too much. He wasn't used to my playing it so close to my pocketbook. But what I was being offered didn't interest me, and the whole point of leaving Universal six years earlier had been so I could have the freedom to choose my own projects. Live New York television was rapidly dying; everything on television was moving west and being put on tape or film, and I didn't want to live in California. I was accustomed to trying to do without and waiting for good work. I'm not sure that made sense to Joe.

We were at opposite poles intellectually and emotionally. I felt he sincerely wanted to take care of me, but he was young (my age), and he didn't have the experience or the emotional and financial resources that he wished, and we struggled. I suppose Joe was at last beginning to believe what I'd been telling him: for lack of a better phrase, how very screwed up I was. I honestly don't know why he stayed. I stayed, I suppose, because when we'd married, I had made a vow before God. But something else unknown was holding us together. I respected his intellect and wanted him to think I measured up a little, which he clearly found difficult to do at times. But we both persevered.

I drank a lot in the evenings during those years, and I was using amphetamines heavily. Joe knew about the drinking, but he didn't know about the amphetamines because I was deeply ashamed. I had ongoing prescriptions in at least three pharmacies, two in New York and one in California. Doctors wrote prescriptions without a word about the side effects, which were little understood at the time, so I took one whenever I felt I needed it, which was most of the time. I had discovered during my studio days that taking a pill before going into a social situation gave me a burst of false courage. I relied on the pills more and more over the years, and by the time I married Joe, I couldn't function very well socially without them and was completely dependent on them to perform. My need had grown so that I'd hide pills in the wings, on the set, or in a costume pocket to have ready when my energy faded. I tried to anticipate my need so that I would always be ahead of it. When doing *Rosemary* and *The Alligators*, terrified that I would not get through the performance, I used to put a pill inside the little changing tent on stage, hidden behind a tissue. I would swallow it down during a performance with the help of a hard candy if water were not available. In the early stage of rehearsals, or if I felt nothing spectacular would be required of me, I would try to cut back on my use for a while, so that when I started performances, I wouldn't have to take as much. In the aftermath of Jim's suicide, I was convinced that the amphetamines kept me from falling into even deeper depression.

Joe didn't know about the pills, but he certainly knew about my nicotine addiction. He had used every kind of bribery imaginable to get me to stop or even cut back on smoking cigarettes. I didn't want to stop. I had no intention of doing so, and therefore I had never tried. I could do nothing without a cigarette in my mouth, except act or make love. I normally had at least three or four going in ashtrays in the same room. I loved lighting them. Cigarettes were an indispensable part of my diet and life. Getting me to quit smoking seemed hopeless, so Joe tried to get me to smoke cigars and not to inhale as a sort of lesser evil, and he finally found a cigar that hit the spot. It was honey-dipped and sweet-smelling like a pipe, nice and fat to hold, with an attached soft wooden filter to bite. A wholly different but nice sensory experience. Joe gave me a few "don't inhale" lessons on how to draw on the cigar very gently. The idea was to wean me away from the nicotine, and eventually it worked. I began to prefer the cigars to cigarettes, and after a while I was smoking only cigars. It never bothered me, I must say, when people stared at me puffing away on a fat cigar. My mother, of course, was outraged. About three years later I stopped the cigars when they made me feel queasy and was surprised to find myself nicotine free.

Nearly two years had passed without any offers of meaningful work, and we were running low on money. Journalists don't make much, and I had spent a good deal of my savings on Bob Richards's legal defense. The financial worry added to the pressure on the marriage, and the months without work ate away at my self-esteem. Then one day I received a script written for TV by a fine writer named David Rayfiel, who once had been married to Maureen Stapleton. The film was called *Something About Lee Wiley* and was to be directed by a very young and unknown Sydney Pollack. It was about the jazz singer Lee Wiley, a popular artist of the 1940s, 1950s, and early 1960s, who'd gone blind for a period of her life. The cast was extraordinary: Claude Rains, Alfred Ryder, Ruth White, and Steve Hill. I couldn't turn down the opportunity to play this unique woman. I decided to do the film, even though it meant going to California.

Joe and I flew to L.A. and stayed at a motel to conserve money. I was feeling anxious about the initial meeting with everyone and explaining my thoughts about the script. It had been a couple of years since I finished shooting *The Hustler*, and I felt very much out of the movie business. I had really regressed in those years. I found myself leaning on Joe like a child and refused to go to the meeting by myself. I begged Joe to go with me, and he did. In retrospect, it was awful that he was there, speaking on my behalf, but at the time I couldn't face it alone.

I sat on the floor at the meeting, leaning against the wall while we talked. Joe sat on the floor near me. Sydney Pollack sat on the floor, too, on the other side of the room. Rayfiel and the producers were in chairs. I felt like a fearful child and was both ashamed and grateful that Joe was expressing my thoughts. I spoke up occasionally when I thought Joe wasn't getting it exactly right, and I also answered no when asked if I wanted to do the singing myself. I really wanted to say yes, but I was afraid again. They hired a band singer to do it, and I always felt I would have done a better job, but I was cowardly. That's a sin in my book.

Even so, it turned out to be a terrific and really interesting show. Sydney was extremely good to work with and had a light touch with the actors. He deservedly was nominated for an Emmy. The best part for me was working with Ruth White again and with that warrior Claude Rains, whose body of work continues to thrill me. I had read how challenging and exciting it was for Bette Davis to work with Rains and still retain her relevance and power within a scene, so I was somewhat prepared for a battle. I decided no tricks; I would be focused on the specifics of the work, intense in my thought processes, listening purely, "using" everything he gave me. Not a moment would be dishonest. If he stole the scene from me with theatrical tricks, I reasoned, what was left of my work would stand on its own, and I would be proud of it. I found the actual experience of working with him exhilarating and fun, though it was a very serious scene. Claude was truly wonderful, and I think I held my own.

Next to working with Claude Rains, I especially treasured the experience of singing all the songs, even though I was lip-synching. Sometimes on breaks, the live band would play for me, and I would sing with them. What a treat! They had brought together some great musicians. It pleased me that a few of them asked why I wasn't singing the songs myself. But it was too late; I had missed the boat.

When we got back to New York after shooting the film, Joe and I became friends with the real Lee Wiley. Lee still has a cult following, but she was a regular gal. The three of us watched the broadcast of the movie together in her apartment. I think we all drank a lot that evening; it was a scary event for all of us. It was too bad we couldn't have used her voice, her recordings in the film, but she no longer had legal control over how her voice could be used, and her recordings were too expensive for the show's budget.

Working again had been very good for me, and it wasn't long before another offer came in. After the intensity of the Lee Wiley show, Joe and I were in Vermont enjoying the fall foliage when a phone call came, offering me the part of Laura in Tennessee Williams's *The Glass Menagerie*. This was to be the twentieth anniversary of the original Broadway production. Assuming things went well, the production would be going to Broadway after a few weeks in New Jersey at the Paper Mill Playhouse. Maureen Stapleton would be playing Amanda; George Grizzard, Tom; and Pat Hingle, the Gentleman Caller. Extraordinary! This would be my first time on Broadway.

I was excited by the opportunity, but I was not overjoyed at playing what I felt was a cliché character, the poor crippled girl. My character was based on Tennessee Williams's schizophrenic sister, and she had long been stereotyped as weak and fragile. Bob Richards came east to work with me and, through our conversations, helped me to have the courage to play her as the person I thought she really might be under all that wispiness. Laura was real, and I played her with the humor and the passions we all have. I also worked very hard on my voice. I was playing an almost nonverbal shy person, something I knew a bit about. It was too easy to tuck my voice inside myself and not be heard. Bob helped me overcome that. With Bob at the other end of my apartment, about three large rooms away, I tried having a conversation with him. I found some muscles in my body, in my belly, that I only used when I truly needed to be heard a distance away. Of course, some good breathing was involved. The emotional content didn't change. I found the most important thing was my brain's desire for me to be heard.

Rehearsals for *The Glass Menagerie* were held in a midtown rehearsal hall. We had three weeks in the rehearsal hall before opening at the Paper Mill. George Keathley, the director, was pleasant and had a light hand. We would be using a reproduction of the original set by Jo Mielziner, and George showed us pictures. Rehearsals went well. The "gentleman caller" scene was such fun to do, with as much joy as riding a merry-go-round. Pat Hingle was terrific. He was slightly too old for the part, but he was so good, it didn't really matter. He gave me so much, and the work seemed to be growing and deepening.

Maureen was supremely intelligent and amazingly strong, but life was difficult for her. Her phobias would sometimes overwhelm her. When we went over to New Jersey to begin previews, I had to hold on to her to keep her from jumping from the car as we rode through the long tunnel. Every night just before the play started, Maureen and I would sit in terror at the little table on stage behind the scrim, grasping hands and belching to relieve the tension. Some nights we were very loud, and we wondered if the audience on the other side of the scrim could hear us. It turned out they could. Maureen was the only one of the cast who had actually seen the legendary performance with Laurette Taylor twenty years earlier. Poor Maureen—she was haunted by Laurette Taylor's performance and couldn't shake her inhibitions until her very last night with us many months later. Her performance that night was one of those recorded in heaven. I was touched by something miraculous being with her on stage that night. She was the most gifted actress I had ever worked with. I loved her very much, and we remained friends for a very long time.

When previews ended in New Jersey, we played about eight or nine months on Broadway, and a lot of friends came to see us. Paul Newman and Joanne Woodward came backstage after one performance, and Joanne wanted to know if all the long hair was really mine. It wasn't. I had added a bit of a "fall" for Laura. Funny what actresses say to other actresses, very little about acting unless we ask for it. But asking takes a lot of courage, and an honest answer could very well damage an actor's self-confidence, so few of us take the risk. Kim Stanley also came to see the show one night, and I sat in Maureen's dressing room afterward chatting with her. She said nothing about our performances but leaned over and whispered in my ear a suggestion that I use brown, rather than black, eyeliner. That was her only "criticism." If she had been critical about the work, it would have destroyed me. Years later she asked to direct me in her *Hedda Gabler*—a dream that never happened.

Some critics (I read them later) couldn't accept my interpretation of Laura and scolded me for it. Others, and more important Tennessee Williams himself, who attended many performances, felt it was the first time his sister had been portrayed properly. His sister was a real person, not just a fragile girl defined by her handicap. He always felt his sister was the strongest one of the whole family.

I often cut back on amphetamines in the early stages of rehearsing a project, saving them for the boost I would need as the actual performances drew near. I had cut back during rehearsals for *Menagerie*, waiting until the preview drew near to begin again. But on our last day in the midtown rehearsal hall, I thought, *The work is going* pretty *well. Hold off a little. Wait as long as possible.* I made a decision to wait until we were actually working in front of the audience at the first preview before starting the pills. On opening night Tennessee Williams and about four hundred people were out there in the audience, waiting for us to begin. My plan, as always, was to take the first pill a short time after the stage manager called half hour. That would be enough time for it to take effect. But I thought about how solid our work in the rehearsal hall seemed to be. A voice in my head said, *Hey, hey, Rosetta, wait a minute, take a chance. Maybe you don't need it. The work is full and good.* I let the half hour slide away. The stage manager called fifteen minutes—and then five. The time was gone. *It's too late. Too late!* I was terrifically excited; I was on my own! I was so high, and filled with self-esteem and God's grace, that when places were called, I knew I was no longer a prisoner and soared through the performance, and then another one the next day, and another. I have sailed, and sometimes fought, through performances and through life for forty-five years now, without once taking another amphetamine. I believe I did my best work after this, and it was all me, good and bad.

I was so ashamed of my secret that I didn't tell Joe about any of it until about three years later. I wanted to be sure that the change was real. It still seems incredible that he didn't know, but he didn't. That amazing experience freed me from the guilt I'd had for a good part of my life, my fear that my gifts were not genuine but chemically produced. It also, not incidentally, protected me from the drug culture years when they came along soon after. I would have been a sitting duck for all that. Instead, because I was too fearful to try even pot, I am the straightest of all my friends. I was so high on clarity and reality that I never lacked for a buzz or a stimulant. Every once in a while, when life is challenging and working hours are long, I drink plenty of water or a cup of tea—and for celebrations, an occasional beer or glass of wine. Once sober, I wanted to see and experience every bit of the real world.

Adding more excitement to our run, the cast of *The Glass Menagerie* was asked to do a command performance at the Lyndon Johnson White House. Maureen and George Grizzard would do the scene when Amanda hears that the Gentleman Caller has been invited to dinner, and Pat Hingle and I would do most of the "gentleman caller" scene.

When we got out of the limo at the White House that afternoon, each carrying our own costumes like traveling players, I was told to find the "bathroom upstairs." I started up the wide stairway, not a soul in sight, and found myself in a spacious hallway where I finally spotted the clearly marked ladies' room. It was a big, sterile-looking room with a large mirror and a small sofa. I proceeded to get out of my dress and into my costume. But after several attempts, I realized it was impossible for me to zip it up by myself. My dresser had always done it for me. It seemed to be caught halfway up, but I couldn't see to uncatch it.

I opened the door and peered out. There was no one in sight. The hall was completely deserted. I called, "Hulloooo—anybody there?" There was no answer. This was creepy. No people! Who was running the country? I came back in and hoped that perhaps Maureen would be coming along soon. I waited. After a while I decided that she must have gone to a different ladies' room. I was beginning to panic. It was almost time to start. What was I going to do?

Suddenly the door opened. I was saved! In came a tiny woman. Of course, I recognized her—anybody would. It was the legendary Helen Hayes, who was to be part of the program. Close to tears and not wasting any time, I said to this tiny icon, "Would you please zip me up?"

"Of course, dear—there you are!" she replied, and zipped me up as if it were nothing. I thanked her and ran down the staircase in time to start my scene.

I think Pat and I were pretty good. Afterward we rubbed elbows with the special guests at the reception and met Lady Bird Johnson, who, as we all know, was charming. She apologized for the president, who had to attend a meeting and "had missed something truly wonderful."

When *Menagerie* was over, I remained friends with Maureen. She adored my husband, Joe, who she thought was brilliant. And so he was. He was now doing movie criticism for *Newsweek* magazine. Sometimes Maureen would call and beg for company or just let off steam about something. Once it was right after she'd thrown all her husband's possessions out the window into the street when she thought he was cheating. Out for a stroll one day, Maureen and I chased my old friend Rock Hudson down Columbus Avenue as he outran us, trying to avoid what he thought were screaming fans. The louder we called "Rock!" the faster he ran without once turning around. Maureen and I remained close until she left the city permanently years later.

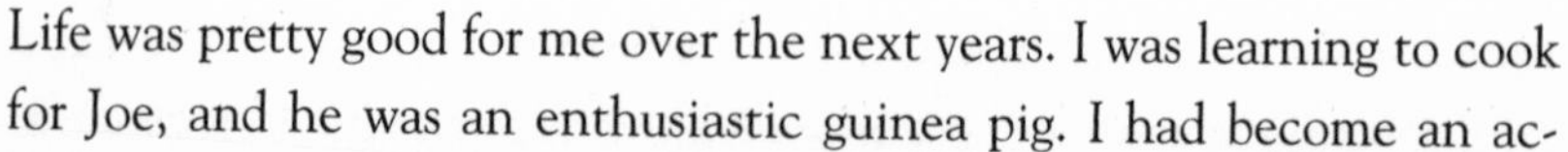

Life was pretty good for me over the next years. I was learning to cook for Joe, and he was an enthusiastic guinea pig. I had become an accomplished bread baker through trial and error; good enough so that Ray Sokolov at the *New York Times* did a half-page piece on my bread baking that included some of my recipes. I was thirty-seven years old, hadn't made a movie in eight years, not since *The Hustler*, and I didn't care.

I decided to give myself a meaningful gift and go back to art school. When I was eleven, my parents had sent my sister and me to art classes at the Otis Art Institute in Los Angeles. I have no idea how they paid for it. We took the Wilshire bus downtown every day during the summer to study design, life drawing, charcoal sketching, perspective, and still life. At fourteen Sherrye was sophisticated and quite developed for her age, so I, in effect, was the only child in those classes, and I had a problem with the life drawing. Too immature to be casual about the nude models, I felt it would be rude to look at them, so I pretended to draw and instead stared at all the adult students to see how they were behaving in these extraordinary circumstances of casual public nudity. Nevertheless, I had continued drawing and painting through high school and always felt connected to the visual arts.

Now, years later, I enrolled at the Art Students League on West 57th in Manhattan. It's a legendary old school, with a history of famous artists as teachers since 1875. I signed up for a life drawing class to limber up my hand and my eye. One day I left my easel and took a little walk in the building, where I noticed a handwritten sign on a wall with an arrow pointing "to the sculpture class." I followed the arrow, which led me to another sign with an arrow pointing down the stairs to the basement. Following the arrow downstairs and through a long corridor, I heard tinkling music in the distance that grew increasingly louder as I walked. It was a heavenly sound, like nothing I'd ever heard before. When I turned a corner, I could see an open room with a small group of people striking on pieces of stone and marble with metal tools, making the loveliest and most original music I'd ever heard while they created their marble treasures. I had never seen people carve stone before. The room looked as if it had been snowing, with men and women of various ages wearing dust masks. As I stood there gazing at the scene, a beautiful young Japanese woman walked up to me, removing her mask and gloves, revealing perfectly manicured long red nails. She said she was Flory, the monitor, and told me, "The maestro will be here any minute."

Just as she spoke, Maestro José de Creeft, a small, wiry man of eighty-five, entered the studio, bursting with electric energy. Waving his arms, he signaled everyone in the room to follow as he critiqued the students' work. I quickly made myself a part of the group and followed him from piece to piece as he expressed himself in a passionate mix of Spanish, English, and hand gestures. He seemed to have forgotten the names of the students as he talked. I was now at his side, not wanting to miss a thing, when he suddenly turned to me and said, "Where is your work? What is your name?"

"I'm Rosetta," I told him. "I don't have anything. I haven't started yet." (I knew already that I would.) The maestro gestured for the group to follow and, turning to me, said with a heavy accent, "Get your boyfriend to get you the biggest piece of marble he can carry, put it in his car, and bring it through the back door. Don't make cookies like these ladies." He pointed to some women who were working on small pieces. I was very excited. Flory told me where to go downtown for a few simple tools and a block of marble.

It was thrilling, picking out my piece of marble. It took me a long time to decide. When I'd made up my mind, it was loaded into the backseat of the car, as Joe and I watched the seat sink under the dense weight. Oh well, it was only a car. When we arrived at the hidden back door of the Art Students League, a secret knock brought two men with a dolly and plenty of muscle. I said goodbye to Joe and followed my beautiful block of Vermont marble into the studio, where it was placed on a pedestal that turned. I spent the next four days walking around it. Admiring it. Loving that I possessed it. The block was about thirty inches high, perhaps twenty inches across. It was so white, with just a tinge of green showing on its flat surface. All my life I had collected rocks and minerals. My specimens of crystals were small and beautiful, from the earth. But this piece of Vermont was majestic, and I loved it more than anything I had ever owned. I met Joe in a restaurant for dinner after class one day and remember talking about the stone's power, its permanence. I felt it could never be destroyed. I felt so calm and happy inside just possessing it.

But it appeared that I was incapable of working on it. I could see no future for it beyond what it was. Every day I would go to class and circle it, touching it occasionally, walking around, not wanting it to change. Finally my classmate Tom Vanderzel, who had been watching me for days, grew impatient and said, "Oh, Rosetta, just chomp into it!"

With that, I thought, *Yes, I'll do that.*

Accepting the push, I took a deep breath, stepped forward, and chomped lightly at the top corner with my chisel and hammer. Off came a chip that revealed a sweet, pale vein, like something from the first extraordinary "in the womb" photographs I had seen. I knew immediately what I would carve. For the next seven months, every day the League was open, eight hours a day, I worked on it. I worked only with hand tools. The maestro, who was a friend and contemporary of Picasso, felt strongly about not using power tools. I could have cut my time from seven months to about one if I'd used them, but the result of using one's hand is very different, the maestro felt, warmer and more alive. I was excited always in this long process, and I never became impatient, roughly blocking the marble; then gently bush hammering so as not to bruise deeply into the stone; then smoothing and filing with metal tools and various textures of stones with water; and finally polishing with many grades of increasingly fine sandpaper and water, until the curves were smooth and the surface felt like silk. It was beautiful seeing the transformation of the stone. I was taught to believe that the form was much more important than the material, but I couldn't suppress the thrill of seeing and studying the crystals as they sparkled in front of me on the rough stone. It was the same thrill I had felt as a child at discovering a pretty rock and breaking it open. I was filled with contentment.

Many months later, when I had finished my first piece, *The Twenty-fifth Day*, the maestro petted and stroked "the baby," as he called it, and wanted it to go into a show at Macy's. I missed the deadline, but the piece had its moment in the sun a few years later in a gallery show with more of my work. It sits in my living room today.

I had discovered in the years since my marriage that there were some perks to being the wife of a movie critic. Seeing movies was part of Joe's job, and after sculpture class I would often meet him for a Chinese dinner and the movie he was covering. In 1967 Joe was asked to do a cover story for *Newsweek* on Charlie Chaplin, who was directing what was to be his last movie: *The Countess from Hong Kong*, starring Marlon Brando and Sophia Loren. The film was being shot in London, so we went to England for several weeks. With all the traveling I'd done, it was the first time I'd ever been there. Each morning I'd buy a red rose or carnation from the hotel flower shop and stick it in the lapel of my new white raincoat. Then I'd go exploring museums while Joe sat on the set.

I don't enjoy going onto other people's sets—an outside person is often quite intrusive—but eventually I couldn't resist this one. I went just one day and saw the headstrong Brando being a pussycat for director Chaplin, who carefully blocked the movements and gestured for Brando to copy, which indeed he did. Brando imitated every movement so very carefully. I couldn't believe it, but I saw it with my own eyes. Obviously he had great love and respect for Chaplin. If there were problems later on, on that day I didn't see them.

Chaplin's producer had promised Joe interview time, but it never came until Joe finally put his foot down. Chaplin agreed but said he would give Joe only fifteen minutes. We were invited to Chaplin's rented country estate on the weekend to do the interview. Bob Goldstein, the surviving twin brother of my dear friend Leonard, insisted that his car and driver take us there. When Chaplin saw the fancy chauffeured car coming up the long drive, he himself came out to greet us. I was wearing my white raincoat with a fresh red rose and was introduced as Rosie, Joe's wife. I chose not to tell Mr. Chaplin we had met when I was fifteen and he was looking for the girl in *Limelight*. He had been warm and charming that day, and I, silent.

Now it was my turn to be charming so that perhaps he'd let us stay longer. It was just the three of us, and Chaplin sat in a big chair with the coffee table separating us. I was the woman in the room, so Chaplin, now in his eighties, spoke directly to me most of the time. It was easy for me to be a good audience; I was completely captivated and listened spellbound, while Chaplin went on and on as we sipped our tea. The promised fifteen minutes came and went, and several hours passed before we said goodbye.

When we returned home and Joe's story came out in *Newsweek*, we heard that Chaplin was hurt and disappointed. After giving us all that time, it was natural that he expected a completely uncritical love letter. I confess I had felt the same way when Joe did his piece on me. And I'd actually slept with the guy! But Joe is very good at what he does and wrote a somewhat balanced "love letter" of Mr. Chaplin.

One evening not long afterward Joe came home from work and told me that, of all people, G. David Schine had called him at the office. David had invited us to have dinner at the Waldorf Towers with him and his wife! I had not seen David in years, not since we parted at the Smoke House in California. I knew he'd married a beautiful Miss Universe from Sweden and had a family. What was on his mind after all these years? The world had not heard from him, and neither had I. Joe and I were too curious to say no, so I put on the only really well-made dress that still fit me, and we went to the Waldorf Towers, which was the Schines' home when they were in New York.

A pale, slightly bent, gray-faced man answered the door. He shook Joe's hand and said, "I'm David Schine. Come in." I couldn't believe that this was David. I was shocked. The apartment was large and luxurious, and his still-beautiful wife joined us a few minutes later. She looked quite harried, followed by about six little blond children, all under the age of eight, going in every direction like little chickens, until they were quickly removed.

At dinner David told us he had become a theatrical manager and wanted Joe to write a piece about his client. Of course, Joe declined and had to explain that he could not be part of a publicity machine. As he and David talked, I looked at the man across the table from me whom I had come so close to marrying years before and thought that I wouldn't have recognized him on the street. It was sad seeing David's transformation from the six-foot-four Adonis I remembered. I can only imagine how difficult his life had been. The change seemed more spiritual than physical. Joe, who was just a fraction under six feet, seemed taller than David that night.

Another time a few years later, our curiosity took us to David's huge Hancock Park home in L.A. for drinks, and later to a hotel where there was a reception for Bobby Kennedy! Kennedy went around to every table and shook hands with every single person in the room. I was surprised to see that when he shook our hands, even Kennedy had the familiar glazed look in the eyes that overworked celebrities get. He looked right through me and past me as he said his "Nice to meet you." I never saw David Schine again after that night. He and his wife and one of their children were killed in a private plane crash in 1996. A sad ending to a sad life.

In 1969 Joe was asked to write a piece for *Newsweek* about the first landing on the moon. Before the launch, Joe and I traveled around the country by car, getting people's opinions about "men going to the moon." Some of his piece would focus on the thoughts of the American Indian. We went to many reservations, talking in depth with people who had original points of view. When we returned to New York, Joe, who was writing on a deadline, asked me to cover a part of the story for him by going downtown to a school for the blind and finding someone to interview. I took a tape recorder and got a truly wonderful interview from a young boy of fourteen who had never seen the moon but had definite and poetic thoughts about the coming event. I was thrilled that a good chunk of my interview was included in Joe's story. Perhaps there was something else I could do in life.

Joe's piece was magnificent, his writing almost equal to the event, which was the most extraordinary happening of my lifetime. I pity the people who are younger and take the miracle of actually touching the moon for granted. What a night!

Somewhere during those first ten years with Joe, I realized I had left Piper Laurie behind and turned into Rosetta Jacobs Morgenstern, who was starting an entirely new life. The real change happened slowly at first, my becoming healthy and clear-headed and learning that self-esteem, a very powerful drug, comes out of purposeful action. Joe and I had struggled together, but many of those years were self-healing and creative for me thanks to Joe's sense of humor, patience, and generosity of spirit. Over the years I think he and I educated each other. I grew to admire and respect the really fine journalists and critics, of whom he certainly was one. In return, I taught him a little bit about how actors feel and what's not useful to them in published criticism. I think I even gave him some happiness. Our life together was good. Professionally, I was yet to do my best and most fulfilling work, and personally, to achieve the greatest rewards.

13.

Woodstock

Joe and I were still living well in my big Central Park West apartment. But finances were becoming a concern. The general feeling in the business that I was no longer interested in acting after I got married was close to the truth. I certainly didn't want to do what was offered. Journalists are not highly paid people, and without me working, we would soon need to make some changes.

I received an offer to do a television pilot in California, and my instinct was to turn it down, but I hesitated; there were two of us now. It wasn't a bad script, and it would pay the bills for quite a long time. My agent assured me it would never be seen by the public, and I would only be gone for two weeks. He was right. I flew to California, had some scenes with my old friend Rip Torn, laughed a lot, and came home. It paid a year's rent and bought us a new car.

While shooting the pilot, an unusual thing happened. I'd been running across a field in front of the camera, proud that I could still run very fast, when suddenly my legs buckled under me, and I fell to the ground. I got up, dusted myself off, and went on with the scene. We shot it one more time, and again I fell. That was all, and afterward I forgot about it. But a week later, when I was back in the city, I found I couldn't walk. One foot was partially paralyzed, and I was in great pain. I went to see Dr. Walter Thompson, the head of orthopedics at New York University Hospital, who diagnosed me with a congenital spinal disease that I never knew I had. He told me the disease was relatively rare and sometimes seen among Eskimos. I immediately imagined my ancestors from Russia canoeing across the Bering Strait and commingling in Alaska, or perhaps the other way around! Dr. Thompson tended to be conservative in his approach and recommended rest rather than surgery. I was sent to lie flat in bed for as long as it took, until the pain went away.

I was a slugabed all day long. I had to be completely flat, so it was a challenge to read. Joe would be gone all day and come home very late in the evening from seeing movies, so I was on my own most of the time. We put a toaster oven on my bed, and sometimes during the long evenings, I would bake my luxurious and only meal: one good-size potato. I had stayed about ten pounds over my moviemaking weight, and I was trying to keep it there. But even with one potato, my metabolism had been screwed up for so long that my weight was going up! I couldn't exercise, I wouldn't dream of taking any pills, and I no longer wanted to smoke. Finally I was allowed to start isometric exercises, and when I was strong enough, I started a strict regimen of swimming on my back almost every day at the Ansonia in the city. My weight gradually stabilized, and after a while I was able to function reasonably well in spite of great restrictions. I could not complain; many people had far greater challenges.

We could no longer depend on my working, so our lifestyle needed to change. I'm sure this was not the life Joe had imagined he'd have with me. We were devastated at having to give up the big apartment that I'd been in when he'd first met me. I tried hard not to dwell on it. We took a tiny one-bedroom apartment in the back of the building with a view that I despised—of the elevator shaft. I yearned so for the view of the park and reservoir that had been the best part of living there. I knew every tree intimately and what it would do during the changes of the seasons.

We began to look for a place in the country and settled on Woodstock, New York, known primarily as an artists' community. At first we rented for a summer. Eventually, we bought a small and beautiful 1700s farmhouse on two acres that had a large barn with a wood-burning stove that became my studio. Joe had his office in the house. He was still writing for *Newsweek* and would go back and forth to the city and stay in our tiny apartment, which we kept until we could no longer afford it.

We settled comfortably into our new life in Woodstock. I spent most of my time carving stone in my studio; my upper body was still strong. I cooked meals for Joe and brought them to his study. I baked our bread, hundreds of loaves of all kinds, experimenting until baker's yeast became my close companion. Sometimes we'd go into Kingston and have a Chinese feast for five dollars. I joined the Y in Kingston and made the thirty-five-minute drive almost daily for a swim, even during blizzards. We met interesting and good people who have remained our close friends through the years—Grace Wapner, an artist and sculptor, and her intelligent, witty lawyer husband Jerry; and Jane Traum, formerly an actress, now in business with her gifted performer-musician-songwriter-teacher husband, Happy Traum, and their "Homespun Tapes." I had close women friends at last, intelligent, talented women.

I didn't care if I ever worked again as an actress. It seemed a shallow, silly thing for a grown-up person to be doing. My teenage idealism had faded with the years, and I no longer believed I had anything special to offer the world as an actress. There were so many people crying out for social justice. I wanted to participate in the civil rights demonstrations, but I couldn't trust my balance in crowds, and sometimes I needed to use a cane. My limp would have come in handy when I was doing *The Glass Menagerie* and *The Hustler*.

I was carving stone and listening to the news in my studio one day, when I heard that my old friend Ronnie Reagan had been elected governor of California. It was mind-boggling. I couldn't believe it. To me, he was just a reasonably bright actor who was a little more attractive than many people in government and was facile at saying something charming in public at the right time. Charm and likability are qualities that young actors worked hard to develop, and he had plenty of both.

The Woodstock Festival came and went, but there was no sign of it in the town itself. The actual festival was sixty miles away in Bethel.

Some of the locals were not comfortable leaving their homes unoccupied, and not knowing what to expect, they didn't go. A lot of people did go, certain friends and musicians whom we knew, but we did not. And yes, I met Bob Dylan very briefly, in the home of a close friend. He'd come to pick up his little girl, who'd been playing there. I was introduced as Rosie, as I was to everyone in those days. I doubt he associated me with the movie star I'd once been.

But then one day, out of the blue, George Keathley put in a call to Piper Laurie. I hadn't been called that in a long time. George had directed me in *The Glass Menagerie* on Broadway and was now working at the Ivanhoe Theater in Chicago. He had called many times wanting me to do a play there. Finally he suggested *The Innocents*, the play version of Henry James's *Turn of the Screw*. It had been five years since I'd worked on stage and almost ten since I'd made a movie. I was very frightened by the prospect of returning to the stage. I did not yet understand intellectually that doing the difficult thing gave me strength. I knew there were many long monologues in the play, and I was worried about learning them. The facility for memorization needs to be exercised, and I was very rusty. But I was being offered an extremely handsome salary for about eight weeks' work. I felt perhaps it would be possible. I could hide my limp for short periods of time. After much deliberation I decided to do it, and Joe agreed.

I looked all over Woodstock for someone with an English accent to hold the book and cue me. I assumed we'd all be using English accents. We would only have two weeks of rehearsal at the theater, and I needed to be pretty solid with the words when I arrived. The only person in all of Woodstock with an English accent turned out to be a lovely young woman named Elaine Frank, an elegant seamstress with a small child, who designed and made clothes. She came to the house every day for about a month and worked with me. She too became one of my closest friends for life, generous and devoted to her friends beyond anyone I know.

Joe and I drove from Woodstock to Chicago for the start of rehearsals. We were put up in a spacious apartment overlooking the giraffes in the Chicago Zoo. If I hadn't been so frightened of doing the play,

I would have enjoyed the animals' proximity. We spent a few months there, though Joe often went back to New York. While I was in Chicago, I had the first serious experience of insomnia not caused by medication in my life. When I did sleep, it was for little more than an hour, and I dreamed of tall skyscrapers falling on me, my feet frozen to the sidewalk, not being able to move. Pretty transparent. Asleep or awake, the experience was a nightmare. I did lose some weight, which was good, but it was from anxiety and pain. Never did I even consider going back on the amphetamines.

The play was full of surprises, none of them good. The text of the play didn't match the reality. For one thing, the child actors, playing beautiful angelic young children, were far too old, and one child was truly nasty and couldn't hide it. It was impossible to ignore the reality of what I was getting from these kids, and it distorted the play and, I'm sure, confused people. Worse, when we started rehearsing, I discovered that I was the only one using an English accent. I kept waiting for the others to start using accents over the course of rehearsals, but it never happened. Joe saw the dress rehearsal and, ever the critic, told me to drop the English accent just minutes before the first performance. I saw Joe's point, but I didn't have the technical facility to just drop it on the spot. I had learned the part with an accent, and I couldn't suddenly remove it under the pressure of opening night. Even the theater itself was a problem. It was in the round, meaning that the actors came down the same aisles the audience used. Occasionally, our elegant "ghosts" would have to walk down the aisle by the side of a housewife with a shopping bag who was arriving late for a matinee. Scary to the housewife, I'm sure, but ridiculous to the audience and distracting for the actors.

I was not unhappy when the production was over. I had successfully survived, so I gave myself a bonus from the salary I'd earned and bought myself a stylish, heavy woolen coat from an upscale Chicago department store.

Shortly after returning from Chicago, I got another phone call, but this one was for Rosetta Morgenstern, and it was infinitely more important than any offer of work. It was from a social worker who said, "I might have some good news for you soon." Her good news was a possible child for us to adopt.

It was not important to me at that point in my life to have a child biologically. Whatever that need is, to replicate oneself, I did not have it. I could have easily conceived at that time, but Joe and I decided to adopt a child. We couldn't afford and didn't want an expensive private adoption, so we'd started working with the Department of Social Services in upstate New York. Our friend Grace Wapner had put us in touch with a caseworker. Grace's children were growing up, and though she remained a sculptor, she had a strong urge to do something in the real world. She had worked in the department for a time. We made it clear to the caseworker that we didn't care about race, gender, or even age, though if we had a choice, we would prefer a younger child.

About ten days after the first call, the caseworker called again and said, "Can you come to the office in Kingston tomorrow and meet someone? The foster parent will be bringing a baby for you to meet. This is only for you to take a look. You're not committed in any way. This little girl is seven months old and has had a cold, and we were waiting for it to be over. She's fine now and ready to be introduced if you can make it."

The next day Joe and I drove to Kingston, to the shiny black office building that was one of the few modern structures in this early American town. We parked and took the elevator to the fourth floor, where we were escorted to a small office. The door was closed sharply behind us. We were told the foster mother would be arriving any minute and would hand the baby over to a social worker and leave. We were not permitted to see the foster mother. The laws dictated we have no contact with her. All we were told was that the baby had gone into a foster home shortly after birth, and been surrounded by a loving family with children and animals.

We were told nothing about the biological parents either, except that the young mother was twenty-one years old. The father was not much older and was, we were told, "artistic." At the time New York state law said an adopted child must be of the same religion as the adoptive parents. There were very few Jewish babies available, and this little girl was not Jewish. The young mother had the generosity and wisdom to write a letter waiving the restriction about religion. The mother wanted only people who would respect the child and allow her to choose her own destiny.

Joe and I sat in the office and waited. There was something solemn and spiritual about this moment. Why, I didn't understand, for this would only be the first in a series of children we would see. Then the door opened, and in she came, resting in the arms of the social worker. A very round, dark-haired little being, who took one look at us and started to howl in a big, beautiful voice. Joe stepped closer, and she howled even louder. Nothing would stop her. Of course not. She was smart enough to know that she had been taken from the comfort of her home to a room full of strangers, and she was protesting. The caseworker kept apologizing about the weeping, but I knew it was to be expected from a bright baby. I reached out and asked to please hold her. A strange, light feeling came over me as I took her to a chair and sat down. She seemed hot, so I took off her little white bonnet and then her soft sweater, and her pretty little dress, and everything I could, leaving just her diaper. She kept howling all the while as I looked at her and smelled her. I don't know why I kept sniffing her like a mother animal; it was instinctual, and I couldn't stop myself. Whose baby was this? Her aroma was not familiar to me at all. Her thick, dark hair was matted on her head, and she smelled so foreign. She was not happy, of course, and I redressed her. Funny, I had never undressed or dressed my dolls.

When they said it was time to end the visit, I felt bereft. "Yes," we said, when the caseworker asked if we would be interested in having this baby visit us at our home the next day. We were told, "Just for a short visit and perhaps more visits later on."

They didn't know there was magic in the air.

Joe put on some Spanish music for the baby's arrival the next day. She made her entrance howling, as usual. The caseworker sat the baby in a little stroller that she had brought with her and asked if she should stay or if we wanted to be on our own for an hour. We told her we'd be fine. The moment the worker walked out, I realized the baby might be hungry; she hadn't stopped crying. She had arrived with several jars of food, so I fed her a little something. She indeed was very hungry, and her crying became softer and intermittent. Picking her up, I took her for a tour of the house, explaining everything to her as we passed.

I held her close as we climbed the stairs, and midway at the landing, hanging above us, was a round, glowing, amber-colored light fixture that had come with the house. She spotted it, and suddenly her face was transformed. She beamed with the most glorious smile, accompanied by two deep dimples, the kind that surprise you and make your heart stop for a moment. She was happy now as I walked into the little room at the front of the house that would be a child's bedroom. We had only gone so far as to buy a crib, a mattress, and plain bedding, since we had no idea who would be sleeping there, or when. She seemed so calm now, and I thought maybe she was a little sleepy, so I put her in the crib and covered her with the small blanket she'd traveled with. I spoke to her for a little while, and she soon went to sleep. I came back a few minutes later, after reporting to Joe about this new development. She had covered her face with the corner of the blanket. I peeked to see if she was all right, pulled the blanket down a little, and tiptoed out again. I came back fifteen minutes later to check, and she had covered her face again. I left the blanket in place this time and went downstairs. This was very exciting.

When the caseworker called to see if it was time to pick up the baby, we explained that the baby was asleep, and the caseworker said she'd call again in a little while. She called several more times, but by now the baby had been asleep for four hours. She seemed to be sleeping and breathing well and looked so relaxed. The caseworker said, "There's no point in waking her and taking her back to the foster home if she wakes up happy and you want her to stay."

I had not given it any thought; there was never a decision to be made. I don't know how or why, but I knew it was destined that she was to be my baby from the first moment in the office. Or perhaps before. I don't understand such things, but she was conceived at about the time

I was carving my first sculpture, *The Twenty-fifth Day*. She was my baby, and she woke up happy and laughing in her new home. We called her Anna, after my grandmother.

As if in a spy movie, Joe went out that first night and met a surrogate for the foster mother on a street corner. A man handed Joe a small suitcase filled with Anna's possessions; some clothes, a note with some instructions, and a few photographs memorializing her first seven months. On the way home, Joe stopped to pick up a supply of baby food.

All night, that first night, Joe and I listened for any sound that might come from her room and didn't sleep a wink. We kept tiptoeing in to check on her, but she slept the whole night through. She coyly lifted a piece of the blanket over her face every time we pulled it down.

The next day Joe went out and got a dozen child care books. I carried our dear Anna in my right arm and a stack of books in my left. I knew very little about taking care of babies, and I had to learn fast.

I had always known that being a parent would be difficult, but I wasn't prepared for the intense joy Anna brought me. It was a kind of love I had never imagined. I loved her so much that I often felt as if I *had* given birth to her, and I still do. In the evenings, when I sat in the rocking chair and held her so close before sleep, I was sure I could have given her my breast. I didn't know then that there was hormone therapy to actually make that possible, but I gave her what I could of myself, which was all of my heart. I held her and the bottle, enjoying our supreme closeness.

Ours was a quiet house except for music, Anna's beautiful trilling laughter, and the sounds from the animals. There were never arguments. Any anger Joe and I felt was swept under the rug. Now that I was sober, I couldn't tolerate a repeat of my parents' home. Joe adored Anna. His feelings were so tender, he wept bitterly in the middle of Tinker Street when he accidentally closed the car door on her thumb one day.

While Joe was working, I would take Anna for walks through the woods. I held her in my arms and showed her all the things in nature that I loved. She liked touching the leaves and smelling the blossoms.

And we would play, rolling in our huge field of thyme with the tiny wild strawberries hidden beneath. I bathed her in the little sink upstairs in *cool water*. The water took a while to warm up, but Anna seemed to prefer it that way: bracing.

She was such an easy child to take care of and raise, especially for older parents. We were forty now and didn't have the stamina of younger parents. Anna was a great traveler, which was wonderful for us because we did so much of it. As she grew older, she was quite content to look at her books, play her music, or look out the window. We would often drive the two hours to the city and sometimes on much longer trips. Never once in her childhood did she say, "Are we there yet?" And, hallelujah, Anna insisted on having nine uninterrupted hours of sleep every night! Can you imagine? She never woke up, except once or twice when she was sick. We could hear her entertaining herself in the mornings on the intercom in our bedroom, singing and talking. She was always happy and excited to see me each morning, but she did like her sleep. There was always at least a three-hour nap in the afternoon. We put an intercom in the kitchen downstairs and one in my studio, which was about twenty feet from the house. While Anna was napping, I worked. I wondered why she went to wherever she went for so long. But when she awoke and was with us again, she was very present.

Anna was a miraculous child. It was like having a mysterious, unknown seed planted in my garden and watching it grow, having no idea what it would look like or become. She bloomed like a rare and wonderful flower, intelligent, talented, and gloriously beautiful. The first piece I did after Anna came to us was in alabaster. It was of Anna's head, with her astoundingly beautiful round cheeks. It is about ten times life size and weighs about a hundred and fifty pounds. I worked on it for about four months, though I couldn't really call it work. Every day, every month, Anna was a new and delightful surprise. I couldn't understand how a child could be that serene and joyous and at peace with herself. I felt so blessed to be her mother. I often had an overwhelming desire to thank her biological mother, to embrace her and show her the beautiful person she had given us. I thought of her so often through the years.

While Joe and I were experiencing the joy of new parents, my sister Sherrye was struggling in the aftermath of her divorce. Her self-esteem was battered, and she was so depressed, she could barely function. We talked on the phone regularly. One day she called and begged me to send her money to have a costly and complicated stomach bypass surgery. At five foot two and four hundred pounds, she had tried all the diets, but nothing had worked. The surgery was very dangerous, and the side effects were horrific; it is rarely done anymore because of the risks. But Sherrye was desperate and said she didn't want to live anymore unless she could do this. I was no longer wealthy, but I had enough money for the surgery, and I sent it. How could I not? If Joe disapproved, he said little about it. Sherrye survived the surgery, and over a period of years she eventually lost all the weight. The procedure made a dramatic difference, and after a time she weighed less than I did and was smashingly beautiful.

It had been years since I'd had an agent, but then one day the quiet rhythm of our life was interrupted. My old agent in the city, Lily Veight, sent me a new play written by John Guare. He was the extraordinary playwright of *House of Blue Leaves*, *Two Gentlemen of Verona*, dozens more plays, later the movie *Atlantic City*, and the play and movie of *Six Degrees of Separation*. I had no idea why they had sent me the play. How did they come to think of me after all these years? I was told they wanted me to come to New York to meet the director, Mel Shapiro. Was this an offer?

I tortured myself for many days with doubts about meeting Mr. Shapiro. The Chicago theater experience had been horrendous. It was the only time I had worked in the last ten years, and I had done it only for the money and to test my courage. I'd been electrified with terror before every performance, and I'd never been able to drop the accent completely. Everything had gone wrong with the production, and I'd felt foolish. Perhaps I simply wasn't a professional any longer. And what about Joe and Anna? When Lily sent me the Guare play, I talked long and hard with my friend Grace about returning to work. Grace knew little about show business; her world was the world of art, but she encouraged me not to be afraid of the play and to do it if I found it and circumstances agreeable. And she felt the question of Anna and Joe was not insurmountable.

So I took the train into the city to meet the director at the Oyster Bar in Grand Central Station. Mel Shapiro was a smart and likable fellow. He said, "We're going to do a workshop on Nantucket all summer long. We'll play in the big auditorium of the high school. Would you like to do it?"

I was very surprised and didn't know what to say, except, "I have a husband. I have a young child—she's almost three. If I can figure out a way to have her with me, I'd like to do it."

I had gone ahead and met with him without really knowing if they wanted me or if it was only a meeting to see what had happened to me during the past almost ten years. Now that I knew they wanted me, I needed to discuss this with Joe. I'd never *really* known what he felt about my working, and we'd been married for thirteen years. Joe said it was fine with him. Lindsay, a lovely person and our first and occasional nanny, agreed to come to Nantucket with us for the summer. So that was that.

We loaded everything into two cars. Lindsay drove her station wagon. We had everything we'd needed for the summer plus our cats and our baby girl. The only thing I lacked was my courage. It was an all-day trip. When we got to Massachusetts, we put our cars on the ferry to travel to Nantucket. It was dusk by the time we drove off the ferry, exhausted.

Suddenly I saw a large man running back and forth, jumping up and down, running around our car in circles like a large puppy dog greeting its master. As he ran alongside the car, he was shouting something and waving his arms. We opened the windows and heard the man say, "Piper Laurie, Piper Laurie! I don't believe it! I don't believe it! You're here! You're here! Piper Laurie is here!" He directed us to follow him in a car.

Joe said, "I think that's John Guare!" I was laughing and crying with excitement.

John directed us to our little bungalow about twenty minutes away, embraced us all, and introduced himself. It was the best greeting I'd ever had in my life. I was filled with his warmth, and some of my fear started melting away.

The play was called *Marco Polo Sings a Solo*, and with it began a great summer. We rehearsed all day in a large hall. Often Lindsay would bring Anna, who was three, to visit at lunchtime. The cast usually walked to nearby restaurants for lunch, so the rehearsal hall was empty. Anna and I could run around and have fun while I nibbled on my lunch from home. In the evening the four of us would have dinner together at the bungalow. Lindsay was a good cook, making lots of the veggies that I loved. Joe stayed, and Joe went back, depending on his work.

I met James Woods for the first time doing this play. It was before he became a movie star, and it may have been his first play. I know he'd never made a movie. He was still in his twenties and flirting with all the girls. Every morning we had a brilliantly improvised stand-up routine from him before we began the day's rehearsal. He could riff as long as he was given the time. Mel Shapiro enjoyed and encouraged Jimmy as much as anyone. It obviously took time from the rehearsal, but none of us had ever seen this kind of brilliance before, and we were spellbound.

It was indeed a workshop, and we all had to be facile and flexible and adapt to major changes in the script every day. John would write new material all the time, and we would do our utmost to put it on its feet immediately. What training this was for all of us, certainly for me! I began to lose my insecurities as the challenges grew. Even when we actually opened and were playing in front of a large audience of perhaps five or six hundred people, we would still get last-minute changes written by hand on the yellow paper tablet John carried. One particular long speech of mine had to be delivered in front of the audience without any rehearsal at all. It was extremely sexual in nature, as my character described her lover's penis in imaginative and grandly vulgar terms. The audience actually gasped while I was doing it. It would have been nice to have worked up to that moment at least once in a rehearsal hall, but it was definitely an exercise in courage and mental discipline. I think we all loved John's creativity and enthusiasm and wanted to take chances with and for him.

Every performance seemed to bring a surprise. In the opening scene of the play, James Woods and I are in a hospital room, both patients, in separate beds facing the audience. We have an exchange of dialogue, and then there is a blackout, and the second scene begins. One night James responded to me as usual, but then continued talking and talking and talking. He went on for what seemed a lifetime. I thought he had lost his mind, or maybe I had. He spoke about lots of things, it seemed, having nothing to do with the play, not even related to him personally. What was happening? Should I run offstage? No, I couldn't do that; I couldn't leave him alone out there if he was having a breakdown. And then he blessedly stopped. He said a line I recognized from the play, and the blackout came. Jimmy had, of course, neglected to tell me about his new speech, assuming someone else had. He later said that while he was delivering his monologue to me, I looked like the proverbial deer caught in the headlights. We were daredevils performing by the seat of our pants. It was thrilling.

After playing Nantucket, I found out my mother's health was deteriorating. Like many women of her generation, Mother found it difficult and embarrassing to see a gynecologist on a regular basis. So by the time it was discovered that she had cancer, it was too late. She and my dad fulfilled a lifelong dream and took a cruise to Alaska. When they returned, I was about to go into the hospital for the major back surgery I could no longer delay, and it was clear she would most likely die while I was recovering. I wanted to see her and say goodbye while she was still alive, so we went to California for a few days.

On the last day in California, Mother was reclining on the couch, propped up by many pillows and making a great effort to hide how very sick she was. I wanted to dress up a little for her; I knew how important it always was to her, to see me looking nice. How she had watched over every detail of my appearance. But because of needing play time in the park with Anna, I wasn't able to get back to our motel to change clothes before I saw her. I had to wear my old Woodstock shawl with fringe, which I knew she wouldn't care for, but it was clean and warm. When we walked in at the beginning of the visit, she was obviously too ill to notice my clothes, and her attention was on beautiful Anna, the apple of her eye. Then Joe and my dad took Anna somewhere so Mother and I could be alone. After a while, when it was time to go, Mother touched my face gently and told me that she loved me. I embraced her and with a true heart, told her that I loved her, too.

My body felt so heavy as I walked to the door. Then Mother called out softly, "Sissy, I like your stole. It's very pretty—with the fringe."

Never in a million years would she have liked my stole; I knew that. She was being kind instead of honest, and I was deeply touched.

A few weeks later Sherrye called to say Mother wanted to speak to me and to hear my voice. I reassured my mother that I was doing well, and she said, "I love you, Sissy . . . I love you . . . I love you," over and over again. Perhaps trying to make peace with my childhood. She died a few days later.

As my surgery drew near, Joe and I agreed that we would have to move. There were no downstairs bedrooms in our beautiful little farmhouse, and stairs would be impossible for a long while, if at all, after the surgery. So Joe and Anna and I moved into a furnished rental closer to town. It had a small downstairs bedroom and bathroom, a nice living room, and Anna and Joe each had a bedroom upstairs. We had a massive garage sale to downsize our belongings. I gave away or sold many beautiful things I had collected over the years. But in truth, it was good to be free of these things.

The surgery brought me healing in so many ways. I had been overwhelmed by a profound feeling of powerlessness. I decided to pray differently, asking God only that "Thy will be done." I never, ever again asked for anything. Instead I worked hard at doing my part as earnestly as I could and then put myself in God's hands. While I was in the hospital, my feeling about the artist's place in the world had started to change again as well. For a while, being an artist had seemed insignificant and indulgent when so many people in the world were deprived of freedom, food, and shelter. But now, after having spent six weeks in a hospital away from my family, I greatly valued all the arts for their gifts of joy and distraction, stimulating insights, beauty, or just the treat of a great big belly laugh.

On the way home, lying on a mattress in a borrowed station wagon with my head close to Joe's, I had found myself dreaming out loud. I said, "It might be enjoyable to work as an actress again in movies." *Had I really come that far? That I could speak out loud about my dreams?*

And Joe had replied, "Too much time has gone by. Nobody's going to hire you after all these years. It's not realistic."

I knew part of what Joe had said was true. It wasn't realistic. It had been so many years since I'd made a movie. Sometimes people would come up to me and say, "Didn't you used to be Piper Laurie?" Or even more bizarre, to my sister Sherrye, "Piper Laurie used to be your sister, didn't she?" We both enjoyed that one. But now I had the arrogance of someone who had recently survived a trauma. Though I didn't say it out loud, I knew that I would work again.

14.

Carrie

Out of the blue I received a call from my former agent Lily. She had a script to send me and hadn't a clue about who had sent it. "Will you read it, Piper?" she asked me. "This is something the new director Brian De Palma is doing." "Of course," I said, almost speechless. The mail arrived a few days later; I read the script and thought it was awful. I was disappointed. That night Joe said, "You know, De Palma often has a comedic approach to his work." So I guessed I had misread the whole thing, that it was satiric; and after reading it again, I began to see how funny the mother's part could be. I called Lily and told her I was interested. She said, "You know, Piper, this is not an offer. You will have to come to the city and be interviewed by the director." *Fair enough*, I thought. I was someone from the past. If he were young, he'd probably never heard of me.

I had been a little hesitant to travel alone since the surgery, but I had been swimming almost every day at the Y in Kingston and felt surprisingly strong. I drove myself across the bridge to the station in Rhinecliff, parked my car, and boarded the train for the city wearing a long black velvet coat that my grandma had made for herself years before. The silk lining was a little worn if you looked closely, but it was still very nice. I wore my hair down and natural. Pauline Kael had encouraged me to stop blow-drying it straight years before, telling me,

"It's in style." So here I was, at forty-five, setting off for an interview as I had twenty years earlier, in another lifetime.

When I was escorted into Brian De Palma's office, I was prepared to explain what I had done in my career, but to my surprise, he asked not one thing about me or what I thought of the script. Instead, he proceeded to tell me a great deal about himself and the work he had done, as if he were seeking a job from me and I were interviewing him. I realized he was trying to make me feel comfortable, and I was quite touched. By the time I left, I was completely charmed, and I hoped that he liked me, too. The trip home took about three hours, and when I came in the door, Joe told me my agent Lily wanted me to call.

Lily said, "Piper dear, Brian De Palma liked you very much, and he wants you to play this part! You will have to fly to California for two weeks of rehearsals next month and then go back again when shooting starts in about two months. They said it would be about three weeks of shooting, and they've offered you ten thousand dollars for the entire movie."

I was stunned and couldn't speak for a moment. Lily misunderstood my silence and said, "If you wish to do the movie, I think you should accept that. We won't get more, my dear. It's been fifteen years, you know."

"Oh, that's fine. I'm happy to have whatever they want to pay." This was going to be fun! I had never before gone into a movie situation thinking and feeling it would be fun. Acting had always been a matter of life or death for me. I thought I had to suffer so. This was new. Could I really enjoy it now?

I think Joe was astounded. He had not believed that I could restart my movie career. I was astounded too at my good fortune, to receive this work just when my psyche was yearning for it. And any money they offered was deeply appreciated. Joe had quit his job at *Newsweek* a few years before and had been struggling with a big writing block, so finances were tight.

What I didn't know was that Marcia Nasatir and Arlene Donovan, friends from New York whom I'd met through Pauline Kael and hadn't seen in years, had whispered my name into Brian De Palma's ear toward the end of the search for Carrie's mother. I heard later on that the producers were thinking of Joan Fontaine for Mrs. White. I have Marcia and Arlene to thank for giving me a third career.

I flew out by myself for the rehearsal period, as if nothing in the world had changed, and was put up at a hotel in Beverly Hills on Pico Boulevard with a pool. It was not too fancy but attractive and clean—it'd be a good place to come back to, when I returned with Anna and Joe for the actual shoot. I had a rental car to get around in, and I drove to Brian's apartment on Fountain Avenue for the first rehearsal. It was in one of those bastardized Spanish buildings with large rooms and interior archways. I was now almost always on time, having lost some of my self-involvement and the stress that came along with it. And motherhood had taught me a great deal about being organized.

When I entered the apartment, Brian introduced me to two other members of the cast, Amy Irving and Sissy Spacek, who had just finished rehearsing a few scenes. Amy left a short while later.

Sissy was very nice and quite serious about the work, though it threw me hearing somebody else being called Sissy. We read through some of our scenes. She knew the lines to many of the scenes because she had made at least one screen test for the part. When I left that day, Brian gave me a taped cassette of Sissy's audio from her screen test to take back to Woodstock. He asked me to learn her natural Texas accent. He thought it would be easier for me to change my speech than for Sissy to change hers. I hadn't thought of these people as having any accent when I read the script, but oh well, why not? It would make them seem even more like outsiders.

On the second day of rehearsal I was given an updated version of the script and noticed to my horror that one of my character's best speeches was missing, presumably cut. It was the scene just before she kills Carrie. I stayed quite calm, though churning inside. *Was this a deliberate editing decision?* It appeared so. Was someone afraid of the rawness of the moment before I'd even played it? I pointed it out to Brian, who said he thought it was probably an accident, a secretary's error. There was no way to know the truth. Brian told me to use my old script for the rehearsal. If I hadn't spoken up, the scene would have been lost. That can happen sometimes with a big production—seemingly small things fall through the cracks. I was relieved and grateful that Brian put it back. I found him to be a sympathetic and sensitive director, and not just because he always said yes to me.

One day at rehearsal Sissy's husband, Jack Fisk, who was also doing the set design, stopped by to see his wife and to speak to Brian. I was standing between the living room and dining room as we said hello. Jack asked me how I was wearing my hair in the movie. I told him, "I guess, as it's been described in the book and script. In a tight bun at the back of my head." Jack said, "Brian, come over here, take a look at this. Look at Piper under that archway. Look at her hair! They're great together!"

Brian said, "Yeah, yeah!"

I think it was Jack who then said to me, "Would you mind wearing it like that in the movie, as it is now, curly and big?" I had personally not been happy to wear it in a bun; it seemed cliché, though I would have done it if Brian had insisted. Would I mind? It was wonderful for me and so easy.

On one of the early days of rehearsal I tried something I thought would be funny, to see if it would work. It was the scene when Carrie is getting ready to go to the prom, and Mother has come to her room, desperately trying everything to keep her from going. The script said, "Mrs. White tears her dress, abuses herself in some way." I knew the costumers would not appreciate my destroying the wardrobe for every take. So midway in the scene I grabbed my hair and used it to pull myself around the room. I figured it would look absurd and funny. When I was about to do it a second time, Brian suddenly stopped me. He said, "Piper, you can't do that. You're going to get a laugh!"

I thought to myself, *Yes, that's right, I hope so. Isn't that the point?* But I could see he was not smiling. He was serious. Oh boy, how could I have gone so wrong? I was embarrassed. He meant the movie to be serious. It was too late to back out, and I was just plain enjoying myself. How to do this? I decided to just move the line of reality slightly. There is a thin line between humor and horror. I toned things down just a little, to a place of possible believability. I pulled my hair, but with deeper *inner* emotional pain, and threw out any attempt at visual comedy. I did that for much of the part. I never told Brian about my misunderstanding. When I got back to New York after the rehearsal period, I went to see every De Palma movie I could, including *Phantom of the Paradise*, which had just opened. Very operatic—he liked that. I needed not be afraid to be big.

When I returned to shoot the movie weeks later, I came back a few pounds lighter and with a Sissy accent. I was not as slim as I wanted to be, but I was rarin' to go. There was something completely enchanting about being on the set. They had the old-fashioned dressing rooms with wheels like they did when I first started at Universal. You had to go outside to use the permanent bathrooms. Elaborate trailers hadn't yet come into vogue except on locations. Making movies seemed much the same, and I felt very much at home. So much so, it came as a loud thunderclap when I suddenly realized *internally* that it had been fifteen years since I'd acted on a set!

It was a very sweet and sentimental time for me. I felt so welcomed by the crew, a few of whom I had known before. I felt embraced by everyone and especially free to do the work. I found my emotional resources were bottomless. It was miraculous to me that I could do this and not bring it home every night. I didn't have to anymore. I could just use myself fully while I was at work, and then leave it there. I had also found a secret weapon that inspired me in the part. I was channeling my vulnerable mother, from the days when she was enraged and on the warpath. Thank you, Mom.

We had been shooting for a while when Brian told me the stunt people were going to put a harness on me under my clothes—it would suddenly jerk me back and down onto the bed when Carrie uses her powers on me. I had kept my back surgery a secret, even from my agent, but I was going to have to take Brian into my confidence now.

He immediately said, "Oh no, we don't have to do this. I'll shoot it from another angle and get a double."

I said, "Wait a minute, let me try on the harness, see what it feels like, where it pulls on me, and then have them very gently and slowly show me what they will do." And that's what we did. It was clear to me that I would be safe, and I worked out a position in which to fall. Brian was frightened for me, but I assured him it would be fine, and it was. Whenever I see that scene, I relive the moment, and my buttocks, stomach, and thigh muscles tighten up to protect me one more time.

When we got to the scene just before Mrs. White tries to kill Carrie, I asked Brian if he minded my not rehearsing. I would get into my physical position on the floor for the director of photography to light, but I wouldn't play until the camera was rolling. Hopefully, I would not have to do the scene more than once. I think my experience with the John Guare play, doing new material as bravely as I could in front of the audience for the very first time, helped prepare me for this. Brian was great. He did everything he could to get the mechanics to work perfectly so I wouldn't have to do it more than once. The cameras rolled, and I let Mrs. White's secret life spill out in front of the camera. Afterward Brian came to me almost in tears and said, "I'm so sorry, Piper, do you think you could do it one more time?" There had been some technical screwup. I did it again, and I think it was as fresh as the first take. A miracle. They printed both. I don't know which take they used.

I had the most fun, and laughed the most, on the day I died. Death by kitchen implements. Just minutes before we were to shoot the scene, I happened to cross paths with Brian on the way to the restroom outside. I stopped him and told him my idea for the mother's death, for her to be in ecstasy rather than agony. Ecstasy because she was at last getting to meet her Savior. He liked the idea, so I was free to play it that way and not worry about being interrupted if he didn't. The special effects required me to wear a steel vest under my costume that covered my entire chest. It reminded me of the contraption the Japanese had improvised for me when I'd gone to Korea twenty-five years earlier. There were little wooden blocks glued to the spots on the steel where the knives and kitchen tools would land. A wire was attached to each wooden block, threaded through a tiny hole in my nightgown, then strung across to the special effects man about twelve feet away. Each time one of the objects moved and hit me, it was in slow motion. The knife or scissors bobbing along on the wire would sometimes take as much as a full minute to reach me. All the while I had to prepare to react both physically and vocally when the object struck its target. Playing the ecstasy, after watching this ridiculously bobbing can opener slowly heading my way, was almost more than I could stand. I roared out my laughter every time we cut.

The day I wrapped, I was given a little party on the set, and a cake that said, "Welcome back, Piper." I was so moved, full of joy and emotion. When I'd finished my last scene, Joe and Anna came to the set for the very first time. As always, seeing her was a moment of pure joy, even if I'd last seen her that morning. She had some juice and cookies, and our picture was taken together with her powdering me with a puff. Sissy, who did not yet have children, was enchanted with Anna and played guitar for her. The next time Sissy and I worked together, we were sisters in *The Grass Harp*, and she and Jack Fisk had two almost-grown-up girls of their own.

I truly had changed inside because of Anna and Joe, and God's grace. Being responsible for another human being and taking pretty good care of another one was very hard work, and it got me outside of myself. In comparison to real life, acting was easy! The ten thousand dollars they gave me was like being paid to go on vacation.

I never wanted to live in California again and assumed we'd move back to New York as soon as I finished the film, but Joe liked California, and he wished to stay for a while. He was learning to fly sailplanes, a lifelong dream of his. He hadn't yet broken through the writing block, and while he wrestled with what he wanted to do with the rest of his life, I was asked to star in another movie, called *Ruby*, to be directed by the avant-garde Curtis Harrington, for which I was offered a hefty salary. It was a strange script, with a couple of genuinely original scenes, in which I would play a woman who runs a drive-in theater and always dresses in red, but it was not what I wanted to be doing. It would, however, pay a lot of bills. We found a large house perched high on a bluff overlooking the ocean. The ad had read "Children and pets welcome." The rent was quite modest because our landlady, who lived in the guesthouse, wanted company. Soon after, we enrolled Anna in kindergarten in Santa Monica. That move cemented us geographically.

We shot *Ruby* at the old Studio Club in Hollywood, designed by the famed woman architect Julia Morgan, who also did the Hearst Castle at San Simeon. While I was shooting, Joe went to the first screening of *Carrie*. He called me afterward on the set and said, "Our lives are never going to be the same." He was very excited.

I saw *Carrie* for the first time at a sneak preview in Westwood at midnight on Halloween. My old friend Bob Richards and our friend Kathy Butterfield, who was out from Woodstock, joined Joe and me for sushi in a restaurant around the corner before the movie. I had at least three or four cups of sake before we walked over to the theater. *Well, nobody's perfect*. The lobby was packed! I saw a lot of the cast from the movie. I can't tell you what I thought of my performance that night. I was well protected by the sake.

But then, some months later, I received another Oscar nomination! Incredible! I was shocked when I heard about it. I was proud of my work in the movie because I had been brave, but it surprised me that the Academy members would even go to see a horror movie. Besides, I had no press agent, and as far as I knew no one had been promoting me. How very nice.

This time Joe and I went to the Academy Awards. I wore an old black velvet skirt with a modest slit, and the beautiful lace blouse that I'd worn for my wedding fifteen years earlier. I thought my work in *Carrie* was the best thing I'd done in front of a camera. I hoped I might win because it would bring more and better work. Though many Academy members tend to dismiss what they consider "horror movies," I confess I still thought I had a chance.

It was hard to look delighted when they announced that Beatrice Straight had won for *Network*. I liked Beatrice personally a lot and just a few weeks before had taken her to a screening of *Funny Girl* because she'd never seen Barbra Streisand. When I heard Beatrice's name, I was disappointed, and it took a little effort to put on a good face. I think it costs actors a lot when we feel we have to do that. Is that nakedly dishonest moment really worth it? Meryl Streep does that moment really well. She appears as though she's genuinely happy whether she wins or not. I think it's real. If not, well, that's why she's been nominated so many times.

Carrie was a huge hit and continues to be so, making millions for many. I remained happy and content with my ten-thousand-dollar fee until years later, when Paul Monash, the producer of the movie, insisted on giving me a tour of his mansion "that *Carrie* built, thanks to your extraordinary performance." That made me just a little sensitive about my simple contract, which Lily had negotiated with no back-end deal. Every once in a while I get a ten-dollar residual check for a TV showing. Though I didn't get rich from it, I got much more. I know what it's like to be rich, and I know what it's like to be poor. Experiencing both has made me feel like a whole person who can make informed choices. I think I would be bored, unhappy, and no longer creative if I were not required to make some effort to survive.

We remained in California, which did not make me happy. Anna stayed in her school, and somewhere down the line Joe finally started writing again, this time screenplays that I was hoping would be for me. But he gave them to famous actresses whom we had met. I pretended I understood, but frankly I didn't.

Luckily worthy roles come from many sources. A couple of years after *Carrie*, the incomparable Eddie Bondi from the Morris office called and said his client Julie Harris had turned down an interesting movie offer. At the risk of losing his job, he had recommended me, a nonclient, to the producer-director Michael Pate.

Pate sent me only the novel, Colleen McCullough's *Tim*, and a forty-page treatment. The film would be shot in Australia. It was a pulpy, romantic story about an older woman and her mentally handicapped young gardener who looks like a Greek god. The boy falls in love with the woman. Eventually she realizes she loves him, and in spite of his handicap and the age difference, they marry.

Once I agreed to do the film, Pate mentioned that his son might play the young and handsome boy. The son was a gifted actor but not one who comes to mind when thinking of Greek gods. I thought the part, not to mention the opportunity to go to Australia for three months, was potentially so exciting that I would take a chance on whomever he cast to play my young lover.

I started making plans for the time in Australia. I knew I would be wearing a bathing suit for an important scene, so I began running and swimming regularly when I could. I was forty-seven years old, and I was supposed to look attractive to an extremely young man. Of course, my family would come. Joe and I had our problems, but we were still friends and good companions. We received special permission to take Anna out of school because of the educational nature of the trip and our promise to bring back Aboriginal artifacts for the school to share and display. My back held up well. Our ex-nanny Lindsay, who was now studying painting in Hawaii, would meet us in Australia.

It was a long flight. It seemed almost as long as going to Korea in the 1950s, though it was actually much shorter by days. We stopped in New Zealand just long enough to have a simple and delicious lunch. When we finally reached Sydney, we were taken to an attractive hotel in the middle of the city. Most of the shooting would take place in the country, no more than an hour away. Later on there would be several overnight locations within a few hours' drive. While I was on location, Joe, Anna, and Lindsay would be out on a rented houseboat.

We settled into the hotel, and the next day I was taken to an exterior location to meet everyone—the director, the young actor, and very importantly the hairstylist who would be entrusted with the care of my white-haired wig. She and I went off to practice putting on the wig for some photos. But she just hadn't had enough experience to make the tiny pin curls and wrap my head so that the wig would slip on easily. She couldn't get it on. The director, Michael Pate, seemed not at all disturbed and said, "That's all right. We'll use your own hair.

That's fine, don't worry about it." He actually seemed happy about it, but I worried that the age difference, an important story point, would be diffused.

The actors were supposed to get into some wardrobe for photos. It would just be myself and the young man, whom I'd not yet met. I hadn't even asked if it was the director's son. I didn't want to know. I would try to accept what I was given and make it work. I was in the wardrobe truck when I was informed that the actor had arrived and would I please come down the steps to be introduced and have our photo taken together. In truth, I had been dreading the moment of meeting the person who I was to have profound feelings for and would be working with in such an intimate way. I was told he was only twenty-three. What if he were not only unattractive but also insensitive and stupid?

I came down the three steps to the sidewalk and saw someone smiling at me. He was blazingly handsome and looked warm as the earth. The assistant director said, "Meet Mel Gibson. This is his first movie." I was struck by the *life*, the intelligence in his face and in his eyes! I was enchanted. *Now, if he can only act.*

Once we began to shoot, it became apparent that my leading man was a serious actor. In fact, he was a very good one, with Shakespearean and theater experience under his belt. He seemed to have wisdom far beyond his twenty-three years, though he was unsure of himself on and around the set. He never asked me, but I found him watching how I would handle something that was new to him. It was very touching. He would take his lunch as I did, on a tray in a little private corner of the set, so as not to waste time, and stretch out wherever he could find a flat spot. I noticed he also started bringing his toothbrush and brushing his teeth after lunch as I did.

The original treatment of the script had run only forty pages, and Pate had promised that a full script would be ready before we started shooting. But when I arrived in Australia, the original forty pages of the script had not grown. One evening Pate assigned Mel and me the task of writing some scenes ourselves in the evenings, telling us he didn't have the time to do it himself. Both Mel and I thought that was too big a challenge to tackle, and we said no. Today I would do it, and I'm sure

Mel would, too; but then I felt we had been deserted by our director. He would often tell us to play scenes and then go off somewhere while we shot them, with no feedback and just the director of photography in charge. I began to be frightened that the movie might not get done.

There were other kinds of behavior that I found extraordinary. Sometimes Pate used Mel as a whipping boy. Pate ridiculed Mel in front of the crew for his inexperience in the technical aspects of movie-making—hitting marks on the floor so as to be in right place in relation to the camera, etc. On at least two separate occasions, I saw Mel reveal the strength of character and restraint of someone much older and wiser. I could see the blood rising in his face as Pate ridiculed him, and I was sure he was going to just haul off and belt Pate, who deserved it. No doubt he'd be fired if he did. I saw this young man decide in about three seconds whether to turn his back on the opportunity of starring in his first movie to become "the kid who's a troublemaker." I'd seen that happen before. Instead, Mel steadied himself, swallowed his twenty-three-year-old pride, which had to be enormous, and moved forward to work. I admired him so for his ability to think beyond the moment.

I indulged myself and allowed the role, with my character's growing affection for Tim, to blossom, and it turned me into a young girl from time to time. I confess I had retained my silly streak, and Mel didn't have to do much to bring it out. I would save my dignity for later. I was having a marvelous time. It was not a bad thing to bring that home with me. Better than the tragedy of poor Sarah from *The Hustler*. It was shameful that I was so enamored of Mel, and I told everyone, including Joe.

Our director asked us to rehearse a lengthy dialogue scene at home on our own the night before shooting. The scene was an emotional one, especially for Mel, as my character attempts to explain what death is to the innocent Tim. By the end of the scene, Tim is weeping, and my character embraces and comforts him as she would a child.

The location hotel made an empty room without furniture available for us to use for the rehearsal. It was just the two of us. We were quite disciplined and got to work right away. We rehearsed the scene sitting on the floor, which was pretty close to how we would be on the actual set. When we got to the climax of the scene, I embraced Mel, and he embraced me. End of scene. I waited a few beats and gently started to pull my arm away, but it was locked there under his, and he didn't move. I waited, but he stayed in the embrace, unmoving, holding me tightly, not letting me go. Was this the scene, or was it something else? Was he telling me something? Was I in trouble? Oh, dear. I had not been so tempted in many years. He seemed to be sorting something out for himself; the wrong decision had the potential of souring our work relationship. Finally he relaxed his arm, and we moved away from each other. A few moments later we said goodnight and returned to our respective rooms.

On one of our last days of shooting, Mel and I were standing on the beach alone, waiting for the crew to set up for the next scene. I was feeling the sadness of the coming to an end. Perhaps Mel was, too. I was very touched by him as an actor and had enjoyed the work with him. I thought our scenes together were very beautiful. Mel picked up a shell from the sand, handed it to me shyly, and said, "A goodbye present." I said I hoped we could share a meal together before we parted. Later that night, at an impromptu wrap party at a café, Mel leaned over the large table and placed his precious cap on my head, a familiar gesture of possession I hadn't seen since high school. I returned the cap before leaving, and our director of photography, Paul Onorato, dropped me back to my room after the party. I took a bath and got ready for bed when there was a knock at my door. It was Mel, wanting to say a proper goodbye.

May God forgive me—I opened the door.

The goodbye was more like a leap over the moon for me, and it ended a long time later with Mel holding me tenderly all night long as we slept, encircling me with both his arms locked behind my back, unwilling to let me go, as if I were a precious teddy bear. When the brilliant Australian sun came through the windows, I didn't even bother pulling the curtains to soften the light on my almost-fifty-year-old body.

When we said goodbye, I knew it would have to be a final one and I made no attempt to stay in touch. But that night was life-affirming, something I would never regret, and Joe would understand, and I carried its glow for years.

Joe, Anna, and I traveled all around Australia. We went to the places the Australians rarely go—Ayers Rock, Alice Springs, the Great Barrier Reef. This was in the 1970s, and things were more rugged and unspoiled. We brought back many things to share with Anna's school. The most precious, besides my family, were a length of thick gold thread spun by a native spider and the memory of the sweet relationship I had with Mel.

Tim was not released in America until Mel had made two more movies. It was almost fifteen years later when I saw him again. It was no surprise to me that he'd become a great movie star, and he had also just won the Oscar for directing *Braveheart*. I was asked to say a few words at a Lifetime Achievement Award banquet for him. Afterward my daughter and I were invited to a small get-together upstairs at the hotel. With great happiness for him, I offered my congratulations and met his wife and close friends. I was astonished that after all this time he seemed so uncomfortable with the trappings of success, as if he couldn't wait to get out of there. Who can know how his devils were operating? I can't even guess.

Now another fifteen years have gone by, and we have all been drawn into his nightmare. Everyone who has cared about him has watched as it happened. I am not wise enough to know who he is now, or why. I still resist acknowledging that the sensitive and courageous Mel I knew has been so thoroughly transformed. I cannot make sense of it.

The old memory however, stays intact, and I have kept the little shell he gave me.

When I returned from Australia, offers continued to come in regularly. Amazing. Not long after I finished *Tim*, Lynne Meadow, the artistic director of the Manhattan Theater Club, a new and exciting part of New York theater, asked me to do the first New York revival of S. N. Behrman's play *Biography*. I was excited to be back on stage, especially in such a good role. Joe and Anna came to New York for a long visit and went back to California before the run was over. I stayed behind a week to see some other shows.

One play I went to see was *Betrayal*, the Harold Pinter play starring Raul Julia, Blythe Danner, and Roy Scheider. I knew Blythe; we were mothers together at Anna's school in Santa Monica, which her daughter, Gwyneth Paltrow, also attended. I always remembered Gwyneth because when it was my turn to help serve salad in the cafeteria at school, the already-exquisite seven-year-old was the only child who wanted any. *Betrayal* was awfully good, and I went backstage afterward to see Blythe. As we chatted, a large presence stepped into the dressing room.

It was John Frankenheimer.

I stopped talking midsentence. We looked at one another for a long moment. There was a table separating us, so we couldn't touch or shake hands. Finally he said, "Rosie."

It was like a mini-Pinter play.

He said, "You look wonderful." I saw that he looked vigorous and still magnetic.

I said, "You look wonderful, too." And he did. I realized later, it had been eighteen years.

Then he said, "Are you here now?"

I said, "No, I was just doing a play."

I turned to look at Blythe, who had said something, and when I turned back, John had disappeared. I left a few minutes later and took a cab back to my hotel.

The next day I got a call from Blythe, who was quite excited and apologetic about not knowing my history with John. She said Roy Scheider had called her that morning and asked what had happened in her dressing room with me and John the night before. She'd said, "Nothing happened. What do you mean?"

Roy told her John had come upstairs to see him, told him he'd just seen me, and proceeded to have an emotional breakdown. Roy said that John had actually collapsed. When he found out I had left the theater, he asked Roy to please go with him to help find me. Roy had convinced him that while he was in that state, it was not a good time for him to look for me, and Roy and someone else had helped to get him home.

I was deeply affected listening to Blythe. Even after all those years, John's passions were like a giant wave that washed over me. Against my better judgment, I called my agent and asked if he could find out where John was. Two days later my agent called back and said that John had gone overseas somewhere to start a movie. Perhaps my good fortune.

Back in L.A. I buried myself in an exciting new TV series called *Skag*. It was about a steelworker played by Karl Malden. I was to play Karl Malden's wife. On the first day of shooting, I had a confrontation with the writer-producer, Abby Mann, who told me my appearance "didn't work for him." He said I was too young-looking, I didn't look lower class enough, and my hair was too clean and pretty. Well, for heaven's sake, he'd already met with me a number of times, and he was the one who had cast me. He hadn't suggested any change at the time. Mann was loud and vulgar and did his best to blame and demean me in front of the crew. I wanted to cry, but the adult in me now would not allow it. I saw red instead—so red I don't remember what I said, but I do know that I held my own. I was as strong and tough as he was—and unlike him, I think I was civil. Several weeks later, when the pilot was over and about to be broadcast, I received a letter from Frank Perry, the director, in which he said (the capitalization is his), "I must tell you, I will never forget your raw COURAGE and GRIT in the face of an insensitivity and abrasiveness which still embarrasses me to think about." The letter meant a lot to me. Of course, he didn't know how much.

At the same time, bad feelings were also growing between Mann and Karl. Mann, whose public face was that of a liberal humanitarian since writing *Judgment at Nuremberg*, was producing disappointing scripts. It got so bad that the network finally hired someone to replace him as the main writer and producer. The new show runner was assigned the task of writing a "bible" for the show, so everyone would know where the stories were going over the long haul. The person who took over Abby Mann's position was Lane Slate, someone whom Karl liked and respected. I met Lane quite briefly when I had to ask one of the studio heads for permission to take a job that would be shot in Paris on my hiatus. The show was to be *The Bunker*, starring Anthony Hopkins, about Hitler's last days. I needed official permission to accept another project during the *Skag* hiatus. I was going to do the asking myself, not have my agent ask on my behalf. It was like the old days at Universal, but now I was not trembling. Before going upstairs to see the big boss, I decided to introduce myself to Lane Slate, and I stopped by his office. Lane was a big bear of a man close to sixty, with mischievous eyes. There was a bubbling spirit in him that I liked. He came rambling over, sat me down, and then sat himself down behind the desk. I told him I was hoping to go to Paris, where I'd never been before, to do a movie, and had to see the guy upstairs to ask for permission. Lane told me he had spent a good deal of time in Paris and wished me well. Afterward I went upstairs to see the big man, who didn't scare me too much. I will confess that I was trembling slightly inside, but unlike the old days, I got my request out very nicely, and he said, "Why not?"

I met Joe for lunch out at the old Getty museum in Malibu to tell him I was going to be able to take the Paris job. He was excited for me and assumed we'd all be going. We had always traveled together, wherever we went, always the two of us until it was the three of us. I hadn't thought about it until that moment, but something made me say, "I want to go alone this time." The few times we'd been separated for short trips of a few days, Joe had been a loving and patient dad who took good care of Anna, as I think I did when Joe was gone. I continued, "It would be nice if Anna could join me in a few weeks."

Joe said he was fine with that. I think we both sensed that things were changing.

A few days later we said our goodbyes, and I flew to Paris, where they put me up at a fancy French hotel. I made no attempt to speak French at first, and the people at the desk were only mildly rude. I had a lot of time on my own between shooting days, and I timidly began to explore the city. I walked rather than take the Métro or a cab so I wouldn't have to speak to people. I was patient with myself about this small setback. I would walk from the hotel to the Louvre and spend the day whenever I could. I spent so much time there, it felt like home.

All that richness caressed my soul as I strolled through the galleries. I knew where everything was kept, even the Rembrandts that were locked away in the top gallery, sealed from the public while waiting for a special wing to be built. I would eat my lunch at the tiny snack bar upstairs and sit on one of the three stools looking out the window where I could see the Jeu de Paume in front of the museum. It had been closed for a long time, and when it finally reopened, I stood with hundreds of others in the long line, waiting to see the Impressionists. I went to many of the places Joe had told me about, the places he particularly loved, like Saint Chapelle, where I was lucky enough to buy a ticket and listen to a concert one evening. Moving around Paris, I slowly began to feel some of the freedom I had experienced once before, when I was nineteen and lost in Tokyo. No one knew where I was, but it was okay. There was none of the childhood panic of feeling alone, the fear that no one would rescue me. I walked and walked, all over the city, and came to realize how small Paris really is. Gradually I became courageous enough to start using my very little bit of French. Struggling to form words brought back memories of my challenge with my first language, and it made me feel a bit of pride in my growth. I no longer had to rely on my mother or on my husband, who was so gifted verbally, to speak for me. Relying on myself to be understood felt good.

Soon it was time to go to work. I had trouble keeping myself together when I was in a scene with Tony Hopkins, who played Hitler so powerfully. As a Jewish woman, I felt a little frightened and outside my character. I had done a lot of research about Hitler's propaganda minister, Joseph Goebbels, and in particular my character, his beautiful wife, Magda. She was one of the few people, perhaps the only person, whom Hitler trusted to cook for him without a "taster." I felt that if indeed Hitler had a physical relationship with a female, it was logical that it was with her, not Eva Braun. My God, I was feeling personally competitive! Magda, her husband, and her four children were in the bunker during Hitler's last days. When the end came, Magda fed her children chocolates laced with poison and tucked them into bed for the last time. I'm sure she loved those children. When I played the scene, I tried to put them to bed in the most loving way possible, not letting any evil intent or pain show. The children were extremely young and not well behaved. One little cherub tried to jab me with a lead pencil. Their bad behavior was effective because it created a sharp contrast to what was really happening in the scene. The show was extremely well received, and Tony Hopkins won a well-deserved Emmy Award as Best Actor for his performance. I was also nominated, for Best Supporting Actress.

As Joe and I had agreed, eight-year-old Anna came to Paris for a visit when I finished shooting. She stayed with me for about a month in a converted photographer's studio I rented in Montmartre. It was pretty exciting. We went to lots of places, with Anna always leading the way and teaching me to use the Métro. We went to museums. We went to a dance concert and met the dancers afterward, sat at outdoor cafés, walked up to the Sacre Coeur, watched the parade at night on Bastille Day. We went to Giverny, Monet's home, where I picked petals from off the ground of Monet's garden. I pressed them into a book that I continue to treasure. Finally, at the end of a trip that I think was more wonderful for me than it was for her, I put her on the plane for home to her dad. I would follow two weeks later.

It was bittersweet, leaving France. I felt whole and clear-headed in a way I never had before. Nothing spectacular had happened while I was in Paris—it seemed like a natural evolution. After my return, both Joe and I acknowledged that after twenty years, though we still loved each other, we had come to the end. We both knew it was remarkable that two people who were so different had managed to maintain a relationship for so long. Perhaps he hadn't been able to save me as he originally wanted to do, but he had given me the stability I needed to save myself. Joe and I remained close friends and partners in raising Anna, and Joe's work at the *Wall Street Journal* flowered. In 2005 he won a Pulitzer Prize for his extraordinary reviews, which "elucidated the strengths and weaknesses of film with rare insight, authority and wit." I was proud to be invited to the celebratory party.

15.

The Great Years

Each decade of my life so far had brought a new beginning for me. At the end of my first decade, I'd left the sanitarium for a new home with my parents in Los Angeles. I'd ended the second decade by leaving Universal for an uncertain career as a free agent. I began the next decade by marrying Joe Morgenstern, and I started my forties by becoming a mother. Each transition had been filled with change and anxiety, and each one had eventually brought growth and a new and better life. As my forties drew toward an end, I was approaching the age when a woman's romantic life and an actress's career often seem to be ending. But instead I found myself fulfilling the dreams I'd had since I was seventeen. I was free as a bird to take a play or do any kind of work that would stretch, challenge, or just plain delight me. I was comfortable enough financially, and though I still hadn't learned to love money, I took enormous pride, probably more than I should, in having solely supported myself since I was eighteen. I managed to keep my daughter close as she grew, and I believed at long last that I could take care of myself without having to lean on someone else.

My family's life was changing, too. My sister had remarried. She'd met a rough, funny, warm-hearted Italian fellow from the Bronx named Al Cimino. Sherrye's children were fond of him, and it appeared he treated them better than their own father had. Sherrye, Al, and her redheaded kids occupied a large Santa Monica apartment not far from me, then moved to Arizona for a time before returning to California. Al never had any money, but he made Sherrye laugh, and he was crazy about her, which was all she'd ever needed.

My father had also remarried four years after my mother's passing. We all attended his wedding at a little chapel in Santa Monica. His new wife was twenty years younger than my mother and was, as my father so memorably described her to his brother Morrie, "built like a brick shithouse." That delighted and startled me; my father had never used such colorful language in front of us. The lady was devoutly of another religion, not Jewish, which also amused me. He had made such a fuss when I dated "non-Jewish" men. But this lady was as talkative as my mother had been, and that must have been a comfort to my dad. We were happy that he now had company, and they traveled together extensively for several years.

When Joe and I separated, he moved into an apartment a block away and continued coming to the house. We hoped to keep Anna's life as unchanged as possible. She seemed to have expected this, perhaps because so many of her friends had divorced parents. Her initial response when we told her was "Is Daddy going to have a pool?" Was it total denial or immediate adjustment? Either way, only time would tell. We had Anna going back and forth from my place to Joe's every few days at first but soon realized Anna did much better spending longer periods with each of us.

I spent a lot of time alone while Anna was in school, walking and meditating down by the ocean. I spent hours working on the six-hundred-pound piece of Georgian marble that was parked on a dolly in a shady place outside the house. Inside the house, I confess I adored not having to share a closet, and I rejoiced in having *all* the space to myself.

After many months on my own, I decided it was time to venture out into the world again. I bought two tickets to see *My Fair Lady* at the legendary Pantages Theater in Hollywood. Weeks went by, but I couldn't think of anyone to invite to go to the performance with me. Most of my women friends were in Woodstock, Anne Strick was out of the country, Elaine was back in England, and all the interesting men I knew were taken. There was no one. Finally, on the day before the performance, I had a thought—what about Lane Slate, the "show runner" for *Skag?* Our hiatus was not yet over, so I hadn't seen him since our initial meeting. I'd heard that he had lost his wife of thirty-five years about four years before. He'd sent me a postcard at the hotel while I was in Paris just to say hello. It was worth a try.

I hadn't been out on a date in twenty years, and I was shaky as a teenager when I picked up the phone to call him. I apologized for the last-minute invitation and said I hoped he could join me. I started to go on with more explanation, but Lane cut me off with "I'd love to, absolutely, I'd love to." I had a date.

I had someone stay with Anna the next evening and drove my car to meet Lane midway. I didn't want a man coming to the house for Anna to see. I parked, he got out of his car and helped me into his, and we went to Hollywood to see the show. Lane was at least six foot four, a *big* guy with a craggy, still-handsome Irish face, graying hair, and dark brows. He was close to sixty, but he behaved like a young kid that night. He was openly delighted to be with me. I was touched, and I also laughed a lot because he struck my funny bone, bull's-eye, every five minutes. He looked at me at intermission as if he could devour me, while he guiltily smoked his cigarette out on the sidewalk. When the show was over, he took me to a small club where they played good jazz, and we had a beer and shrimp cocktail. Then he took me back to my car, and while standing in the street before helping me in, he gave me a feeling-full kiss.

It was the beginning of a long romance with a wonderful man. Lane was respectful and admiring of my work as an actress, and he himself was quite a brilliant writer, producer, director, and painter. He was also a birder, spoke many languages, designed furniture, and worshipped the flowers outside his house. Friends told me how deeply and faithfully he had loved his wife during their long marriage. He was, as his son later told me, "a servant of the truth: brilliant, sensitive, and kind." After our first date Lane wrote me a hand-printed letter or postcard every single day and sent it through the mail. They were sometimes ardent, never heavy, frequently funny, and always delightful. I was a little overwhelmed with his show of feelings for me. I didn't know what to do with them. I tried to slow things down a little, and I waited a fairly long time before becoming intimate with him. I could no longer be casual, as I had been when I was a very young woman. It was a big step for me. Lane never pressed me, but his interest was clear. And when I was ready, it was everything I could have dreamed of. We had a powerful cerebral and physical connection. The mind is the main thing, isn't it? He was a passionate and imaginative lover. He adored my body, whether my weight was up or down. When I walked down the street with him, I felt so protected by his presence, electrically charged at the sight of him. And always there was the humor. Lane wanted us to marry when I was legally free, but I didn't want marriage. I loved him, but I don't think I ever really wanted that with anyone, and now I was wise enough to know it. Lane and I were lovers and friends for most of the next ten years. Rich years.

My professional life continued to thrive as well. Nearly thirty years after the *Twelfth Night* fiasco, I was excited to have another crack at Shakespeare. This time I'd play Lady Macbeth opposite Jeremy Brett, who had great success as Sherlock Holmes on TV. We would rehearse it as a play, with the performance filmed as part of a series made for distribution to colleges. Arthur Allan Seidelman was our director. We rehearsed for about four weeks on stage in an enormous old semi-abandoned theater in a fairly rough section of downtown L.A. I had vague memories of having played there when I was a kid during the Second World War, singing and dancing with my sister to sell war bonds. I don't think I spoke to anyone of my awareness of the theater's history and its connection to my past.

At the end of the month's rehearsal, we shot the play from beginning to end on a soundstage, stopping the filming for a break between the acts. I don't know how successful we were. Because of the limited nature of the distribution for many years, there was little feedback. But it was a great exercise and gave me a chance at a classic role that certainly gave life to many things I played after that.

I loved becoming fifty. I was amazed and felt so blessed to have arrived there. I gave myself a birthday party and invited twenty special friends for a sit-down dinner. My friend Lilah Kan, a superb professional Chinese chef, flew out from New York and made a Chinese banquet for me at home. We created a very long table in the big living room to accommodate everyone, and I bought a length of pretty fabric to cover it. Everyone wore formal clothes. Lane looked delicious in a tux; Joe was handsome and dressed up, accompanied by a small and lovely Asian girl. He had taken a job with the *L.A. Herald-Examiner* by then, writing an interesting column several days a week and doing well. My dear friend Bob Richards was there, and of course, my darling Anna. Lane and his son Webster had a birthday cake made that said "Actress, Sculptor, and Foxy Lady." My health was good, I think I was looking well, and I was happy.

I renewed my friendship with Jean Simmons when we were both cast in *The Thorn Birds*. I'd known her since we'd played sisters in *Until They Sail* in 1957. Jean now lived very near me in Santa Monica, and we often took long walks together, sometimes passing our ex-husbands' apartments in the same neighborhood. They didn't know each other, but we thought it would be great fun if they came out so that we could wave as we passed. Jean and I were both nominated for Emmys for Best Supporting Actress in 1983 and went to the ceremony together, each with our own beau, mine being Lane. For one wild moment, we considered wearing identical gowns with a large stuffed bird on one shoulder but settled for something a bit more conservative. Jean won the Emmy that night. If it wasn't going to be me, I was glad it was beautiful Jean.

I was regularly offered miniseries and movies of the week on TV, and though the roles weren't always challenging, they paid the bills. Then in the mid-1980s, an interesting film came along. More than forty years after the original *Wizard of Oz* with legendary Judy Garland, I was offered the chance to play Auntie Em in an *Oz* story entitled *Return to Oz*. It was a British-American production to be shot in England. Eight-year-old Fairuza Balk, a genuinely nice little girl, was cast as Dorothy, along with Nicol Williamson and Jean Marsh in key roles.

My friend the great Freddie Francis was the director of photography for only the first half of the movie and moved on after my scenes were shot. I was never quite sure why. David Watkin took over and is the only DP credited. I had the pleasure of being directed by the extraordinary Walter Murch, Academy Award–winning film editor and sound designer and, incidentally, son of the fine painter Walter Tandy Murch. Walter is a tall, gentle, shy man with a passion for the works of Frank Baum. *Return to Oz*, unlike the *Wizard of Oz* movie, was a dark story in which Dorothy is put in a mental institution to "cure her" of her delusion that she has been to another world. Although the film was too dark for some people's taste, it attracted a strong cult following that appreciated its relationship to the original *Oz* stories.

We shot the film in England, and I was there for many weeks. Some of our time was spent in the country, shooting exteriors and staying in old inns with three-foot-thick walls. I saw Stonehenge for the first time on that trip. At times the wind was so cold and strong on the moors that between takes I had to wear a large cardboard box over my head with eyeholes cut out, to keep my wig and my face from flying away.

My part was relatively small, so I had free time to wander around London and hang out in my hotel room, reading the travel magazines in the room. One afternoon I was lying on the bed, enjoying myself, devouring the photographs of quaint Scottish villages and beautifully thatched cottages. I was daydreaming, wishing that one day I could see them for real, when I was suddenly thunderstruck by what should have been obvious—why was I looking at pictures when I could be there?! I had ten days before I had to shoot my next scene.

I went to the train station and purchased a ticket for thirty-five dollars that could take me all over Scotland by train, ferry, or bus, anywhere I wanted to go within the span of eight days. It was a wonderful decision and I had a glorious time.

I decided to use my professional, Scottish-sounding name for the trip. It seemed appropriate I don't think any of them had ever heard of me as an actress. They saw almost no American movies.

The last night I spent at an inn, I went into the pub after dinner. It was a small, softly lit room with a bar large enough for just a few people. As I stood chatting with friends I'd made from the village, two very young men barely in their twenties drifted over to me and asked in a flirtatious manner what I was doing there. (I credit the soft pink lighting in the room for their interest.) I told them I was on vacation.

Then one of them asked, "What kind of work do you do?"

I said, "I'm an actress."

One of the boys said, "Oh, what's your name?"

"It's Piper Laurie."

"Is that your real name?" the other boy asked.

I said, "Oh no, it's completely made up."

At that moment the boys' proper Englishman father, whose attention had been elsewhere, said, "Of course it's made up—that's the name of that ancient movie star!"

I turned to face the father squarely, knowing I would treasure this moment forever. Taking a deep breath from the bottoms of my feet up, I said in the grandest way I knew how, "Sir—I *am* that ancient movie star!"

I left Scotland with considerable reluctance. I had an amazing trip and was overwhelmed by the warmth and hospitality of the people I met along the way.

When I arrived back in London, the studio driver had lots of gossip for me. The first big news item was that there had been an armed holdup at the *Oz* office on the lot, and our producer had managed to get away by running down the back stairs. The other big news was that our beloved director, Walter Murch, had had a temporary loss of confidence and been fired. The driver said some of Walter's pals had flown over to insist he be rehired and stayed to support him by their presence. Indeed, when I came through the soundstage door, sitting "inconspicuously" in directors' chairs in the corner were Walter's "pals"—George Lucas, Francis Coppola, and Phil Kaufman! They stayed long enough for Walter to get his second wind. How's that for appreciation and friendship?

Later I would return to Europe for a miniseries based on F. Scott Fitzgerald's *Tender Is the Night*. I was shooting in France and invited my once-bold sister to meet me in Paris for a week. I knew she wouldn't come, she had never traveled anywhere before, but I asked anyway. She called me back and said, "Surprise! I'm coming, I'm coming!"

That was the beginning of a precious, sweet time with my older sister. I waited for her at the Paris airport as I had for eight-year-old and fearless Anna a few years before. I saw Sherrye come up that same ramp, looking so frightened before she spotted me, yet I knew she was actually very brave to come. When she finally saw me, she began to relax, and I took her to our quaint little hotel. She was enchanted with all the small inconveniences, including having to use a bathroom down the hall. She was a little uneasy at first, being in a separate room and on a different floor from me, but she quickly relaxed. I took her under my wing and had the joy of showing off as I showed her Paris, my knowledge of the city, and getting by with my French. She was so impressed. She always seemed to have taken my other successes for granted, but this was different somehow, and her admiration meant a lot to me. We had such a good time. We both feasted on the memory of that trip for years afterward.

There was great release in being able to do fine supporting roles, traveling all over the world, often with my daughter, Anna, and not being burdened with the trappings of publicity and physical perfection.

My body, however, was beginning to revolt and show signs of the abuse I'd given it when I was a kid. I had joyously done all those movie stunts and falls from horses and high places, and now I was told I needed a hip replacement. The surgery was relatively rare at that time with someone my age, so I kept it secret from my agent and people in my profession because I didn't want to limit prospective work. Of course, my family knew, and Lane, who was my first visitor at the hospital. Using my body creatively had been the most fun in building characters, and I didn't want to be deprived of that tool. I did exercises in the early morning hours to keep limber and strong before going to work.

I had a new challenge in 1985 when I was offered a role in the movie version of the play *Children of a Lesser God.* It starred William Hurt,

Philip Bosco, and Marlee Matlin in her first film role. I played Marlee's mother. I would need to learn sign language for the part, and I worked very hard on it. Weeks before shooting, my teacher, Bob Daniels, a profoundly deaf man who could speak quite well and later became a friend, arrived at my apartment to begin teaching me. On that first day he didn't speak to me at all, just used hand and body movement to tell me what he wanted. I was forced into inventing my own body-sign language on that first day, serving him tea and getting a visceral sense of what sign language was about. But after that beginning I had to learn properly. We met regularly, and I got very good at signing. But since my character was supposed to be rusty and reluctant to sign, I stopped the lessons well before we started to shoot.

Our director for the film was Randa Haines, who was directing her first feature. Randa was the first woman film director I'd ever worked with, and I thought she was very good. She had definite ideas of what she wanted, and I liked them, too, even to the eye makeup my character would wear, a hard line near the lashes, as many women did at that time. It made sense to me. I arbitrarily decided to wear no makeup at all in the scenes when Marlee comes home in the middle of the night. Randa must have approved because she said not a word. She also allowed me some creative input in my dialogue. There had been many attempts to write an important speech my character gives to her daughter in one of the last scenes, but none of the revisions seemed right. Randa didn't like them, I didn't like them, and the fine writer, who was worn out by then, didn't like them, either. We were getting to the day when we'd have to shoot the speech, so I made a stab at it, boiling it down to its essential truth. It was much shorter and to the point. Everyone liked it, so that's what we did. I found that as one gets older, people more readily accept their ideas simply because they're older. It's really not fair—I had good ideas when I was twenty, but people wouldn't listen.

It was a fine film and received many honors. Bill Hurt was handsome in an old-movie-star way and very creative. I loved his intensity and his courage as an actor. I thought Marlee and Bill were wonderful together, and I believed Bill should have gotten the Academy Award for his performance, just as Marlee did. When the movie was over,

Bill sent me yellow roses and a special note that I still have. Then, an amazing surprise—I received my third Oscar nomination! Not bad for an ancient actress! I must admit I was excited, and I had great fun at the ceremonies with Lane.

In 1986 Glenn Jordan offered me a role in the very beautiful *Promise,* one of the best shows Hallmark has ever produced. Glenn is one of the most accomplished directors I've ever worked with. He is also the only director who consistently hired me after I stepped over the threshold into a certain age. I consider him a friend and trust his judgment enough to call him from time to time for insight into a character I'm playing. *Promise* is a powerful and touching film about two brothers, played by James Garner and James Woods, one of whom is mentally ill. The two Jameses were quite brilliant. I played opposite James Garner, a very grown-up and sexy actor, a dream come true. I got to work with the extraordinary James Woods again. We had a special bond, having worked together so closely on stage in Nantucket many years before.

The completed film was powerful and deservedly nominated for many Emmys. Glenn Jordan won for Best Direction, James Woods for Best Actor, Richard Friedenberg for Best Screenplay, and the movie for Best Show. I won, too, for Best Supporting Actress. I was pleased by the honor but had no expectations of winning, having been nominated at least a dozen times in the past, not because my acting was particularly good, but because I'd chosen parts and shows well. I was on the road doing a play at the time of the Emmy Awards ceremony, so I asked James Woods to accept for me, "just in case." I was sitting on a couch in my hotel room, having just finished dinner, watching the awards show with our stage manager and his assistant, when I heard my name called out as the winner. *What?!* The stage manager jumped up and threw his body on top of mine, knocking the wind out of me; his assistant threw herself on top of both of us; and we all screamed with delight! They pulled themselves away in time for us to watch James give an acceptance speech on my behalf. James was clearly very excited that I'd won, and I was so proud that it was he who was there for me. Not long afterward our little group—Glenn Jordan, James Garner, and myself—was invited to James Woods's very large wedding. My father was my escort. As far as I could tell, out of hundreds of guests, I was the only actress there. I took it as some kind of honor.

I continued to receive offers for roles that allowed me to travel to places I had never seen. In 1988 I was thrilled to go to Israel to shoot Agatha Christie's *Appointment with Death*, with a large cast of distinguished actors, including Sir John Gielgud, Peter Ustinov, Carrie Fisher, and the legendary Lauren Bacall. She told me to call her Betty and said, "We're two Jewish girls going to Israel for the first time together." I found her to be terrifically funny and vulnerable, and she made me laugh a lot. On one of our last days in Jerusalem, I'd been walking around happily buying souvenirs to take to friends and family back home, when I heard the unmistakable husky voice of Lauren Bacall.

"Piper! My God, girl! What are you doing?!" She threw herself at me from behind, almost knocking me over a jewelry counter. "Your *skirt*, for God's sake! It's tucked into your pantyhose! Your whole bottom is exposed!" Betty pulled and tugged at my clothes. "Oh, Piper, can't you be trusted to go anywhere?" *Apparently not!*

My friend Jean Simmons gave lavish teas, and at one of them I met Charles Nelson Reilly, whose public persona was that of a funny man. He was in reality a very serious man, a splendid acting teacher and director. He asked me if I would be interested in doing William Luce's *Zelda*. Charles had had a great Broadway success directing Julie Harris as Emily Dickinson in Luce's *The Belle of Amherst*, and he hoped he could do the same with Zelda Fitzgerald and me.

When I agreed to do *Zelda*, later called *The Last Flapper*, Charles asked me to learn the words before we began rehearsing. No thought, no motivation, no emotion, just the words by rote, as a child learns. He told me to take all the time I needed. We had no deadline, no schedule. Only when I was ready would we begin to stage it. That made it seem possible, and I didn't panic. There were two hour-long acts to memorize. My sister came to me each day and held the script while I slowly began to learn, and only when my brain and tongue felt they would explode and I could absorb no more did we stop. It took four full months working every day to master the solid two hours of talking. My patience as a stone carver helped me with this.

When I felt absolutely sure about the text, we rented an inexpensive rehearsal studio on Hollywood Boulevard. I was quite terrified. At first, in the new environment, the words left me, hiding somewhere in my brain. After I relaxed and settled down, I found they were still there.

Charles had no staging planned. We had a couple of large movable blocks to use as furniture if it became necessary. I'd just be saying the words and moving instinctually around the space. Charles was brilliant. He never looked at the script or at me. I'd be talking, talking. He'd be walking around quietly, looking down the hallway, over to a table, out the window, but never, or seldom, at me. It was as if he were just keeping me company. Every once in a while I would hear Charles say, "Oh, that's good." So somehow he was taking in what I was doing, I don't know, perhaps through his skin. But it was totally nonjudgmental and allowed me to find my way. What a gift of freedom. Every actor can understand that.

I never thought about the words; they were simply there naturally, as they are in life when you express a thought. This experience changed my way of working forever.

It was during performances of *The Last Flapper* that I had the astonishing experience of breaking the sacred fourth wall and finding it no longer terrifying. I was speaking directly to all those strangers out there who had frightened me so while I was growing up. I began to love it, especially when I was forced to improvise and interact with the audience, or even just offer a paper cup of water from my pitcher on stage to someone coughing badly. I could easily, for the evening, bring them into the play. No fortune was great enough to pay for this experience.

Through my research I began to know the Fitzgeralds so intimately that for a time, I felt haunted by Zelda and Scott. My visualization of Scott, to whom Zelda speaks occasionally in the course of the play, became so intense that one night, for a fleeting instant toward the end of the performance, I thought I saw Scott standing in the wings, a bit shorter than I had imagined, looking at me with interest. I have never spoken of this, nor have I had a moment like that since. The brain is an interesting trickster.

Back home in L.A. again, I found that Lane had become very ill with what are called cluster headaches. At first he'd thought they were a side effect of trying to stop smoking. There is no cure for these headaches. They are so horrific that there is a very high suicide rate among the often brilliant people who suffer from them. The experimental drugs that were used to treat Lane's headaches ultimately caused several aneurysms. When he didn't improve, he sold his house in Pacific Palisades and bought a ranch outside of Tucson to hide his illness away from people. After a time he seemed to recover and was able to work again. We still saw each other whenever we could. Sometimes he'd come to L.A., and sometimes I'd go to his ranch in Arizona. When we were together, he was as vital and stimulating as ever in every way. Once his health improved, he continued to ask me to marry him and tried to entice me to move to the ranch by building a structure that would be my studio. I continued to say no. I loved him, but I didn't want to be anyone's wife.

Then one day I had an epiphany of sorts. I'd been shopping at my local market, and for a moment I thought I spotted Lane. When I realized it wasn't him, I had such a deep yearning to be with him that I rushed home and called him in Arizona to tell him I had changed my mind: I wanted to marry him. I never got the words out. He spoke first and told me he had been about to call me, to tell me he was getting married to some lady he knew from the East, years before his first marriage. I felt a flood of pain and embarrassment but said, "That's wonderful . . . I wish you . . ." and wept when I hung up because our timing was doomed, as Lane had once said. *Why did I not have the courage to speak the truth about my yearning for him at that moment?* I suppose because he might have called my bluff, and I would really have had to face the question of marriage—or even worse, that he loved her more.

16.

Peaks and Valleys

Though I never pursued projects that would become cult favorites, as it turned out, they found me. Fifteen years after *Carrie* jump-started my career and assured me immortality among followers of horror films, I was offered a part in a quirky gothic melodrama named *Twin Peaks*. David Lynch's darkly comic venture into series television attracted a rabid following that rivaled fans of *The Rocky Horror Picture Show*.

I first met David Lynch at a small dinner party, and he was not what I had expected. I'd seen all his work, including *Eraserhead*. He was not weird at all, but quiet and friendly, and I liked him very much.

Months later I was sitting in the reception area in David's West Hollywood office. There was a stunningly beautiful Asian girl sitting there, waiting with me. I would meet Joan Chen later. Right now I thought she looked tense. I can't say I was. I liked David and was actually looking forward to seeing him. I had read the pilot script and didn't care that my part was very small; I wanted the experience of working with David. While I waited, I noticed a few men who obviously worked there moving about, coming in and out of doors, looking busy. I kept thinking there was something a little odd about the picture before me. Then I realized they were all wearing their hair very much like David's: blondish and very high. I supposed the imitation was unconscious.

After a few minutes I was escorted into the office. It was tiny, but like the tresses of the men who inhabited the place, it too had a vaulted ceiling. Everything was ultra-stainless steel and stark white. Both David Lynch and Mark Frost, who was David's partner and cowriter, were standing there looking really happy to see me, and so of course I was very happy, too. I stayed maybe five minutes, no more, leaning against the wall. None of us sat down. I agreed to do their pilot for *Twin Peaks* and left. Though I was sure it was a one-time thing, I had to sign on for a possible series. These things almost never go forward, and I was not interested in being tied up. As things turned out, the pilot was a spectacular success, and I was contractually committed to work on the series. I shut my eyes and threw myself into it. My part grew, and with the exception of the long hours, I enjoyed the work tremendously.

The exteriors for the pilot were filmed in the state of Washington on exquisite locations in the pines. The actual *Twin Peaks* studio and soundstage were in a converted warehouse deep in the San Fernando Valley, with the lodge painstakingly re-created indoors. While we were on the lush locations, we fancy stars slept not in the lodge but in third-rate motels with views of the gas station.

It was a pleasure working with David. He had a low-key, quiet style on the set, sounding, I thought, a little bit like Jimmy Stewart. One had to listen closely or they might miss the flashes of great wit. His mind was fearless and creative, like a child who has never experienced the dark.

My body behaved well, and I made few adjustments. I had to tone down the required wild dancing to moderately wild dancing for my character Catherine in one scene. I confided in our director for that episode, former dancer and choreographer Lesli Linka Glatter, whom I was confident would keep my secret. Cleverly, I traveled with ice packs on my legs as I drove myself home at night.

My sister asked me if I was aware that my romantic leading man, Richard Beymer, was fifteen years my junior. She proceeded to tell me that I appeared younger-looking because I had good health and skin, and because I rarely drank. She knew almost nothing about my past since we'd been children, and I had no need to tell her. Sherrye was having a good time enjoying my newfound celebrity. Every relative and friend I possessed was watching the show, which had not always been the case. Clearly, we were a hit.

The crowning glory came after we wrapped up the first season. David called me at home and said, in his Jimmy Stewart drawl, "Rosie, I want you to give some thought to the next season. Your character was last seen at the fire in the sawmill. We don't know whether Catherine escaped or not. When we come back, I want the audience to think you died in the fire. Your husband, Jack Nance, will think you're dead. Everyone will think you're dead, and we'll take your name off the credits of the show."

It crossed my mind for a millisecond that this was David's original way of telling me I was being fired.

But he continued, "Now, Rosie, this is the part I want you to think about. You will return in some sort of disguise, as a man, and you'll spy on the town and create trouble for everyone—your husband, your lover, everyone. You should probably be a businessman. I want you to decide what kind of businessman you would like to be. Maybe a Frenchman or a Mexican. Think about it for a while and let me know."

I was so enchanted with the open possibilities and the power of being able to choose my part. Who was the child now? I decided I'd be a Japanese businessman because I thought it would be less predictable. I was so filled with excitement and laughter; this was joyful children's play. There was no argument from David when I told him my choice, no attempt to influence me. He simply accepted it. Then came the hard part. David wished me to keep it a secret from the entire cast and crew. Not even my agent or my family was to know. That was important to him. I wasn't to tell a soul.

There was so much preparation involved in pulling off the subterfuge. There were secret makeup and wardrobe tests at a laboratory in the Valley. Paula Shimatsu-u, who was Mark Frost's assistant and one of the few people who knew, was helpful in making tape recordings of Japanese friends reciting my lines. I practiced imitating them while driving to and from work. I had assumed that, of course, the placement of my voice would be electronically altered, but they had given it no thought and were not prepared on the morning of my first scene. I am trained to keep going no matter what, and when I realized I was on my own, I ended up going to a place in my chest and throat to get that appropriate guttural sound. It turned out to be painful to sustain, and I sipped liquids constantly between takes. I shall never do that again for fear of injuring my voice permanently.

I've skipped the enchanting part. Paula Shimatsu-u also dealt with the press and released a bio about "the new cast member": **"Fumio Yamaguchi is a Japanese star who has worked primarily with Kurosawa. He has flown over especially to work with David Lynch. His English is a little shaky; therefore he needs an interpreter and learns his lines phonetically."**

The cast, crew, and all guest directors knew nothing; nor did my family. My name came off the credits, and Fumio Yamaguchi's was put on. Because I wouldn't talk about it when asked, my poor sister and her friends assumed I'd been fired. Sherrye was so upset that she started having asthma attacks, and I had to take her into my confidence.

I was introduced to Paula's brother Derick, whom I hired to act as a much-needed personal assistant, and whom David later hired to appear on camera as "Fumio's" assistant in the show. Derick would pick me up at three in the morning in Santa Monica and drive me to the special makeup lab way out in the Valley, about twenty minutes from our studio. There I would spend four hours being made up and dressed for my new identity. From the moment the studio van arrived for me, I was Fumio Yamaguchi. The driver, whom I knew personally, had no idea whom he was picking up. When the long day was over, I would be driven back to the lab and spend at least an hour and a half removing the prosthetics before Derick drove me home. Wisely, they never scheduled consecutive days for me. I needed at least three days for my face to heal until the next time the prosthetics were glued on.

The enchantment continued for me, though certainly not for the guest directors, who were not told what was up and had their hands full. I was flying! I constantly improvised conversations with Derick, my so-called assistant-interpreter on the set; I spoke fake Japanese in a very low voice, and Derick responded in real Japanese. Every time the poor director gave me a direction, I caused a five-minute delay while my assistant and I thrashed things out. I would instruct Derick to say to the director, on my behalf, things such as "This is not the way Kurosawa works!" When it appeared that the director was about to quit or have a stroke, he would be given a heads-up, quietly. But even then he didn't know who I was. This was my life's Harpo moment! And I did not deny myself.

I learned that suppressing laughter all day long while I stayed in character was actually physically difficult. Even if I went to a private place like the bathroom (I had a locked private one next to some offices), I could crack and ruin the makeup by laughing. So I stayed controlled, and I was too tired when I got home to whoop and holler in the wee hours.

The regular cast on the set bought the act at first. They were a little intimidated initially by the strange foreigner and were told to be very respectful to me. Jack Nance, the innocent, who played my husband on the show, went to David and Mark at the end of the first day and said, "Boy . . . is that new actor *weird!*"

When the cast got used to me being around, they looked a little more closely and could see I was wearing very heavy makeup. Later most of the actors said they knew something was up, but they never revealed that in front of me. And no one suspected "Fumio" was me. I heard that Peggy Lipton was convinced I was Isabella Rossellini. Jack Nance and I had a number of important scenes together, but he didn't know it was me until weeks later, when he read the "reveal" scene in his script.

Matt Roush, the journalist and critic who was then a reporter for *USA Today*, was a special fan of my character Catherine Martell. He wanted to know if it was true that Piper Laurie was no longer on the show. He said he missed me. Paula Shimatsu-u said she couldn't discuss it but could arrange an interview with the new star from Japan. Roush had seen the "new actor" in several episodes and said he would be interested. And so Paula invited Roush to come out to the studio to interview "Fumio Yamaguchi."

A time was set for a meeting in Mark Frost's office. If this were a close, face-to-face meeting, Roush would immediately spot the heavy makeup, so when he arrived, he was told, "Mr. Yamaguchi is exhausted from yesterday's work and wished to rest at home, but he has offered to speak to you on the telephone. He has his interpreter with him at home."

Roush agreed and began an interview with me on the telephone while I was actually just downstairs in an office. Derick and Paula were by my side as I spoke in my guttural voice and broken English. I don't remember if it was Roush or me who brought up baseball, but for some reason it became an important part of the conversation—that, and in what ways David Lynch was different from Kurosawa, who was then still very much alive. Every once in a while I'd put Derick on the phone to pretend to explain things for me, and after a good half hour the interview ended. Roush thanked me in an extremely formal and nice way. Moments after hanging up, I walked upstairs to Mark Frost's office and said, "Hi, Mark, I just dropped by to say hello." (Of course, Mark was expecting me.)

Mark introduced me to Roush, who said, "I'm so relieved to see you here, Ms. Laurie. I presume this means you'll be doing more episodes. I was getting concerned—I really loved your character."

"Oh, thank you," I replied sweetly.

The conversation went on for quite a while, and I made myself comfortable on the couch, flirtatiously close to Mr. Roush. Mark joined in the conversation, and I drifted into talking about baseball and quoted the reporter and myself in a subtle way from our phone conversation.

Finally, and it was just an exquisite moment, the lightbulb went on. Mr. Roush suddenly turned whiter than he was, looked squarely at me, his eyes wide, his face turning rose red. Jumping up, he threw himself on the floor, kicking and screaming, "No . . . no . . . no . . . I don't believe it!" He got himself up off the floor and fell back onto the couch again shouting, "Oh . . . no . . . no!" He was hitting himself and laughing, and we all had such a long, deep, wonderful laugh together. It made up for all the times I couldn't laugh while I was working. Matt Roush was such a good sport and wrote two good pieces about the show for *USA Today*.

When *Twin Peaks* ended, I was nominated for an Emmy and also a Golden Globe for my performance. I went to the Foreign Press's Golden Globe ceremony out of loyalty to David Lynch. I didn't expect to win anything. It was awfully nice that they always seemed to nominate me whether I deserved it or not, and every year it was the same: I never won. My agent was my escort. Everyone from *Twin Peaks* who had been nominated sat together, having dinner at one large table. Before the ceremony started, feeling a bit trapped behind a railing and between colleagues, I felt lazy and didn't bother going to the ladies' room to tidy my hair for the possibility of a camera spotting me. Happy to be one of the crowd, I sat back and made myself comfortable, leaning on the railing. My category came early in the show, and we were all poised to applaud enthusiastically for whomever, when suddenly I heard my name. *Oh dear God, no!*

I shot out of my seat as if reporting for duty, afraid to waste anybody's time, not stopping to hug or kiss anybody. It seemed to take forever to squeeze past the railing and find a pathway to the stage, and I cringed as I approached the microphone. I had always dreaded this possibility and frankly always preferred losing because of it. *Some things never change completely*. There were lots of smiling faces looking up at me, among them Van Johnson, of all people, with whom I'd made a movie and hadn't seen in decades, looking so happy for me and applauding! I have no recollection of what I said, and I'm certain I was hyperventilating.

Afterward I exited upstage as instructed, quickly carrying my prize through the narrow white fabric tunnel that led to the press room—and saw Whoopi Goldberg coming fast toward me in the tunnel from the other direction. Wasn't this one-way? I had always admired and loved Whoopi Goldberg, but we'd never met. I stopped short, and so did she. There was barely enough room for us to pass. We both laughed, threw our arms around each other like long-lost friends, then continued on. George C. Scott told me that he and Donald O'Connor, whom he greatly admired, once passed each other in a country club foyer.

Big George, well over six feet, and small slender Donald also threw themselves into each other's arms. I've never had the opportunity to ask Whoopi why she was traveling in the wrong direction. But then, why wouldn't she?

I was still shooting *Twin Peaks* when I was asked to work opposite Gregory Peck in *Other People's Money*, the film adaptation of the stage hit. The *Twin Peaks* producers were terrific with their scheduling in allowing this to work. I was picked up in a limo and driven across town from set to set, removing my makeup for the one while en route. Being accommodated in this way made me feel useful and appreciated—very different from the pouring out of conveniences thrown at me when I was a kid.

The notion of working with Gregory Peck was as unreal as anything I'd experienced in my career. I'd never met him, nor did I ever expect to, for he was obviously not mortal. I had seen him and his gloriously beautiful wife, Veronique, at a number of Hollywood events over the years. He could easily be spotted towering over most people in a crowd, and your eye couldn't help but catch the magnificent couple. Every woman I knew, even the most sophisticated, was envious of me, including Lauren Bacall, who had known and worked with him in the past. Wouldn't you know, he turned out to be the warmest, slightly imperfect, regular guy. Gregory was authentically a fine human being who took the world very seriously and did much to make it better, but he was a real laugher when he had the chance—I suppose because he knew so much. We had one scene in which we were not at all the focus, just sitting around the big family dinner table, chuckling on cue in the background. Our laughter was always genuine and sometimes almost out of control.

Our director, Norman Jewison, who had made one of my favorite movies, *Moonstruck*, decided that he wanted me to look older and dowdier *after* we had begun to shoot. Norman hadn't said a word about my looks when he'd cast me. This was not the first time this had happened. Abby Mann had made an ugly scene, but Norman was a gentleman. He even wore a lapel pin that said "It's only a movie." So I made a point of enjoying my meals and wore clothes and hair that were not terribly flattering, which may have been a career mistake. If so, it was worth it. I'd never have missed getting to know Gregory, whom I could never quite bring myself to call "Greg." Through the years I remained friends with him and Veronique and had the privilege of performing as his reading partner at the downtown L.A. Library reading series that he created.

Some things in my life were coming full circle. I played opposite Albert Finney in a movie, *Rich in Love*, and he told me that he had had a crush on me in his youth. Lane had divorced his new wife after six weeks of marriage. We picked up as if nothing had changed, except I'd gotten cold feet again about marriage, as you might suspect. We took lots of the driving trips that we both loved, and sometimes I stayed at his ranch in Arizona.

Other things were changing as well, and some of the changes were painful. My beautiful, independent Anna decided it was time for her to live her own life. Shortly after high school, she got a job and moved into a tiny place of her own a few miles from us, with a young boy she had met while in high school. Neither Joe nor I was thrilled with her decision, but it was her life, and we knew we had to let her live it. The most painful moment for me was walking into Anna's room for the first time after she'd left. Of course, her clothes were gone. But the closet door was open, and the dozens of stuffed animals she'd collected through the years, that had lived on the top shelf seemingly forever, were also gone. That was a surprisingly powerful symbol of my loss and her growth. I appreciated that she still wanted those soft, cuddly things with her. I could have used a few myself.

Lane continued to write and paint in Arizona, sometimes visiting me in L.A., but by the second season of *Twin Peaks*, he had become very ill. We spoke almost every day while I was working, until his son called to tell me he was in the hospital. I went to Arizona to visit him. Webster picked me up at the Tucson airport and drove me to the hospital. We visited for a long while. I took it upon myself to break my word to David Lynch and explained the disguise to Lane, telling him about my scenes as the Japanese businessman. I knew he'd enjoy the whole charade, but I also feared he might not live to see it. I acted out some of the scenes for Lane, playing all the parts, and we both laughed a lot. He was discharged from the hospital and sent home for a while, and I went back to L.A. to work.

Some weeks later I flew again to see Lane, who was back in the hospital. When I walked into his room, the change was shocking. He was pathetically thin and frail, the color of pale marigolds. There was little flesh on his face, but it revealed his fine bone structure. This great huge man looked ethereal. He actually looked quite beautiful and almost on the other side.

I sat on Lane's bed and kissed him gently on the cheek. Suddenly he sat up and kissed me ferociously, fully on the mouth like a young lover, as if to tell me his passion for me—for life—was great, and he was still part of it. By holding on to his sexuality, he was holding on to life.

That night I slept in Lane's bed at the ranch, surrounded by his distinctive aroma of aftershave and old cigarettes. I touched all the beautifully made, perfectly pressed shirts hanging in the closet that were all ready to go out on the town. I soaked up all that I could, together with his spirit, and took it with me when I left in the morning.

His son Webster called me on the set a few days later to tell me that Lane was gone. They let me go home early that day.

Lane's body was sent to his family in Massachusetts. I met his many East Coast relatives later on, when I flew to New York to attend Webster's wedding. I was so touched that Webster wanted me there.

Four months after Lane died, I had a big-numbered birthday. I wished Lane were around to tease me and make me laugh about myself. The remedy for so much sadness was to throw myself a little party, just a few good friends. I took everyone to a good restaurant in Santa Monica for dinner. There were about a dozen of us: my sister and her husband, Al; Anna and her boyfriend; Joe and his date; Glenn Jordan and his partner, Michael; Happy and Jane Traum, who were out from Woodstock and who celebrated my birthday with me every year. I sent a limo to South Central to pick up Bob Richards and his mother. Bob had been fighting cancer for years by then and was almost unrecognizable that night, extremely bloated from medication and not well, but determined to join us and have a good time. Champagne was poured for everyone. I took a sip and, uninvited, made a clumsy little impromptu speech to commemorate the event and to acknowledge my superior age. I actually invited myself to make a speech. This was indeed progress.

Six months later my dear friend Bob, my long-ago lover and my collaborator since I was sixteen, was also dead. He had fought the cancer for fifteen years. I had a memorial celebration for him at my new little home at the foot of the Hollywood Hills. We had elegant food, and I baked good bread in his honor. His elderly mother joined us. My darling Anna, sensing that she might hear something she might not want to know about me, stayed in the kitchen while I read aloud something I had written about Bob. In a strange way, Anna and I had become much closer since she'd left home. She was on her way to becoming a woman. However, that day she stayed there in the kitchen with a well-meaning friend who was carefully cutting the six-inch stems off the deluxe strawberries.

Death had become a regular part of life for me by then, as it does for those of us blessed with a long life, and I was learning to embrace it. I was glad that both Lane and Bob were no longer in pain, and I assumed God was watching over them, even though I knew they'd both been agnostics in life. Well, perhaps now they would know whatever there is to know. As for me, often I felt I knew nothing, and I constantly struggled to keep my spiritual foundation.

Back in L.A., Marshall Mason, a sensitive and creative director, invited me to meet him at a café. I already knew that Larry Kramer, the justifiably angry playwright of *The Normal Heart*, had written a new play called *The Destiny of Me*. Colleen Dewhurst was the actress they had originally cast, but she had since passed away, and I was amazed and honored when Marshall told me that they wanted me. As we sat under a giant tree outside the café, he told me we'd be playing at the Lucille Lortel Theater, a historic off-Broadway house. As much as I appreciated the offer, I told Marshall that I couldn't take the job because my daughter, Anna, would be having her first child around the time the play was scheduled to open in New York, and I wanted to be in L.A. for the birth.

When Anna heard I'd turned down the play, she told me that when she had her child, she definitely wouldn't want me in the delivery room. She might not even want me in the waiting room. She was determined to do this on her own. The child's father would be in the delivery room with her. She strongly encouraged me to take the play, saying she didn't need or want me there. After the baby was born would be soon enough. That was admirable and good for her, but it was sad for me. I so wanted to be there. I wasn't sure what to do. But I had to believe that what she was telling me were her true feelings, so I told Marshall I'd do the play, but only if I could immediately fly to L.A. as soon as Anna went into labor, for one day at least. He agreed.

I flew to New York and checked into the old Wyndham Hotel, where actors used to love to stay. A friend I hadn't seen in years was also staying at the hotel and invited me to join him for dinner with the Sir Laurence Oliviers. I could hardly believe that after all these years, I would finally get to meet Olivier.

Sir Larry answered the door of their apartment himself and put his hand out to me, saying, "It's so wonderful to see you again." Overwhelmed, I blurted out the truth, that we'd never met. He blushed just a little and then said, with the charm that only the greatest actor could make believable, "Oh, my dear, it's because I've seen you in so many things I've adored, I felt as though we were dear old friends." *He sold me*.

He sat next to me at the restaurant and took off the sweater that was under his jacket and put it over my shoulders when I said I was a little chilly. It was terrific! I remembered how I was so in awe that I had frantically and successfully avoided meeting him many times in the 1950s when I was with Christopher Plummer.

Our rehearsals of *The Destiny of Me* went well, even though Larry Kramer insisted on being at all of them. At first it made us all quite nervous. The author is the king in the theater. Not a word can be changed without his consent. My part was a long one. I was playing a woman from her twenties into her nineties with no makeup changes and only minimal costume changes, using mostly my body and emotion to convey the aging process. I was in a quandary about how to do a particular long scene. The writing for my part was very interesting, but I thought it lacked a clear through line. I experimented at home, rearranging the speeches. I showed what I'd done to Marshall, our director, at the next rehearsal. Marshall agreed it was good but felt it should be presented carefully to Larry Kramer, with whom we were all quite respectful. He must have explained my ideas to Larry brilliantly, for Larry agreed to them, especially after he saw how well they worked in execution. Larry Kramer turned out to be such a warm and accessible person, and I considered it a huge compliment that he approved my small contribution.

Toward the end of the rehearsal period, I got the call that Anna was in labor. I was on the first flight to L.A., but the baby had already arrived, and they were back home in their tiny pink house when I got there. A car and driver waited outside to take me back to the airport while I met my grandson. I had less than an hour to spend with Anna and her little boy, Ian. They were both healthy and happy, and since I had no camera with me, I made a little sketch to take with me that I still keep in my datebook. My daughter having this child, the fact of my becoming a grandmother to Anna's child, somehow made me feel biologically related to this baby. It's illogical, I know, but that's what I felt. I flew back to New York so proud of being a part of it, bursting with the joy of the miracle.

There was something about doing *The Destiny of Me* that was so satisfying. Essentially it was tragic and angry but not entirely. There was a scene toward the end of the play in which I, the ninety-year-old mother, come to visit my son, who is dying of AIDS in the hospital. Something would come over me, Rosetta, when I'd put the skirt from the old country over my other clothes and dance for my son. I'd feel my own grandma invade my body, and I bent it and twirled as my old grandma would have, a little off balance, feeling the music in my limbs and head. One night the audience came with me into the dance; I don't know how else to explain it. They chuckled affectionately and laughed during the dance, and when I began to speak to my son, the laughter grew inexplicably with every line. Whatever I said, the giant waves of laughter grew louder and louder. It was thrilling, but I didn't know why what I was doing brought that response. Afterward no one could tell me, and I never found out. In a way I loved that it *was* a mystery, that there was no sure formula for moving an audience, that one would be forever seeking, keeping things alive. It was always a nice and funny scene, but it was never quite that way again.

I found out that Joe had sneaked into the theater to see the show, because he stayed to see me when it was over. He knew it upset me to know he was out there. I think I'm finally over that. And my dear friend and director Micki Dickoff brought the extraordinary Sunny Jacobs to my last performance. I am proud that Sunny and I have remained close and treasured friends for more than eighteen years now.

When I got home, Sean Penn sent me a great little note along with his screenplay *The Crossing Guard*. Sean was relatively new to directing at the time, but it was very nice working with him. He was sensitive to the actors' needs. We had lots of rehearsal time, occasionally using the written script as a starting point and improvising from there. Eventually the scenes took shape, and the dialogue was pinned down. Though I found it fun working that way, ultimately I don't think our dialogue was necessarily better than his, but he used what he wanted of it. It turned out to be an interesting and very successful movie, and he survived and grew in spite of all the pressure put on him.

I've worked with lots of first- and second-time directors who don't survive. New or young directors are often very rigid, not sufficiently prepared, or sometimes overprepared. Occasionally they can get trampled on by overbearing actors and lose control of the movie. The bottom-of-the-barrel directors are the ones who think that unless they are overtly "directing" the actors, telling them what to do and how to do it, they will not be respected by them, or the crew. These types also presume to know the emotional makeup of an actor they've just met.

I've found the best directors for actors are the ones who cast wisely and then trust that the actor knows what he's doing. They're not afraid to accept something they hadn't thought of. If they are also the writer, they can even accept a different line reading than they imagined. They welcome it. And every decent actor loves a good suggestion presented in the manner of just that, a suggestion. Sometimes an actor needs to adjust or physically move for the sake of the camera, to help motivate another actor, or for aesthetic composition within the frame. That's the director's decision, and assuming the director is not an idiot, I believe the actor must find a creative way inside his head and body to adjust and make it happen.

If he wants, I imagine Sean will become a great director. As an actor, he is braver than almost anyone else when it comes to choosing roles, and heroic in the way he plays them. As a human being, I think he's beyond heroic. I admire him and worried a lot about him during his selfless efforts in Haiti.

I had been fortunate in getting so much work when many actresses my age didn't. I had even bought a charming house for myself in the Hollywood Hills. I'd been in it for almost four years when in 1994 my world was shaken up once again—this time, literally.

I was lying in bed in the early hours before dawn, sound asleep, when the earth, my house, my room, became violently angry. They shook and shook with such rage! *What had I done?* I grabbed my pillow and put it over my head seconds before the heavy crystal lamp on my bedside table crashed over me. Furniture was moving in the room; I could hear it, but I couldn't see anything. It was very dark. The security alarm began blaring away.

Finally the movement stopped, and with a wildly beating heart, I found a flashlight in my bedside drawer. Glass had broken, so I shook out my shoes before putting them on and carefully moved in the direction of the living room, but I could see little in the narrow beam of my flashlight. It was clear that large objects were not where they belonged, and rather than risk falling, I decided to crawl back into bed and wait there until it was light. The security alarm finally stopped, and I pulled the phone onto the bed and tried calling Anna. The line was dead, all power gone; it was utterly black and silent.

Now, in the darkness, I had the task of believing that God would take care of me and my family. I became calm and knew I needed to stay calm. I don't know how long I lay there in the dark when suddenly there was the blessed sound of the telephone ringing next to me, a sound I usually hated. I picked it up, trying not to hang up on myself in the dark. It was Joe, calling to see if I was all right! I was so grateful to hear his voice. He told me that he was fine, he had telephone power, and that Anna, who was at her home in Santa Monica with little Ian, was also fine. He said he'd call me again in a little while, when it got lighter.

Finally it was daylight, and I made a cursory inspection. I still couldn't call out on the phone, but things weren't too bad. An alabaster sculpture had fallen onto the lap of an antique chair and broken its arm, but only the sculpture's base was damaged. A glass vase I had purchased in New York when I was twenty-five and carried with me all those years had slipped off its little table and was cradled safely on a fluffy rug. I saw no structural damage in the house at all, but there was no water. Then I heard loud pounding on my front door. It was an impromptu neighborhood group going from house to house, checking on everyone, followed soon by John Dye and his brother Gere, who lived a mile away and wanted to be sure I was all right. I waved to them through my window and thanked them. Then I got dressed, got into my car, and headed for the little grocery store at the end of the road, where I got some bottled drinking water. I was among the first there and felt guilty. The phone was working in a few hours, and I spent the day speaking to those close to me.

The next day I received an offer to work on a new TV series shooting in Vancouver, playing George C. Scott's wife. I didn't even ask to read the script. Joe and Anna were safe, and so was my grandson. I packed in two hours and was gone.

17.

Surprises

I had been working steadily for a very long time, far longer than I had had the right to expect since returning to the third career of my life with *Carrie*. In my seventh decade, with the twentieth century nearing its end, my professional longevity was a blessing for which I never ceased to be grateful. But as I got older, the parts inevitably got smaller. They were often fine parts, good enough to get me Academy Award nominations. With the exception of what I did in the theater, however, I was no longer being offered leading roles. I had stopped expecting them.

Then one day when I must have been doing everything right, I received a call telling me that I was wanted for the lead role of Dolly in *The Grass Harp*, a film based on the Truman Capote novella. Joan Plowright, who had originally been cast as Dolly, had been delayed making another movie. Charles Matthau, Walter's son, who was directing, had wanted me for something else years before, also with his father, but I wasn't available at the time. I would be playing opposite Walter Matthau, Jack Lemmon, Mary Steenburgen, Nell Carter, Charles Durning, Joe Don Baker, Bonnie Bartlett, my old friend Roddy McDowall, and my former comrade in *Carrie*, Sissy Spacek. This time I would be the good, sweet one, and Sissy would be the horror. It was a deeply spiritual day for me, one of disbelief and of thanksgiving. All day long my body was quivering with excitement.

I stepped in about a week before we started. A hurried luncheon meeting was called at a country club, where I met the producers, the writer, and the director, none of whom I knew. They all seemed very pleased that I'd be doing the part and that Sissy Spacek and I would be playing sisters instead of mother and daughter, as we had in *Carrie*. That afternoon I went to a wardrobe fitting at the very upscale costumer's and met the designer, Albert Wolsky, who is truly an artist and a gentleman and has had more awards and nominations than anyone I know. Albert is so trusted and respected; people from all over the country, perhaps the world, send him antique clothes in hard-to-find sizes from which to select. Lucky for me—I was almost never as slender as I would have liked. My character, Dolly, always wore pink. (I secretly loved pink, too.) One of Albert's contacts sent a beautiful antique pink wool coat with a little black embroidery for me to wear in the film. It fit perfectly. Albert designed the rest of my clothes, and they were wonderful for the character. I was bursting with gratitude for all this, a lot of thanking God for such a lovely happening at this time in my life.

I had seen Walter Matthau once years before, but we'd never met. I did, finally, in the fitting room at the costumer's. I was going out as he was coming in. He looked down at me with such surprise and warmth—no, it was a lot more than warmth. It was pleasure, and I don't know what else, but whatever it was, it was good, very good, and we both knew we would be good together. Walter immediately planted a great big smackaroo on my mouth.

Long before I met Walter, I had heard plenty about him, especially about his wife, Carol, from Maureen Stapleton. Maureen thought that Carol (who had once been married to William Saroyan) was the most perfect person in the world. According to Maureen, Carol was the most beautiful, had the best taste, was rich and smart, and knew how to do everything better. On the plane going to Alabama to shoot the film, I sat next to Walter, and it was clear he, too, thought that Carol was perfect. He talked endlessly about her and their son Charley, the director, whom he adored and called his best friend. They even lived next door to each other. Walter's eyes lit up when he spoke of his Carol. His monologue went a little bit like this: "Carol needed more room to put her things, so we added ten thousand more feet to the house. She loves those things—the towels, the sheets, the gowns. She's so beautiful, just beautiful. She's a good writer—she's writing a book. She puts that weird white makeup on her face—have you ever seen it? I don't know why she does that. Beautiful woman, quite a woman." I had seen Carol in public, and indeed she was eccentric with her stark white makeup. I was touched that Walter was aware of it but loved even that about her.

Working with Walter was an experience. Two days before we were to start shooting, I walked into the makeup trailer to find an argument going on between Walter and everybody else, including his son. Walter had his heart set on wearing a white wig that had been made for him when the film was first cast. Now that he would be playing opposite me, however, everyone thought his own natural dark hair would be more appropriate. Walter stubbornly insisted he needed the white wig in order to feel more in character as the judge. Suddenly he picked up a straight razor that was sitting nearby and removed about three inches from the front of his hairline while we watched, mesmerized. Now he *had* to wear the wig! Other than that, there was no temperament from him, just fun and operatic music in the trailer in the mornings. He would blab away with his jokes before all the takes, even after the director had said "action." It was a lovely way to keep everyone relaxed.

We were all put up at a big motel. I shared a two-bedroom suite and kitchen with Merry Traum, daughter of my good friends Jane and Happy, who was there as my assistant. It was a small suite but comfortable, and we made our breakfasts and most of our dinners in the room. If my call wasn't too early or if it was a Saturday night, Merry and I would go out to eat at one of two possible restaurants. Occasionally in the evening we'd see Jack Lemmon and Walter sitting at a little table together in a restaurant, silently eating their dinner, hardly aware of each other, like some married couples, as if there were nothing more to say. We were there during Thanksgiving and had a traveling feast in various motel apartments. At Christmastime we were allowed to go home for a week. While we were on break, the actress who was to play the woman behind the counter in the cigar store had a fatal heart attack in New York while shopping, and was replaced with Doris Roberts, who hadn't yet become famous on *Everybody Loves Raymond*.

The location was very cold, and it was even colder inside the large, dusty Victorian house. There was no heat at all. Only the crew could dress for the weather; the actors on camera had to remain in costume. Sissy and I wore thin cotton summer dresses on top of thin silk underwear and huddled in a small room with a space heater between takes. Many of us caught nasty colds during the filming, including me. I had deliberately pitched my voice in a higher register for the childlike Dolly, but because of my cold I had to speak even *higher* in order to get any sound out. I was promised an opportunity to dub my strange-sounding voice when we got home, so I continued to work, no matter what, to keep the show from shutting down.

Despite the challenges of the climate, it was fabulous being listed as number one on the call sheet. Being listed first meant you had the biggest or most important part, though not necessarily the best one. It's a meaningless thing, but I admit I got a kick out of it. It had been many years since I'd been treated like a movie star, and I enjoyed it thoroughly. I never had before. In the past I had either taken it for granted or thought I didn't deserve it.

I think the character I was playing, the sweet, innocent Dolly, also influenced people's behavior toward me. John Alonzo, our director of photography, treated me like a princess and often photographed me like one. That rarely happens to a mature woman. When I was a kid and didn't really need it, hours would be spent lighting my close-ups. At the time my face was bland and not very interesting, and by the time they lit me, there was really nothing left, but the studios insisted on it. Alas, it's still pretty much the same way; the young and perfect get the super-duper treatment. This time, though, John not only took time in lighting me; he often took my hand and kissed it when he wanted me to move a few inches from place to place. It was delicious to be treated so royally.

While we were still shooting, my close friend Grace Wapner came down from New York to spend a week on location with me. Grace is an artist and sculptor who is interested in the world in general. Grace was the one responsible, many years earlier, for our meeting beautiful Anna, whose middle name is Grace after our friend. Though we'd been very good friends for well over thirty years, Grace had never been on a movie set. It was fun having her intelligent, wide-eyed face there witnessing the work. I became surprisingly angry, though, when I found out someone had taken the liberty of giving my script to Grace to read when she had expressed interest in seeing it. My copy had my notes in it, more private to me than a diary. These were the precious secret keys to my work. I had never let anyone look at my notes, not even Bob, who knew more about my inner process than anybody. Once these secrets are known to the world, you have given away their power. They are useless. I would never dream of looking at someone else's script, not even a technician's or a crew member's. I was so upset when I found out Grace had seen it—not at Grace, who couldn't have known, but because I'd lost an important part of my work. When I looked at the script later that night however, I saw that it was filled with little chicken scratches, half-words, abstract sketches, little clues for me—nothing that anyone could possibly have deciphered. Much ado over nothing.

Months later, when the shooting finished, Walter came to my room to say goodbye while I was packing. Our affection and admiration for each other was mutual and he gave me quite a passionate goodbye kiss. I suspect he didn't realize I was sharing the suite with Merry and thought I was alone, or perhaps he didn't care. My hearing aid whistled because of the close proximity, and he jumped back, thinking it was his pacemaker! That took care of that.

Out of the blue, sometime later Walter sent me a postcard with his bold hand printing that said, "DEAR ROSIE, I SAW *THE HUSTLER* THE OTHER NIGHT AND I MUST SAY YOU ARE UNIQUE! I LOVE YOU TOO. XXX. WALTER."

Postproduction on the film, unfortunately, did not go as I had expected. There were some bad feelings between Walter and the movie company. Walter had made an ill-advised phone call to columnist Army Archerd, the substance of which was printed in a long column in the trade papers. Walter was highly critical of the money people and what he considered their cheapness and inappropriate pressure on his son. The company was angry to be criticized so openly in the press and appeared to drop their support for the film in a dramatic way. I was not given enough time to redo most of the soundtrack of Dolly's voice from the days when I'd been so sick. They gave us only a few hours, when we should have had a couple of days. I made a terrible scene, the first one in many years, when they told us that our time was up, that we had to leave the sound studio. I must have embarrassed and scared the poor studio representative, who was only following orders. When the movie was released, the studio ran a few modest newspaper ads but not a single television commercial, a necessary thing for this day and age. It was heartbreaking to me personally and professionally.

Despite the studio's lack of support, the film got quite good reviews, and I got some magnificent ones. (I was told it was safe to read them!) This was the first time Joe didn't excuse himself from reviewing a movie I was in; he was open about the fact that he had once been married to me, charitable to the movie, and loving to me. Nevertheless, the movie was pulled from the theaters after three weeks. Most of my friends didn't even know it had opened. I still think it's a slightly imperfect but lovely film that is slowly getting its due from being seen on television.

I was surprised to receive a handwritten postcard from Gregory Peck: "Dear Piper, This card is meant to be a small tribute to your beauty in *Grass Harp*. And to the beauty of your performance. It was a series of revelations moving and true. My love to you, Greg P." During the years after we worked together, Gregory had sent me several postcards, all of which I've kept, of course. The first one had said, "Dear Piper—I miss you and long to begin another picture with you. Thank you for giving so much. With love from Greg." Forgive my vanity in sharing these.

Between amusing film roles such as in Robert Rodriguez's *The Faculty* in 1998, which probably made more money than many others I'd done put together, I worked in television throughout the 1990s, doing an occasional guest role on some popular series. Some of the parts were less than memorable, but they paid bills. One day I got a call from my agent telling me George Clooney needed a mother for his role as Doug Ross on *ER*, the most popular drama on television at the time. Playing his mother turned out to be a learning experience for me on several levels.

The first surprise came when I arrived at the studio. In the years since I'd been there last, Warner Bros. had become a fortress. It used to be so casual getting in the gate. Now I had to prove who I was before they would let me in, and I had a lot of trouble doing it. The guards didn't know me, and I didn't have photo ID with "Piper Laurie" on it. All my identification listed my legal name. It took a good thirty minutes just to prove I belonged there and get admitted.

Meeting George Clooney wasn't what I expected, either. I was seated in the fake restaurant waiting for him that first day, when he made a rather grand entrance onto the set. This was before George had become a movie star and "the sexiest man alive," according to *People* magazine. I was astounded at how cocky he seemed. I was also astonished at how good-looking he was, the jawline unbelievably chiseled, too perfect. So far I didn't like him. He entertained the crew and extras as he made his way to the small table where I sat waiting for him. But the moment he sat down and interacted with me in the scene, he became a serious actor and person—a serious actor that I think he went to some effort, oddly enough, to hide from the camera. He had a funny way of keeping his chin down, peering out only when he had to. As we worked together, I found I really liked him, perhaps because I was playing his loving mother, but I don't think it was that. I thought he was quite decent and sensitive under all that flash. And a lot more, as we have all learned in the ensuing years.

The real learning experience, however, came when we shot the next episode, for my eyes were opened then to how other people sometimes perceive me. In this episode we were being directed by one of the actors, Anthony Edwards. It was a kitchen scene, and I was to prepare dinner for George as we talked. I had come to the set the day before and asked the prop man for lots of green beans; they would be relatively noise free as an independent activity during the scene. The first-class prop man, who had the budget that goes with a successful show, had a lug of green beans waiting for me on the day we shot. My character begins the dialogue for the scene, and when we rolled for one of the takes, I stood pinching off the ends of the beans, waiting for Anthony Edwards to say, "Action." I waited for what seemed forever, pinching the beans, but there was still no cue to start. A very long time went by, and I finally looked up at Anthony, who was standing near the camera, and at George, who was in front of me at the table. They were both looking at me with expressions that said *What's going on?*

I said, "Why are we waiting?"

They said, "We're waiting for you."

"Me?!" I did not usually need my hearing aid for work, but that day I had not heard Anthony's softly spoken "Action." They had both thought I was doing some kind of special acting preparation, starting only when it felt right. I would normally not indulge myself in that way except perhaps during rehearsals, almost never on a set, and certainly not for this chatty green-bean scene, but they didn't know that. And they were quite happy to wait for me. How flattering, how kind, how funny! I laughed so, and they did too.

It was a nice job. It would have been extended into many more episodes, but the actor playing George's father wanted more money, the network refused, and the story line was dropped. I ran into George a year or so later, when he had just become a movie star. He showed me a great deal of warmth, hugging and kissing me and telling me he missed his mom and that I should come back and do some more shows. "Tell them you'll come back!" he told me. Flattering.

It wasn't uncommon for those of us fortunate enough to continue working to be reunited with old friends in new roles. In 1999 I was once again cast opposite George C. Scott in a television production of *Inherit the Wind*, directed by Daniel Petrie. George was playing the character based on William Jennings Bryan; I would play his wife. George had just played the Clarence Darrow–based role for months on Broadway, but this time around Jack Lemmon would be doing that plum part. George's part was a brand-new one for him; same play, completely different role. Both parts were long and difficult. How George, who was now extremely ill, had managed to learn the new role so quickly was beyond me. The physically powerful man I had feared decades before had lost his bodily strength but was still a demon of brilliance on camera. I sat in the courtroom in the front row all day long for many days, watching these two men battling it out, but the real battle was with their own bodies and minds. Without fail, after the last shot of every day, Jack and George would slowly make their way to the back of the courtroom to go home, and two hundred extras would break into thunderous and sustained applause.

Jack Lemmon was very fine in his performance, but he struggled often with some of his lines. I didn't know then that he was hiding his own illness. Often he'd go blank in the middle of a long speech, as we all have done. Unfortunately, his memory lapses were usually in the middle of a miraculous performance given by George C., which meant that the whole thing would have to be done again. But George continued to work fully in all these aborted takes. He wanted to support his fellow actor. George was consistently compelling and brilliant, but many of the takes could not be used. By the time the camera came around to film a close-up of George, he was exhausted and forced his performance. As a result, his close-ups looked a bit over the top and lacked the nuances and colors of what he'd been doing for hours. It was ironic and unfair that George C. did not also win the Emmy for his performance, as Jack did. Sadly, it was the last part George C. would play. Incredibly, Jack went on to do one more, *Tuesdays with Morrie*.

I continued to work on stage when opportunities arose, and I was pleased to receive word that the gifted Daniel Sullivan, who was the director of almost all the current hits in New York at the time, wanted to meet me and had arranged for me to fly to New York. He was interested in discussing a new Lincoln Center production for Broadway called *Morning's at Seven*, to be rehearsed at Lincoln Center and performed at the exquisite old Lyceum Theater. The script was delivered to me just as I left for my flight to New York. I read what I could of it on the plane. I was put up at a hotel near Lincoln Center and met with Dan the next morning for breakfast in the coffee shop. He was easy to talk to, and I liked him. He wanted to know what I thought of the play. I told him the truth: that I hadn't quite finished reading it, but what I'd read, I liked. He told me that three of the four sisters had already been cast with Estelle Parsons, Frances Sternhagen, and Elizabeth Franz. All great actresses. He had also cast Christopher Lloyd, Buck Henry, William Biff McGuire, Julie Hagerty, and Stephen Tobolowsky in the remaining roles. I was being considered for the fourth sister. I checked out of the hotel and flew back to California after the meeting, but before I left my room, I got a call from my agent telling me that Dan wanted me to do the part.

It took me a while to understand how hard the role was going to be, though I suppose that if I had known before we started, I still would have chosen to work with these fabulous actors and Dan. Part of the problem was the lines themselves. The dialogue was written in the way the playwright's own family actually spoke. The construction of the sentences was a bit awkward and unnatural. If you're doing Shakespeare, you expect that, but we were doing modern colloquial speech, and the unusual arrangement of the words tripped me up. My cousin Pamela, cousin Marvin's daughter, was helping me, but I found my part very difficult to memorize. I found out later that all the actresses were having the same problem with their lines.

Though I was close to being the youngest, I was playing the eldest sister. I was overweight then and couldn't disguise anything in the fitted dress of the period, which came to midcalf, displaying my ankles, which were quite swollen at the time. I wore unbecoming shoes and a gray wig. It would be an exercise in courage to go out on stage. Letting go of all my vanity, I was up for it.

I had a little more dialogue than the others, but unlike the other characters, my role was ill defined. The other sisters had an arc to their stories, something emotional that one could hook into. My character, in contrast, seemed bland and somewhat manipulative, as if her primary purpose were filling in exposition for the writer. I couldn't get a clear sense of who she was. At the first table read at Lincoln Center, I said in front of everybody, "I have no idea of who this woman is," which was a stupid thing to confess. It must have frightened Dan Sullivan to hear me say that, but at least he didn't fire me. I struggled a lot during the first weeks of rehearsal. The old monster, fear of being fired, had reared its ugly head. Dan did not give a lot of positive feedback. As a matter of fact, he gave none, as far as I knew. Once he passed me in the hallway and gave me a little pat on my shoulder as he walked by. I lived on that pat for weeks. The others weren't getting any more than I was, but we were grown-ups and carried on.

It took me a long time to find the core of this woman. In the end I invented one. I just brought all the energy, joy, fun, and love of life I could find, and overlaid that into her and into my relationship with everyone on stage. Only when we were out of the rehearsal hall and into the theater, and I was more secure with the words, did my performance begin to come together. My goosed-up energy and joy seemed to work for much of the time, especially in my scenes with Christopher Lloyd and Estelle Parsons. Christopher was unpredictable, sometimes the cartoonish man and sometimes simple and real. It was exciting working with him either way, and my laughter and joy on stage with him were entirely genuine.

After we'd been playing for a while, some discerning people told me that my character was their favorite of the sisters, which seemed incredible to me. But I didn't charm the Tony committee. I was the only sister not nominated, and I confess my feelings were hurt. I suppose because I'd worked so hard, and the character I ended up with was so far from my own Russian soul, almost complete invention. I was proud of that. I got many letters from people who had seen the play, expressing their outrage that I had been "overlooked." I let them comfort me. In the meantime Estelle Parsons, whom I became very fond of and who always burst into my dressing room without knocking like a real sister, encouraged me to go to the party for the Tony nominees anyway. She and her husband took me along with them, and I put on a good face, pretending I didn't give a shit. I also went to the Tonys with them a few weeks later, and had a genuinely good time.

Toward the end of the run, Paul Newman and Joanne Woodward, who were friends of Estelle's and of our superb stage manager, Roy Harris, came to see the play. I hadn't seen Paul in quite a few years, though we'd spoken a few times. I think he and Joanne came out of duty, but they seemed genuinely surprised at how much fun this production was and were very pleased with us. I was told that everyone backstage had watched as Paul and I embraced and chatted. Roy, who was a theater and movie buff, later said, "It was like watching movie history!" We all left the theater together. Paul told me he liked my black straw hat as he took my arm, and we walked to find me a cab. Joanne trailed behind with Roy, thoughtfully letting us have a moment.

Another night Rosemary Harris came backstage. The last time I'd seen her was in my apartment on 55th Street in the late 1950s, when she'd tried to get me to come back to do *Twelfth Night*. I was standing outside my dressing room, almost ready to go home, when I saw a lovely lady with beautiful white hair tied back in a ponytail standing about fifteen feet away. I recognized her immediately. It was an emotional moment as we walked toward each other and embraced. So many years, so much drama.

It was while I was doing the play that another of the central dramas of my life finally reached its climax. Some ghosts are never completely put to rest, and John Frankenheimer had long been one of my familiar spirits. Given our shared profession, it was almost inevitable that we would eventually run into each other again, and so we had over the years. The first time was in a local restaurant not long after my divorce. I had gone to pick up Chinese food that I'd ordered for Anna and myself from a restaurant in Santa Monica. I hadn't bothered to put on makeup or fix myself up. Who dresses up to pick up Chinese takeout? As I waited for my food, I was sitting at a large round table in an alcove at the front of the restaurant where the employees usually sat when they ate. The alcove was in semidarkness. It was a busy night, and the tables were filled. There was another woman waiting on a chair near me at the door. She was wearing a beige trench coat and looked familiar, like a blond dancer I used to know. She seemed tired. I'd been waiting perhaps ten minutes when the door opened and a man walked in and looked around, his eyes adjusting to the darkness. It was John

Frankenheimer. He wasn't more than five feet away. The woman stood up and walked over to him. John looked around and said, "Is there someplace we can sit while we're waiting?"

"You can sit here with me!" I said. *Had I said that?* Obviously the devil had entered my body. They both looked in my direction, not able to make out who was speaking from the darkness. They came closer, and I repeated the offer.

John said, "Rosie! What are you doing here?" I told him I lived around the corner. He said he had an office nearby and introduced me to his wife. Just then my food arrived. I felt an urgency to get out and stood up.

John said, "Is the food any good here? What's good here?" He was making conversation, perhaps to delay my departure.

I said, "I always order the spicy string beans. I like them." And I left, feeling as if I were escaping with my life.

When I got home, I told Anna I had just run into an old boyfriend. She said, "See, Mommy, I told you always to look nice. You should wear something nice and fix your hair."

I told her I thought she was right, but this night it had been all right not to look my best because it didn't really matter that much. *Really?*

Over the next years I saw John briefly several more times. One time he asked me through my agent to attend a retrospective of his work at the Directors Guild and stay for the Q-and-A for *Days of Wine and Roses*. We were both seated on the little stage, and I felt happy and at ease in his presence as we talked about the work we'd done together. At the reception he had introduced me to his "fiancée," a tall and elegant young blond girl who wore her hair in a bun at the nape of her neck, just as I had in the last scene of *Days of Wine and Roses*. It had been a long time since I'd seen the show, and I was struck by how busy my face was in the last scene. I compulsively mentioned it to John as he held the door open when we were leaving the auditorium.

He said, "No, it wasn't. It was wonderful. Just right."

I gather the engagement ended because he went back to his wife again sometime later. I had heard many stories about John leaving his wife and being with other women over the years, but he always seemed to go back to her.

I saw John again around 1997 when I was asked to be on a Q-and-A panel at the Motion Picture Academy. The panel included all of "we survivors" who had worked on live TV. Everyone was there, from Charlton Heston to Cliff Robertson. We all gathered in a room at the Academy for a reception before the event. About twelve feet away stood John Frankenheimer by himself, looking at me. I nodded and then tried to look away, but I couldn't, and then I wouldn't. I indulged myself and stayed there, looking into his eyes and his spirit that had brought me such pleasure. I was aware that I was revealing more than I should. I don't know how long we both stood there, connecting with each other, passing years of feelings between us. It went on, and it felt like a commitment of some sort was being made.

Someone spoke to me, and the spell was broken for the moment. Then John came over and said, "Rosie, will you tell me how to reach you? Will you give me your number?" He had a little pad, and I wrote my number down for him.

Even though we sat on opposite sides of the stage for the symposium, I felt the ease and power I always felt in John's presence. I spoke easily to the audience and even had the chutzpah to ask Charlton Heston, who was sitting next to me, if he would tell the audience what he personally felt like in those minutes leading to the moment of being on the air live. Charlton said, incredibly, that he was never nervous; he'd done it so many times that it never bothered him. I didn't believe it. No one is that brave.

John called me first thing the next morning and said, "I want to see you. What is your life like? When can we see each other?"

I told him I was on my way to New York and would be gone for a few weeks. He asked when I'd be back and said, "I'll call you the day you return."

To my surprise, he did. I don't remember how many weeks had gone by in the interval. He'd begun to shoot the fabulous *George Wallace* film starring Gary Sinese and asked if I'd come to the set and have lunch with him in his trailer. That wasn't where I would have liked a reunion, but I said I would. I was so curious about his life during those years. I had a thousand questions. I had heard that he was a recovering alcoholic and wondered how all that had happened. I wanted to know about his years living in France. I had heard he'd gone to school at the Cordon Bleu, and I used to fantasize about baking the bread for his fabulous dinners. I wondered if he knew I was a baker and that I was a pretty good cook now myself. That I had become a sculptor. That I had a marvelous daughter and grandson. There was so much I wanted to know about him and to tell him about me. He was, after all, the person who had known me best in the first part of my life.

On the day I was to visit, I got a call from John's assistant, telling me they were breaking for lunch early that day. Could I come right away? I knew it would be impossible, but I said I'd be there as soon as I could. I drove up to the huge mansion where they were shooting and parked. It was raining a little as I walked through the gate and found someone to show me to John's trailer. It was parked on the grounds a half-block behind the house. My guide knocked on the trailer door, stuck his head in, and said, "You have a visitor." There was a brief pause, and I was told to go in. I stepped up out of the mud and into the trailer and saw John moving toward me.

"I'm sorry, Rosie, we had to break early. I've already eaten." There was a quick and stiff embrace. He sat down at the far end of the long trailer, at the table near his tray covered with empty dishes, and offered me the only other vacant spot to sit—pretty much where I was standing, near the door. I kept my coat on. It was very cold. And it wasn't just the weather. John didn't ask if I wanted something to eat, didn't even offer me a cup of coffee.

Something was wrong. Perhaps it was the work. Whatever it was, I felt we probably wouldn't have much time, so I started with a bold, important question: Why had I never known he had an alcohol problem during the years we had been close? Probably a mistake to lead off with something so personal. Instead of giving me a real answer, John began to talk as if he were at a twelve-step meeting; it was almost a speech. He talked as if I were no longer there, and I began to wonder why I was.

He asked nothing about me, what my life had been like. After about a half hour, someone knocked on the door and said the crew was back from lunch.

"Please, Rosie, come to the set," he told me. "I'd like you to see what we're doing." I reluctantly agreed. We stepped out of the trailer and followed the AD to the set. As I walked behind them, I noticed that John was taking very strange little mincing steps, so peculiar to him. I thought then it might have been because of the mud and puddles. It even crossed my mind that he might be in pain. We went into the mansion. I asked to use the bathroom and said I'd meet him upstairs, where they were shooting. I joined him a couple of minutes later. He introduced me quickly to Gary Sinese and Angelina Jolie and asked me to sit and watch the work. He had a high director's chair ready for me right in front of the TV monitor. John walked away, then came back with earphones and helped me to adjust them. When he left, I sat and watched the rehearsal.

About five minutes went by, and I was so uncomfortable. I hated visiting other people's sets. I had come to see John, not to watch a rehearsal. *Did he expect me to sit there watching the entire day? If so, then what? Would he become his old self and bring me into an untenable situation that I could not resist? Or would the day just go on and on and I simply not know when to leave?* I would be a victim either way. I took off the headphones, walked to where John was giving instructions to someone, gave him a kiss on the cheek, and said, "I have to go." He looked astounded, but I just kept moving.

Afterward I often wondered what had happened to him between the moment we had connected at the Academy and my visit weeks later. *Why did he have that funny walk? Was he ill? Did he know it?*

We were well into the run of *Morning's at Seven* when, on my day off from performing, I went to Lincoln Center to see Barbara Cook in concert. Barbara had been to our show twice and invited us to come see her. I had been a fan of hers since the 1950s and was so looking forward to hearing her sing. I invited Caroline, a friend of a friend, to come with me to the concert that afternoon.

We arrived a little early and waited in our seats for the concert to begin. I was thinking of Barbara's pure voice, only half-listening while Caroline made small talk when she said, "I've been so busy lately, I've hardly had time to read the paper. I watched the TV news. Did you hear that that director died—did you ever work with him? What's his name, John Frankenheimer?"

It seemed my heart stopped—I couldn't breathe. It was not possible. Dead. I wanted to shout out, *No! There's unfinished business! So much I need to know! So much to resolve and talk about!* I'd not lost my passion for my phantom lover. The adolescent in me was still alive and well.

Just at that moment Barbara Cook came out and started her first song. I was trapped in a public place, unable to escape, as I had been fifty years before, when I'd gotten the news that my friend Leonard had died. And again I remained where I was, until the concert was over. Frozen, the music going through my body, trying to stay with the living. Afterward I rushed backstage even before the applause had died, to say a hurried "Thank you . . sorry I have to run . . I'll tell you later" to Barbara. Then I fled to a cab and my hotel, closed the heavy door to my room, and let out my rage.

"AAAAHHH! . . . AAAAHHH!" I kept bellowing from my gut, "DAMN! DAMN! DAMN!!" stomping my feet. I was close to seventy, but at that moment I was a child having a tantrum! I sobbed and cursed, furious at God, furious at John for leaving before it was time, before we'd had a chance to at least work together. I was so sure we'd work together again. That had been our great partnership.

I don't remember if I had a performance the next day. For a number of weeks I was so tightly wound that I isolated myself from everyone except when I was on stage. The fantasy of the play was the only thing real to hold on to. Each day I marched down Sixth Avenue toward the beautiful old Lyceum on West 45th Street, thinking of nothing but John with every step. I usually looked at people's faces, but now it was just the pavement and my thoughts. *How would the world be without him? Without my person to shine for? Where was his soul right now? Why had I asked him that irrelevant question the last time I was with him?* I had really screwed up that last time, and now there would never be a chance to make it right.

When it was time to go on stage, I became frightened to make my entrance and had to ask either God or John to hold my hand and go out there with me. Once I was out there, I was all right. My dresser, Lynn Bowling, who was a sensitive man, asked if there was something he could do. He knew something was wrong. I thanked him, but my feelings were still too raw. I didn't dare speak of what I felt. I avoided everyone for fear someone would ask me something about John or mention his name, and I would break—never to put myself together again. I had to keep my mourning private. How pitiful that I felt I had to. A part of the child forever remains.

I struggled through the performances as best I could for the remainder of the run. Anna and my grandson, Ian, flew east to see our last few performances and stood in the wings for the final curtain call. The curtain was not really completely down when they both stepped forward onto the stage and embraced me. *How daring,* I thought.

Loss was now a recurring theme in my life. I knew that my old friend Roddy McDowall would be leaving us soon. I had known Roddy since I was seventeen and had first started to smoke. He had asked me to save empty Parliament boxes for him to store his wire recording—it was that long ago. In the days before he passed, Roddy had a number of little dinners to say goodbye to his close friends, never more than three or four people. He would sit at the small table with a dispenser of morphine next to his plate, pressing it from time to time. No need to be discreet. We all knew how ill he was and why we were there. The evening I was there, I brought a fine bottle of wine, and we celebrated our friendship a little. Sitting in his wheelchair, Roddy made an effort to pick out some personal possessions for me to take home as I was leaving.

A memorial gathering for dear Roddy was held at Elizabeth Taylor's house. It was an elegant affair with a wide mix of people, from Gregory and Veronique Peck to David Hockney. All of us had been touched by Roddy in an important way. We were standing around the pool having refreshments when Elizabeth appeared wearing a red gown. She spoke with the aid of a microphone to the group of perhaps sixty people. She was having a difficult time. A few others spoke after Elizabeth, followed by the sound of a bagpiper, who came out of the house in full dress, playing an old Scottish air. It was chilling. He walked completely around the pool piping, and some of us couldn't help but weep for the loss of the brilliant child actor and loyal adult friend we had loved. When the piper disappeared into the house, we could still hear him playing for a minute, and then utter silence fell except for the occasional bird chirping. We were all very quiet, stirred beyond anything we could have imagined. No one was willing to break the silence.

Suddenly a voice rang out—"Hip, hip, hurray! Hip, hip, hurray!" It was the unmistakable voice of Doris Roberts, who was holding her glass in the air at the end of the pool. Then all of us raised our glasses, and together we toasted our friend, "Hip, hip, hurray!"

A few weeks after Roddy was gone, someone dropped off a gorgeous silk scarf and a potted peach rosebush from his garden with a little handwritten note. It said "For Rosie, my posy."

Roddy's passing was another reminder of how precious our friends are, especially old friends. Over the years I had kept in touch with Donald O'Connor, my first leading man when I was just a teenager, and when I got back from New York, I went to visit him. Donald and his terrific wife, Gloria, were living in Sedona, Arizona, at the time. The three of us watched *The Milkman* for the first time in about fifty years, and the first thing Donald said as our soft-shoe routine began was, "Oh, look how graceful she is. Oh my, isn't she graceful?" He was the same kind friend who had encouraged me when I was a frightened teenager dancing on screen for the first time.

Donald and Gloria moved back to L.A. when his health began to fail, and eventually he moved into the Motion Picture Home. I was able to go out there and spend time with both Donald and Gloria during his last days. Despite his illness, Donald enjoyed being outdoors and would ask the nurses to take him outside for walks. While walking with one of his nurses one morning, Donald collapsed. The nurse told me that she caught him as he was dropping and held him for a moment while she waited for help to come. Suddenly she felt his body lighten by about eight or nine pounds, as if something, "perhaps his spirit," had left his physical body. This was a common phenomenon, she said, that other nurses had told her they'd experienced. I thought to myself that it was not the first time Donald's remarkable spirit had soared, lifting his body into extraordinary places.

I was fortunate to still have my dad in my life, long after my mother passed on. My father had remained remarkably healthy in his old age, but as his ninetieth birthday approached, he began to show signs of Alzheimer's. Unfortunately, when the first signs of the disease appeared, his wife grew helpless and had him removed to a "home," where she rarely went to see him. When the family became aware of what was going on, Sherrye's older son, Michael, took my dad to Arizona, where Sherrye and Al were then living. We found a very lovely "guest" home for Dad that was just fifteen minutes from Sherrye's house and an hour's flight for me. I visited often, staying in a nearby motel. Sometimes I brought Anna and Ian with me. Despite his condition, my dad always seemed to know who I was, and he praised me sometimes as he never could when I was younger. He told a fellow guest how hard I had studied to be a good actress and how difficult it was to be a movie star. I was so touched to hear these things filter through the Alzheimer's. Nature can be very kind at times. My dad lived in the guest home for about a year before he passed away at ninety-three. He welcomed death and told me so several times at the end, saying with calm pleasure, "I'm ready to go now." One day an attendant found him outside in the backyard. He had thrown off his clothes and was trying to push himself into the dry earth and saying, "I want to go. I want to go now." And he did go soon after that, quite peacefully.

After years of ill health, Sherrye's husband, Al, also passed away. It was a huge adjustment for Sherrye, who had never lived alone. She had gone straight from our parents' home into her first marriage, and when her first husband divorced her, she continued to live with her three children. The children had still been living at home when she met Al. But by the time Al passed away, her children were grown, and at close to seventy, Sherrye had never spent a night alone. She tried to get by on her own for almost a year, but she often had falls and had to send for paramedics to rescue her. Finally her eldest son invited her to come live with his family, and she did for a good long while. During those years we often talked in the mornings. I called her almost every day to chat while I had my coffee. Sherrye never touched the stuff, but our morning chats were a ritual that we both enjoyed. Our life experience and education couldn't have been more different, but we became much closer in those years.

In 2003 I shot *Eulogy*, playing Debra Winger's mother. Shortly after, I came down with a bad case of the flu. On Sunday, January 9th, I was hunkered down in bed feeling sorry for myself because it was my daughter's birthday and I wasn't well enough to see Anna and Ian or my friends the Traums, who were in town. I felt so miserable that I hadn't even bothered to brush my hair for days. I'd hardly been out of bed. I was propped up watching *Meet the Press* when I noticed a slow and powerful shoving at my back. It felt as if the whole wall were pressing against me. It was. I glanced quickly out of the corner of my eye toward the window and realized with a shock that the hill behind my house was moving toward me, a giant wall of mud pushing its way straight into my bedroom. I hadn't heard it.

I moved faster than I ever imagined I could. I grabbed my backpack with wheels, threw in my purse, camera, vitamins, and car keys, and rushed to the front door. I couldn't get through. Water and mud were rushing against it too swiftly. I went to the side door, where the rushing mud was even worse, but at least there was an iron handrail by the steps to hold on to. I clung to the railing and navigated my way down the steps, then slipped across the patio and made it into the side door of my garage. My car started, the garage door opened—thank God—and I was out into the street, headed for any place of shelter. The closest place turned out to be the parking lot of the Beverly Garland Holiday Inn. I had my blessed cell phone with me and called my cousin Pamela, who lived close by, and asked if she could please come check me into the Holiday Inn. I was wet and muddy, wearing only my big cotton nightgown, and I had the hair of a wild woman. While I waited for Pamela, I speculated on what could have happened. We were in the middle of a rainy season, but I'd lived in my house for twelve years, through many rainy seasons, and I'd never had a problem. The hill behind my house had been stable for decades before that. There were ancient trees holding the soil in place and deeply rooted ivy as a ground cover. A mystery.

Pamela arrived to check me in, and then her dad, Marvin, drove me back to my house to see what was going on. There we were greeted by an emergency crew from the fire department. They told me that during the night a city tractor clearing the road above my house had accidentally "mowed down" a fire hydrant, which had then gushed down over my property all night, causing the hill and two retaining walls to fail. I peered at the back rooms of my house. What was still intact seemed to exist in a cave of mud, blocking out all light. The bedroom was completely destroyed. It had been hit first and hardest. I thanked God for *Meet the Press*, and that I had been awake.

Life was crowding me and showing me its power in so many ways. A week after I found myself a gypsy, my sister, Sherrye, died. It was not unexpected, but she left a big vacant spot in my heart. I spent a long week at the motel, trying to get over my flu and shock. Cousin Pamela loaned me some dry clothes, but even in bed, wearing three or four sweaters, I couldn't seem to get warm. It was one of those moments when I would have loved someone strong and warm to cuddle with. Sometimes there's no glory in being independent.

Wonderful Rosa, who has worked for me for more than fifteen years, helped me sneak into part of my house and salvage some clothes to wear. When my young next-door neighbors Pam and Colby Jensen, who now lived a few blocks away, offered me the use of their guesthouse, I gratefully accepted. I took advantage of the Jensens' hospitality for well over a month. It gave me some time to regain my bearings and to mourn my sister's passing.

The city took full responsibility for the catastrophe and said they would rebuild, restore my home as it had been before the mudslide, and pay for temporary housing. I looked around and found a small, sterile, but adequate apartment nearby, rented some sterile furniture, and moved in. I stored everything that I cared about, everything that I had created with my own hands, including all of my sculpture and ceramics, and my papers, books, paintings, photographs, scripts, films, and awards.

It was a strange and surreal time for me. The city kept its promise, but the pace was slow, to put it mildly. Rebuilding my home took more than four years.

Meanwhile there I was—a lady in temporary storage, with nothing familiar to identify the space I lived in as mine. I had only a roof over my head and a clean bed to sleep in.

I had spent much of my childhood longing for nothing more than to go home. Now I had no home to go to. But living lots of years has its blessings as well as its challenges, and I had learned a few things on the way to this point in my life. The trauma of my early years had forced me to discover that home is not a place. It's something else. We have to have fortitude to find it. On a brief visit to Reslocks fifty years after I had left the sanitarium as a frightened and confused child, the place I had hated and feared was gone, the buildings destroyed by the ravages of time and the elements. Only nature had endured. The small tree I'd planted had sunk its roots deep, learned to bend with the wind and the rain, and never stopped reaching. Like me, with the passing of the years, my tree had grown tall and unafraid. And like me, when the storms came, it did not break. It learned to dance.

18.

Zero Hour

The great film director Guillermo del Toro has said he sees catastrophe as a moment of opportunity. I learned that for the first time in sculpture class when a seemingly destroyed piece could have an even greater life by simply turning it upside down and starting anew. I knew that if I was to survive the chaos, the missing of familiar objects that told me I had lived a life, I would have to look elsewhere. I chose to open myself to the world's possibilities, and in return, I was showered with a burst of creativity that took me to places I'd never imagined.

My drive to fill the void took my love of a James Lasdun short story called "Property" and showed it to me obsessively in my mind's eye. This perfect story was told on twelve bejeweled pages. Lasdun's work was described by the *New York Times* as "an elegant pathology report on the modern soul." I yearned to see the story off the page and filled with rich colors and vulnerable people. With the gift of ignorance I had no hesitation, no asking myself if I could do this. Like a passionate fool, I just put one foot in front of the other to make it happen. I secured the rights, wrote the screenplay, and found the funding. All of this of course took many months. My screenplay added dialogue, monologues, and some visuals that revealed some of the intimate life of the main character, whom I decided *not* to play myself. Better not, first time out. I used my friend Michael McNamara's production company, with Michael himself as coproducer and first assistant director. I borrowed a house, designed all the sets, dressed them with new paint and rental furniture, and searched all over town (in addition to my own closet) for clothes to fit my leading lady. I looked for months for impossible-to-find props described in the story. I hired composer Paul Robinson to do original music and Larry Boothby from Nashville as cinematographer. Merry Traum, my former assistant, had become a fine makeup artist and was also one of the producers. I hired a terrific caterer to serve at least two great meals each day (a low-budget must). With the actors in place, we shot the film in five days. I felt calm and prepared throughout the shoot. After all, I'd been watching very closely for almost sixty years.

Of course, there were unforeseen problems. One of my cast members had an anxiety attack on the first day and couldn't remember a line. I sent the whole crew, including our unbelieving and alarmed producer–first AD, out of the house, while I worked to create a zone of comfort for this actor. That used a big chunk of the morning, but it was necessary. I adjusted my plans accordingly and did many short takes instead of the long ones I had planned on. The owner of the house we used also complicated matters, insisting we be out by five every day, which meant a very short workday, and in the mornings we found that some of our props had been moved on the "hot" sets. Despite the problems, we ended up covering everything and finishing on time. It's great to be the boss.

I had an opportunity to show my small creation on a big screen for my supercritic ex-husband, Joe Morgenstern, who has never had a problem telling bad truth to me. He admired it, even used the word "daring" to describe an element, and kept asking himself why I hadn't started doing this a long time before. I had another discerning audience. I was invited to the Port Townsend Film Festival in Washington State to be interviewed on stage by Robert Osborne before a screening of *The Hustler*, and the festival sponsors asked if I'd mind if they showed *Property* as a special event while I was there. Of course, I said yes, though I wasn't sure it would be everyone's cup of tea. My grandson, Ian, came with me for the four-day trip as my escort. Can you imagine? Talk about fulfillment! I even met someone briefly who made my heart beat a little faster for the first time in a long while. I was very gratified when my little film actually won the audience award at the festival. It is the first of what I hope will be a trilogy of short films based on Lasdun's work that I have already written and expect to direct.

I was still in my sterile little apartment, but my life was being rebuilt in ways I would never have foreseen. Not long after I finished *Property*, my friend Jim Brochu, an actor-writer whom I greatly admire, invited me to observe the beginnings of a one-person play he was writing for himself about the extraordinary Zero Mostel, whom we both had known. I had met Zero several times and seen him in almost everything he'd done on stage, including *Ulysses in Nightown* and *Rhinoceros*, and of course, I'd seen all his movies. I'd even sat and had lunch with him at the old Tip Toe Inn on upper Broadway one day in the 1950s, when I'd come by to visit my uncle Morrie, who worked there behind the deli counter. Jim Brochu had borrowed a little theater space in Los Angeles to work on *Zero Hour*, and that first day he simply sat on stage and read the play as I watched, acting it when he could get away from the page. I found myself mesmerized. As the work evolved, he invited me to a number of readings and then performances in front of small audiences, and a few times it was just the two of us working alone in my apartment. I was always invited to say what I thought about the shape of the play and threw out a few suggestions about performance that Jim said he found useful. Sometime before Jim played Florida on tour, I became the play's official director.

I joined Jim on tour in Washington, D.C., where *Zero Hour* received over-the-top reviews that gave me much more credit than I deserved. There were a few weeks off before going to New York for the opening at the Theater at St. Clements in midtown on West 46th Street. Naturally, we feared we'd be squashed down in New York like other "regional" successes.

Jim, however, had continued to grow and refine the work as an actor, until his performances became little short of magnificent. He won the Helen Hayes Award in Washington, received a nomination for the Lortel Award in New York, and won the prestigious Drama Desk Award for Best Solo Performance (on or off Broadway). We had superb reviews, full houses, and along the way I found myself getting more offers to direct. Isn't life amazing? I'm back where I started when I made my directing debut in the school play when I was eleven.

A few weeks after the opening of *Zero Hour* in New York, I made the ritual trip to Woodstock to celebrate Thanksgiving with my old friends. It was impossible not to think of the last time I'd made the trip, not long after John's death. My daughter and grandson had been with me in the car. We'd made the usual stop at H&H Bagels on upper Broadway to buy freshly baked hot bagels for the road. The day was exquisite, and we were on our way to visit dear friends. No schedule, no half-hour warning before curtain, no lines to remember after months of rigid discipline. I coudl feel some of the pain lifting and the beginning of acceptance that John was gone. Not the phantom John, but the real one who loved me so passionately at a crucial time in my life and taught me how to love someone else without reservation.

Luxuriating in the warm sunlight streaming through the car window and feeling my children physically close to me, I tried not to weep. I was so filled with emotion and with the healing my family brought me. This was the precious core of my life. Their warmth was bringing me even closer to my own mother—my complicated mother who instinctively pointed me in the right direction.

I was awakened by a phone call from my mother in a dream the other night. "Are you all right, Sissy?" she asked me, her voice and breath so close to my ear. It was not her far-off telephone voice but her very present and beautiful voice from when she was young. She was clearly anxious. I awoke with a flood of emotion that stayed with me all day.

> *Yes, Mother, I'm all right . . . Alas, despite the good fight, my body has morphed into something a little like yours, the sturdy Russian woman, and there's nothing to be done except embrace it. . . . Do you know that after you left us I began to act again? I suspect that pleases you. And mother . . . I haven't realized dear Uncle Schmule's expectations for me of a perfect and blessed life, but I've*

been useful. And I've had an awful lot of fun, more than you ever allowed yourself.

And Mother . . . do you know that long ago . . . I stopped being that frightened child you saw gazing out of the train window, yearning only to be a part of the speaking world?

I suspect you do.

Acknowledgments

My thanks to all the people that made this book possible. My attorney Chuck Hurwitz, who showed my original manuscript to literary agent Adam Chromy. To my team at Crown Publishers: Mary Choteborsky, Mary Jane Ross, Janet Steen, Tricia Wygal, Luisa Francavilla, Songhee Kim, Meredith McGinnis, and Ellen Folan.

My gratitude to my cousin Pamela; my dear friend Anne; and to Donald, my very own George Cukor; for their encouragement and not letting me lose heart. With great respect and thanks to my many-faceted super-assistant Dave Child, and apologies to my precious four-legged companions over the years, especially Sukoshi and Luck, who were tragically ignored in this tome.

Index